The OECD Multilateral Instrument for Tax Treaties

The OECD Multilateral Instrument for Tax Treaties

Analysis and Effects

Edited by

Michael Lang
Pasquale Pistone
Alexander Rust
Josef Schuch
Claus Staringer

Wolters Kluwer

Published by:
Kluwer Law International B.V.
PO Box 316
2400 AH Alphen aan den Rijn
The Netherlands
E-mail: international-sales@wolterskluwer.com
Website: lrus.wolterskluwer.com

Sold and distributed in North, Central and South America by:
Wolters Kluwer Legal & Regulatory U.S.
7201 McKinney Circle
Frederick, MD 21704
United States of America
Email: customer.service@wolterskluwer.com

Sold and distributed in all other countries by:
Air Business Subscriptions
Rockwood House
Haywards Heath
West Sussex
RH16 3DH
United Kingdom
Email: international-customerservice@wolterskluwer.com

ISBN 978-90-411-8836-6

e-Book: ISBN 978-90-411-8916-5
web-PDF: ISBN 978-90-411-8847-9

Editors

Prof. Dr DDr h.c. Michael Lang is Head of the Institute for Austrian and International Tax Law of WU (Vienna University of Economics and Business) and academic director of both the LLM Program in International Tax Law and the Doctoral Program in International Business Taxation (DIBT) of this University. He is the president of the Austrian Branch of the International Fiscal Association (IFA) and has been visiting professor at Georgetown University, New York University, Sorbonne, Bocconi, Peking University (PKU), University of New South Wales (Sydney), and at other universities.

Prof. Dr Pasquale Pistone holds the *Ad Personam* Jean Monnet Chair on European Tax Law and Policy at the Institute for Austrian and International Tax Law, WU (Vienna University of Economics and Business) and is the Academic Chairman of IBFD, Amsterdam. He is also an Associate Professor of Tax Law at the University of Salerno, and an honorary professor at both the Ural State Law University and at the University of Cape Town. He is the editor-in-chief of the World Tax Journal and the IBFD Doctoral Series.

Prof. Dr Alexander Rust is a Professor of Tax Law at the Institute for Austrian and International Tax Law, WU (Vienna University of Economics and Business). He previously worked as a Professor of Tax Law and director of the Master's Program in European and International Tax Law at the University of Luxembourg, as an acting assistant professor at New York University, and as an assistant at the University of Munich. He is a member of the editorial board of Intertax and Internationale Steuer-Rundschau, as well as co-editor of *Klaus Vogel on Double Taxation Conventions: Commentary*. His main research interests are tax treaty law, European tax law and tax policy.

Prof. Dr Josef Schuch received his Doctorate in Law in 1998 for his thesis on expenses and losses under tax treaty law, and his PhD in 2002 for his work on timing issues under tax treaty law. His research and publishing activities mainly focus on international tax law. He has been a Professor in International Tax Law at the Institute for

Austrian and International Tax Law, WU (Vienna University of Economics and Business) since 2002, and is a partner at Deloitte Austria.

Prof. Dr Claus Staringer is a professor at the Institute for Austrian and International Tax Law, WU, and a principal consultant with the law firm Freshfields Bruckhaus Deringer.

Contributors

Nathalie Bravo received her law degree from the Universidad Católica Andrés Bello in 2004, and obtained an LLM in International Tax Law with honours from the Institute for Austrian and International Tax Law, WU (Vienna University of Economics and Business) in 2012. Additionally, she has more than eight years of relevant professional experience at various law firms in Venezuela, where she advised domestic and foreign corporations on domestic and international tax matters. Since September 2014, she has been studying for her doctorate degree in the Doctoral Program in International Business Taxation at WU. She also is a recipient of the DOC Fellowship of the Austrian Academy of Sciences.

Robin Damberger, after receiving a Bachelor's in Business Administration, received a Master of Science in Accounting and Taxation from WU (Vienna University of Economics and Business). He works as a research and teaching associate at the Institute for Austrian and International Tax Law, WU.

Sriram Govind is a lawyer who graduated in 2013 from Symbiosis Law School in Pune, India. Following graduation, he worked for over two years at the law firm, Nishith Desai Associates in Mumbai, India as a senior member of the international tax practice. In 2016, he received his LLM in International Tax Law from the Institute for Austrian and International Tax Law of WU (Vienna University of Economics and Business). His areas of expertise include tax treaty law, tax policy and dispute resolution in tax matters. Since September 2016, he has been a research and teaching associate at the Institute for Austrian and International Tax Law, WU, and is pursuing his doctoral studies in the Doctoral Program in International Business Taxation at WU.

Raphael Holzinger holds academic degrees in Business Administration (BSc and MSc) as well as Business Law (LLB and LLM) from Vienna University of Economics and Business. In addition, he received another LLM in Tax Law and Accounting from the University of Vienna. Raphael is currently enrolled in the Doctoral Program in Business Law at WU, and works as a research and teaching fellow at the Institute for Austrian and International Tax Law, WU. Besides his scientific work, he gains practical experience as an assistant tax consultant at Grant Thornton Unitreu.

Benedikt Hörtenhuber, after receiving a Bachelor's in Business Law, continued the Master's Program in Taxation and Accounting at WU (Vienna University of Economics and Business), ultimately receiving an MSc. He works as a research and teaching associate at the Institute for Austrian and International Tax Law, WU.

Mag. Andreas Langer, received a Mag.iuris in Law from the University of Vienna. He works as a research and teaching associate at the Institute for Austrian and International Tax Law of WU (Vienna University of Economics and Business).

Alexandra Miladinovic received an LLM and LLB in Business Law as well as a BSc. in Business Administration, from WU (Vienna University of Economics and Business). She works as a research and teaching associate at the Institute for Austrian and International Tax Law, WU.

Jean-Philippe Van West holds a Master's degree in Commercial Sciences from the Economic University-College of St Aloysius (EHSAL) and a Master's degree in Law from the Free University of Brussels (VUB). For both degrees, the focus of his studies was taxation. Later, he received an LLM in International Taxation from WU (Vienna University of Economics and Business). During his studies, he has worked in the tax department of several multinationals. After obtaining his LLM degree, he worked for three years in the tax department of a leading Belgian law firm. In September 2016, he began his studies in the Doctoral Program in International Business Taxation at WU.

Svetlana Wakounig received a Mag.iuris in Law at the University of Vienna. She works as a research and teaching associate at the Institute for Austrian and International Tax Law, WU (Vienna University of Economics and Business).

Benjamin Walker received his degrees in law and finance from the University of Otago, New Zealand. He received his LLM in International Taxation from WU (Vienna University of Economics and Business) in 2013. He has almost three years of international tax experience working for Ernst & Young in Australia and the United Kingdom. He gained additional experience working in Germany with the German Ministry of Economics & Technology. Since September 2015, he has been studying for his doctorate degree in the Doctoral Program in International Business Taxation at WU. Furthermore, whilst pursuing his doctoral studies, he works for Henkel, a major German multinational company.

Christiane Zöhrer received an LLM in Business Law from WU (Vienna University of Economics and Business). She works as a PwC Research Associate at the Institute for Austrian and International Tax Law, WU.

Summary of Contents

Table of Contents

Preface

Several OECD BEPS measures require the amendment of the worldwide tax treaty network. Action 15 of the OECD BEPS Action Plan aims to amend tax treaties by developing a Multilateral Instrument (MLI), which will coexist alongside the already established tax treaty network. The OECD released the final version of the MLI on 24 November 2016, and it was signed by over seventy jurisdictions on 7 June 2017. The MLI will lead to the modification of numerous tax treaties. As tax treaties can have different wording, terminology and structure, a great challenge is to find a proper way to accomplish their modification without distorting the underlying framework or triggering undesirable effects.

In order to analyse possible techniques that the MLI can implement in order to effectively modify tax treaties and thereby contribute to a better understanding of the relationship between bilateral and multilateral treaties, the 24th Viennese Symposium on International Tax Law was held on 26 June 2017 at the Vienna University of Economics and Business (WU). Renowned professors from Austrian and foreign universities, tax researchers from the WU and tax experts from various countries participated in this symposium. In the presence of Jessica di Maria, of the OECD Centre for Tax Policy and Administration, the speakers presented their findings, including a detailed analysis of the procedural mechanisms on how the new measures aimed at preventing BEPS will interact with, and complement existing tax treaties. The authors completed their papers using input received during the symposium, and these papers have become the chapters of this book. The authors offer an in-depth analysis along with the most recent scientific research on their topics.

The editors would like to thank Renée Pestuka and David Orzechowski, who were mainly responsible for the organization of the symposium and made essential contributions to the preparation and publication of this book. The editors would also like to thank all the authors who have patiently revised their contributions in order to enhance the quality of this book, and Constance McCarthy, who contributed greatly by linguistically editing the authors' texts.

Above all, sincere thanks to the publishing house Kluwer, which agreed to include this publication in its catalogue.

Michael Lang
Pasquale Pistone
Alexander Rust
Josef Schuch
Claus Staringer
Vienna, October 2017

CHAPTER 1

Scope of the Multilateral Instrument

Robin Damberger

1 ASSESSING THE SCOPE OF THE MULTILATERAL INSTRUMENT

The OECD's Base Erosion and Profit Shifting (BEPS) project has given rise to significant changes in international tax law. The main focus of the BEPS project is to prevent BEPS through a series of fifteen actions. In order to implement the tax treaty-related BEPS measures, the development of a Multilateral Instrument (MLI) to swiftly modify bilateral tax treaties was proposed in BEPS Action 15.[1] The OECD released the final version of the MLI on 24 November 2016.[2]

Especially for tax practitioners it is critical to understand the limits of the scope of the MLI in order to assess the instrument's impact on international taxation. This chapter will evaluate the scope of the MLI. It begins by providing an overview of the scope of the MLI. One reason behind this approach is that the MLI is a complex instrument. Thus, it is essential to grasp how the framework of the instrument works in order to provide a foundation for the subsequent analysis. The main focus of this chapter, however, is responding to legal questions concerning the scope of the MLI. This provides for an evaluation of which treaties are covered by the MLI and deals with the question as to which conditions must necessarily be fulfilled by the contracting states in order for the MLI to be applicable. Besides those technical questions, this chapter analyses who can ratify the MLI.

1. OECD, *Developing a Multilateral Instrument to Modify Bilateral Tax Treaties – Action 15: 2015 Final Report*, OECD/G20 Base Erosion and Profit Shifting Project (2015).
2. OECD, *Multilateral Convention to Implement Tax Treaty Related Measures to Prevent Base Erosion And Profit Shifting* (2016).

2 THE SCOPE OF THE CONVENTION

2.1 The Framework of Articles 1 and 2 of the MLI

Part 1 of the MLI deals with 'Scope and Interpretation of Terms'. This section of the MLI contains the relevant conditions that must be fulfilled for the application of the MLI. The basic idea of the MLI is to implement treaty-related BEPS measures into the tax treaty network. The MLI will not replace existing tax treaties, but rather will be applied alongside those tax treaties.[3] Article 1, which governs the scope of the MLI, states that the MLI modifies all covered tax agreements as defined in Article 2(1)(a). This provision indicates that the scope of the MLI is limited to modifications through the MLI. However, Article 1 of the MLI does not specify for which conventions the MLI is applicable.

Article 2(1)(a) defines the term 'covered tax agreement' as referring to 'an agreement for the avoidance of double taxation with respect to taxes on income (whether or not other taxes are also covered)...'. Thus, an agreement may fall under the scope of the MLI only if this criterion of Article 2(1)(a) of the MLI is fulfilled.[4] From a legal perspective, it is highly interesting to explore in greater detail what exactly constitutes 'an agreement for the avoidance of double taxation'. Section 3 of this chapter will therefore deal with this question and analyse the wording of the provision.

However, agreements that meet the conditions set forth in Article 2(1)(a) of the MLI are not automatically modified by the MLI. Instead, the parties must take action and make a notification in order for the instrument to apply to a specific bilateral or multilateral agreement. Finally, Article 2(a)(i) of the MLI requires that an agreement be in force between two or more parties to the MLI. In this context, the term 'party' refers to a state or jurisdiction that has signed the MLI, and for which the MLI has entered into force.[5] As a result, the scope of the MLI extends only to agreements that meet the formal criteria set forth in Article 2 of the MLI.

Therefore, it appears accurate that the personal scope of the MLI is identical to the personal scope of the specific covered tax agreement. Consequently, defining an agreement's scope is of critical importance. Many tax treaties follow either the OECD or UN Model Tax Convention on Income and Capital (hereinafter 'OECD Model' and 'UN Model'). Under Article 1 of the OECD Model, the 'Convention shall apply to persons who are residents of one or both of the Contracting States'.[6] Article 1 of the UN Model has the same wording as the OECD Model. The only requirement set forth in these provisions for the application of a tax treaty is that a person be a resident of one or both of the contracting states. A person is defined in Article 3(1)(a) of the OECD Model and includes both individuals and companies, as well as any other body of persons.

3. OECD, *Explanatory Statement to the Multilateral Convention to Implement Tax Treaty Related Measures to Prevent Base Erosion and Profit Shifting* (2016), para. 13.
4. OECD, *Explanatory Statement to the MLI* (2016), *supra* n. 3, para. 25.
5. *See* OECD, *Explanatory Statement to the MLI* (2016), *supra* n. 3, para. 34.
6. *OECD Model Tax Convention on Income and on Capital* Art. 1 (2014).

Assuming that a person falls within the scope of a tax treaty, the legal consequence is that the right of taxation for cross-border transactions is separated between the contracting states.[7]

2.2 Notification Requirement

Article 2(1)(a)(ii) of the MLI requires that 'each such party' have made a notification to the Depositary[8] listing which it wishes to be covered by the MLI. This provision reflects the situation in which there might be circumstances where a party wishes not to cover a specific tax treaty in the scope of the MLI.[9] It is therefore possible not to include all tax treaties in the scope of the MLI because only tax treaties that have been specifically identified in a notification to the depositary are covered by the scope of the MLI. Furthermore, each contracting party to a tax treaty must notify that it wishes to have the treaty be covered by the scope of the MLI. If only one party to a tax treaty wishes to cover a specific treaty, the MLI is not applicable until the second contracting party decides to notify the treaty to the depositary. This approach prevents the unilateral modification of a tax treaty by the MLI. Furthermore, notifications help to identify the agreements along with any other instrument that has been amended by the MLI.[10]

Under Article 2(1)(a)(ii) of the MLI, the parties must notify 'the agreement as well as any amending or accompanying instruments thereto (identified by title, names of the parties, date of signature, and, if applicable at the time of the notification, date of entry into force)'. This approach ensures clarity as to the content of the agreement at the time it is modified by the MLI.[11] Pursuant to the principle of reciprocity, the notifications must correspond to each other. If a mismatch occurs (e.g., the parties notify a different accompanying instrument), the agreement may not fall within the scope of the MLI because the formal criteria for the application of the MLI are not fulfilled. Otherwise, there could be disagreement between the parties about the scope of the MLI. To minimize such disagreements, the depositary (who collects the notifications) requires the parties to report the notifications prior to the ratification of the MLI. The depositary compares those notifications and gives the parties the opportunity to discuss any mismatches and correct them prior to finalization of the lists.[12] Another requirement for the application of the MLI is that – under Article 2(1)(a)(i) of the MLI – the agreement be in force. However, the MLI gives the parties the opportunity to include an agreement in their list of notified agreements under Article 2(1)(a)(ii) of the MLI which has not yet entered into force.[13]

7. R. Prokisch, *DBA Doppelbesteuerungsabkommen*, Art. 1, para. 4 (K. Vogel & M. Lehner eds., 5th edition, Beck 2008).
8. The depositary is managed by the OECD. It collects all reservations and notifications, and makes them available for the public.
9. OECD, *Explanatory Statement to the MLI* (2016), *supra* n. 3, para. 14.
10. OECD, *Explanatory Statement to the MLI* (2016), *supra* n. 3, para. 26.
11. OECD, *Explanatory Statement to the MLI* (2016), *supra* n. 3, para. 33.
12. OECD, *Explanatory Statement to the MLI* (2016), *supra* n. 3, para. 18.
13. OECD, *Explanatory Statement to the MLI* (2016), *supra* n. 3, para. 32.

2.3 Flexibility with Regard to the Substantive Provisions of the MLI

An agreement falls within the scope of the *MLI* only if it cumulatively fulfils the criteria set forth in Article 2 of the MLI. However, this does not automatically mean that all substantive provisions of the MLI are applicable to a covered tax agreement, as one of the essential characteristics of the MLI is that it allows the contracting states a certain degree of flexibility.[14] By allowing the contracting states to choose between different sets of alternative provisions, the MLI provides for a considerable amount of flexibility.

The MLI contains opt-out clauses, opt-in clauses and provisions where the contracting jurisdictions may choose between different alternatives.[15] In this context, opt-out clauses mean that a contracting party is bound by the provision of the MLI unless it explicitly expresses at the time of ratification of the MLI that it does not wish to be bound by the provision. The parties must make a reservation in such cases in order to ensure clarity about the content of the MLI. In contrast to opt-out clauses, opt-in clauses are measures where a contracting jurisdiction decides to apply a specific additional and non-compulsory provision of the MLI. However, provisions that contain options are usually applicable only when both contracting states notify that they wish to apply the same option.[16] This approach follows the principle of reciprocity in international law. Thus, a precise analysis is necessary to figure out which substantive provisions of the MLI are applicable in a specific covered tax agreement.

3 AGREEMENT FOR THE AVOIDANCE OF DOUBLE TAXATION AS COVERED TAX AGREEMENT

3.1 General Remarks

Under Article 2(1)(a) of the MLI the term 'covered tax agreement' refers to 'an agreement for the avoidance of double taxation with respect to taxes on income (whether or not other taxes are covered)'. This wording also includes agreements that covers capital taxes and taxes on capital gains beside income taxes. However, agreements that deal solely with shipping, air transport or social security, are not intended to fall under the scope of the MLI.[17] The discussion below considers which types of agreements fulfil the criteria set forth in Article 2 of the MLI and have the potential to fall under the scope of the MLI.

3.2 Taxes on Income

A requirement for the application of the MLI is that the agreement cover taxes on income.[18] The MLI itself does not contain a legal definition of 'taxes on income'.

14. OECD, *Explanatory Statement to the MLI* (2016), *supra* n. 3, para. 14.
15. OECD, *Explanatory Statement to the MLI* (2016), *supra* n. 3, para. 14.
16. OECD, *Explanatory Statement to the MLI* (2016), *supra* n. 3, para. 12.
17. OECD, *Explanatory Statement to the MLI* (2016), *supra* n. 3, para. 25.
18. OECD, *Explanatory Statement to the MLI* (2016), *supra* n. 3, para. 25.

Therefore, it is not clear which understanding of the term was intended by the drafters of the MLI. Considering that the term 'taxes on income' is used frequently, one could argue that there is a commonly accepted definition of the term.[19] Nevertheless, the MLI does not contain an indication of such a common understanding. However, the MLI provides a rule in Article 2(2) that clarifies how the terms of the MLI are to be interpreted in case of doubts. Under that rule, 'any term not defined herein shall, unless the context otherwise requires, have the meaning that it has at that time' under the relevant covered tax agreement. Under this interpretation rule, it is arguable that the 'income tax' definition of the covered tax agreement applies also for the MLI. However, it must be admitted that an interpretation, following the underlying covered tax agreement, may result in different understandings of the term 'taxes on income', as definitions may vary among covered tax agreements. It is questionable whether this approach reflects the intention of the drafters of the MLI, as this approach may lead to different views regarding the interpretation of an essential term of Article 2(1) of the MLI.

However, the interpretation rule of Article 2(2) of the MLI offers another solution to clarify the meaning of particular words used in the MLI. Considering the wording of the interpretation rule and specifically the phrase 'unless the context otherwise requires', it could be argued that the definition of 'taxes on income' may be derived from the context of the MLI. The MLI was drafted by the ad hoc group in order to implement tax treaty measures that were developed by the OECD.[20] The wording 'taxes on income' which is used in Article 2 of the MLI corresponds to the wording which is used in Article 2 of the OECD Model (2014). As both instruments were drafted in connection with an OECD project and the wording of both instruments is identical, it can be assumed that the term 'taxes on income' is to be afforded the same meaning. Therefore, considering the second part of the interpretation rule, recourse to definitions laid down in the covered tax agreement does not seem necessary.

Although Article 2 of the OECD Model (2014) clarifies which taxes are covered by the treaty, this provision does not provide a precise definition of the term 'tax'.[21] Rather, Article 2 of the OECD Model (2014) merely indicates the meaning of the respective term, as these provisions describe the term in a more general way.[22] Article 2(1) stipulates that 'taxes on income and on capital' are be imposed 'on behalf of a Contracting State or its political subdivision or its political subdivisions or local authorities irrespective of the manner in which they are levied'.[23] The reference to

19. F. Sutter, *Der sachliche Anwendungsbereich des ErbSt-MA*, Erbschaftsteuern und Doppelbesteuerungsabkommen, at 57 (M. Lang ed., 1st edition, Linde 2002).
20. OECD, *Explanatory Statement to the MLI* (2016), *supra* n. 3, para. 6.
21. R. Ismer & A. Blank, *Klaus Vogel on Double Taxation Conventions*, Art. 2, at 156 (K. Vogel & A. Rust eds., Vol. 1, 4th edition, Kluwer Law 2015); M. Lang, *'Taxes Covered' – What Is a 'Tax' According to Article 2 of the OECD Model?*, 59 Bull. Intl. Taxn. – Tax Treaty Monitor, at 216 (2005).
22. Lang, *supra* n. 21, at 216.
23. *OECD Model Tax Convention on Income and on Capital: Commentary on Article 2(2)* (2014).

'imposed' allows for no other conclusion than that 'taxes' are restricted to mandatory levies. Generally, taxes are considered to be 'compulsory, unrequited monetary payments to the government'.[24] However, as the scope of the MLI is restricted to taxes on income, the instrument requires a more precise definition of the term.

Article 2(2) of the OECD Model (2014) provides a tautology which describes the term 'taxes on income and on capital'. Under this provision, 'taxes imposed on total capital, or on elements of income or of capital, including taxes on gains from the alienation of movable or immovable property, taxes on the total amounts of wages or salaries paid by enterprises, as well as taxes on capital appreciation' are regarded as taxes on income and capital. Nevertheless, the term 'income' is not be described in more detail through Article 2(2) of the OECD Model. However, the context of the distribution rules of Articles 6–21 of the OECD Model (2014) must also be taken into consideration, as the aforementioned provisions provide distribution rules for income taxes.[25] Therefore, the distribution rules of Articles 6–21 may be used for the interpretation of the term 'income', and a fall back to domestic definitions under Article 3(2) of the OECD Model (2014) would not be necessary.[26] Thus, 'income' encompasses undoubtedly business profits (Article 7 of the OECD Model), capital gains (Article 13 of the OECD Model), excess profits, as well as salaries and wages (Article 15 of the OECD Model).[27] Moreover, gross receipts from dividends (Article 10 of the OECD Model) and interest (Article 11 of the OECD Model) can also constitute 'income'.[28] This broad definition in Article 2(2) of the OECD Model allows the coverage of a great number of income taxes because the list of taxes is not exhaustive. This seems to be in line with the intention of the drafters of the MLI to modify the maximum number of tax treaties.[29] In contrast, consumption taxes, like value added taxes or expenditure taxes, are not considered as 'income taxes' as they do not fulfil the 'income' criterion.[30]

3.3 Income Tax Treaties

The MLI is designed to modify agreements for the avoidance of double taxation. Double taxation arises because most states levy taxes on all sources of income, i.e., income generated at home and abroad. In order to prevent double taxation, states enter into bilateral agreements for the avoidance of double taxation. Double taxation agreements (hereinafter 'tax treaties') allocate the taxing rights between the jurisdictions that are parties to the tax treaty.[31] Tax treaties may differ significantly from each other, as they reflect varying political positions and special national characteristics. However, the

24. Ismer & Blank, *supra* n. 21, at 156.
25. K. Vogel, *DBA Doppelbesteuerungsabkommen*, *supra* n. 7, Art. 2 tn. 22.
26. Lang, *supra* n. 21, at 216.
27. M. Tumpel, *DBA-Kommentar*, Art. 2 tn. 11 (D. Aigner, G. Kofler & M. Tumpel eds., 1st edition, Linde 2017).
28. Ismer & Blank, *supra* n. 21, at 159.
29. OECD, *Explanatory Statement to the MLI* (2016), *supra* n. 3, para. 6.
30. Tumpel, *DBA-Kommentar*, *supra* n. 27, Art. 2 tn. 13.
31. K. Holmes, *International Tax Policy and Double Tax Treaties*, at 57 (2nd edition, IBFD 2014).

OECD[32] and the UN[33] developed model conventions[34] that are of enormous practical relevance today. The aim of these models is to offer guidance to countries wishing to enter into tax treaties. However, these models are not legally binding on the parties.[35] The OECD has summarized the purpose of tax treaties as being 'to promote by eliminating international double taxation, exchanges of goods and services, and the movement of capital and persons. It is also a purpose of tax conventions to prevent the avoidance of evasion'.[36]

Tax treaties are primarily designed to prevent double taxation with respect to taxes on income.[37] As analysed above, income taxes are within the scope of treaties that follow the OECD Model. The same is true for treaties that are based on the UN Model, as both the OECD Model and the UN Models contain the same definition of taxes on income. For this reason, treaties that are based on one of the model conventions fulfil the income tax criterion of Article 2 of the MLI.

Another requirement for the application of the MLI is that the underlying instrument be an 'agreement'. In international law, Article 2(1)(a) of the Vienna Convention on the Law of Treaties stipulates that a treaty is 'an international agreement concluded between States in written form and governed by international law'. The conclusion of a tax treaty falls under this definition of a treaty, as it is usually concluded in a bilateral manner between different states.[38] These treaties are an independent source of law that regulates the legal relationship between countries in international tax law.[39]

Tax treaties undoubtedly fulfil the criteria for the application of the MLI. They deal with the prevention of double taxation with respect to income taxes. This wording covers the criteria for the application of the MLI which are set down in Article 2 of the MLI. This conclusion reflects the intention of the drafters of the MLI because the MLI is specifically designed to implement anti-BEPS measures in the tax treaty network.[40] Furthermore, the application of the MLI is not restricted to treaties that follow the OECD Model, as this is not a requirement of Article 2. In order to clarify which rules are relevant for the application of the MLI, the MLI paraphrases those rules.[41] This systematic approach ensures that provisions which differ in their wording from the

32. *OECD Model Convention on Income and Capital.*
33. *United Nations Model Double Taxation Convention Between Developed and Developing Countries.*
34. K. Vogel & A. Rust, *Klaus Vogel on Double Taxation Conventions*, Introduction, at 20 (K. Vogel & A. Rust eds., Vol. 1, 4th edition, Kluwer Law 2015); Lang, *supra* n. 21, at 216.
35. Holmes, *supra* n. 31, at 65.
36. *OECD Model: Commentary on Article 1* para. 7 (2014).
37. Holmes, *supra* n. 31, at 57.
38. Vogel & Rust, *supra* n. 34, at 24.
39. V. Kluge, *Das Internationale Steuerrecht*, at 646 (4th edition, Beck 2000).
40. OECD, *Explanatory Statement to the MLI* (2016), *supra* n. 3, para. 2.
41. These compatibility clauses describe which provisions of a covered tax agreement are affected by the clause. This approach makes sure that the provisions of the underlying tax agreement will be identified if the wording differs from the MLI. Moreover, these clauses describe the legal consequences of a situation where a covered tax agreement does not contain a provision affected by a compatibility clause.

OECD Model nevertheless fall within the substantive scope of the MLI where the MLI refers to the underlying tax treaties.[42] As a result, a tax treaty undoubtedly can become a covered tax agreement under the MLI.

3.4 Multilateral Tax Treaties

In order for an agreement to be covered by the MLI, Article 2(1)(a)(i) thereof requires that the treaty be in force between two or more parties. This raises the question as to what is meant by the expression 'between two or more parties'.[43] Tax treaties are usually intended to eliminate double taxation in a bilateral manner. Therefore, almost all tax treaties in force are ratified between two parties. However, there are multilateral tax treaties with more than two contracting parties. One reason for including the expression 'between two or more parties' could be that the more states involved in an agreement, the lower the chances of concluding an agreement.

Even though there are only a limited number of multilateral tax treaties currently in force, these treaties can undoubtedly have significant importance for the contracting parties of such a treaty.[44] This is why it makes sense for the MLI to modify also these multilateral tax treaties. The MLI enables the modification of such treaties by its use of the wording 'between two or more parties' in Article 2(1)(a)(I).

From a European perspective, the agreement between the Nordic countries for the avoidance of double taxation with respect to taxes on income and capital (hereinafter 'the Nordic Convention') is a significant example of a multilateral tax treaty.[45] The Nordic Convention is ratified between Denmark, Finland, Iceland, Norway, Sweden and the Faroe Islands. Another multilateral treaty has been ratified between the Member States of the South Asia Association for Regional Cooperation (SAARC). SAARC members that are parties to the SAARC Limited Multilateral Agreement on the Avoidance of Double Taxation and Mutual Administrative Assistance in Tax Matters are Bangladesh, India, Maldives, Nepal, Pakistan and Sri Lanka. Additional multilateral tax treaties are in force in South America (Andean Community Income and Capital Tax Convention) and Africa (West African Economic and Monetary Union Tax Treaty).[46]

In addition to the already mentioned multilateral tax treaties, the Arbitration Convention[47] between the EU Member States may also fulfil the criteria for application of the MLI. The Arbitration Convention is an international law convention which is

42. S. Bendlinger, *Multilaterales Instrument zur automatischen Anpassung bestehender Doppelbesteuerungsabkommen*, 27 SWI, 2, 7 (2017).
43. Article 2(1)(a)(i).
44. N. Mattsson, *Multilateral Tax Treaties: A Model for The Future?*, 28 Intertax, at 301 (2000).
45. Mattsson, *supra* n. 44, at 301.
46. K. Vogel & M. Lehner, *DBA*, Vermeidung der Doppelbesteuerung durch multilaterale Abkommen, tn. 40a (K. Vogel & M. Lehner eds., 6th edition, Beck 2015).
47. EU Arbitration Convention (1990): Convention 90/436/EEC of 23 July 1990 on the Elimination of Double Taxation in Connection with the Adjustment of Profits of Associated Enterprises, OJ L225/10 (20 August 1990).

independent from EU law.[48] The purpose of the Arbitration Convention is to eliminate double taxation which may occur from a profit adjustment in one Member State without a corresponding adjustment in the other Member State.[49] Therefore, it seems possible that the Arbitration Convention could be classified as an 'agreement for the avoidance of double taxation' in light of the MLI. As income taxes fall within the scope of the Arbitration Convention,[50] it fulfils the criteria for application of the MLI under Article 2 of the MLI.

In order to apply the MLI to these multilateral tax treaties, the same criteria as discussed above must be fulfilled to be treated as a covered tax agreement. Multilateral tax treaties usually differ from the wording of many treaties, as they deal with cases where more than two countries may be involved. An analysis by Mattsson as regards the Nordic Convention shows that there are many similarities between bilateral and multilateral tax treaties.[51] However, if those treaties have the purpose of preventing double taxation with respect to income taxes, they can undoubtedly be notified to the depositary in order to apply the MLI to those treaties.

Nevertheless, there are some specialities and unique aspects to be considered before a multilateral tax treaty is modified by the MLI. There could be situations where not every contracting party to the underlying multilateral tax agreement ratifies the MLI. At this point, one could may ask what would happen if, for example, Norway and Sweden were to ratify the MLI while the other parties to the Nordic Convention do not. Has the MLI modified the relation between Norway and Sweden in such situations? What legal consequences arise for the relations between states which ratify the MLI and those which do not?

Unfortunately, the MLI does not contain an explicit rule regarding treaties between more than two parties. However, it is possible that the wording of the MLI contains a hint on the modification of treaties between more than two states. Under Article 2(1) of the MLI, the MLI modifies agreements that are in force between two or more parties. But one requirement for the application of the MLI is that 'each such party' have made a notification to the depositary. The wording 'each such party' indicates that it is necessary that every party to a treaty notify that multilateral treaty to the depositary. As a consequence, treaties between more than two parties cannot be modified by the MLI when not every party to such a treaty ratifies the MLI and notifies that treaty to the depositary. A unilateral application of the MLI in relation with another party to a tax treaty will be prevented by this approach.

---

48. P. Plansky, *The EU Arbitration Convention*, Introduction to European Tax Law on Direct Taxation, at 261 (M. Lang, P. Pistone, J. Schuch & C. Staringer eds., 4th edition, Linde 2016); L. Hinnekens, *The Uneasy Case and Fate of Article 293 Second Indent EC*, 37 Intertax, at 602, 604 (2009).
49. Plansky, *supra* n. 48, at 258.
50. Article 2 Arbitration Convention.
51. Mattsson, *supra* n. 44, at 304.

4 FURTHER POTENTIAL AREAS OF APPLICATION

4.1 General Remarks

The MLI is designed to modify covered tax agreements in order to implement the BEPS-related measures into the tax treaty network.[52] Thus, it seems that only tax treaties for income taxes which undoubtedly fulfil the criteria of Article 2 of the MLI, fall under the scope of the MLI. This section analyses whether the MLI may also be applicable to agreements and other instruments that do not primarily aim at preventing double taxation with respect to income taxes.

The MLI modifies substantive provisions of tax treaties that fall under the scope of the MLI. Thus, the MLI focuses on the modification of the distribution rules which are governed by Articles 6–21 of the OECD Model (2014). If agreements other than income tax treaties were to fall under the scope of the MLI, the instruments' effects would be limited, as those agreements might not contain provisions which are modified under the MLI. However, this view does not hold for every provision included in the MLI, as the MLI also contains provisions which could be relevant for the application of other agreements such as the mutual agreement procedure (Article 16) and the preamble. For example, Article 6 of the MLI contains the preamble which clarifies that tax treaties are intended to eliminate double taxation 'without creating opportunities for non-taxation'.[53] This text of the preamble is remarkable because it clarifies for the first time that the purpose of a covered tax agreement is to not create opportunities for non-taxation. Regarding Article 6 of the MLI, the preamble has a significant importance for the interpretation of treaties under Article 31 of the Vienna Convention on the Law of Treaties. Parties to the MLI may therefore have an interest in implementing those provisions in agreements other than tax treaties.

4.2 Tax Agreements on Estates and Inheritance and on Gifts

In practice, tax treaties may significantly deviate from the OECD Model. As a result, their scope is no longer identical to Article 2 of the OECD Model. Furthermore, some treaties may not deal exclusively with taxes on income. Instead, they may also contain provisions that apply to taxes on capital or taxes on inheritance and on gifts.[54] Under Article 2(1)(a) of the MLI, the fact that a specific treaty also applies to other taxes (e.g., taxes on inheritance and on gifts) does not preclude its application to the MLI. In such cases, it appears to be obvious that the agreement may fall under the scope of the MLI because the income tax criterion is fulfilled.

In addition to the OECD Model, the OECD has published a Model Double Taxation Convention on Estates and Inheritances and on Gifts (hereinafter 'the OECD Model on Estates and Inheritances and on Gifts'). The OECD Model on Estates and

52. OECD, *Explanatory Statement to the MLI* (2016), *supra* n. 3, para. 6.
53. Article 6(1) MLI.
54. For example, tax treaty between the Federal Republic of Germany and the Kingdom of Sweden, Federal Law Gazette Germany, Part II, 1994/686.

Inheritances and on Gifts is the only model convention that was developed for the prevention of double taxation with regard to inheritance, gifts and estates. The number of inheritance tax agreements is very low compared to the number of income tax treaties.[55] The OECD Model on Estates and Inheritances and on Gifts was published three years after the first OECD Model. Its aim was to close gaps in the scope of the OECD Model.[56]

The Commentary on the OECD Model on Estates and Inheritances and on Gifts stipulates which taxes are covered by that Convention. Under the definition provided therein, taxes on estates and inheritance include 'all taxes which are imposed by reason of death in the form of taxes on the corpus of the estate, taxes on inheritance, transfers duties and donations mortis causa. ... Taxes on gifts inter vivos include all taxes which are levied on gifts ... or other gratuitous transfer of property'.[57] This definition deviates from the definition of 'taxes on income' under Article 2 of the OECD Model.[58] Thus, the MLI does not apply to treaties that follow the OECD Model on Estates and Inheritances and on Gifts because the income tax requirement of Article 2 of the OECD Model is not fulfilled.

If there were two separate tax treaties – one concerning taxes on income and on capital, and the other concerning taxes on estates and inheritance and on gifts, and no overlap between the respective agreements can be identified – it seems that the MLI would be applicable only to the treaty concerning taxes on income and on capital. However, this result may be different in practice, as the parties to a specific inheritance tax agreement may extend its scope to taxes which also reflect elements of income taxes. In such situations, it is possible that the MLI may be applicable to tax agreements on estates and inheritance and on gifts if both parties notify the agreement to the depositary.

Another noteworthy issue concerns the question as to whether it is possible for there to be an overlap of agreements following the OECD Model on Estates and Inheritances and on Gifts and treaties that are based on the OECD Model. In this context, Sutter, after analysing the scope of both agreements, concluded that no such overlap is possible, as these conventions cover different kinds of taxes.[59] Conversely, Lang highlighted that overlaps between the scope of income tax treaties and inheritance tax agreements can occur as – in practice – the design of taxes may deviate considerably from the definitions set forth in the OECD Model on Estates and Inheritances and on Gifts. By means of an Austrian example, he described that it is arguable that income tax treaties as well as tax agreements on estates and inheritance and on gifts are applicable if a payment is subject to a tax which contains elements of income and inheritance taxes which fall under both treaties. In such situations,

55. F. Sutter, *Erbschaftsteuern und Doppelbesteuerungsabkommen*, Der sachliche Anwendungsbereich des ErbSt-MA, at 43 (M. Lang ed., 1st edition, Linde 2002).
56. Sutter, *Der sachliche Anwendungsbereich des ErbSt-MA*, *supra* n. 19, at 54.
57. *OECD Model Convention on Estates and Inheritance and on Gifts: Commentary on Art. 2* para. 2 (1982); a gift *mortis causa* is one in prospect of death, while a gift *inter vivos* refers to a transfer of goods during the donor's lifetime.
58. Sutter, *Der sachliche Anwendungsbereich des ErbSt-MA*, *supra* n. 19, at 57.
59. Sutter, *Der sachliche Anwendungsbereich des ErbSt-MA*, *supra* n. 19, at 58.

taxpayers must apply both treaties simultaneously. This approach is possible because both tax treaties aim at reducing a person's tax liability and they do not have a contradictory aim.[60] In case of an overlap of the two conventions, one could argue that the MLI is partially applicable to the tax agreements on estates and inheritances and on gifts if the MLI is applicable to the underlying income tax treaty. However, the partial application of the MLI would be limited to the overlapping provisions.

4.3 Agreements for Diplomatic Relations and Immunity

In order to foster diplomatic relations between states, various types of privileges in the host country are granted to diplomatic representatives.[61] For example, diplomatic and consular representatives benefit from tax exemptions in other states under the principle that 'one government should not be taxed by another government'.[62] Regarding tax exemptions for diplomats, several legal sources should be considered.

The Vienna Convention on Diplomatic Relations of 1961[63] was concluded after preparatory work of the UN in Vienna. Article 34 of this Convention provides that '[a] diplomatic agent shall be exempt from all dues and taxes, personal or real, national, regional or municipal'. This tax exemption does not apply to indirect taxes, taxes on private sources of income; inheritance taxes; registration, court or record fees; mortgage dues; and stamp duty, nor to charges levied for specific services rendered.[64] Furthermore, Article 28 provides for an exemption with regard to '[t]he fees and charges levied by the mission in the course of its official duties'. Furthermore, the Vienna Convention on Consular Relations (1963) was ratified and contains similar tax advantages for consular representatives.[65] It is questionable whether these Conventions fulfil the criteria for the application of the MLI under Article 2.

The phrase 'exempt from all taxes' indicates that 'income taxes' that would be levied in the host country are also included in the exemption. Thus, this finding suggests that those agreements cover taxes on income. Furthermore, another criterion is that the purpose of those agreements must be the prevention of double taxation. The preamble of the Vienna Convention on Diplomatic Relations indicates that its purposes is 'the maintenance of international peace and security, and the promotion of friendly relations among nations'. Moreover, the preamble clarifies that the benefits for diplomats have 'to ensure the efficient performance of the functions of diplomatic missions as representing States'. This approach can be justified by the concept of

60. Lang, *supra* n. 21, at 223.
61. C. Zeileissen, *Die abgabenrechtlichen Privilegien in den diplomatischen und konsularischen Beziehungen*, at 1 (1st edition, Braumüller 1971).
62. P. Fischer & H. Köck, *Völkerrecht*, at 228 (6th edition, Linde 2004).
63. *Vienna Convention on Diplomatic Relations* (1961), available at https://treaties.un.org/doc/Publication/UNTS/Volume%20500/v500.pdf (accessed 5 June 2017).
64. M. Richtsteig, *Wiener Übereinkommen über diplomatische und konsularische Beziehungen*, at 80 (1st edition, Nomos 1994).
65. *Vienna Convention on Consular Relations* (1963), available at https://treaties.un.org/doc/publication/UNTS/Volume%20596/v596.pdf (accessed 3 May 2017); *see* Art. 32 (Exemption from taxation of consular premises), Art. 49 (Exemption from taxation), Art. 60 (Exemption from taxation of consular premises), Art. 66 (Exemption from taxation).

representation, which means that one sovereign does not tax another sovereign. Furthermore, tax exemptions have a functional necessity which should help diplomats in performing their duties independently.[66] In addition, the Convention does not contain any hint that the intention of the drafters was to eliminate double taxation. However, the host country is prevented from taxing diplomats, as they are usually already taxed in their home country. Thus one could argue that diplomatic agreements constitutes agreements for the 'avoidance of double taxation' under Article 1(a) of the MLI.

Nevertheless, it is unrealistic for them to fall under the scope of the MLI. The reason for this is that each contracting party[67] must notify to the depositary that it wishes to apply the MLI to the agreement. Such a political commitment is quite unrealistic because the Vienna Convention on Diplomatic Relations has been ratified by over 150 sates.[68] Moreover, several tax treaties contain provisions covering members of diplomatic and consular missions.[69] Those agreements can, of course, fall under the scope of the MLI when the parties notify the agreement to the depositary.

It is common practice for international organizations to set up treaties that regulate privileges and immunities for the organization. For example, the United Nations set up the Convention on the Privileges and Immunities of the United Nations.[70] Other organizations have more or less copied this convention for their own purposes. Under this Convention, representatives of the UN enjoy the same tax exemptions as diplomats under the Vienna Convention on Diplomatic Relations. Moreover, the United Nations is exempt from all direct taxes on its assets, income and other properties.[71] These tax privileges are necessary for the fulfilment of the purposes of the organization and not for the prevention of double taxation. Furthermore, tax exemptions prevent organizations from annexing part of the common funds for purposes of paying taxes in a specific country, which would undermine the concept of equality of UN members.[72] Moreover, international organizations enter into so-called headquarter agreements with their host countries.[73] Under these agreements, the host countries grant tax exemptions to the respective organizations and their employees.[74]

66. D.S. Smit, *General Report*, in *Tax Rules in Non-Tax Agreements*, at 3 (M. Lang, P. Pistone, J. Schuch, C. Staringer & A. Stork eds.,1st edition, IBFD 2012).
67. Article 2(1)(a)(ii) MLI.
68. Richtsteig, *supra* n. 64, at 80.
69. Zeileissen, *supra* n. 61, at 38.
70. *Convention on the Privileges and Immunities of the United Nations*, available at http://www.un.org/en/ethics/pdf/convention.pdf (accessed 5 June 2017).
71. Smit, *supra* n. 66, at 8.
72. Smit, *supra* n. 66, at 9.
73. For example Austria has several agreements with seventeen organizations that have premises in Austria, such as the *Agreement Between the Republic of Austria and the Organization of the Petroleum Exporting Countries regarding the Headquarters of the Organization of the Petroleum Exporting Countries* (BGBl 382/1974), and the *Agreement Between the Republic of Austria and United Nations regarding the Seat of the United Nations in Vienna*, available at http://ilmc.univie.ac.at/uploads/media/HQ_Agreement_UN_-_Austria.pdf (accessed 3 May 2017).
74. For example, sections 24 and 37 of the *Agreement Between the Republic of Austria and United Nations regarding the Seat of the United Nations in Vienna*.

In light of the MLI, it remains debatable as to whether those treaties may fall under the scope of the MLI, as they deal with tax exemptions that help to prevent double taxation for the employees of international organizations. Therefore, diplomatic agreements of international organizations and headquarter agreements fulfil the criteria for the application of Article 2(1)(a) of the MLI, as they deal with income taxes and help to prevent double taxation, despite the fact that the agreements are not ratified between states, as international organizations do not fulfil the statehood criterion.[75] It is significant that international organizations are not states, as under Article 2(1)(b) of the MLI, a party to the MLI must be a state or a jurisdiction. At first glance, international organizations do not seem to fulfil this criterion, with the result that the MLI is not applicable to agreements of international organizations. However, this conclusion may well be called into question, as international organizations are considered to be states under international customary law.[76] As a result, the MLI is theoretically also applicable to such agreements. The practical impact of this reasoning is limited, as the agreements do not aim at preventing double taxation. Therefore, it seems highly unrealistic that political consensus will be reached such that the MLI would apply to those agreements.

5 CONTRACTING JURISDICTIONS

5.1 General Remarks

Article 2 of the MLI stipulates a number of prerequisites that must be fulfilled by an underlying tax agreement, and it defines the term 'party'. Under Article 2(1)(i) of the MLI, a covered tax agreement must be in force between parties, jurisdictions or territories. Under Article 2(1)(b)(ii), parties are states and jurisdictions for which the MLI has entered into force. This raises the question as to how to interpret these terms, and requires a close examination of the legal requirements that must be fulfilled to become a party to the MLI.

5.2 States as Parties to the MLI

The MLI clarifies that states for which the MLI has entered into force, are parties to the MLI. However, the MLI does not contain a definition of the term 'states'. Under international law, states are considered to be sovereign entities that need not accept any other authority unless they choose to do so. International customary law has come up with a list of criteria that can be used when assessing the legal classification of an entity.[77] These criteria are codified in the Convention on the Rights and Duties of

75. *See* section 5.2.
76. K. Daxkobler & M. Seiler, *Austria*, in *Tax Rules in Non-Tax Agreements*, at 69 (M. Lang, P. Pistone, J. Schuch, C. Staringer & A. Stork eds., 1st edition, IBFD 2012).
77. J. Klabber, *International Law*, at 69 (1st edition, Cambridge 2013).

States,[78] which was signed at a conference of American States in Montevideo. Even though this agreement was ratified only by American states and is therefore applicable only between the contracting parties, this agreement serves as a significant tool for interpreting the statehood criteria. Under that Convention, states must have population, a territory, an effective government and the capacity to enter into relations with other states.[79]

The first requirement set forth in the Convention on the Rights and Duties of States is that a state must have a population. It is irrelevant how the population got there or how large it is.[80] The second criterion is that the state must have a certain territory in which the population claims the power of disposition and organizes its existence. The Convention on the Rights and Duties of States does not require a minimum size of a territory. Furthermore, as long as a state has a core territory, border disputes are not detrimental to an entity's statehood.[81] The first two requirements of this Convention - namely territory and population - are more or less formal, as a state either has them or does not. The remaining criteria are more substantive and therefore are much more noteworthy from a legal perspective.[82]

Another essential requirement in order to qualify for statehood is that the territory have an effective government. In the Island of Palmas case, the arbitrator Huber asserted the opinion that effective government is reflected in the fact that a state is capable of guaranteeing that law and order are upheld.[83] As long as law and order are ensured in a territory, international law is satisfied. In this context, one should bear in mind that this concept applies regardless of the form of government (e.g., democracy, dictatorship).[84]

Regarding the state requirements it is important that the territory be governed completely independently.[85] This means, in effect, that a state may make independent decisions concerning its internal and external relations, and has the capacity to enter into international relations. Therefore, the last of the aforementioned requirements was particularly significant in the days of colonialism, as in the past many territories lacked the sovereignty under international law to enter into international relations. Colonialism gave rise to various types of relations between the colonizers and the colonized. Some colonized territories were entirely dominated by the colonizer, while others were afforded varying degrees of sovereignty.[86] Even today, some territories do not have the capacity to enter into international relations. In general, another state may then be responsible for the entity's international relations. Furthermore, Article 7 of the

78. *Convention on Rights and Duties of States*. As this Convention was signed in Montevideo, it is known as the Montevideo Convention.
79. Klabber, *supra* n. 77, at 70.
80. Klabber, *supra* n. 77, at 70.
81. A. Verdross & B. Simma, *Universelles Völkerrecht*, at 224 (3rd edition, Duncker & Humblot 1984).
82. Klabber, *supra* n. 77, at 71.
83. *Island of Palmas (United States v. Netherlands)*, sole arbiter Max Huber, 2 UN Rep. Intl. Arb. Awards 829.
84. Klabber, *supra* n. 77, at 71.
85. Verdross & Simma, *supra* n. 81, at 225.
86. Klabber, *supra* n. 77, at 71.

Vienna Convention on the Law of Treaties, which is relevant for the interpretation of the MLI, requires that every state possess 'capacity to conclude treaties'.

Territories that fulfil the statehood criteria have the ability to ratify the MLI under Article 27(1)(a) of the MLI. Parties to the MLI are states that have ratified the MLI, and for which the instrument has entered into force under Article 34 of the MLI.[87] Moreover, within its substantive provisions, the MLI uses the term 'contracting jurisdiction' instead of the more commonly used expression 'contracting state'. Contracting jurisdictions are parties to covered tax agreements that are notified to the depositary. However, the term 'contracting jurisdictions' refers not only to states, as it also includes jurisdictions and territories that are parties to a covered tax agreement. This indicates that the MLI is designed not only for states.[88] Furthermore, this wording should enable jurisdictions with fiscal sovereignty but without sovereignty in international law to ratify the MLI.[89]

5.3 Non-state Jurisdictions

The MLI recognizes situations in which territories do not fulfil the statehood criteria because they lack sovereignty in international law, and allows them to nevertheless apply the MLI. Thus, Article 2(1)(b)(ii) stipulates that covered tax agreements may also be agreements between 'jurisdictions or territories which are Parties to an agreement described above and for whose international relations a Party is responsible'. As a result, such jurisdictions can become a party to the MLI when the state that is responsible for their international relations notifies to the depositary that the jurisdiction wishes to join the MLI. The notifications that a state makes for the jurisdiction the international relations for which it is responsible, can differ from its own notifications.[90]

However, non-state jurisdictions cannot ratify the MLI without meeting the conditions set forth in Article 27. This provision sets forth specific rules that must be fulfilled by signatories of the MLI. Article 27(1) of the MLI provides that the MLI is open for signature by:

> 1. As of 31 December 2016, this Convention shall be open for signature by:
>   a) all States;
>   b) Guernsey (the United Kingdom of Great Britain and Northern Ireland); Isle of Man (the United Kingdom of Great Britain and Northern Ireland); Jersey (the United Kingdom of Great Britain and Northern Ireland); and
>   c) any other jurisdiction authorised to become a Party by means of a decision by consensus of the Parties and Signatories.

As a result, the MLI is explicitly open for signature for Guernsey, Isle of Man and Jersey. These islands are known as Crown dependencies, as the United Kingdom is

87. OECD, *Explanatory Statement to the MLI* (2016), *supra* n. 3, para. 34.
88. OECD, *Explanatory Statement to the MLI* (2016), *supra* n. 3, para. 35.
89. Bendlinger, *supra* n. 42, at 7.
90. *See* Art. 29(2).

responsible for their international relations.[91] The inclusion of a certain jurisdiction in the list of jurisdictions that are eligible to ratify the MLI must be authorized by the state that is responsible for its international relations, and it must also be agreed upon by the ad hoc group. Article 27(1)(b) of the MLI exhaustively enumerates all non-state jurisdictions for which the MLI is open for signature by 31 December 2016.[92]

Article 27(1)(c) of the MLI provides for the opportunity to authorize further non-state jurisdictions that do not fulfil the statehood criterion, to nevertheless become parties to the MLI. However, this requires a unanimous decision by the parties to the MLI. Therefore, a non-state jurisdiction may become a party to the MLI only if no party objects.[93] Under this provision, one party to the MLI has the power to prevent the ratification of the MLI for a specific non-state jurisdiction that is not mentioned in Article 27(1)(b) of the MLI. In addition, Article 27(1)(c) of the MLI refers not only to non-state jurisdictions for which another party is responsible for their international relations. Therefore, also non-state jurisdictions that act on their own behalf may refer to this provision.

5.4 Jurisdictions with Limited Recognition of Statehood

The analysis here considers whether jurisdictions with limited recognition of statehood may ratify the MLI. The MLI does not explicitly refer to such jurisdictions in its Article 27(1), as this provision is specifically designed to set out rules for states and non-state jurisdictions. In the context of the MLI, it is critical for jurisdictions with limited recognition of statehood to know whether or not they are considered as states or non-state jurisdictions, as different rules apply to each.[94] This is especially relevant considering that Article 27(1)(c) of the MLI stipulates that any party may object to a non-state jurisdiction's admission and may therefore prevent a non-state jurisdiction from becoming eligible to ratify the MLI.

In practice, jurisdictions that do not fulfil the statehood criteria will not be recognized by the international community of states as equal partners. However, political considerations must also be taken into account as – in some cases – states do not have an interest in recognizing another state, irrespective of the existence or non-existence of the criteria of statehood. Therefore, it is possible that states may have a different view concerning the recognition of statehood for a specific jurisdiction. For those jurisdictions, the legal consequences of the non-recognition are less clear. Generally, in international law, the academic discussion concerning the legal effects of the recognition of statehood is known as the 'great debate' between the declaratory theory and the constitutive theory.[95] The declaratory theory regards the recognition of statehood as a political act that is independent from the existence of a state in

91. *See* House of Lords, Brexit: the Crown Dependencies, 19th Report of Session 2016-17, 7 (HL Paper 136).
92. OECD, *Explanatory Statement to the MLI* (2016), *supra* n. 3, para. 261.
93. OECD, *Explanatory Statement to the MLI* (2016), *supra* n. 3, para. 262.
94. OECD, *Explanatory Statement to the MLI* (2016), *supra* n. 3, paras 261 and 262.
95. Klabber, *supra* n. 77, at 72.

international law. On the other hand, the constitutive theory suggests that a state is created only after the recognition of its statehood.[96]

However, this debate is not useful in the context of the MLI, as the MLI provides its own framework. Thus, under the rules of Article 27(1)(c) of the MLI, a consensus of the parties is required if a non-state jurisdictions wants to ratify the MLI. In light of this provision, it is obvious that the rules of Article 27(1)(c) of the MLI apply for jurisdictions with limited recognition of statehood. But, what happens if only a limited number of parties do not recognize a jurisdiction as a state because there is no consensus among the parties of the MLI as to whether the jurisdiction constitutes a state in international law? Is there also a consensus needed in such situations under Article 27(1)(c) of the MLI or not?

Differing views concerning the statehood quality of a jurisdiction leads to the situation where not all parties to the MLI recognize a jurisdiction as an equal partner for the MLI. Therefore, there are strong reasons to apply the more specific rule of Article 27(1)(c) of the MLI, which is especially designed for non-state jurisdictions in such a situation, as well. Only this approach ensures that the same view of all signatories of the MLI is reached concerning the ability of jurisdictions with limited recognition of statehood to ratify the MLI. Moreover, this consensus is of utmost importance, as the MLI must be understood as a multilateral convention of equal partners which follows the principle of reciprocity. Thus, jurisdictions with limited recognition of statehood should be classified as non-state jurisdictions under Article 27(1)(c) of the MLI. If a consensus is not reached under Article 27(1)(c) of the MLI, a non-state jurisdiction cannot ratify the MLI. However, the non-state jurisdiction may adopt the outcomes of the MLI on a bilateral basis instead.

6 CONCLUSION

Summing up, the MLI has the potential to considerably change international taxation. With one modification of the treaty network, the MLI implements the income tax treaty-related BEPS Actions into the treaty network. However, the application of the MLI is restricted to agreements that fulfil specific criteria set forth in Article 2 of the MLI. Under that rule, the scope of the MLI is limited to agreements 'for the avoidance of double taxation with respect to taxes on income' for which each party has made a notification to the depositary. Therefore a specific agreement is within the scope of the MLI only if the parties to the treaty explicitly wish to do so. This approach follows the principle of reciprocity in international law, as it prevents a unilateral modification of a treaty by the MLI. Furthermore, the MLI contains numerous options that can be exercised by the contracting jurisdiction. Such options give contracting parties the opportunity to adjust the impact of the MLI on their covered tax agreements based on their own preferences.

Moreover, Article 2 of the MLI requires that the underlying covered tax agreement cover 'taxes on income' within its scope. Although the MLI does not contain a

96. J. Crawford, *The Creation of States in International Law*, at 28 (1st edition, Oxford 2006).

definition of the term 'taxes on income', it can be derived from the context of the MLI that the income tax definition under Article 2 of the OECD Model (2014) should apply to the MLI. What is more, the explanatory statement of the MLI clarifies that treaties that cover capital taxes and capital gains may also fall within the scope of the MLI as long as income taxes are covered. However, agreements that deal solely with other types of taxes, air transport or social security are not intended to fall under the scope of the MLI.[97]

Under Article 2 of the MLI, the multilateral convention modifies agreements for the avoidance of double taxation. Thus the application is not limited to agreements for the avoidance of double taxation that follow the OECD Model, as there is no such requirement for the application. Therefore all tax treaties that deal with 'taxes on income' can potentially be modified through the MLI. This includes both bilateral and multilateral income tax treaties. Regarding multilateral tax treaties like the Nordic Convention, special attention should be given to the requirement that each party to this convention must notify the instrument to the depositary individually. An analysis of this article has shown that agreements for diplomatic relations and immunities theoretically fulfil the requirements of Article 2 of the MLI, as they provide tax exemptions for diplomats and potentially also have the ability to fall under the scope of the MLI. However, this seems unrealistic in practice. In contrast, the MLI is not applicable to tax agreements on estates and inheritance and on gifts, as they are not concerned with taxes on income, which constitutes a requirement for the application.

The MLI is open for signature for all states, and any other non-state jurisdictions that are authorized by a decision of the signatories of the MLI. Under international law, states are considered to be sovereign entities that fulfil the criteria for statehood, namely a population, a territory and the capacity to enter into relations with other states. Under Article 27(1)(c) of the MLI, each party to the MLI has the power to hinder a non-state jurisdiction from ratifying the MLI, as a unanimous decision of all parties is required with regard to non-state jurisdictions. States with limited recognition of statehood can also ratify the MLI; however as they are not undoubtedly classified as states, this also requires a consensus of the parties.

97. OECD, *Explanatory Statement to the MLI* (2016), *supra* n. 3, para. 25.

CHAPTER 2

Interpretation of Terms Used in the Multilateral Instrument

Svetlana Wakounig[*]

1 INTRODUCTION

The Multilateral Instrument (MLI) is part of the OECD base erosion and profit shifting (BEPS) Package. The OECD BEPS Package, which contains fifteen Actions, aims at preventing BEPS. The MLI that results from Action 15 was published on 24 November 2016 and has been open for signature since 31 December 2016. The MLI has been described by the OECD Secretary General Angel Gurria as 'a turning point in tax treaty history'.[1] The purpose of the MLI is to modify existing tax treaties to implement the tax treaty-related measures developed through the BEPS Project. Therefore, it can be regarded as a tool to prevent BEPS. The MLI was presented together with an Explanatory Statement in which the OECD explains in more detail the operation of the MLI.[2]

The MLI contains many specific terms. These terms can be divided into two groups: terms that are defined by the MLI and terms that are not explicitly defined by the MLI. The Vienna Convention on the Law of Treaties (hereinafter 'the Vienna Convention') states that a special meaning is to be given to a term if it is established that the parties so intended. Thus, any definition of a term given to it by the MLI overrides any other definition the term may have. Terms defined by the MLI do not need any further interpretation. However, the MLI also contains terms that are not

* The author would like to thank Univ.-Prof. Dr DDr h.c. Michael Lang for his encouragement, comments and supervision.

1. OECD, *Remarks at Adoption Ceremony of the BEPS Treaty, Remarks by Angel Gurria, OECD Secretary-General in Paris, France 24 November 2016* (2016).
2. OECD, *Explanatory Statement to the Multilateral Convention to Implement Tax Treaty Related Measures to Prevent Base Erosion and Profit Shifting* (2016).

explicitly defined by it. As an interpretation rule of the MLI, terms that are not explicitly defined in any provision in the MLI should have the meaning that they have under the relevant covered tax agreement, unless the context otherwise requires. The critical question concerns what the *context* means. This chapter deals with the interpretation of the terms used in the MLI and offers an overview of the main interpretation rules provided by the Vienna Convention. Finally, it focuses on Article 2(2) of the MLI and the effects that this article has on the interpretation of terms.

The Vienna Convention provides numerous interpretation rules. However, interpretation is never a mere formalistic procedure. Therefore, the interpretation rules of the Vienna Convention should not be overestimated. When interpreting, the primary goal must be always kept in mind. The main question concerns what is the content of the provision.[3]

2 GENERAL INTERPRETATION

2.1 The Vienna Convention on the Law of Treaties

The MLI is an international treaty. For international treaties, the main interpretation rules are codified in the Vienna Convention.[4] Usually, only parties are bound by an agreement. This is the result of the rule *pacta tertiis nec nocent nec prosunt*. The interpretation rules codified in the Vienna Convention are considered as international customary law.[5] Even if a state has not ratified the Vienna Convention, the codified interpretation rules are applicable to treaties concluded by that state. The International Court for Justice applies the interpretation rules contained in the Vienna Convention to all international treaties.[6] In addition, the Vienna Convention is limited to treaties concluded between states in written form.[7] The MLI is an international treaty that is concluded by states and is in written form. Therefore, the interpretation rules codified in the Vienna Convention are applicable to the MLI.

The interpretation rules under the Vienna Convention are found in Articles 31 and 32.

Article 31(1) of the Vienna Convention states the general rule of interpretation, stipulating that 'a treaty shall be interpreted in good faith in accordance with the ordinary meaning to be given to the terms of the treaty in their context and in the light of its object and purpose'. Therefore, the provision clearly indicates that the starting

3. H.F. Köck, *Vertragsinterpretation und Vertragsrechtskonvention: zur Bedeutung der Artikel 31 und 32 der Wiener Vertragsrechtskonvention 1969*, at 67 (Duncker und Humblot 1976).
4. For Austria, *see* Wiener Übereinkommen über das Recht der Verträge, Bundesgesetzblatt (BGBl) 40/1980.
5. M. Lang, *Die Auslegung des multilateralen Instruments*, Steuer und Wirtschaft International (SWI) 1, at 11 (2017).
6. H. Loukota, *Die rechtliche Relevanz von BEPS im Lichte der Wiener Vertragsrechtskonvention*, SWI, at 436, 437 (2016).
7. C. Binder & K. Zemanek, *Das Völkervertragsrecht*, in *Österreichisches Handbuch des Völkerrechts*, para. 235 et seq. (A. Reinisch ed., Manz 2013).

point is the term and its ordinary meaning.[8] The so-called ordinary-meaning rule is primary, but when a word has more than one ordinary meaning, the meaning must be chosen that is reasonable within the context.[9] Thus, the grammatical interpretation offers a framework for any subsequent interpretation; it is the beginning of the interpretation. A special meaning can be attributed to a term if it is established that the parties so intended.[10] The final part of Article 31(1), the object and the purpose, focus on the teleological element. The main issue relating to object and purpose concerns what these terms stand for, how they are to be identified and what use is to be made of them.[11]

Article 31(2) defines the context of a treaty for the purpose of the interpretation. The text of a treaty must be read as a whole. This is called the systematic interpretation.[12] The preamble and the annexes are also of critical importance.[13] Therefore, the preamble indicates the purpose of the MLI, which is of critical importance when engaging in interpretation.

Article 31(3) of the Vienna Convention indicates that there it is also necessary to take into account any subsequent agreement between the parties regarding the interpretation, any subsequent practice regarding the interpretation and any relevant rules of international law.[14] This rule is very significant for agreements found in the mutual agreement procedure defined in Article 16 of the MLI or through the conference of the parties, defined in Article 31 of the MLI. Lang has noted that those agreements *must be taken into account*. This does not give them more weight than any other agreement.[15] Tax treaties not only bind the two parties; they also have an impact on taxpayers. Therefore, they must meet high constitutional standards in most countries.[16]

Alongside constitutional standards, the separation of power must also be considered. The separation of powers forbids an administration from legislating or changing existing regulations, and is of even greater importance with regard to tax law. In most countries, the conclusion of tax treaties requires the approval of the legislature. One must be very careful when taking into account any subsequent agreement between two different parties, except a case where the legislature has approved the agreement found in the mutual agreement procedure.[17] It has been suggested that Article 31(3) of the Vienna Convention (and so also any agreement found through the mutual agreement procedure) should be viewed as significant only when there are still open questions

8. M. Lang, *Auslegung von Doppelbesteuerungsabkommen und authentische Vertragssprachen*, Internationales Steuerrecht (IStR), at 403, 408 (2011).
9. Köck, *supra* n. 3, at 86 et seq.
10. Article 31(4) Vienna Convention.
11. Lang, *Die Auslegung des multilateralen Instruments*, *supra* n. 5, at 11.
12. R.J. Nimmervoll, *Das Strafverfahren*, at 2 et seq. (LexisNexis 2010).
13. Article 31(2) Vienna Convention.
14. Article 31(3) Vienna Convention.
15. Lang, *Die Auslegung des multilateralen Instruments*, *supra* n. 5, at 12.
16. M. Lang, *Doppelbesteuerungsabkommen und innerstaatliches Recht*, at 86 et seq. (A. Orac 1992).
17. M. Lang, *Art 3 Abs 2 OECD-MA und die Auslegung von Doppelbesteuerungsabkommen*, Internationale Wirtschaftsbriefe (IWB), at 281, 284 (2011).

with regard to the interpretation. Any agreement or practice between two parties should not have any impact on a multilateral (tax) treaty.[18]

Article 31(4) of the Vienna Convention defines that a special meaning is to be given to a term if it is established that the parties so intended. When the MLI uses terms that are already defined in the MLI, this rule is significant, as the parties' definition of a term is then superior to any other definition of the term.

Under Article 32 of the Vienna Convention, the *travaux préparatoires* are to also be taken into account. This refers to the materials that had a preparatory function and that are significant for the historic interpretation.[19] The main function of those *travaux préparatoires* is to confirm the interpretation carried out in accordance to Article 31 of the Vienna Convention; to sort out any ambiguities or uncertainties; or to resolve any meaningless or unreasonable outcomes.[20] In conclusion, like any other international treaty, the MLI must be interpreted in accordance with Articles 31 and 32 of the Vienna Convention.

2.2 Explanatory Statement

The MLI was introduced together with an Explanatory Statement. The Explanatory Statement aims at clarifying the approach that is taken in the MLI and how singular provisions covered by the MLI will be affected.[21] The Explanatory Statement clearly states that it does not address the interpretation of the underlying BEPS measures, except for the mandatory binding arbitration provisions.[22]

The MLI is open for signature, but the Explanatory Statement is not part of the signed MLI. States (contracting jurisdictions) can be bound only by contracts or instruments that the state has approved.[23] Because the Explanatory Statement is not part of the signed agreement, the contracting jurisdictions are not bound by it and therefore the Explanatory Statement cannot have a legally binding character.

In the past, the legal status of the Commentary on the OECD Model has been analysed on multiple occasions. Mostly, the Commentary on the OECD Model was classified as either a special meaning given to a term under Article 31(4) of the Vienna Convention[24] or as circumstances of a treaty's conclusion under Article 32 of the

18. Lang, *Die Auslegung des multilateralen Instruments, supra* n. 5, at 12.
19. Lang, *Art 3 Abs 2 OECD-MA und die Auslegung von Doppelbesteuerungsabkommen, supra* n. 17, at 283.
20. Lang, *Die Auslegung des multilateralen Instruments, supra* n. 5, at 11; Köck, *Vertragsinterpretation und Vertragsrechtskonvention: zur Bedeutung der Artikel 31 und 32 der Wiener Vertragsrechtskonvention 1960, at* 93.
21. OECD, *Explanatory Statement to the MLI* (2016), *supra* n. 2, para. 11.
22. OECD, *Explanatory Statement to the MLI* (2016), *supra* n. 2, para. 12.
23. Binder & Zemanek, *supra* n. 7, para. 247.
24. *See also* M. Lang, *Wer hat das Sagen im Steuerrecht? Die Bedeutung des OECD-Steuerausschusses und seiner Working Parties*, Österreichisches Steuerzeitung (ÖStZ), at 203, 205 (2006); R. Prokisch, *Fragen der Auslegung von Doppelbesteuerungsabkommen*, SWI, at 52, 54 et seq. (1994); M. Lang, *Die Bedeutung der 1995 erfolgten Änderung des OECD-Musterabkommens*, in *Die Weiterentwicklung des OECD-Musterabkommens*, at 27, 29 et seq. (M. Lang, H. Loukota & D. Lüthi eds., Linde 1996); H. Jirousek, *Kritische Anmerkungen zur Auslegung von Doppelbesteuerungsabkommen*, SWI, at 112, 113 (1998).

Vienna Convention.[25] These findings can be analogously applied to the discussion regarding the Explanatory Statement and the BEPS Actions.[26] The Explanatory Statement and the BEPS Actions can thus be either subsumed under Article 31(4) or Article 32 of the Vienna Convention. Article 31(4) states that a special meaning is to be given to a term if the parties so intended. The special meaning will override any other definition of this term. The International Law Commission stated that this article '... provides for the somewhat exceptional case where, notwithstanding the apparent meaning of a term in its context, it is established that the parties intended it to have a special meaning'.[27] The advantage of subsuming the Explanatory Statement and the BEPS Actions under Article 31(4) of the Vienna Convention is that they are not classified as subsidiary interpretation material.

Classifying the Explanatory Statement and the BEPS Actions as supplementary means of interpretation under Article 32 of the Vienna Convention would give them a subsidiary meaning, but still a meaning when interpreting. Having recourse to those supplementary means of interpretation is possible only when the interpretation under Article 31 of the Vienna Convention: (i) leaves the meaning ambiguous or obscure; or (ii) leads to a result that is manifestly absurd or unreasonable. The subsumption of the Explanatory Statement and the BEPS Actions would therefore give them solely a subsidiary meaning.

The Explanatory Statement and the BEPS Actions are classified as interpretation material under either Article 31(4) or Article 32 of the Vienna Convention, and are a significant tool when engaging in interpretation. Neither has a legally binding character, but both are of great significance when engaging in interpretation.

3 INTERPRETATION UNDER THE MLI

3.1 Lessons to Be Learned from Article 3(2) of the OECD Model

The MLI's interpretation rule is found in its Article 2(2). Article 2(2) states that any term not defined in the MLI is to have, unless the context otherwise requires, the meaning that it has under the relevant covered tax agreement. Article 2(2) can be

---

25. J.M. Mössner, *Zur Auslegung von Doppelbesteuerungsabkommen*, in *Liber Amicorum Professor Ignaz Seidl-Hohenveldern*, at 403, 411 et seq. (K.H. Böckstiegel et al. eds., Kluwer Law Intl. 1998); M. Lang, in, *Aktuelle Entwicklungen im Internationalen Steuerrecht*, at 15 et seq. (W, Gassner, M. Lang & E. Lechner eds., (Linde 1994); Lang, *Wer hat das Sagen im Steuerrecht?*, *supra* n. 24, at 204. For a dissenting opinion, *see* H. Loukota, *Die rechtliche Relevanz von BEPS im Lichte der Wiener Vertragsrechtskonvention*, *supra* n. 6, at 440; C. Gloria, *Das steuerliche Verständigungsverfahren und das Recht auf diplomatischen Schutz*, at 90 et seq. (Duncker und Humblot 1998); M. Lang, *Die Bedeutung des Musterabkommens und des Kommentars des OECD-Steuerausschusses für die Auslegung von Doppelbesteuerungsabkommen*, in *Aktuelle Entwicklungen im Internationalen Steuerrecht* (W. Gassner, M. Lang & E. Lechner eds., Linde 1994), at 13, 15.
26. These are BEPS Action 2, BEPS Action 6, BEPS Action 7 and BEPS Action 14. The Explanatory Statement refers to the BEPS Actions.
27. Commentary to the ILC Final Draft, 17 U.N. Conference on the Law of Treaties, U.N. Doc. A/CONF. 39/Add 2, 7, at 37.

regarded as the MLI's 'equivalent' to Article 3(2) of the OECD Model.[28] Article 3(2) of the OECD Model states that any term not defined in the tax treaty is to have, unless the context otherwise requires, the meaning that it has at that time under the law of that state for the purposes of the taxes to which the treaty applies. The equivalency between those two articles justifies taking at first a look at Article 3(2) of the OECD Model. The discussion with regard to Article 3(2) of the OECD Model is of major importance for Article 2(2) of the MLI. Questions that will be raised with regard to the MLI's interpretation rule have already discussed with regard to Article 3(2) of the OECD Model.

One discussion concerns the term *application*. Avery Jones raises the argument that a state 'reads' a treaty when the state wants to find out whether it is entitled to tax income. An application occurs when the state uses a treaty's provision to reach a different taxation result than it would have under the state's own domestic law. If the state notices that its own right of taxation is not limited, the state applies domestic law.[29] The MLI does not limit any taxation rights. It instead implements the changes that have been made through the BEPS Project, and thus it changes (existing) tax treaties. If the conclusions of Avery Jones were to be applied to the discussion regarding the MLI, it could mean that an application of the treaty occurs only if the provisions of the MLI materially derogate a bilateral treaty provision or add another provision to the bilateral treaty.[30] But when the result is that there is no change in the tax treaty because the bilateral treaty provisions already correspond to the provisions of the MLI, no 'application' would be deemed to take place.

At least regarding Article 3(2) of the OECD Model, this opinion is not prevailing.[31] Opinions have been offered that if a state's authority comes to the conclusion that the treaty does not limit the states' taxation rights, this is also a result of the application of the treaty. When a state comes to the conclusion that a tax treaty leaves its taxation right unaffected, this is of course also a result of an application. It would be artificial to make a distinction regarding the fact that in this case the state would only read the treaty.[32]

Another discussion concerns the renvoi to national law. Also Article 3(2) of the MLI states that 'any term not defined herein shall, unless the context otherwise requires, have the meaning that it has at that time' under the relevant covered tax agreement. The consequence is that one must look into the covered tax agreements. But the critical question concerns the point when recourse to the covered tax agreement is required. Article 3(2) of the OECD Model states as follows:

28. D.W. Blum, *The Relationship Between the OECD Multilateral Instrument and Covered Tax Agreements: Multilateralism and the Interpretation of Undefined Terms*, forthcoming.
29. J.F. Avery Jones, *Qualification Conflicts: The Meaning of Application in Article 3(2) of the OECD Model*, in *Libercorum Beusch*, at 43, 47 (H. Beisse, M. Lutter & H. Närger eds., Gruyter 1993).
30. M. Lang, *The Interpretation of the Multilateral Instrument*, in *Skattepolitisk Oversigt* (2017), forthcoming.
31. K. Vogel, *DBA-Kommentar*, Art. 3, para. 65 (3rd edition, C.H. Beck 1996). *See also* M. Lang, *Die Bedeutung des innerstaatlichen Rechts für die DBA-Auslegung*, in *Außensteuerrecht, Doppelbesteuerungsabkommen und EU-Recht im Spannungsverhältnis: Festschrift für Helmut Debatin zum 70. Geburtstag*, at 283, 286 (G. Burmester & D. Endres eds., C.H. Beck 1997).
32. Lang, *The Interpretation of the Multilateral Instrument*, *supra* n. 30.

> As regards the application of the Convention at any time by a Contracting State, any term not defined therein shall, unless the context otherwise requires, have the meaning that it has at that time under the law of that State for the purposes of the taxes to which the Convention applies, any meaning under the applicable tax laws of that State prevailing over a meaning given to the term under the laws of that State.

The meaning of the reservation under which the renvoi to domestic law is possible, is controversial. In particular, tax administrations share the opinion that the phrase 'unless the context otherwise requires' has almost no relevance. If a definition that is not specified in the treaty is being used, under Article 3(2) of the OECD Model the renvoi to the domestic law of the applying state is to be made; the recourse may be avoided only in exceptional cases.[33]

The contrary view gives special significance to the phrase 'unless the context otherwise requires'. The context represents not only the systematic interpretation, but also the grammatical, historical and teleological interpretations. This emphasizes again that tax treaties are to be first interpreted on their own accord under consideration of all interpretation rules. If the grammatical, systematic, historical and teleological interpretations do not lead to any result, a renvoi to domestic law is to be made.[34] Usually, using all possible interpretation methods leads to a satisfying result, so when interpreting tax treaties this should also be the case.[35] It has been stated in the literature that Article 3(2) of the OECD Model is not primary a renvoi to domestic law. Instead, it is another emphasis that the interpretation of a treaty must include all interpretation methods, and thus also the systematic interpretation that places the context of a treaty into focus.[36] This is the only way that leads to a consistent interpretation of a tax treaty in both states.[37] A recourse to domestic law should be made only when the interpretation would otherwise fail.[38]

33. *See also* H. Loukota, *Grundsätze für die steuerliche Behandlung international tätiger Gastprofessoren*, SWI, at 465 et seq. (1998); H. Loukota, *Vermeidung von Irrwegen bei der DBA-Auslegung*, SWI, at 559, 563 (1998); at: Supreme Admin. Ct. (*Verwaltungsgerichtshof*, VwGH) 12 December 2006, 2005/15/0158.
34. *See also* M. Lang, *Die Maßgeblichkeit des innerstaatlichen Rechts für die DBA-Auslegung in der jüngsten Rechtsprechung des VwGH*, SWI, at 199, 205 et seq. (2007). Also, the Austrian Supreme Administrative Court rejected the recourse to national law in its decision 2005/15/0158 of 13 December 2006.
35. M. Lang, *Die Auslegung von Doppelbesteuerungsabkommen als Problem der Planungssicherheit bei grenzüberschreitenden Sachverhalten*, in *Handbuch der internationalen Steuerplanung*, at 1351 (S. Grotherr ed., C.H. Beck 2011).
36. *See also* M. Lang, *Die Bedeutung des originär innerstaatlichen Rechts bei Auslegung und Anwendung von Doppelbesteuerungsbakommen*, SWI, at 61, 62 (1999); Lang, *Die Maßgeblichkeit des innerstaatlichen Rechts für die DBA-Auslegung in der jüngsten Rechtsprechung des VwGH*, *supra* n. 34, at 206; Lang, *Art 3 Abs 2 OECD-MA und die Auslegung von Doppelbesteuerungsabkommen*, *supra* n. 17, at 291.
37. Lang, *Die Auslegung des multilateralen Instruments*, *supra* n. 5, at 14.
38. Lang, *Art 3 Abs 2 OECD-MA und die Auslegung von Doppelbesteuerungsabkommen*, *supra* n. 17, at 291.

Vogel takes a position somewhere in between. Only in convincing cases is the context to be of importance, and usually a recourse should be made to domestic law of the applying state.[39]

All this illustrates how much confusion Article 3(2) of the OECD Model creates. Prokisch and Vogel therefore suggested the deletion of Article 3(2) from the OECD Model.[40]

3.2 Article 2(2) of the MLI

Article 2(2) of the MLI is the interpretation rule codified in the MLI, and provides that any term not defined in the MLI is to have, unless the context otherwise requires, the meaning that it has under the relevant covered tax agreement.

The MLI contains some specific definitions, including 'covered tax agreement' and 'party'.[41] In the absence of a definition, recourse should be had to covered tax agreements, provided that the context does not require otherwise. Usually, a provision similar to Article 3(2) of the OECD Model can be found in covered tax agreements. If an expression is used in the MLI but not defined therein, recourse should be had to covered tax agreements, unless the context does not require otherwise. If the expression is not defined in the covered tax agreement either, recourse to domestic law should be made - again, provided that the context does not require otherwise.

The recourse is also explicitly mentioned in the Explanatory Statement to the MLI, which states as follows:

> With respect to a term not explicitly defined in the Convention or in the relevant Covered Tax Agreement, Covered Tax Agreements generally provide that any term not defined shall, unless the context otherwise requires, have the meaning that it has at the time the Covered Tax Agreement is being applied under the domestic law of the Contracting Jurisdiction applying the Covered Tax Agreement, the meaning given to that term under the tax laws of that Contracting Jurisdiction prevailing over a meaning given to the term under other laws of that Contracting Jurisdiction. Where this rule is present in a Covered Tax Agreement, it would apply for the purposes of determining the meaning of undefined terms in the Convention, unless the context requires an alternative interpretation. For this purpose, the context would include the purposes of the Convention, as described in the preamble as modified by Article 6 (see paragraphs 21 to 23 above, related to the preamble of the Convention, and paragraph 76 below, related to Article 6).[42]

The questions arise as to what the word 'context' even means, and when does that context otherwise require. The determination of the term 'context' must be done

39. K. Vogel, *DBA*, Introduction MC 56 (3rd edition, C.H. Beck 1996); Vogel, *DBA*, Art. 3, para. 70 (3rd edition, C.H. Beck 1996).
40. K. Vogel & R. Prokisch, *IFA Cahiers - Volume LXXVIIIa. Interpretation of Double Taxation Conventions*, General Report, at 55 et seq. (IFA 1993).
41. *See* section 4.
42. OECD, *Explanatory Statement to the MLI* (2016), *supra* n. 2, Art. 2, para. 38.

in accordance with international law principles of interpretation. Taking the object and the purpose of the MLI into account, leads to a broad understanding of the term 'context'. The MLI can fulfil its purpose (i.e., the modification of existing tax treaties to implement the tax treaty-related changes developed through the BEPS project) only if the terms used in the MLI are understood in the same way. The fall-back to covered tax agreements could be in conflict with this purpose. Because of this, the concept of context in Article 2(2) MLI should be understood broadly. The context should therefore comprise all interpretation materials set out in Articles 31 and 32 of the Vienna Convention.[43] There is no limitation of the 'context' to the object and purpose of a treaty or used expressions, if they are used in either the MLI or in the Explanatory Statement.[44]

The OECD Model is also part of the context of the MLI as sketched out above. For example although the term 'permanent establishment'[45] is used in the MLI, the term is not defined therein. The provision regarding permanent establishments was drafted with regard to Article 5(1) and (2) of the OECD Model.[46] The provision of the MLI corresponds to the provision of the OECD Model. Thus, consultation of the OECD Model can be required because of the context of the MLI. When recourse is had to the OECD Model out of the context of the MLI, there could still be some terms that cannot be defined by the context. In this case, the consultation of domestic law can be necessary.

Even the consultation of domestic law can happen out of the context of the OECD Model and its provisions. Article 9 of the MLI concerning capital gains from alienation of shares or interests of entities deriving their value principally from immovable property, speaks of immovable property that is situated in a contracting jurisdiction. The OECD Model does not define the term, but states that the term is to have the meaning that it has under the law of the contracting state in which the property in question is situated. It is therefore the contracting jurisdiction's domestic law that indicates what can be regarded as 'immovable property'.[47] The context of the provision includes not only the OECD Model[48] and the OECD's considerations in the BEPS Action

43. M. Lang, *Introduction to the Law of Double Taxation Conventions*, para. 116 (IBFD 2010). *See also Doppelbesteuerungsabkommen: DBA*, Art. 3, para. 121 (K. Vogel & M. Lehner eds., 5th edition, C.H. Beck 2008).
44. S. Austry et al., *The Proposed OECD Multilateral Instrument Amending Tax Treaties*, 70 Bull. Intl. Taxn. 12, at 683, 684 et seq. (2016).
45. *See also* section 5.1.
46. Blum, *supra* n. 28.
47. The relevance of domestic law is derived by the particular provision found in Art. 6(2) of the OECD Model and not by Art. 3(2) of the OECD Model.
48. Lang, *Art 3 Abs 2 OECD-MA und die Auslegung von Doppelbesteuerungsabkommen*, *supra* n. 17, at 290; M. Lang, *Das Verhältnis zwischen Abkommensrecht und innerstaatlichem Recht in der Definition des unbeweglichen Vermögens nach Art. 6 Abs. 2 OECD-MA*, Zeitschrift für Internationales Steuerrecht (ISR), at 41, 44 et seq. (2015).

6 Final Report,[49] but also in the broadest sense the domestic law of the contracting jurisdiction.[50]

As sketched out above, the concept of 'context' in Article 2(2) of the MLI must be understood broadly. In the absence of a definition, Article 2(2) of the MLI requires the consultation of covered tax agreements unless the context otherwise requires. Recourse to domestic law is instead possible if: (i) the covered tax agreement does not define the used term; and (ii) again all possible interpretation methods do not lead to a satisfying result. Once a term is not used in the covered tax agreement, recourse to domestic law is not possible.[51] Direct recourse to domestic law is not possible because the wording of Article 2(2) of the MLI states that an undefined term is to have the meaning that it has under the relevant covered tax agreement. Even if the undefined expression used in the MLI does have a definition in the domestic law of the applying state, the fall-back to domestic law in order to define a term that is not explicitly mentioned in the covered tax agreement is not possible.[52]

Following the view that the covered tax agreement and domestic law should govern the interpretation, it must be clarified how the recourse is to be understood. It is pivotal to understand whether the legal framework existing at the time of the conclusion of the MLI should govern the interpretation or the legal framework existing at the time of the recourse. A recourse to different legal frameworks could lead to different results in the interpretation. To prevent any misunderstandings with regard to the reference, since 1995 the OECD Model has clearly stated that the reference must be understood dynamically and not statically.[53] Article 2(2) of the MLI, as the MLI's equivalent to Article 3(2) of the OECD Model, clearly states that 'any term not defined ... shall ... have the meaning that it has at that time' under the relevant covered tax agreement. Because of the phrase 'at that time', the recourse is to be made dynamically, meaning that the legal status existing at the time of the recourse governs the interpretation.

4 TERMS DEFINED IN THE MLI

4.1 General Remarks

Under Article 31(4) of the Vienna Convention, a special meaning is to be given to a term if it is established that the parties so intended.[54] The MLI itself defines some specific terms. When a rule is being applied that contains a term already defined by the MLI, that specific definition has priority over any other definition of the term.

49. Article 9 of the MLI is found in Part 3. Part 3 seeks to implement tax treaty-related changed developed through BEPS Action 6 – Preventing the Granting of Treaty Benefits in Inappropriate Circumstances.
50. Blum, *supra* n. 28.
51. Lang, *Die Auslegung des multilateralen Instruments*, *supra* n. 5, at 15.
52. Lang, *Die Auslegung des multilateralen Instruments*, *supra* n. 5, at 15.
53. Lang, *Introduction to the Law of Double Taxation Conventions*, *supra* n. 43, para. 119.
54. Lang, *Art 3 Abs 2 OECD-MA und die Auslegung von Doppelbesteuerungsabkommen*, *supra* n. 17, at 282.

4.2 Covered Tax Agreement

Article 2(1) of the MLI states that a 'covered tax agreement':

> means an agreement for the avoidance of double taxation with respect to taxes on income that is in force between two or more Parties ... and/or jurisdictions or territories ... with respect to which each party has made a notification to the Depositary listing the agreement ... as an agreement which it wishes to be covered by this Convention.[55]

The MLI aims to modify tax treaties that are in force between two or more parties. Agreements that cover, in addition to taxes on income, also capital taxes or taxes on capital gains should be included, but not agreements that are exclusively applicable to shipping and air transport or to social security.[56] To be modified by the MLI, an agreement must be specifically listed in a notification to the depositary[57] by each party to the agreement. There is also no obligation that every agreement by the parties to the MLI be covered by the MLI. Indeed, the MLI also does not foresee such an obligation.[58] There are various reasons why a party might not want an agreement to be covered by the MLI. Reasons could include that the agreement was recently renegotiated to implement the changes made through the BEPS Project or is presently being renegotiated.[59] The MLI does not forbid any further amendment of the agreement.[60]

4.3 Party

Article 2(1) defines the term 'party' as either a state for which the MLI is in force or a jurisdiction that has signed the MLI.[61] The Explanatory Statement declares that this term is used for states and jurisdictions that have signed the MLI and that, in contrast to signatories, the MLI is also already in force for them. The term refers to states and jurisdictions for which the MLI is already in force. The MLI enters into force for states and jurisdictions individually[62] on the first day of the month that is followed by the expiration of three calendar months. The counting of those three calendar months begins at the time of the deposit by a signatory of the MLI of ratification, acceptance or approval.[63]

---

55. Article 2(1)(a) MLI.
56. OECD, *Explanatory Statement to the MLI* (2016), *supra* n. 2, Art. 2, para. 25.
57. Under Art. 39(1) of the MLI, the depositary is the Secretary General of the OECD.
58. L.E. Schoueri & R.A. Galendi Jr., *Interpretative and Policy Challenges Following the OECD Multilateral Instrument (2016) from a Brazilian Perspective*, 71 Bull. Intl. Taxn. 6 (2017).
59. OECD, *Explanatory Statement to the MLI* (2016), *supra* n. 2, Art. 2, para. 26.
60. OECD, *Explanatory Statement to the MLI* (2016), *supra* n. 2, Art. 2, para. 33.
61. Article 2(1)(b) MLI.
62. There is also a general entry into force from the MLI. Under Art. 34(2) MLI, the MLI enters into force on the 'first day following the expiration of a period of three calendar months beginning on the date of the deposit of the fifth instrument of ratification, acceptance or approval'.
63. Article 34(2) MLI.

4.4 Contracting Jurisdiction

Article 2(1) of the MLI defines the term 'contracting jurisdiction' as a party to a covered tax agreement. The term 'contracting jurisdiction' was intentionally used instead of the more common expression 'contracting state'. The definition could have led to confusion, as there can also be non-state jurisdictions that are parties to a covered tax agreement. The expression 'contracting party' would also have been inaccurate, as the term 'party' refers to states or jurisdictions that have signed the MLI and those for which the MLI is already in force.[64]

4.5 Signatory

The last expression that is found in Article 2(1) of the MLI is the definition of the term 'signatory'. This term refers to a state or a jurisdiction that has signed the MLI, but the MLI is not yet in force for it.[65] The MLI has been open for signature since 31 December 2016 for all states, certain territories (such as Guernsey and Isle of Man) and other jurisdictions that are authorized to become a party to the MLI.[66] Signature of the MLI is to be followed by ratification, acceptance or approval, depending on national legal requirements.[67]

4.6 Qualified Person

Article 7(8) defines a qualified person, stating that, under certain conditions, a resident of a contracting jurisdiction of a covered tax agreement should not be entitled to a specific benefit granted by the covered tax agreement unless the person can be regarded as a 'qualified person'. Given the fact that the term is of great significance for simplified limitation-on-benefits provisions, it is not surprising that an explicit definition of the term is provided. First, it is of importance that the person be regarded as a resident[68] of a contracting jurisdiction at the time the benefit would be accorded. Furthermore, a qualified person is:

(1) an individual;
(2) that contracting jurisdiction, or a political subdivision or local authority thereof, or an agency or instrumentality of any such contracting jurisdiction, political subdivision or local authority;
(3) a company or other entities, if the principal class of its shares is regularly traded on one or more recognized stock exchanges;[69]

64. OECD, *Explanatory Statement to the MLI* (2016), *supra* n. 2, Art. 2, para. 35.
65. Article 2(1)(d) MLI.
66. Article 27(1)(c) MLI.
67. Article 27(2) MLI. *See also* OECD, *Explanatory Statement to the MLI* (2016), *supra* n. 2, Art. 27, para. 263.
68. The term 'resident' will be analysed later.
69. The term 'recognized stock exchanges' is analysed under section 4.7.

(4) a person, other than an individual, that:
   - is a non-profit organization of a type that is agreed to by the contracting jurisdictions through an exchange of diplomatic notes; or
   - is an entity or arrangement established in that contracting jurisdiction which is treated as a separate person under the tax laws of that contracting jurisdiction and which (i) is established and operated exclusively or almost exclusively to administer or provide retirement benefits and ancillary or incidental benefits to individuals and which is regulated as such by that contracting jurisdiction or one of its political subdivisions or local authorities or (ii) is established and operated exclusively or almost exclusively to invest funds for the benefit of entities or arrangements referred to in (i); or

(5) a person other than an individual if, on at least half the days of a twelve-month period that includes the time when the benefit would otherwise be accorded, persons that are residents of that contracting jurisdiction and that are entitled to benefits of the covered tax agreement under one of the above four primary points, own, directly or indirectly, at least 50% of the shares of the person.[70]

The definition was first established in the BEPS Action 6 (Preventing the Granting of Treaty Benefits in Inappropriate Circumstances) Final Report.[71] The simplified limitation-on-benefits provision of Article 7(8) through (13) is based on Article X (Entitlement to Benefit) of the OECD Model as produced in the Action 6 Final Report.

4.7 Other Definitions

The MLI also defines the following terms:

- A 'recognized stock exchange' is: (i) any stock exchange established and regulated as such under the laws of either contracting jurisdiction; or (ii) any other stock exchange agreed upon by the competent authorities of the contracting jurisdictions.[72]
- A 'principal class of shares' is the class or classes of shares of a company that represent the majority of the aggregate vote and value of the company or the class or classes of beneficial interests of an entity that represent, in the aggregate, a majority of the aggregate vote and value of the entity.[73]
- The legal definition of 'equivalent beneficiary' refers to any person that would be entitled to benefits with respect to an item of income, accorded by a contracting jurisdiction to a covered tax agreement under the domestic law of

70. Article 7(9) MLI.
71. OECD, *Preventing the Granting of Treaty Benefits in Inappropriate Circumstances – Action 6: 2015 Final Report*, OECD/G20 Base Erosion and Profit Shifting Project (2015).
72. Article 7(13)(a) MLI.
73. Article 7(13)(b) MLI.

that contracting jurisdiction, the covered tax agreement or any other international instrument which are equivalent to, or more favourable than, benefits to be accorded to that item of income under the covered tax agreement. For the purposes of determining whether a person is an equivalent beneficiary with respect to dividends, the person is deemed to hold the same capital of the company paying the dividends as such capital the company claiming the benefit with respect to dividends holds.[74]
- The term 'shares' includes interests that are comparable to shares, in the case of entities that are not companies.[75]
- Two persons are deemed to be 'connected persons' if one owns, directly or indirectly, at least 50% of the beneficial interest in the other or another person owns, directly or indirectly, at least 50% of the beneficial interest in each person. In any case, a person will be deemed to be connected to another if, based on all the relevant facts and circumstances, one has control of the other or both are under the control of the same person or persons.[76]

A negative definition, i.e., a specification of what should not be classified as an active conduct of a business, is also given. This definition applies for the purposes of the simplified limitation-on-benefits provision. Accordingly, the active conduct of a business does not include the following activities or a combination thereof:

- operating as a holding company;
- providing overall supervision or administration of a group of companies;
- providing group financing (including cash pooling); and/or
- making or managing investments, unless these activities are carried on by a bank, insurance company or registered securities dealer in the ordinary course of its business as such.[77]

5 TERMS NOT DEFINED IN THE MLI

5.1 Theoretical Considerations

Terms that are used but not defined in the MLI must be interpreted. The MLI's independent interpretation rule is found in its Article 2(2). In the case of the use of an undefined term, recourse to covered tax agreements may be made unless the context otherwise requires. As outlined above, the concept of 'context' is to be understood as broadly as possible.

If one denies that the context otherwise requires, recourse should be made to covered tax agreements. If a term is used but not defined in the covered tax agreement,

74. Article 7(13)(c) MLI.
75. Article 7(13)(d) MLI.
76. Article 7(13)(e) MLI.
77. Article 7(10)(a) MLI.

this leads to the application of Article 3(2) of the covered tax agreement. The question here concerns whether the context of the covered tax agreements requires a treaty-autonomous interpretation or whether recourse should be had to the applying state's domestic law.[78] The question is whether domestic law prevails over the treaty-autonomous interpretation. If one again denies that the context otherwise requires, domestic law governs the interpretation.

Covered tax agreements do not always follow the OECD Model, and deviations are common. There can and will be deviations in the definitions of particular terms. Keeping in mind that the purpose of the MLI is the modification of existing tax treaties to implement the tax treaty-related measures developed through the BEPS project, one can question whether the interpretation of terms governed by individual covered tax agreements or even domestic law was intended. The MLI can properly fulfil its purpose only if tax authorities of both contracting jurisdictions understand terms the same way. A fall-back to domestic law when interpreting undefined terms (that are used in the MLI) would definitely conflict with this purpose.

5.2 Permanent Establishment

Article 10 (Anti-abuse Rule for Permanent Establishment Situated in Third Jurisdictions) uses the term 'permanent establishment', but does not define it. Thus, the MLI does not provide a definition of the term itself. The article offers two options that offer a negative definition of the term 'permanent establishment'.[79] Under the interpretation rule stated in Article 2(2) of the MLI, unless the context otherwise requires, recourse to the covered tax agreement is possible. Thus, one must first take a look at the context of the provision itself. Article 10 is situated in part 4 of the MLI, which aims to implement the tax treaty-related measures made through BEPS Action 7. BEPS Action 7 aims to prevent artificial avoidance of permanent establishment status.[80] There are two different ways to find a solution.

One way is via the broad context. Lang argued that the context is to be of major importance, stating that a reference to covered tax agreement is to be considered only if all possible interpretation methods do not lead to a satisfying result. Considering that all possible interpretation methods (i.e., meaning the systematic, teleological and grammatical interpretations) are to be taken into account, this case is extremely rare.[81] In particular, there is a close connection between the MLI and the OECD Model. The term 'permanent establishment' is directly connected with the definition of this term in

78. E. Reimer & A. Rust, Art. 3 General Definitions, in *Klaus Vogel on Double Taxation Conventions*, para. 108 et seq. (E. Reimer & A. Rust eds., Wolters Kluwer 2015); Lang, *Art 3 Abs 2 OECD-MA und die Auslegung von Doppelbesteuerungsabkommen*, *supra* n. 17, at 281 et seq. (2011).
79. The MLI comes with flexibility, this is the reason why contracting jurisdictions have options regarding the implementation of some provisions. In this case the parties can choose if they want to implement either option A (*see* Art. 13(2)), Option B (*see* Art. 13(3)) or neither of them.
80. OECD, *Preventing the Artificial Avoidance of Permanent Establishment Status – Action 7: 2015 Final Report*, OECD/G20 Base Erosion and Profit Shifting Project (2015).
81. Lang stated this in relation to Art. 3(2) of the OECD Model, but – as demonstrated above – the discussion can be shifted one-to-one onto the discussion regarding the interpretation rules of the MLI. Lang, *Introduction to the Law of Double Taxation Conventions*, *supra* n. 43, para. 76.

Article 5 of the OECD Model. The context in which Article 10 of the MLI was drafted was the OECD Model provision regarding permanent establishment.[82] Thus, the provision of the MLI is connected to the provision of the OECD Model. The context makes it necessary to take a closer look at the OECD Model. Recourse to the OECD Model is made because of the general interpretation rule that states that also the context of the MLI must be taken into account, and not because of the recourse required under Article 2(2) of the MLI. Under this hypothesis Article 5 of the OECD Model is of relevance. One can assume that a permanent establishment must be understood in accordance with Article 5 of the OECD Model.

Another way to find a solution for the definition of this term is via the reference in Article 2(2) of the MLI; in particular the tax administration is apparently following the view that the context is to be of minor importance and the recourse to covered tax agreements is to be made primarily.[83]

Under the last mentioned hypothesis, the permanent establishment definition under the covered tax agreement becomes relevant. When bilateral tax treaties are negotiated, usually the OECD Model or the UN Model (which are to a large extent similar) are typically used as a starting point. However, often there are deviations from Article 5 of the OECD Model. In these cases, it makes a difference whether one attempts to find a solution from the context, or immediately looks into the tax treaty. Keeping in mind the purpose of the MLI, it is essential to interpret the treaty autonomously in order to fulfil the purpose of the MLI in its broadest sense.[84]

5.3 Dividend

Article 5(4) of the MLI (Application of Methods for Elimination of Double Taxation) uses the term 'dividend'. This article is placed in part 2, which seeks to implement the tax treaty-related changes made through BEPS Action 2.[85] BEPS Action 2 aims to neutralize the effects of hybrid mismatch arrangements. The term 'dividend' is not defined in the MLI itself. The term dividend is another good example of

82. *See also* Blum, *supra* n. 28.
83. This has been said with regard to Art. 3(2) of the OECD Model, but as explained above the discussion can be shifted on to one. Loukota, *Grundsätze für die steuerliche Behandlung international tätiger Gastprofessoren, supra* n. 33, at 465 et seq.; Loukota, *Vermeidung von Irrwegen bei der DBA-Auslegung, supra* n. 33, at 563.
84. As explained above, tax treaties do not always follow the OECD Model, so deviations are common. For example the Austria-Qatar tax treaty requires for a permanent establishment that the building site, the construction assembly, the installation project or any supervisory activity in connection with such site or project last more than six months within a twelve-month period. On the one hand, there is a deviation regarding the time requirement (twelve months versus six months within a twelve-month period), while on the other hand, the Austria-Qatar tax treaty also lists supervisory activity that is in connection with a building site or an installation project explicitly as constituting a permanent establishment. A supervisory activity is not directly listed in Art. 5(3) of the OECD Model, but is still covered by it, according to the Commentary on the OECD Model. A recourse to this tax treaty would lead to deviations in the application of the MLI. Therefore, the treaty-autonomous interpretation should be preferred.
85. OECD, *Neutralising the Effects of Hybrid Mismatch Arrangements – Action 2: 2015 Final Report*, OECD/G20 Base Erosion and Profit Shifting Project (2015).

treaty-autonomous interpretation and interpretation because of recourse to the covered tax agreement on the basis of Article 2(2) of the MLI. The relevant passage that uses the term 'dividend' provides as follows:

> Provisions of a Covered Tax Agreement would otherwise exempt income derived by a resident of a Contracting Jurisdiction from tax in that Contracting Jurisdiction for the purpose of eliminating double taxation because such income is treated as a dividend by that Contracting Jurisdiction shall not apply where such income gives rise to a deduction for the purpose of determining the taxable profits of a resident of the other Contracting Jurisdiction under the laws of that other Contracting Jurisdiction.

As explained above, the OECD Model can be regarded as part of the context of the MLI. So when doing an interpretation, it can be necessary to consult the OECD Model. The consultation of the OECD Model should happen when a provision in the MLI directly refers to domestic law or rather to covered tax agreements. In this case, the term 'dividend' is directly connected (such income is treated as a dividend by that contracting jurisdiction) with the definition of this term in the OECD Model. Thus, the provision in the MLI is linked to the provision in the OECD Model. Thus, already the context can require making recourse to the OECD Model. The recourse is made because of the interpretation rule under which also the context of the MLI must be taken into account, and not because of the recourse provision found in Article 2(2) of the MLI. In this case, Article 10(3) of the OECD Model should be consulted. Article 10(3) of the OECD Model provides as follows:

> The term 'dividend' as used in this Article means income from shares, 'jouissance' shares or 'jouissance' rights, mining shares, founder's shares or others rights, not being debt-claims, participating in profits, as well as income from other corporate rights which is subjected to the same taxation treatment as income from shares by the laws of the State which the company making the distribution is a resident.

The interpretation should be done as treaty autonomous. The definition of the term 'dividend' can be split into three parts. The first part contains the terms income from shares; jouissance shares or jouissance rights; mining shares; and founder's shares. Pursuant to the second part of the definition, the term 'dividend' also includes 'income from ... other rights, not being debt-claims, participating in profits'. The first and second parts of the definition do not contain a recourse to domestic law. Regarding the third part of the definition, 'income from other corporate rights', domestic law can be of importance.[86] Article 10(3) of the OECD Model states that 'the term "dividends" ... means ... income from other corporate rights which is subjected to the same taxation treatment as income from shares by the laws of the State of which the company making the distribution is a resident'. Thus, this is the recourse to domestic law of that residence state of the company that is making the distribution.[87] The

86. M. Lang, *Der Begriff der 'shares' in Art. 13 Abs 4 OECD-MA*, in *Estudos de Direito Tributário em Homenagem ao Professor Gerd Willi Rothmann*, at 267, 272 et seq. (L.E. Schoueri & J.F. Bianco eds., Quartier Latin 2016).

87. The term 'residency' is defined in Arts 1 and 4 of the OECD Model. For the definition of the term 'residency' under the MLI, *see* section 5.4.

definition of the term 'income from other corporate rights' is governed by the recourse made in the provision. Furthermore, the recourse to domestic law is possible only with regard to the residence state of the company. The residence state of the person that is receiving dividends from that specific company is bound by the classification of the term by the residence state of the company.[88] Thus, the recourse is made because of Article 10(3) of the OECD Model and not because of the recourse required in Article 3(2) of the OECD Model.

Furthermore, all three parts of the definition interact. Because the second part of the definition states 'other rights, not being debt-claims, participating in profits', one should bear in mind that shares; jouissance shares or jouissance rights; mining shares; and founders' shares are also rights that are not debt-claims. The third part of the definition refers to 'other corporate rights'. On the basis of this phrase, only those shares and other rights (as defined in the first and second part of the definition) that are 'corporate rights' should be understood as a 'dividend'.[89]

Following the view that emphasizes the recourse, the following can be said: Because there is no definition of the term 'dividend' in the MLI, the recourse to covered tax agreements via Article 2(2) of the MLI is to be made. If the term is fully defined in the covered tax agreement, a recourse to domestic law via Article 3(2) of the OECD Model may not be made. Otherwise, recourse to domestic law of the applying state can be necessary with regard to Article 3(2) of the OECD Model.[90]

Again, the treaty-autonomous interpretation should be favoured in order to achieve a coherent solution. Only in this way can the purpose of the MLI be completely fulfilled.

5.4 Immovable Property

The term 'immovable property' (also referred to as real property) is used in Article 9 of the MLI (Capital gains from alienation of shares or interests of entities deriving their value principally from immovable property). Article 9(1) provides as follows:

> Provisions of a Covered Tax Agreement providing that gains derived by a resident of a Contracting Jurisdiction from the alienation of shares or other rights of participation in an entity may be taxed in the other Contracting Jurisdiction provided that there shares or rights derived more than a certain part of their value from immovable property (real property) situated in that other Contracting Jurisdiction ... .

88. Lang, *Art 3 Abs 2 OECD-MA und die Auslegung von Doppelbesteuerungsabkommen*, *supra* n. 17, at 290.
89. Lang, *Der Begriff der 'shares' in Art. 13 Abs 4 OECD-MA*, *supra* n. 88, at 272 et seq.
90. Deviations can be found in different tax treaties. The Germany-Iceland tax treaty, for example, does not list in its Art. 10(5) jouissance shares or jouissance rights as dividends. The Germany-New Zealand tax treaty lists only 'income from shares' and 'income assimilated to income from shares' as 'dividends' in its Art. 10(3). A recourse to these tax treaties would lead to deviations in the application of the MLI. Therefore, the treaty-autonomous interpretation should be preferred.

The MLI does not define the term 'immovable property'. Thus, one must carry out an interpretation of this term. If, again, following the view that the context is of major significance, the provision must be interpreted also systematically. The provision of the MLI refers back to contracting jurisdictions. So in the broader context, the OECD Model is significant for the interpretation of this term. Again, Article 6(2) of the OECD Model deals with immovable property and provides as follows:

> The term 'immovable property' shall have the meaning which it has under the law of the Contracting State in which the property in question is situated. The term shall in any case include property accessory to immovable property, livestock and equipment used in agriculture and forestry, right to which the provisions of general law respecting landed property apply, usufruct of immovable property and rights to variable or fixed payments as consideration for the working of, or the right to work, mineral deposits, sources and other natural resources; ships, boats and aircraft shall not be regarded as immovable property.

Although there is a specification as to what is, in any case, to be included in the definition of the term, there is no precise definition of the term itself. Instead, it is stated that the definition of the term is to be derived from the meaning that the term has under the law of the contracting state in which the immovable property in question is located. This passage indicates that for the definition of the term, the classification by the state in which the property is situated is paramount. Vogel does not see this as carte blanche for a recourse to domestic law. He argues that this is rather another element for the treaty-autonomous interpretation of terms.[91] Article 6(1) of the OECD Model mentions that the term 'immovable property' should include 'income from agriculture or forestry'. Article 6(2) of the OECD Model provides a list of property and assets that should always be classified as 'immovable property' (e.g., 'property accessory to immovable property') or that should never be classified as 'immovable property' (ships, boats and aircraft). Lang states that the relevance of domestic law in this case is not derived from Article 3(2) of the OECD Model ('... any term not defined therein shall, unless the context otherwise requires, have the meaning that it has under the law of that State ...'), but from the more particular provision in Article 6(2) of the OECD Model. This is another emphasis on the treaty-autonomous interpretation.[92]

The other view would be that recourse to the covered tax agreement should be made via Article 2(2) of the MLI. Assuming that the provision in the covered tax agreement follows the OECD Model, the relevance of domestic law would be derived by the specific provision in Article 6(2) of the OECD Model (... shall have the meaning which it has under the law of that Contracting State ...). Otherwise, the recourse under Article 3(2) of the OECD Model to domestic law should be made, provided that the covered tax agreement does not define the term.

If the individual covered tax agreement does not fully follow the OECD Model, there can and will be deviations. This is another sign that the interpretation of terms

---

91. Vogel, *Doppelbesteuerungsabkommen: DBA*, *supra* n. 43, Art. 6, para. 64.
92. Lang, *Art 3 Abs 2 OECD-MA und die Auslegung von Doppelbesteuerungsabkommen*, *supra* n. 17, at 290; Lang, *Das Verhältnis zwischen Abkommensrecht und innerstaatlichem Recht*, *supra* n. 48, at 44 et seq.

used in the MLI should be done autonomously. Otherwise, there is again the possibility that the purpose will not be fulfilled to the greatest extent.

5.5 Residence

Article 4 of the MLI contains rules for dual resident entities. The first sentence of this article provides as follows:

> Where by reason of the provision of a Covered Tax Agreement a person other than an individual is a resident of more than one Contracting Jurisdiction, the competent authorities of the Contracting Jurisdictions shall endeavour to determine by mutual agreement the Contracting Jurisdiction of which such person shall be deemed to be a resident for the purposes of the Covered Tax Agreement, having regard to its place of effective management, the place where it is incorporated or otherwise constituted and any other relevant factors.

The MLI itself does not provide a definition of the term 'resident' or 'residency'. Again, there are two different ways to interpret the term 'resident' or 'residency'.

The OECD Model can be regarded as part of the context of the provision found in the MLI. Thus, again the context requires having recourse to the OECD Model. Article 4 of the OECD Model ('Resident') stipulates that as regards the term 'resident of a contracting state', any person should be understood that is liable to tax because of such person's domicile, place of management or any other criterion of a similar nature. Article 1 of the OECD Model ('This Convention shall apply to persons who are residents of one or both of the Contracting States') and Article 4(1) of the OECD Model both deal with resident persons. One must bear in mind that the OECD Model does not define either tax debtor or object of taxation. Both must be defined by domestic law. When the OECD Model refers to a resident, then, it refers to the legal entity that is taxable under domestic law. Thus, only taxable subjects that are obliged by domestic law may be resident persons. Furthermore, Article 4 of the OECD Model even states that only persons that are liable to tax in a domestic state are to be considered as a person in terms of a 'resident of a contracting state'. This phrase is a recourse to domestic law. The recourse to domestic law for the definition of a 'resident person' is made because of the treaty-autonomous interpretation, meaning the recourse is made because of the context of the provision and not because of the OECD Model's own recourse provided for in Article 3(2) of the OECD Model.[93]

The other view is that the recourse to the covered tax agreement should be made via Article 2(2) of the MLI. Assuming, that the covered tax agreement follows the OECD Model, the relevance of domestic law would be derived from the specific provision in Article 4(1) of the OECD Model ('... the term "resident of a Contracting State" means any person who, under the laws of that State, is liable to tax ...'). Regarding Article 4(1) of the OECD Model, the relevance of domestic law is not derived from the recourse

93. Lang, *Art 3 Abs 2 OECD-MA und die Auslegung von Doppelbesteuerungsabkommen*, *supra* n. 17, at 290.

stated in Article 3(2) of the OECD Model, but again because of the provision itself that refers to domestic law.[94] The definition thus refers to the concept of residence that is adopted in domestic law.

6 CONCLUSION

The interpretation of terms used in the MLI does not follow any other rules than the interpretation of any other treaty. Indeed, one must always keep in mind the interpretation rules codified in the Vienna Convention. The grammatical, systematic, historical and teleological interpretations are always the starting point of the interpretation.

The Explanatory Statement, which is to be regarded as the 'commentary' on the MLI, has legal relevance. One must take into account in the interpretation according to the Vienna Convention. To be safe, states should nevertheless adopt the Explanatory Statement at the moment of the signing of the MLI.

The individual BEPS Actions will also play a significant role in the interpretation of the MLI, as, substantively, they are the significant part, not the MLI. This, as mentioned, should be important only when formal questions arise.

The implementation of a provision similar to Article 3(2) of the OECD Model into the new MLI has led to even more confusion than there had already been regarding Article 3(2). All the discussion that was going on regarding Article 3(2) of the OECD Model can now be shifted one-to-one to the MLI. This proves to be rather dangerous. Because of the recourse made in the MLI to the covered tax agreements, and then the recourse made in the covered tax agreements to national law, there is a danger that there will be a drifting apart of the application of the MLI. Besides, the purpose of the MLI, namely the standardization of existing tax treaties with regard to the tax treaty-related BEPS measures, could be torpedoed by different interpretation results when making recourses to domestic law. Lang still notes that a definition not defined in the MLI should be interpreted treaty-autonomous.[95]

94. M. Lehner, in *Doppelbesteuerungsabkommen: DBA*, *supra* n. 43, Art. 4, para. 2.
95. Lang, *Die Auslegung des multilateralen Instruments*, *supra* n. 5, at 14.

CHAPTER 3

The Relevance of the Conference of the Parties for the Interpretation and Amendment of the Multilateral Instrument

Raphael Holzinger

1 SETTING THE SCENE: THE CONFERENCE OF THE PARTIES OF THE MULTILATERAL INSTRUMENT AND LEGAL PROBLEMS

When speaking of the relevance of the conference of the parties for the interpretation and amendments of the Multilateral Instrument (MLI), three aspects can be seen as potential legal problems, namely:

- the legal character of the conference of the parties itself;
- general and specific aspects of treaty interpretation and amendments in international law and
- the interplay between the conference of the parties of the MLI and these general aspects.

All of these legal problems are interrelated with the sovereignty of states, which is a major principle in international law. The significance of the sovereignty of states becomes particularly evident with regard to the general rule '*par in parem non habet imperium*'. Under this rule, states cannot bind other states against their will, if not otherwise agreed.

In this regard, states must consent to be legally bound by a certain treaty, an interpretation (i.e., a subsequent agreement on interpretation) or an amendment to a treaty.[1] Given these aspects, it is questionable as to what extent the conference of the

1. J. Brunnée, 'Consent', in *The Max Planck Encyclopaedia of Public International Law*, at 5 (R. Wolfrum ed., Oxford University Press 2010).

parties of the MLI can influence the interpretation or amendments of the MLI. This chapter seeks to answer this core question.

2 THE CONFERENCE OF THE PARTIES OF THE MLI UNDER REVIEW

2.1 The Legal Character of the Conference of the Parties and Other Governing Bodies of the MLI

Throughout recent decades there was a trend, according to which 'multilateral treaties increasingly provide for their continuous governance through an association of the parties', often referred to as the conference of the parties.[2] The main intention of the conference of the parties in various multilateral treaties is simply to ensure proper governance or execution of the treaty itself. Therefore, a conference of the parties generally constitutes or enables an institutionalized (based on procedural rules of the given treaty), intergovernmental cooperation.[3]

However, in comparison to other governing bodies of multilateral treaties or international organizations, the conference of the parties - even though it is institutionally separate from the parties to certain conventions - cannot constitute an own will. Moreover, the conference of the parties does not have its own legal personality. Rather, it must be seen as an institutionalized body acting on behalf of the states that are parties to a convention.[4] With regard to the MLI, the term 'conference of the parties' can be found in the Articles 31, 32 and 33. Article 31(1) of the MLI provides as follows:[5] '*The Parties may convene a Conference of the Parties* for the purposes of taking any decisions or exercising any functions as may be required or appropriate under the provisions of this Convention'.

Given the wording of the underlying paragraph, the conference of the parties is not intended to be permanent in nature, but rather an ad hoc governing body of the MLI. Regarding Article 31(1), the Explanatory Statement to the MLI[6] provides very little information concerning the question as to whether the conference of the parties is a permanent or ad hoc governing body. However, from a systematic perspective, the

2. V. Röben, 'Conference (Meeting) of States Parties', in *The Max Planck Encyclopaedia of Public International Law*, *supra* n. 1, at 1.
3. Röben, *supra* n. 2, at 1.
4. Röben, *supra* n. 2, at 1. According to Röben, any kind of decision-making powers of the conference of the parties must be provided for in the respective treaty. In this regard, the provided decision-making powers are delegated powers (derived directly from the parties), which are limited to the extent of that delegation. Regarding specific aspects of the Aarhus Convention and its conference of the parties, *see* T. Weber, *Umweltschutz durch Rechtsschutz?*, at 14–25. (Verlag Österreich 2015).
5. OECD, *Multilateral Convention to Implement Tax Treaty Related Measures to Prevent Base Erosion And Profit Shifting*, Art. 31(1) (2016) (emphasis added).
6. OECD, *Explanatory Statement to the Multilateral Convention to Implement Tax Treaty Related Measures to Prevent Base Erosion and Profit Shifting* (2016).

interpretation derived from the wording of Article 31(1) of the MLI is perfectly in line with the description of the formal procedure on the convening of a conference of the parties.[7]

Other than the conference of the parties, there is just one additional governing body, namely the depositary, which only carries out various formal functions (e.g., convening of the conference of the parties under Article 31(2) and (3) of the MLI, notification procedures and maintaining various lists).[8] Under Article 39(1) of the MLI, the Secretary-General of the OECD is to be the depositary of the MLI and of any further protocols to the MLI (e.g., based on Article 38 of the MLI). The fact that the Secretary-General of the OECD is to be the depositary of the MLI strongly indicates the close relation between the MLI and the OECD.[9] Concerning the interrelation between the conference of the parties and the depositary, Article 31(2) of the MLI provides that the conference of the parties should be served by the depositary.[10]

2.2 Parties to the Convention and the Conference of the Parties

When speaking of the parties to the Convention and the conference of the parties, the MLI uses two different phrases which, in fact, have different meanings. Article 2(1)(b) of the MLI states that the term 'party' means:[11]

> i) A *State* for which this Convention is *in force* pursuant to *Article 34* (Entry into Force); or
> ii) A *jurisdiction* which has *signed* this Convention pursuant to *subparagraph b) or c) of paragraph 1 of Article 27* (Signature and Ratification, Acceptance or Approval) and for which this Convention is *in force* pursuant to *Article 34* (Entry into Force).

When comparing the wording of (i) and (ii), which are the two different ways to be treated as a party for purposes of the MLI, Article 27 plays the major role. This is caused by the fact that both paragraphs reference Article 34 of the MLI concerning the entry into force, which means that the difference between the two options can only be described by an analysis of Article 27 of the MLI. Article 27(1) of the MLI provides as follows:[12]

> As of 31 December 2016, this Convention shall be open for signature by:
>
> a) all *States*;
> b) Guernsey ...; Isle of Man ...; Jersey ...; and

7. Article 31(3) MLI. For details on the procedural aspects, *see* section 2.4.
8. Article 39 MLI. *See also* Arts 3, 4, 5, 6, 7, 8, 9, 10, 11, 12, 13, 14, 16, 17, 18, 23, 24, 26, 28, 29, 31, 33, 35, 36 and 37 MLI.
9. M. Lang, *Die Auslegung des multilateralen Instruments*, Steuer und Wirtschaft International (SWI), at 11, 20 (2017). The close relation between the OECD and the MLI could eventually also have implications on the interpretation of the MLI, especially regarding contextual issues.
10. *See also* OECD, *Explanatory Statement to the MLI* (2016), *supra* n. 6, Art. 31(2) and (3).
11. Article 2(1)(b) MLI (emphasis added).
12. Article 27(1) MLI (emphasis added).

c) any other *jurisdiction authorised to become a Party* by means of a *decision by consensus of the Parties and Signatories*.

If one analyses the interplay between Article 2(1) and 27(1) of the MLI from an overall perspective, one can conclude that – irrespective of whether the given party is subsumed under Article 2(1)(b)(i) or under Article 2(1)(b)(ii) – states, different territories and other jurisdictions can become parties to the Convention.[13] Accordingly, one can conclude that the MLI generally has a broad understanding of (potential) parties to the Convention.

Based on this understanding, the interrelation between signatories and parties must be evaluated. Under Article 2(1)(d) of the MLI, the term 'signatory' means a state or jurisdiction that has signed the MLI but for which the MLI is not yet in force. Accordingly, the term 'signatory' has a broad understanding as well, thus including the same states and jurisdictions as Article 27(1) of the MLI.[14] However, the sole difference between the status of being a party or a signatory is interlinked with the entry into force of the MLI for the respective jurisdiction.[15] Once a jurisdiction has signed the MLI, it becomes a signatory, and as soon as the MLI enters into force for this jurisdiction under Article 34 of the MLI – which is mostly based on the national ratification, acceptance or approval procedures – the signatory becomes a party.[16] However, it is also possible for a state to sign the MLI (thus being a signatory) but not carry out the ratification procedure under its domestic law; accordingly, the respective state is not a party.[17]

Based on this understanding, one could ask whether signatories have the right to participate in the conference of the parties. Given the clear meaning of the term 'conference of the parties', signatories do not automatically have a right to participate in the conference of the parties, as they are not yet parties. This interpretation is also supported by the Explanatory Statement to the MLI, which states that '[t]he Parties may decide to invite Signatories to participate in a Conference of the Parties'.[18]

13. This interpretation based on the wording of the articles is also supported by the Explanatory Statement to the MLI regarding Art. 27(1) of the MLI ('given that certain non-State jurisdictions have concluded tax agreements under the arrangements with the State responsible for their international relations, the Convention is open for signature by jurisdictions listed in subparagraph b). ... Finally, subparagraph c) provides that the Parties and Signatories may decide to authorise other non-State jurisdictions to become Parties to the Convention following its opening for signature on 31 December 2016'.).
14. Even though Art. 2(1)(d) of the MLI – in contrast to Art. 27(1) of the MLI – does not explicitly mention Guernsey, Isle of Man and Jersey, they are implicitly included by the wording, as they are jurisdictions.
15. Article 2(1)(b)(i) and (ii) of the MLI both explicitly use the phrase 'for which this Convention is in force pursuant to Article 34 (Entry into Force)', whereas Art. 2(1)(d) of the MLI states that 'the Convention is not yet in force'.
16. Article 27(2) MLI ('[t]his Convention is subject to ratification, acceptance or approval'.). *See also* OECD, *Explanatory Statement to the MLI* (2016), *supra* n. 6, Art. 27(2) ('The appropriate term will depend on domestic legal requirements. Once the domestic procedures have been completed, an instrument of ratification, acceptance or approval must be deposited with the Depositary and this is the event which triggers the rule for the entry into force of the Convention pursuant to Article 34 of the Convention.').
17. As the MLI does not provide a mechanism under which signatories automatically become parties after a certain period, it is possible that a signatory might never become a party.
18. OECD, *Explanatory Statement to the MLI* (2016), *supra* n. 6, Art. 31(1).

Therefore, signatories are generally subject to the discretion of the parties to the Convention when it comes to their participation in the conference of the parties (thus becoming part of the decision-making process within this institutionalized governing body of the MLI).

However – contrary to this interpretation, an analysis of the wording of Article 27(1)(c) of the MLI, where it states that 'by means of a decision by consensus of the Parties and Signatories',[19] could lead one to conclude that signatories automatically play an important role in the decision-making process of the MLI or the conference of the parties.[20] If one further analyses the interrelation between Article 31(1) and Article 27(1)(c) of the MLI, two different lines of argumentation can be brought forward:

- First, Article 27(1)(c) of the MLI does not address which type of decision-making process must be chosen to come to the envisaged consensus decision. Accordingly, one could argue that the way to come to the decision, which is subject to Article 27(1)(c) of the MLI, can be freely chosen by the parties and the signatories, as long as the decision is based on consensus of all parties and signatories. Consequently, the decision-making under Article 27(1)(c) of the MLI need not be carried out during the course of a meeting of the conference of the parties, but rather must be formally distinguished from the decision-making of the conference of the parties (under Article 31 of the MLI).[21] While signatories do not have an important role in the decision-making process of the conference of the parties (i.e., they only might be invited to participate in the conference of the parties), signatories are on par with the parties to the Convention for purposes of decision-making under Article 27(1)(c) of the MLI.
- Second, one could also argue – at least from a the perspective of a first glance – that Article 27(1)(c) of the MLI constitutes an exception from the general rule of Article 31(1) of the MLI (i.e., only parties have the automatic right to participate in the conference of the parties), thus generally expanding the conference of the parties to a conference of the parties and signatories.

19. Decision-making by means of consensus is often incorporated in the rules of procedure of international conferences. In general this mechanism has three main features: (i) it is not the same as unanimity; (ii) it could be joined by a state even if it could not vote in favour of the treaty and (iii) it is not incompatible with indicative voting. In this regard, the mechanism is also often referred to as the 'absence of any formal objection'. For details, *see* A. Aust, *Handbook of International Law*, 2nd edition, at 58 (Cambridge University Press 2010); K. Schmalenbach & C. Schreuer, in *Österreichisches Handbuch des Völkerrechts: Band I – Textteil*, 5th edition, at 243 (A. Reinisch ed., Manzsche Verlags- und Universitätsbuchhandlung 2013); E. Klein & S. Schmahl, in *Völkerrecht*, 7th edition, at 304 (W. Vitzthum & A. Proelß eds., De Gruyter Studium 2016).
20. For details on the tasks of the conference of the parties and its decision-making process, *see* sections 2.3 and 4.
21. Decisions of the conference of the parties must be taken during the course of a meeting of the conference of the parties, whereas decisions under Art. 27(1)(c) of the MLI could also be taken in any other way. At least from a practical perspective, it is very likely that decisions under Art. 27(1)(c) of the MLI will be made at the same time as decisions of the conference of the parties. However, in order to safeguard legally binding decision-making, it must be assured that all parties and signatories participate in the decision-making process under Art. 27(1)(c) of the MLI, even though some of the signatories may not be invited to participate in the conference of the parties.

However, the fact that the term 'conference of the parties' is not used in Article 27(1)(c) of the MLI at all, and the fact that Article 27(1)(c) of the MLI provides for an own decision-making quorum (i.e., consensus), contradict this second line of argumentation.[22]

From an overall perspective, the better arguments can be brought forward with regard to the first line of argumentation. The clear meaning of the phrase 'Conference of the *Parties*' and the teleological argument, under which 'Parties may decide to invite Signatories to participate in a Conference of the Parties' for purposes of conference of the parties decisions,[23] do not leave much interpretational room, which would support the second line of argumentation stated above. Accordingly, one can conclude that the MLI does not just provide for a decision-making process using a conference of the parties (i.e., under Article 31 of the MLI), but rather also provides for an additional decision-making process (i.e., under Article 27(1)(c) of the MLI) which is supposed to deal only with the question of authorizing 'any other jurisdiction'[24] to sign and ratify the MLI.[25] Whereas signatories are automatically part of the decision-making process under Article 27(1)(c) of the MLI,[26] they are subject to the discretion of the parties with regard to their potential participation in the conference of the parties (i.e., they only might be invited to participate in the conference of the parties).

The interpretation - according to which the MLI provides two different and separate decision-making processes - is also in line with the general understanding of Article 31(1) of the MLI, as it explicitly states that the parties 'may' convene a

22. Accordingly, Art. 27(1)(c) of the MLI cannot be used in order to derive a right of signatories to automatically participate in the decision-making process of the conference of the parties subject to Art. 31 of the MLI.
23. OECD, *Explanatory Statement to the MLI* (2016), *supra* n. 6, Art. 31(1).
24. Article 27(1)(c) of the MLI addresses those jurisdictions that cannot be subsumed under the term 'States' under Art. 27(1)(a) of the MLI or which are not a jurisdiction listed in Art. 27(1)(b) of the MLI.
25. This interpretation is also supported by the Explanatory Statement to the MLI regarding Art. 2(1) ('there are two ways in which the Convention may cover tax agreements concluded by non-State jurisdictions or territories: ... jurisdictions may become Parties to the Convention by being listed by name in the text of Article 27(1)(b) at the time of adoption of the text of the Convention or by *being subsequently authorised to sign and ratify the Convention by a decision by consensus of the Parties and Signatories pursuant to Article 27(1)(c)*' (emphasis added).). *See also* OECD, *Explanatory Statement to the MLI* (2016), *supra* n. 6, Art. 27(1) ('subparagraph c) provides that the Parties and Signatories may decide to authorise other non-State jurisdictions to become Parties to the Convention .... This decision must be made by consensus, meaning that any jurisdiction which is not listed in subparagraph b) *can only become a Party to the Convention if no Party or Signatory objects*' (emphasis added).). Accordingly, jurisdictions or territories with an internationally disputed legal status (e.g., Kosovo, Turkish Republic of Northern Cyprus, Palestine, Taiwan) may become parties to the MLI only if no party or signatory to the MLI objects.
26. Given this understanding, parties may - by no means - exclude signatories from the decision-making process under Art. 27(1)(c) of the MLI. A legally binding decision concerning the authorization of 'any other jurisdiction' to sign and ratify the MLI is subject to a consensus decision of all parties and signatories.

conference of the parties for the purposes of taking any decisions. Accordingly, parties are not legally obliged to carry out a decision-making process only by means of a conference of the parties.[27]

In addition to the aspects noted above, the wording of Article 31(1) of the MLI must be further analysed. This article provides that the 'Parties may convene a Conference of the Parties …'.[28] From a logical perspective, the meaning of the term 'convene' a conference of the parties, indicates that there is no legally binding obligation for a party to participate in the conference of the parties.[29] Accordingly, the terms 'parties to the Convention' and 'conference of the parties' are based on the same definition of 'parties', but do not necessarily include the same number of parties.[30]

2.3 The Tasks of the Conference of the Parties and Other Governing Bodies of the MLI

Under Article 31(1) of the MLI, a conference of the parties may be convened for the purposes of '*taking any decisions* or *exercising any functions* as may be *required or appropriate* under the provisions of this Convention'.[31] From the perspective of a first glance, the terms used in Article 31(1) of the MLI indicate broad competences of the conference of the parties, as the conference of the parties may take 'any' decision or exercise 'any' functions that may be required or appropriate under the provision of the MLI. However, the significance of the term 'any' must not be overestimated. This is because 'any decisions' and 'any functions' are logically restricted by the prerequisite of being 'required' or 'appropriate' under the provisions of the MLI. Accordingly, the conference of the parties cannot act arbitrarily, as both a material (required or appropriate) and a formal prerequisite (under the provisions of this convention) must be fulfilled.

Especially the formal requirement is of major importance, as it establishes the limits of the competences of the conference of the parties. In this regard, the wording of Article 31(1) of the MLI gives information about systematic interpretations of the competences of the conference of the parties by making a broad reference to 'the provision of the MLI'. Other than Article 31 of the MLI, only Articles 32 and 33 deal with the conference of the parties – which means that the term 'the provisions of this

27. Accordingly, the decision-making process of the conference of the parties – where only parties have a vote with regard to interpretational questions and amendment issues – must be formally distinguished from the decision-making process laid down in Art. 27(1)(c), under which parties and signatories must come to a consensus concerning envisaged potential signature of 'any other jurisdiction'.
28. Article 31(1) MLI (emphasis added).
29. Even though there is no legally binding obligation that parties to the convention participate in the conference of the parties, it is very likely that parties will participate in the conference of the parties, as the conference of the parties is, in fact, the only governing body that can have a material influence on the MLI (e.g., interpretation and amendments). For the tasks of the conference of the parties, *see* section 2.3.
30. A participant in the conference of the parties automatically must be a party to the Convention. Vice versa, a party to the Convention need not necessarily participate in the conference of the parties.
31. Article 31(1) MLI (emphasis added).

Convention'[32] can be seen as a reference to only these articles. This understanding is also supported by the Explanatory Statement to MLI as regards Article 31(1). There it states that tasks being required or appropriate under the provisions of the MLI could include a 'Conference of the Parties to address questions of interpretation or implementation of the Convention as foreseen in Article 32(2) or to consider a possible amendment to the Convention as foreseen in Article 33(2)'.[33] Accordingly, the conference of the parties generally has two different tasks:

- interpretation and implementation under Article 32 of the MLI; and
- amendments under Article 33 of the MLI.[34]

While the tasks of the conference of the parties have a material character, as they are directly interrelated with the interpretation, implementation or the amendment of the MLI, the depositary has only a formal function. As mentioned, its major tasks are to carry out various notification procedures and to maintain various lists.[35] However, the depositary is also engaged in the convening of the conference of the parties under Article 31(2) and (3) of the MLI.[36]

2.4 Procedural Aspects: The Conference of the Parties between Request and Outcome

From a procedural perspective, Article 31(2) and (3) of the MLI must be explained in detail. Article 31(2) of the MLI provides that the 'Conference of the Parties shall be served by the Depositary' - which indicates the significant role of the depositary in the overall convening procedure. However, from a procedural perspective, Article 31(3) of the MLI is the most significant provision and provides as follows:

> Any Party may request a Conference of the Parties by communicating a request to the Depositary. The Depositary shall inform all Parties of any request. Thereafter, the Depositary shall convene a Conference of the Parties, provided that the request is supported by one-third of the Parties within six calendar months of the communication by the Depositary of the request.[37]

Starting with the first procedural step, a request must be made by any party to the Convention to the depositary. The topic of this request can be related either to interpretational and implementation issues under Article 32 of the MLI or to amendment issues under Article 33 of the MLI. However, other topics cannot be addressed to

32. Article 31(1) MLI.
33. OECD, *Explanatory Statement to the MLI* (2016), *supra* n. 6, Art. 31(1).
34. As the tasks of the conference of the parties include 'amendments' of the MLI, the conference of the parties could have further tasks in the future, as the MLI could simply be amended accordingly. However, to this end, the conference of the parties has only two material tasks.
35. *Supra* n. 8.
36. OECD, *Explanatory Statement to the MLI* (2016), *supra* n. 6, Art. 31(2) and (3).
37. In addition to the different steps that must be carried out in order to properly convene a conference of the parties, parties to the Convention and participants in the conference of the parties do not necessarily have to be the same, as not all parties to the Convention must participate in the conference of the parties.

the conference of the parties. This request is then forwarded by the depositary to all parties to the Convention so that they are informed about the request.

As soon as the depositary has communicated the request to all parties to the Convention, a six-month response period commences. In this regard, the parties to the Convention may support the request, express their displeasure or simply do nothing. If the request is supported by at least one-third of all parties to the Convention, the depositary 'shall' convene a conference of the parties.[38] While the wording of Article 31(3) of the MLI uses the phrase 'the Depositary shall convene', the Explanatory Statement to the MLI regarding Article 31(3) uses a slightly different wording and states that the 'the Depositary will convene' a conference of the parties. Given the fact that the conference of the parties is materially convened by the parties to the Convention[39] (the task is just formally carried out by the depositary) and based on the understanding that the depositary should only 'serve' the conference of the parties[40] (which logically cannot be interpreted as making the decisions as to whether a conference of the parties should be convened), the term 'shall convene' does not lead to any discretion for the depositary. Accordingly, if the one-third support requirement is fulfilled within a period of six months, the depositary even 'has' to convene a conference of the parties.

In this regard, the conference of the parties need not take place in the form of a physical meeting of delegates of the various parties to the Convention, but may also be organized remotely, for example by 'using videoconference or teleconference, by taking decisions through written procedure or by any other means decided upon by the Parties'.[41]

2.5 General Aspects of Treaty Interpretation in International Law

The goal of treaty interpretation is to determine the meaning of the provisions based on the intention of the contracting states.[42] As the MLI is a written international treaty,[43] the interpretational rules of the Vienna Convention on the Law of Treaties (hereinafter 'the Vienna Convention') are generally applicable.[44] As the interpretational rules set forth in the Vienna Convention reflect pre-existing customary international law, the principles of those interpretational rules are also applicable when one of the parties to the MLI has not signed or ratified the Vienna Convention.[45] Under the Vienna

38. OECD, *Explanatory Statement to the MLI* (2016), *supra* n. 6, Art. 31(3).
39. Article 31(1) MLI; OECD, *Explanatory Statement to the MLI* (2016), *supra* n. 6, Art. 31(1).
40. Article 31(2) MLI; OECD, *Explanatory Statement to the MLI* (2016), *supra* n. 6, Art. 31(2).
41. OECD, *Explanatory Statement to the MLI* (2016), *supra* n. 6, Art. 31(1).
42. C. Binder & K. Zemanek, in *Österreichisches Handbuch des Völkerrechts: Band I – Textteil*, *supra* n. 19, at 71–75.
43. Vienna Convention on the Law of Treaties, Arts 1 and 2(1) (23 May 1969), T.S. 18232 (hereinafter 'the Vienna Convention') (the Vienna Convention 'applies to treaties between States'; a treaty 'means an international agreement concluded between States in written form …'.). For details, *see* K. Schmalenbach, in *Vienna Convention on the Law of Treaties: A Commentary*, at 19–25 and 27–48 (O. Dörr & K. Schmalenbach eds., Springer-Verlag 2012).
44. Articles 31–33 Vienna Convention.
45. Lang, *supra* n. 9, at 11. *See also* O. Dörr, in *Vienna Convention on the Law of Treaties: A Commentary*, *supra* n. 43, at 523. Presently, the understanding of international treaty

Convention, Article 31 provides the general rules of interpretation, Article 32 indicates different supplementary means of interpretations and Article 33 deals with interpretational issues of multilingual treaties.[46]

Under Article 31(1) of the Vienna Convention, a 'treaty shall be interpreted in *good faith* in accordance with the *ordinary meaning* to be given to the terms of the treaty in their *context* and in the light of its *object and purpose*'.[47] In this regard, the wording is not the sole basis for the interpretation of an international treaty, but rather forms its starting point.[48] Furthermore, the 'context' sets forth the relevance of a systematic interpretational approach and the 'object and purpose' promotes other teleological considerations that must be considered during the course of the interpretation.[49]

Moreover, Article 32 of the Vienna Convention provides that also historical aspects must be included.[50] In this regard, the historical interpretation has limited importance just from the perspective of a first glance, as Article 32 of the Vienna Convention states that historical means of interpretation may be used only if the interpretation based on Article 31 of the Vienna Convention, either '[l]eaves the meaning ambiguous or obscure' or '[l]eads to a result which is manifestly absurd or unreasonable'.[51] In fact, this understanding also seems to be consistent if one reads the heading of Article 32, which states 'supplementary means of interpretation'.[52]

However, Article 31(4) of the Vienna Convention provides that a 'special meaning shall be given to a term if it is established that the parties so intended'. From a systematic perspective, the interrelation between Articles 31 and 32 of the Vienna Convention can be understood only in a way such that historical considerations cannot be seen as a sole supplementary mean of interpretation, but rather form an integral part of legal interpretation, which is based on a case-by-case evaluation of different interpretational arguments.[53] Accordingly, one can conclude that international treaty interpretation is in general similar to usual legal interpretation, thus being based on grammatical, teleological, systematic and historic interpretation.[54]

---

interpretation can be seen as a hybrid between the objective and subjective theories, meaning that one generally must apply a pragmatically modified form of the objective theory when it comes to international treaty interpretation. For details, *see* Binder & Zemanek, *supra* n. 42, at 71–75. *See also* M. Herdegen, *Interpretation in International Law*, in *The Max Planck Encyclopaedia of Public International Law*, *supra* n. 1, at 5–12.

46. Herdegen, *supra* n. 45, at 7–12.
47. Article 31(1) Vienna Convention (emphasis added).
48. Lang, *supra* n. 9, at 11; Dörr, *supra* n. 45, at 541.
49. Lang, *supra* n. 9, at 11. *See also* Herdegen, *supra* n. 45, at 12–16.
50. Lang, *supra* n. 9, at 11. *See also* Herdegen, *supra* n. 45, at 16–20.
51. Article 32 Vienna Convention ('Recourse may be had to supplementary means of interpretation, including the preparatory work of the treaty and the circumstances of its conclusion, in order to confirm the meaning resulting from the application of article 31, or to determine the meaning when the interpretation according to Article 31: (a) Leaves the meaning ambiguous or obscure; or (b) Leads to a result which is manifestly absurd or unreasonable.').
52. For details, *see* Dörr, *supra* n. 45, at 571–585.
53. *See also* Lang, *supra* n. 9, at 11 et seq. For details concerning special meaning instead of ordinary meaning, *see* Dörr, *supra* n. 45, at 568–569. For purposes of determining the meaning under Art. 32 of the Vienna Convention, *see* Dörr, *supra* n. 45, at 583–585.
54. Lang, *supra* n. 9, at 12; Dörr, *supra* n. 45, at 541–552.

Moreover, Article 31(3) of the Vienna Convention provides that (i) any subsequent agreement, (ii) any subsequent practice regarding the interpretation of a treaty and (iii) any relevant rules of international law applicable in the relations between the parties, 'shall be taken into account, together with the context'.[55] Given the wording of this Article 31(3), those subsequent practises or agreements 'shall' be taken into account, which indicates only that they must not be ignored on the merits.[56] However, especially the use of the term 'shall' rather indicates that such agreements can, of course, have a significant role in terms of interpretation, but they do not have a higher relevance compared to other interpretative arguments.[57]

2.6 Specific Interpretational Aspects of the MLI

In addition to the general interpretational rules under the Vienna Convention, the MLI itself also provides specific interpretational provisions. Under Article 2(2) of the MLI, '[a]s regards the application of this Convention at any time by a Party, any term not defined herein shall, unless the context otherwise requires, have the meaning that it has at that time' under the relevant covered tax agreement. The interpretational aspects concerning this provision are discussed in another chapter of this book and are therefore not dealt with here.[58]

However, in addition to Article 2(2) of the MLI, Article 32 of the MLI also addresses issues of interpretation and provides as follows:

> 1. Any question arising as to the interpretation or implementation of provisions of a Covered Tax Agreement as they are modified by this Convention shall be determined in accordance with the provision(s) of the Covered Tax Agreement relating to the resolution by mutual agreement of questions of interpretation or application of the Covered Tax Agreement (as those provisions may be modified by this Convention).
> 2. Any question arising as to the interpretation or implementation of this Convention may be addressed by a Conference of the Parties convened in accordance with paragraph 3 of Article 31 (Conference of the Parties).

Given the structure of Article 32 of the MLI, one can distinguish between two procedures. While Article 32(1) deals with interpretational and implementation issues regarding covered tax agreements[59] and generally proposes a bilateral resolution via a mutual agreement procedure (MAP), Article 32(2) directly focuses on interpretational and implementation issues of the MLI itself and provides for the possibility to address the conference of the parties with these questions. From the perspective of a first glance, one could argue that Article 32 of the MLI paves the way for two different general scenarios:

55. Dörr, *supra* n. 45, at 552–568. *See also* Herdegen, *supra* n. 45, at 18–20.
56. Lang, *supra* n. 9, at 12.
57. Lang, *supra* n. 9, at 12.
58. For details on the interpretational issues with regard to Art. 2(2) of the MLI, *see* Chapter 2 of this book.
59. Article 2(1) MLI (the 'term "Covered Tax Agreement" means an agreement for the avoidance of double taxation with respect to taxes on income …'.).

- if a covered tax agreement of two parties to the MLI is applied in their bilateral relations and a question regarding the 'interpretation or implementation of provisions of a Covered Tax Agreement as they are modified' by the MLI arises, the parties to the convention 'shall' try to resolve the issue on a bilateral basis;[60] and
- in a situation when a 'question ... as to the interpretation or implementation of ... [the MLI arises]', the parties to the MLI 'may' address the conference of the parties with this question.[61]

Given this understanding, it is questionable as to whether both procedures are interrelated with each another, meaning that both procedures may be applied subsequently in order to address the same interpretational issue. When analysing the wording, one can conclude that both procedures deal with '[a]ny question arising as to the interpretation or implementation ...'. However, under Article 31(1) of the MLI, these questions address 'provisions of a Covered Tax Agreement as they are modified by this Convention', whereas under Article 32(2) these questions are concerned with 'this Convention'.

In this regard, one could argue that every interpretational question that arises under Article 32(1) of the MLI, could also arise under Article 32(2), as both of them deal with the same provision.[62] To this end, one could therefore conclude that the MLI establishes a two-step procedure for purposes of resolving interpretational issues, under which the first step 'shall' be carried out and the second step 'may' be taken.[63]

However, in fact one could generally question the overall relevance of Article 32(1) of the MLI, as the issue of dispute resolution by means of a MAP is already addressed by Article 16 of the MLI, thus being implemented to all covered tax agreements accordingly.[64] Concerning the purpose of Article 32(1), the Explanatory Statement to the MLI states: '[p]aragraph 1 clarifies the mechanism for determining questions of the interpretation and implementation of Covered Tax Agreements, as *opposed to questions of* the interpretation and implementation of the *Convention itself*'.[65] Given this sentence in the Explanatory Statement, it is obvious that the drafters concluded that 'question[s] arising as to the interpretation ... of provisions of a Covered Tax Agreement'[66] and 'question[s] arising as to the interpretation ... of this

60. Article 32(1) MLI.
61. Article 32(2) MLI.
62. Example: A covered tax agreement between State *A* and State *B* was modified by the MLI. During the course of the application of the bilateral covered tax agreement, a question as to the interpretation of a modified provision arose. In a first step, State *A* and State *B* 'shall' try to resolve the interpretational issue based on a MAP. However, irrespective of whether they were able to resolve the issue via a MAP, State *A* and/or State *B* 'may' address the conference of the parties with this question. This is mainly caused by the fact that the provision, which modified the covered tax agreement, is also a provision of the MLI. This means that the interpretational issue between the two States could eventually be relevant for all parties to the MLI.
63. Article 32(1) and (2) MLI.
64. Lang, *supra* n. 9, at 18.
65. OECD, *Explanatory Statement to the MLI* (2016), *supra* n. 6, Art. 32(1) (emphasis added).
66. Article 32(1) MLI.

Convention'[67] are not the same. With regard to the scope of application of Article 32(1), the Explanatory Statement to the MLI notes as follows:[68]

> Accordingly, the usual mechanisms foreseen by the Covered Tax Agreement should be used to determine questions of interpretation and implementation of the provisions of the Covered Tax Agreement which have been modified by the Convention. This would include questions as to how the Convention has modified a specific Covered Tax Agreement *pursuant to the compatibility clauses* and *other provisions set out in the Convention*. The competent authorities of the Contracting Jurisdictions can therefore agree on the application of the Convention to their Covered Tax Agreements, as long as the agreement reached is consistent with the provisions of the Convention.

The comments in the Explanatory Statement imply that the scope of application of Article 32(1) and (2) of the MLI should not overlap. However, ultimately, it is questionable why 'questions as to how the Convention has modified a specific Covered Tax Agreement pursuant to the compatibility clauses and other provisions set out in the Convention'[69] should not be subject to the interpretational competence of the conference of the parties.[70] As noted, the question as to whether the provisions of a certain covered tax agreement - as it is modified by the MLI - is in line with the MLI, is also a question concerning the interpretation and implementation of the MLI itself, thus being generally open to a conference of the parties procedure under Article 32(2). However, one could argue that the drafters of the MLI took a cautious position with regard to possible interference in the sovereignty of the parties to the Convention, thus limiting the competence of the conference of the parties accordingly.[71]

From an overall perspective, one can conclude that the two mechanism to address interpretational questions laid down in Article 32 of the MLI are intended not to overlap concerning the scope of application. Accordingly, Article 32(1) is meant to be applicable with regard to interpretational questions of a covered tax agreement, whereas Article 32(2) is applicable when it comes to interpretational questions of the MLI itself.[72] However, as the MAP procedure is already addressed in Article 16 of the MLI, thus being implemented to the covered tax agreements, Article 32(1) has only declarative relevance. This declarative relevance can be seen in the clarification that Article 32(2) should be applicable only in those cases when the questions as to the interpretation or implementation does not just address questions as to the

67. Article 32(2) MLI.
68. OECD, *Explanatory Statement to the MLI* (2016), *supra* n. 6, Art. 32(1) (emphasis added).
69. OECD, *Explanatory Statement to the MLI* (2016), *supra* n. 6, Art. 32(1).
70. *See also* Lang, *supra* n. 9, at 21.
71. Lang, *supra* n. 9, at 21. Concerning the interference of the sovereignty of a party to the Convention, one could argue that the competence of the conference of the parties could be overwhelming, thus leading to situations where the conference of the parties declares its position on interpretational issues of bilateral situations.
72. Accordingly, interpretational issues of a certain provision of a covered tax agreement - as it is modified by the MLI - are subject to a bilateral MAP (e.g., interpretational issues concerning the interplay between the 'new' article in the covered tax agreement with the remaining articles of the covered tax agreement), whereas interpretational questions of the MLI itself (e.g., broader interpretational questions concerning the general understanding of MLI provisions or concerning procedural rules of the MLI) may be addressed by a conference of the parties.

interpretation and implementation of covered tax agreements.[73] Accordingly, it was not intended by the drafters of the MLI to provide a two-step procedure which could eventually be applied subsequently in order to address 'the same' interpretational questions; the MLI rather provides (clarifies) that there are two different mechanism to deal with interpretational issues.

2.7 General Aspects of Treaty Amendments in International Law

When speaking of amendments to treaties, Article 39 of the Vienna Convention generally provides the legal basis in international law.[74] Similar to the principles of interpretation, most scholars agree that at least parts of Article 39 of the Vienna Convention - especially those parts under which treaties can be amended at all - presently are part of customary international law, thus being applicable also with regard to parties to the MLI that have not signed or ratified the Vienna Convention.[75] Article 39 of the Vienna Convention provides as follows: 'A treaty may be amended by agreement between the parties. The rules laid down in Part II apply to such an agreement except in so far as the treaty may otherwise provide'.

With regard to multilateral treaties, the situation may arise where not all parties want to become parties to an amended international treaty. In this regard, the principles of Article 30 of the Vienna Convention can be applied.[76] Concerning the question as to whether Article 30 of the Vienna Convention reflects rules of international customary law, a perfectly clear answer cannot be given. In fact, there are only very few decisions by international tribunals. However, from an academic perspective, most scholars agree that Article 30 of the Vienna Convention codifies well-established principles of customary international law (e.g., lex posterior principle),[77] thus being applicable also in cases when one of the parties to the MLI has not signed or ratified the Vienna Convention.

The lex posterior principle[78] is set forth in Article 30(3) and (4) of the Vienna Convention and is applicable if 'a treaty neither terminates an earlier treaty in its entirety nor defines its relation with other treaties through compatibility clauses'.[79] In fact, this means that - under Article 30(3) of the Vienna Convention - when 'all the parties to the earlier treaty are parties also to the later treaty but the earlier treaty is not terminated or suspended ..., the earlier treaty applies only to the extent that its provisions are compatible with those of the later treaty'. However, the lex posterior principle follows another understanding if not all parties to the earlier treaty are parties to the amended (later) treaty. In this regard, Article 30(4)(b) of the Vienna Convention

73. Lang, *supra* n. 9, at 18–22.
74. Binder & Zemanek, *supra* n. 42, at 76–77.
75. K. Odendahl, in *Vienna Convention on the Law of Treaties: A Commentary, supra* n. 43, at 701–702.
76. Binder & Zamalek, *supra* n. 42, at 76–77.
77. Odendahl, *supra* n. 75, at 508–509 with further references.
78. Binder & Zemanek, *supra* n. 42, at 91 at seq.
79. N. Bravo, *The Multilateral Tax Instrument and Its Relationship with Tax Treaties*, 8 World Tax J. 3, at 279, 287 (October 2016).

states that: 'As between a State party to both treaties and a State party to only one of the treaties, the treaty to which both States are parties governs their mutual rights and obligations'.

Accordingly, the main question regarding amendments of a certain treaty is the question as to whether the parties to the earlier treaty accept the amendments, thus being parties to the later treaty, as well. In other words, it is necessary to evaluate whether a party has consented to be bound by an amendment.[80]

2.8 Specific Issues Regarding Amendments of the MLI

With regard to amendments, Article 33 of the MLI provides as follows:

> 1. Any Party may propose an amendment to this Convention by submitting the proposed amendment to the Depositary.
> 2. A Conference of the Parties may be convened to consider the proposed amendment in accordance with paragraph 3 of Article 31 (Conference of the Parties).

Under Article 33(1) of the MLI, any party may propose an amendment to the Convention by following the procedural process set forth in section 2.4.[81] Given the clear wording of the paragraph, Signatories are excluded from initiating an amendment procedure, as they cannot be subsumed under the term 'party'. However, as already discussed in section 2.2, signatories may be invited to participate at the respective conference of the parties.[82]

Moreover, Article 33(2) of the MLI provides that a conference of the parties may be convened to consider the proposed amendment under Article 33(1) of the MLI. Again - also in this regard - the procedural aspects of Article 31(3) of the MLI must be followed.[83] In comparison to the interpretational competences of the conference of the parties under Article 32 of the MLI, the systematic interrelation between Article 33 and other provisions of the MLI or covered tax agreements is more clear-cut, as there is basically no overlap. Even though an amendment of the MLI could eventually result in an amendment of a covered tax agreement, Article 33 does not explicitly address the issue of two different mechanism[84] in order to carry out an amendment (e.g., bilateral or multilateral).

Moreover, also the phrase '[a] Conference of the Parties may be convened to *consider* the proposed amendment'[85] implies that the conference of the parties need not come to a decision regarding the proposed amendments. Accordingly, the paragraph

80. K. Schmalenbach, in *Vienna Convention on the Law of Treaties: A Commentary*, *supra* n. 43, at 44; Aust, *supra* n. 19, at 59.
81. OECD, *Explanatory Statement to the MLI* (2016), *supra* n. 6, Art. 33(1).
82. OECD, *Explanatory Statement to the MLI* (2016), *supra* n. 6, Art. 31(1) ('[t]he Parties may decide to invite Signatories to participate in a Conference of the Parties'.).
83. OECD, *Explanatory Statement to the MLI* (2016), *supra* n. 6, Art. 33(1).
84. Even though Art. 32 of the MLI addresses two different mechanism in order to overcome interpretational issues, those mechanism do not constitute a two-step procedure, as they do not overlap.
85. Article 33(2) MLI (emphasis added).

merely provides the possibility to discuss the respective issue at an institutionalized governing body, thus easing the decision-making process.

3 THE CONFERENCE OF THE PARTIES AND ITS RELEVANCE FOR THE INTERPRETATION AND AMENDMENTS OF THE MLI

3.1 General Aspects Concerning the Relevance of the Conference of the Parties

Given the distinction between the scope of application of Article 32(1) and (2) of the MLI, the relevance of the conference of the parties for the interpretation of the MLI is mostly based on Article 32(2). Regarding the amendment competence of the conference of the parties, Article 33(2) serves the same purposes. Both competences of the conference of the parties are subject to the procedural aspects under Article 31(3) of the MLI.[86] In this regard, Article 31(3) provides as follows:

> Any Party may request a Conference of the Parties by communicating a request to the Depositary. The Depositary shall inform all Parties of any request. Thereafter, the Depositary shall convene a Conference of the Parties, provided that the request is supported by one-third of the Parties within six calendar months of the communication by the Depositary of the request.

Irrespective of whether a party to the Convention makes a request under Article 32(2) of the MLI or proposes an amendment under Article 33(2), at least one-third of the parties to the Convention must support the interpretations request or proposed amendment within six months upon notification by the depositary.[87] As noted, the depositary may not convene a conference of the parties if the one-third quorum is not reached within six months or if the quorum is reached only after the six-month period.[88] Assuming that a conference of the parties was properly convened, it is questionable how decisions concerning interpretational aspects or concerning proposed amendments are to be taken. In fact, neither the wording of the MLI itself nor the Explanatory Statement give information about procedural aspects of decision-making by the conference of the parties.[89]

From a systematic perspective, the MLI is strongly interrelated with the OECD. This mainly results from the facts that: (i) the MLI is generally based on the OECD's work on BEPS Action 15; and (ii) there is a strong organizational link between the OECD and the MLI, as for example the Secretary-General of the OECD is the depositary

86. Article 32(2) MLI.
87. Article 31(3) MLI. *See also* OECD, *Explanatory Statement to the MLI* (2016), *supra* n. 6, Art. 31(3); Lang, *supra* n. 9, at 19.
88. *See also* section 2.4.
89. Only Art. 27(1)(c) of the MLI provides for a specific decision-making mechanism (i.e., consensus of parties and signatories). However, as discussed in section 2.2, the mechanism under Art. 27 of the MLI rather must be seen as another type of decision-making process within the MLI which is not interrelated with decisions of the conference of the parties.

of the MLI.[90] Accordingly, the Convention on the Organisation for Economic Co-operation and Development[91] (hereinafter the OECD Convention) can generally be considered relevant from a systematic perspective, when it comes to the interpretation of the MLI.[92] Article 6 of the OECD Convention provides as follows:

> 1. Unless the Organisation otherwise agrees unanimously for special cases, decisions shall be taken and recommendations shall be made by mutual agreement of all the Members.
> 2. Each Member shall have one vote. If a Member abstains from voting on a decision or recommendation, such abstention shall not invalidate the decision or recommendation, which shall be applicable to the other Members but not to the abstaining Member.
> 3. No decision shall be binding on any Member until it has complied with the requirements of its own constitutional procedures. The other Members may agree that such a decision shall apply provisionally to them.

Given the wording of Article 6 of the OECD Convention, especially paragraph 1 is of major significance, as it states that mutual agreement of all members is relevant, unless the members unanimously agree on other decision-making requirements.[93] In light of Article 6 of the OECD Convention, one could conclude that decisions of the conference of the parties must be made by mutual agreement.[94] However, two main arguments can be brought forward against this interpretation:

- even though the MLI has a close interrelation with the OECD in general, the OECD Convention is – by no means – directly applicable to the MLI. Moreover, the MLI is also not limited to signing and ratification by OECD member countries;[95] and
- also the decision-making requirements of conferences under international law have generally changed over previous decades, meaning that the former focus on unanimity has shifted to a two-thirds decision-making requirement,[96] at least with regard to the adoption of the text of a specific treaty.[97]

---

90. OECD, *Developing a Multilateral Instrument to Modify Bilateral Tax Treaties – Action 15: 2015 Final Report*, OECD/G20 Base Erosion and Profit Shifting Project (2015). *See also* Art. 39 MLI.
91. *Convention on the Organisation for Economic Co-operation and Development* (14 December 1960) (hereinafter 'OECD Convention').
92. Lang, *supra* n. 9, at 20.
93. C. Thiele, *Regeln und Verfahren der Entscheidungsfindung innerhalb von Staaten und Staatenverbindungen – Staats- kommunalrechtliche sowie europa- und völkerrechtliche Untersuchung*, 1st edition, at 273 et seq. (Springer-Verlag 2008). *See also* K. Schmalenbach & C. Schreuer, in *Österreichisches Handbuch des Völkerrechts: Band I – Textteil*, *supra* n. 19, at 240–243. *See also* Lang, *supra* n. 9, at 20 with further references.
94. *See also* Lang, *supra* n. 9, at 20.
95. Lang, *supra* n. 9, at 20.
96. Article 9(2) Vienna Convention. For historical background and negotiating history, *see* F. Hoffmeister, in *Vienna Convention on the Law of Treaties: A Commentary*, *supra* n. 43, at 137–146. *See also* Aust, *supra* n. 19, 91.
97. Hoffmeister, *supra* n. 96, at 142 (in the aftermath of the Conference on the Law of the Sea, on 27 June 1974, 'it became a general practice to strive for consensus … and to allow the adoption of a treaty with a two-thirds majority as a fallback, if no consensus can be achieved'.). *See also* P. Daillier, M. Forteau & A. Pellet, *Droit International Public*, 8th edition, at 188–192 (LGDJ 2009).

3.2 Evaluating the Relevance of the Conference of the Parties for Amendments of the MLI

Article 9(2) of the Vienna Convention provides as follows: 'The adoption of the text of a treaty at an international conference takes place by the vote of two thirds of the States present and voting, unless by the same majority they shall decide to apply a different rule.' The focus of this Article 9(2) is on the 'adoption of the text of a treaty', which is per se interrelated with an amendment of the MLI under Article 33 of the MLI.[98] Accordingly, when it comes to proposed amendments of the MLI, one can conclude that the decision-making - regarding the adoption of the amended text - requires a two-thirds majority of the conference of the parties based on an understanding of Article 9(2) of the Vienna Convention.

However, the adoption of the text of the treaty 'does not constitute in any sense an expression of the State's consent to be bound by it'.[99] In addition, the adoption of the text of the amended treaty by two-thirds of the conference of the parties does not make the amended text unalterable.[100] Ultimately, the pure adoption of the text does not lead to any kind of legally binding force at all.

The two-thirds adoption of the amended text rather must be seen as the first step of an amendment procedure that must be followed by the parties' consent to be bound in order to have an amended treaty.[101] However, this does not imply that the amended agreement must include all parties to the earlier treaty.[102] The amending agreement rather binds only those parties that sign and ratify the amending agreement.[103] Ultimately, the parties to the MLI are free to accept or reject the alterations of the MLI that are suggested by the conference of the parties - even by means of a two-thirds adoption of an amended text of the MLI.

In light of recent developments with regard to such amendment clauses in other treaties,[104] one should bear in mind that they strongly differ from each other, but are usually based on some of the following cornerstones:[105]

- the number of parties that must support an amendment before it is subject to decision-making;
- the specific majority that is necessary to make a decision;
- a clause regarding the ratification or acceptance of the amendment;
- the number of parties that must ratify or accept the amendment;

98. Hoffmeister, *supra* n. 96, at 141 at seq.
99. Hoffmeister, *supra* n. 96, at 145 with further references.
100. Hoffmeister, *supra* n. 96, at 145 with further references. The text of a treaty can be changed as long as it is not authenticated under Art. 10 of the Vienna Convention. For details, *see* Hoffmeister, *supra* n. 96, at 147 at seq.
101. In fact, the adoption and authentication of amendments often take place at the same time, thus giving information about the parties' consent to be bound.
102. Odendahl, *supra* n. 75, at 706–707 with further references.
103. Odendahl, *supra* n. 75, at 715–717.
104. For details, *see* Aust, *supra* n. 19, at 92, *citing* H. Blix & J. Emerson, *The Treaty Maker's Handbook*, at 225 et seq. (Oceana Publications 1973).
105. Aust, *supra* n. 19, at 92.

- a clause indicating whether the amendment may be adopted by tacit agreement; and
- a clause that clarifies whether also those parties are bound that have not accepted the amendment.

Given these aspects, the MLI simply provides for the number of parties that must support an amendment before it is subject to decision-making.[106] Other than this, there are none of the above-mentioned specific clauses.

3.3 Evaluating the Relevance of the Conference of the Parties for the Interpretation of the MLI

When speaking of the interpretation under Article 32 of the MLI, there is obviously no such close link to the 'adoption of the text of a treaty' as described in section 4.2. This means that it is questionable from the perspective of a first glance whether the two-thirds decision-making requirement can be applied also for purposes of interpretation of the MLI.

Given the fact that both provisions, namely Articles 32(2) and 33(2) of the MLI, refer to Article 31(3) of the MLI concerning the procedural aspects of convening of the conference of the parties, one can conclude, from a systematic perspective, that also with regard to interpretation and implementation of the MLI, the conference of the parties' decision-making process is subject to a two-thirds majority.[107] Moreover, also based on an argumentum *a maiore ad minus*, one can conclude that the required decision-making quorum of the conference of the parties must not be higher with regard to interpretational issues compared to amendment issues, as interpretation tends to have lower impact on the understanding of the MLI than an amendment. To this end, one can conclude that interpretational decisions of the conference of the parties are based on a two-thirds majority, as well.

However, in fact the MLI includes a specific support requirement, namely the one-third support requirement in order to convene a conference of the parties under Article 31(3) of the MLI. Based on this, one could question whether this one-third support requirement could eventually be interpreted to be a relevant quorum in terms of decision-making. However, the use of this one-third support requirement in terms of decision-making of the conference of the parties (either with regard to amendments or regarding interpretation and implementation) could eventually lead to diverging statements[108] of different blocs within the conference of the parties, which means that none of these statements could claim the authority of being the decision of the conference of the parties. Accordingly, the better arguments can be brought forward with regard to the conclusion that the one-third requirement is relevant only as kind of 'margin of respectability' in order to avoid addressing the conference of the parties with unreasonable questions or proposals.

106. Article 31(3) MLI.
107. Lang, *supra* n. 9, at 20.
108. Concerning diverging statements, *see also* Lang, *supra* n. 9, at 20.

Assuming that a conference of the parties was convened and came to a decision (based on a two-thirds quorum) concerning the interpretation of the MLI, it is questionable whether this interpretative result of the conference of the parties has legal relevance at all. In this regard, Article 32(2) of the MLI provides only that '[a]ny question arising as to the interpretation … of this Convention *may be addressed* by a Conference of the Parties …'.[109] The term 'may be addressed' itself does not constitute a legal relevance of the interpretational results of the conference of the parties, as it establishes only the general possibility to discuss such an issue at a conference of the parties at all.[110] Save for this provision, the MLI itself does not give any further indication as to the potential legal relevance or legal character of such interpretational results of the conference of the parties. In addition, regarding Article 31, the Explanatory Statement to the MLI provides only very little information regarding the legal relevance or legal character.

However, regarding Article 32(2), the Explanatory Statement to the MLI states that the 'word "may" is used … since there could be other means by which to address questions of interpretation … of the Convention, such as the competent authorities *agreeing between themselves* on how the Convention will operate in relation to a particular Covered Tax Agreement'.[111] In this regard, the phrase 'agreeing between themselves' can be interpreted as a reference to the legal character of a 'subsequent agreement of interpretation' under Article 31(3) of the Vienna Convention. Regardless of whether the drafters of the MLI intended to highlight the legal character of the interpretational results of the conference of the parties, those results must be in line with the interpretational rules of the Vienna Convention in any case in order to potentially claim legal relevance in terms of interpretation.[112]

Given the different interpretational rules of the Vienna Convention, one can conclude that interpretational results of the conference of the parties of the MLI cannot have legal relevance on the basis of Article 31(1), (2), (4) and Article 32 of the Vienna Convention, as those provisions refer to documents and context, as well as object and purpose in 'connection with the conclusion of the treaty' or 'the circumstances of its conclusion'.[113] However, this temporal focus is not relevant with regard to Article 31(3) of the Vienna Convention, as the provision explicitly targets 'subsequent agreement[s]', 'subsequent practice[s]' and 'relevant rules of international law applicable in the relations between the parties'.

In this context, one can hardly subsume the interpretative results of a conference of the parties under 'relevant rules of international law applicable in the relation

109. Article 32(2) MLI (emphasis added).
110. Lang, *supra* n. 9, at 21.
111. OECD, *Explanatory Statement to the MLI* (2016), *supra* n. 6, Art. 32(2) (emphasis added).
112. *See also* Lang, *supra* n. 9, at 21; M. Lehner, in *Doppelbesteuerungsabkommen*, 6th edition, at 191–198 (K. Vogel & M. Lehner eds., C.H. Beck 2015).
113. For details, *see* Dörr, *supra* n. 45, at 533–540 & 541–552. *See also* M. Lang, *Wer hat das Sagen im Steuerrecht?*, Österreichische Steuerzeitung (ÖStZ), at 207 (2006); M. Lang, *Die Bedeutung des OECD-Kommentars und der Reservations, Observations und Positions für die DBA-Auslegung*, in *Nationale und internationale Unternehmensbesteuerung in der Rechtsordnung: Festschrift für Dietmar Gosch*, at 238 (J. Lüdicke, R. Mellinghoff & T. Rödder eds., C.H. Beck 2016); Lang, *supra* n. 9, at 21.

between the parties',[114] which means that only the 'subsequent agreement' and 'subsequent practice' are vital possibilities in order to classify the interpretative results as being potentially relevant for purposes of interpreting the MLI. However, when it comes to 'subsequent practices', only a real existing practice could eventually constitute a 'subsequent practice' in the sense of Article 31(3) of the Vienna Convention.[115] In fact, such a practice need not be carried out by all parties to the Convention in order to fall under the scope of Article 31(3)(b) of the Vienna Convention, but must be at least accepted[116] by all parties to the MLI. However, even if the conference of the parties is of the opinion that they simply summarize a 'subsequent practice' when they come to an interpretative result, this is per se not important at all as long as there is no real evidence of an existing 'subsequent practice'. The need for evidence of an existing 'subsequent practice' cannot be replaced by the interpretative result of the conference of the parties.[117]

Accordingly, the most viable option in order to categorize the interpretative results of the conference of the parties with regard to its legal character, is the 'subsequent agreement between the parties regarding the interpretation of the treaty or the application of its provisions' under Article 31(3)(a) of the Vienna Convention. However, even this option is subject to some pitfalls, as a subsequent agreement on interpretation requires 'an agreement' between all parties to the Convention, whereas the interpretative result of the conference of the parties is subject to a two-thirds majority.[118] In addition, another pitfall of a categorization as a legally relevant 'subsequent agreement on interpretation' could be that the parties to the Convention are not necessarily the same as the participants in the conference of the parties.[119]

Accordingly, the legal relevance of the interpretative result of the conference of the parties as a 'subsequent agreement on interpretation' under Article 31(3)(a) of the Vienna Convention is subject to the following four criteria:[120]

- all parties to the Convention participate in the conference of the parties;
- there is an agreement between the participants of the conference of the parties concerning the interpretational questions;
- the participants of the conference of the parties intended to conclude a 'subsequent agreement on interpretation'; and

114. For details on Art. 31(3)(c) of the Vienna Convention, *see* Dörr, *supra* n. 45, at 561–568. *See also* Herdegen, *supra* n. 45, at 22–25.
115. Lang, *supra* n. 9, at 21; Lehner, *supra* n. 112, at 194. *See also* Dörr, *supra* n. 45, at 554–560.
116. Herdegen, *supra* n. 45, at 18; Dörr, *supra* n. 45, at 557–558.
117. Lang, *supra* n. 9, at 21. According to Dörr, *supra* n. 45, at 555–560, there is no particular form required with regard to a subsequent practise. In this regard, 'official statements or manuals, diplomatic correspondence, press releases, transactions, votes on resolutions in international organizations are just as relevant as national acts of legislation or judicial decisions' could constitute a subsequent practice.
118. Dörr, *supra* n. 45, at 553–554. *See also* section 4.1.
119. *See* section 2.2.
120. Lang, *supra* n. 9, at 21–24.

- the interpretative result of the conference of the parties is within the boundaries of interpretation and therefore does not constitute an amendment of the MLI.

If one of the four criteria is not fulfilled, the interpretative result of the conference of the parties cannot be classified as a 'subsequent agreement on interpretation' under Article 31(3)(a) of the Vienna Convention, but could eventually be seen as an expert opinion concerning the interpretation of the respective provisions of the MLI. However, also if all four criteria are fulfilled and the interpretative result of the conference of the parties can be seen as a legally relevant 'subsequent agreement on interpretation' under Article 31(3)(a) of the Vienna Convention, the relevance of this agreement must not be overestimated. In fact, the agreement only 'shall be taken into account, together with the context'[121] and the wording, as well as the object and purpose of the MLI, which means that it obviously does not have a higher priority than other interpretational arguments.[122]

4 CONCLUSION

The conference of the parties of the MLI is an institutionalized, ad hoc governing body that neither has its own will nor its own legal personality, but rather must be seen as a governing body acting on behalf of the parties to the Convention.

The conference of the parties generally may address two different tasks, namely questions regarding the interpretation of the MLI itself and issues regarding proposed amendments of the MLI. In order to address these issues at a conference of the parties, the formal requirements under Article 31(3) of the MLI must be followed.

Regarding interpretational issues, the conference of the parties has competence only with regard to the interpretation of the MLI itself, whereas questions arising as to the interpretation or implementation of covered tax agreements are subject to a bilateral MAP between parties to the Convention. Assuming that the conference of the parties came to an interpretative result by means of a two-thirds majority, the legal relevance of this interpretative result is subject to four criteria, namely: (i) all parties to the Convention participated in the conference of the parties; (ii) there is an agreement between the participants of the conference of the parties concerning the interpretational questions; (iii) the participants of the conference of the parties intended to conclude a 'subsequent agreement on interpretation'; and (iv) the interpretative result of the conference of the parties falls within the boundaries of interpretation and therefore does not constitute an amendment of the MLI. If these criteria are fulfilled, the interpretative results of the conference of the parties can be seen as 'subsequent agreements on interpretation' under Article 31(3)(a) of the Vienna Convention. If they are not fulfilled, the interpretative result of the conference of the parties, could eventually only be seen as an expert opinion with regard to the interpretation of a certain provision of the MLI.

121. Article 31(3) Vienna Convention.
122. Lang, *supra* n. 9, at 22.

With regard to the amendment of the MLI, the two-thirds requirement set forth in Article 9(2) of the Vienna Convention is relevant only with regard to the adoption of the amended text of the MLI, which does not necessarily mean that the parties also consent to be bound by the amendment. Parties that do not consent are not bound by the amendment of the MLI. In this regard, the general rules of Articles 30, 39 and 40 of the Vienna Convention must be considered.

Ultimately, the relevance of the conference of the parties for the interpretation and amendment of the MLI is limited to a certain extent:

- With regard to interpretational issues, the decision of the conference of the parties could be seen only as an agreement of interpretation or an expert opinion, which are only one aspect or the entire interpretation process, as other grammatical, systematic, teleological and historical arguments must be considered, as well.
- Regarding amendments, the decision of the conference of the parties cannot bind parties that do not consent. Accordingly, it is questionable to what extent amendments will be carried out at all.

CHAPTER 4

Authentic Languages and Official Translations of the Multilateral Instrument and Covered Tax Agreements

Josef Schuch & Jean-Philippe Van West

1 INTRODUCTION

The authentic languages of the Multilateral Convention to Implement Tax Treaty Related Measures to Prevent Base Erosion and Profit Shifting (commonly referred to as the multilateral instrument, MLI) are French and English, both languages being equally authentic.[1] The MLI (potentially) modifies hundreds of bilateral double taxation conventions (hereinafter 'tax treaties'). These tax treaties have their own authentic languages, often the official languages of the contracting states, which might be different from French and English. This leads to complicated situations. For example, Austria and Italy have indicated that they wish to modify the 1981 Austria-Italy tax treaty by the MLI. The authentic languages of that tax treaty are German and Italian.[2] As a consequence, when one wants to consult the Austria-Italy tax treaty as modified by the MLI, the original provisions of the tax treaty are authentic in German and Italian, whereas the provisions modified by the MLI are authentic in French and English. As a result, it is possible that some paragraphs of a certain provision of the tax treaty are

1. Testimonium of the Multilateral Convention to Implement Tax Treaty Related Measures to Prevent Base Erosion and Profit Shifting ('Done at Paris, the 24th day of November 2016, *in English and French, both texts being equally authentic,* in a single copy which shall be deposited in the archives of the Organisation for Economic Co-operation and Development' (emphasis added).).
2. Unofficial translation of the testimonium of the Austria –Italy tax treaty (Concluded on 29 June 1981, entry into force on 6 April 1985) available from the IBFD tax treaties database ('Done at Vienna, on 29 June 1981, in duplicate, *in the German and Italian languages, both texts being equally authentic*' (emphasis added).).

authentic only in German and Italian, while some other paragraphs of that provision as modified by the MLI are authentic only in French and English. Immediately questions arise as to how one should interpret those tax treaties which do not have French and English as their authentic languages and which are modified by the MLI, and how interpretation issues related to different authentic language versions should be resolved. This chapter will provide answers to these questions.

This chapter consists of four sections. First, a historical overview is provided regarding the issue of the authentic languages during the development process of the MLI (section 2). During this process the OECD noted that 'language issues may arise with respect to the modification of bilateral tax treaties authenticated in languages different from the authenticated language(s) of the multilateral instrument'.[3] The question arose as to the number of languages in which the MLI should be concluded (e.g., in only English or French; in English and French; in English, French and other common languages, such as Arabic, Chinese, Russian or Spanish; in all official languages of the participating states) and which language(s) should be authentic. Second, attention is given to the means by which public international law deals with language issues related to multilateral treaties (section 3). Many multilateral treaties have more than one authentic language, and international law offers several solutions to deal with language issues. Third, an analysis is presented of the consequences of the choice of English and French as the authentic languages of the MLI for the interpretation of tax treaties concluded in other languages and potential interpretation issues are highlighted (section 4). Finally, the authors present their conclusions and some critical remarks (section 5).

2 REFERENCES TO THE ISSUE OF THE AUTHENTIC LANGUAGES DURING THE DEVELOPMENT PROCESS

During the development process of the MLI, the OECD published several documents on the different BEPS Actions. Regarding BEPS Action 15 on the development of the MLI, the OECD published the following reports relevant to this chapter:

- Action 15 Deliverable (published September 2014).[4]
- Action 15 Final Report (published October 2015).[5]
- Action 15 Discussion Draft (published May 2016)[6] and Comments Received on the Action 15 Discussion Draft (published July 2016).[7]

3. OECD, *Developing a Multilateral Instrument to Modify Bilateral Tax Treaties – Action 15: 2015 Final Report*, at 22 (2015).
4. OECD, *Developing a Multilateral Instrument to Modify Bilateral Tax Treaties – Action 15: 2014 Deliverable*, OECD/G20 Base Erosion and Profit Shifting Project (2014).
5. OECD, *Action 15: Final Report*, *supra* n. 3.
6. OECD, Discussion Draft, *BEPS Action 15: Development of a Multilateral Instrument to Implement the Tax Treaty related BEPS Measures* (2016).
7. OECD, *Comments Received on Public Discussion Draft – BEPS Action 15: Development of a Multilateral Instrument to Implement the Tax Treaty related BEPS Measures* (2016).

These documents provide an overview of the legal issues related to the development of the MLI and deal with the language issue.

2.1 BEPS Action 15: Deliverable and Final Report[8]

During the development process, it was still an open issue which should be the authentic languages of the MLI. The position of the OECD can be summarized as follows.[9] The OECD acknowledged that language issues might arise with respect to the authentic language(s) of the MLI. Tax treaties are usually authenticated in the official language(s) of the contracting states. If the MLI were to be concluded in only a limited number of authentic languages, the authentic languages of the MLI would have been different from the authentic languages of several tax treaties. The OECD referred to international law where issues regarding the authentic language(s) of multilateral treaties have already been discussed, and which offers various solutions. One possible solution would be to have official texts of the MLI in all languages used in tax treaties. However, the OECD expressed its preference to have only a limited number of authentic languages of the MLI. The OECD stated that 'drafting a multilateral instrument in a number of languages would increase its cost, the risk of conflict between versions in different languages and practical challenges in its administration'.[10] Furthermore, the OECD mentioned the option to have a limited number of authentic languages, but to prepare unofficial translations of the MLI into other languages. States could do this individually, they could work together (e.g., all states having Spanish as their official language could work together, or all German-speaking states could do the same) or translation could be prepared by the depositary.[11]

The preference of the OECD for a limited number of authentic languages is not surprising. Many scholars have already highlighted the increased complexity and risk of interpretation issues of multilingual treaties.[12] The more authentic languages, the greater the risk that there will be differences between the different language versions and the greater the risk of interpretation issues having their source in different language versions. Obviously, to avoid any issues related to different language versions, a treaty

8. As the information that can be found in the Action 15 Deliverable on possible language issues is similar to the information in the Action 15 Final Report, both documents will be analysed together.
9. What follows is a summary of the Action 15 Deliverable, at 20–21 & 60–61, and the Action 15 Final Report, at 22 & 52.
10. OECD, *Action 15 Final Report*, *supra* n. 3, at 22.
11. Article 39 of the MLI states that '[t]he Secretary-General of the Organisation for Economic Co-operation and Development shall be the Depositary of this Convention'.
12. *See* e.g., D. Shelton, *Reconcilable Differences? The Interpretation of Multilingual Treaties*, 20 Hastings Int'l. Comp. L. Rev., at 611, 612 (1997) ('The probability of errors in translation or misunderstandings in negotiations increases as additional languages are added to the number of authentic texts. These problems can have important consequences for multilingual treaties, where the degree to which obligations are understood is crucial to compliance.'). *See also* O. Dörr & K. Schmalenbach, *Vienna Convention on the Law of Treaties: A Commentary*, at 592 (Springer 2012) ('Beside the official languages of all of the parties, *which of course is only reasonable when their number is limited*, the choice is normally one or some of their languages, or a third language (today often English)' (emphasis added)).

should have only one authentic language. In the authors' opinion, the OECD kept this option open during the development process of the MLI by referring to 'the authentic language*(s)*' of the MLI in the Action 15 Deliverable and the Action 15 Final Report (emphasis added).[13] However, this option was not ultimately chosen.

2.2 BEPS Action 15: Discussion Draft and Comments Received on the Discussion Draft

The OECD released a discussion draft in May 2016, soliciting input on technical issues surrounding the implementation of the MLI.[14] One of the issues referred to was:

> *Modifying bilateral treaties in multiple authentic languages.* The multilateral instrument is being negotiated in English and French, and is expected to be concluded in only those two authentic languages, but will modify bilateral tax treaties concluded in many authentic languages. It will be important to ensure consistent application to those bilateral treaties despite differences of language.

Important here is that the OECD stated that it is expected that the MLI will be concluded in French and English only. This is different vis-à-vis the Action 15 Deliverable and Final Report, neither of which made such a statement.

The OECD received several comments on the language issue which can be summarized as follows:

- Some commentators expressed the need for official texts of the MLI in languages other than English and French, ideally in all the languages used in tax treaties.
- Some commentators expressed the need for clarity. The MLI should contain a provision that for the interpretation of a provision of a tax treaty that has been modified by the MLI, the wording of the English language version should prevail when there is an interpretation issue. Another request was that the MLI state that it is to be interpreted in accordance with Articles 31–33 of the Vienna Convention on the Law of Treaties (hereinafter 'the Vienna Convention') or those provisions should be included in the MLI, because not all the (potential) parties to the MLI have ratified the Vienna Convention.
- Some commentators referred to the consequences of the choice of French and English as the authentic languages of the MLI for the interpretation of tax treaties that are amended by the MLI, and highlighted possible issues.

These comments reveal that, on the one hand, there is a demand for translations of the MLI into languages other than French and English. Such translations should be carefully prepared in order to reduce – to the greatest extent possible – the risk of differences between the English version of the MLI, the French version of the MLI and the translations. On the other hand, there is a demand for clarity as to how to deal with

13. OECD, *Action 15 Deliverable, supra* n. 4, at 21; OECD, *Action 15 Final Report, supra* n. 3, at 22.
14. *Supra* n. 6.

different language versions and how to interpret the MLI in the event of divergence between the French and English language versions. Ideally, the MLI or the Explanatory Statement would provide rules or guidelines on how to interpret tax treaties modified by the MLI and how to resolve interpretation issues related to different language versions.

2.3 Conclusion

Already in the first BEPS documents on the development of the MLI, the OECD noted that language issues might arise when the MLI modifies bilateral conventions that have different authentic languages than the MLI. The OECD expressed its preference to conclude the MLI in only a limited numbers of languages. A discussion draft was issued in order to solicit input on, for example, possible technical issues of the MLI. Several commentators expressed their concerns regarding the potential language issues. On the one hand, they mainly expressed a preference for translations into other languages than French and English of the MLI. On the other hand, they requested guidelines on how to interpret tax treaties concluded in different languages that will be modified by the MLI, and on how to resolve interpretation issues related to different language versions.

3 MULTILINGUAL TREATIES AND LANGUAGE ISSUES: GENERAL PRACTICE

3.1 The Authentic Language(s) of Multilateral Treaties: A Brief Overview

In public international law, there is no general rule that stipulates in what language(s) treaties must be concluded.[15] The equality of states implies that every state is, in principle, entitled to conclude treaties in the language(s) it prefers.[16] This could be the official language(s) of the states concerned, or any other language. Often, the final clause or the testimonium of a treaty stipulates the authentic language(s).

Initially, and until the end of the nineteenth century, treaties were mostly concluded in only one language – initially in Latin, later on in French.[17] Concluding a treaty in only one language has several clear advantages compared to a multilingual treaty. Translation costs are limited and risks of different meanings between different authentic language versions are eliminated. However, this does not mean that no linguistic issues can arise when a treaty is concluded in only one authentic language. Linguistic issues could still arise if the authentic language is alien to one or more of the contracting states, or even when the authentic language is the official language of all

15. U. Linderfalk, *On the Interpretation of Treaties: The Modern International Law as Expressed in the 1969 Vienna Convention on the Law of Treaties*, at 355 (Springer 2010).
16. Lord Mc Nair, *The Law of Treaties*, at 30 (Oxford University Press 1961); Dörr & Schmalenbach, *supra* n. 12, at 591 (2012); Shelton, *supra* n. 12, at 612.
17. J.K. Gamble, *Choice of Language in Bilateral Treaties: Fifty Years of Changing State Practice*, 3 Indiana Int'l. Comp. L. Rev., at 233, 236–237 (1993); Dörr & Schmalenbach, *supra* n. 12, at 589.

the contracting states.[18] For example, a certain term can have a different meaning under American English and British English. Furthermore, languages are not static and they develop in place and time. A term that initially had a similar meaning in two states, might - over time - come to have a different meaning in the two states.

After the First World War the dominant position of the French language as the model diplomatic language declined,[19] and from the beginning of the twentieth century it became more frequent to conclude treaties in more than one language.[20] Presently, multilateral treaties are often drafted in two or more languages.[21] The International Law Commission concluded that 'The phenomenon of treaties drawn up in two or more languages has become extremely common and, with the advent of the United Nations, general multilateral treaties drawn up, or finally expressed, in five different languages have become quite numerous'.[22] It is important when a treaty is drafted in more than one language, that there be only one single treaty that consists of all the different languages in which the treaty is concluded.[23]

Drafting a treaty in multiple languages can resolve interpretation issues, yet can also be a source of interpretation issues.[24] On the one hand, when the meaning of a term or phrase in one language is unclear, a comparison with another language version can help in determining the meaning of this term or phrase. On the other hand, every language has its own characteristics, and certain terms or phrases cannot be translated. Or the translated terms or phrases can have a different or ambiguous meaning in the other language. Furthermore, states have different legal traditions and systems, and some legal terms might simply not exist in the other jurisdiction(s). An increase in the number of authentic languages of a treaty increases the complexity of the treaty.

When dealing with a multilingual treaty, it is critical to distinguish between the different legal statuses that the language versions of a multilateral treaty can have. Each

18. G. Maisto, *Introduction*, in *Multilingual Texts and Interpretation of Tax Treaties and EC Tax Law*, at xxi (G. Maisto ed., IBFD 2005).
19. J. Hardy, *The Interpretation of Plurilingual Treaties by International Courts and Tribunals*, 37 Brit. Y.B Int'l. L 1961, at 72 (Oxford University Press 1962).
20. Gamble, *supra* n. 17, at 237.
21. A. Aust, *Modern Treaty Law and Practice*, at 250 (2nd ed., Cambridge University Press 2007).
22. Draft Articles on the Law of Treaties with Commentaries, Report of the ILC to the General Assembly on the work of the 8th Session (1966), 2 Yearbook of Intl. Law Commission, at 224–226, para. 1, U.N. Doc A/6309/Rev. 1. Presently, UN treaties are generally concluded in six languages.
23. *See* e.g., D.B. Hollis, *The Oxford Guide to Treaties*, at 695 (Oxford University Press 2012).
24. Yearbook of the Intl. Law Commission 1966-II, at 225, para. 6 ('In practice, the existence of authentic texts in two or more languages sometimes complicates and sometimes facilitates the interpretation of a treaty. Few plurilingual treaties containing more than two articles are without some discrepancy between the texts. The different genius of the languages, the absence of a complete consensus ad idem, or lack of sufficient time to co-ordinate the texts may result in minor or even major discrepancies in the meaning of the texts. In that event the plurality of the texts may be a serious additional source of ambiguity or obscurity in the terms of the treaty. On the other hand, when the meaning of terms is ambiguous or obscure in one language but it is clear and convincing as to the intentions of the parties in another, the plurilingual character of the treaty facilitates interpretation of the text the meaning of which is doubtful.').

language version of a treaty can have the status of authentic text, official text or official translation. An authentic text is accepted by the parties to be authoritative, whereas an official text has been signed by the states concerned, but not accepted to be authoritative. An official translation is also not authoritative. Rather, it is a mere translation prepared by the parties or a single government, or by a body of an international organization.[25] Discrepancies may arise between texts of equal authority, or texts of unequal authority. For a discussion of how divergences between the different language versions are to be resolved, *see* section 3.3.

3.2 Some Examples of the Authentic Language(s) of Multilateral Treaties

3.2.1 Multilateral Treaties Having a Single Authentic Language

Although today most multilateral treaties have more than one authentic text, there are some treaties that have been concluded in only one language. One example is the Central European Free Trade Agreement (between the Czech Republic, Hungary, Poland and Slovakia) of 1992 which has only English as its authentic language.[26]

3.2.2 Multilateral Treaties Having Two or More Equally Authentic Languages

A distinction can be made between treaties that are concluded in two or more equally authentic texts, and treaties that are authenticated in other language versions after the conclusion of the treaty.

3.2.2.1 Original Authentic Texts

Today, most multilateral treaties are concluded in more than one authentic language. For example the treaties concluded under the framework of the United Nations are usually authentic in the six official languages of the United Nations (Arabic, Chinese, English, French, Russian and Spanish).[27] It is possible for a treaty to be drafted and negotiated in one or a limited number of languages, and – before the signing of the treaty – translated into the other authentic languages.[28] When a treaty has more than one authentic language, there is a possibility that one language will prevail in case of

25. Yearbook of the Intl. Law Commission 1966-II, at 224, para. 1. *See also* Dörr & Schmalenbach, *supra* n. 12, at 593.
26. Testimonium of the Central European Free Trade Agreement (1992) ('Done at Kraków this 21st day of December 1992 in a single authentic copy in the English language which shall be deposited with the Government of Poland.').
27. Article 28 International Convention for the Suppression of Acts of Nuclear Terrorism (2005) ('The original of this Convention, of which the Arabic, Chinese, English, French, Russian and Spanish texts are equally authentic, shall be deposited with the Secretary-General of the United Nations, who shall send certified copies thereof to all States.').
28. Aust, *supra* n. 21, at 250–253.

divergence.[29] This practice can help to overcome interpretation issues related to the divergence of authentic language versions.[30]

3.2.2.2 *Authentication of Other Language Versions*

Authentication of other language versions at a later time can be done pursuant to the original treaty or by subsequent agreement. In the first situation, the treaty itself provides for the authentication of other languages.[31] In the latter situation, the authentication of other language versions is based on a new agreement.[32]

3.2.2.3 *A Special Case: The European Union*

Seldom, especially were a large number of states are involved, multilateral treaties are authentic in all the official languages of the states involved. A significant exception is the treaties of the European Union. The Treaty of the European Union and the Treaty on the Functioning of the European Union are concluded in all official languages of the Member States. In addition, there is a specific clause that foresees that these treaties may be translated into other languages.[33] Every time that a new Member State with a

29. For example Art. 22.6 Free Trade Agreement between the Government of the People's Republic of China and the Government of the Republic of Korea (2015) ('This Agreement shall be done in Chinese, Korean, and English. The three texts are equally valid and authentic. In case of any divergence, the English text shall prevail.').
30. Aust, *supra* n. 21, at 253.
31. For example Art. 15.5 Agreement between the European Union and the United States of America on the Processing and Transfer of Financial Messaging Data from the European Union to the United States for purposes of the Terrorist Finance Tracking Program (2009) ('Done at Brussels this day 30 of November 2009, in two originals, in the English language. This Agreement shall also be drawn up in the Bulgarian, Czech, Danish, Dutch, Estonian, Finnish, French, German, Greek, Hungarian, Italian, Latvian, Lithuanian, Maltese, Polish, Portuguese, Romanian, Slovak, Slovenian, Spanish, and Swedish languages. Upon approval by both Parties, these language versions shall be considered equally authentic.').
32. For example Arts 1 & 2 Protocol on The Authentic Trilingual Text of the Convention on International Civil Aviation (1968) ('Article 1: The text of the Convention in the French and Spanish languages annexed to this Protocol, together with the text of the Convention in the English language, constitutes the text equally authentic in the three languages as specifically referred to in the last paragraph of the Convention. Article 2: If a State party to this Protocol has ratified or in the future ratifies any amendment made to the Convention in accordance with Article 94(a) thereof, then the text of such amendment in the English, French and Spanish languages shall be deemed to refer to the text, equally authentic in the three languages, which results from this Protocol.').
33. Article 55 TEU (2007) ('1. This Treaty, drawn up in a single original in the Bulgarian, Czech, Danish, Dutch, English, Estonian, Finnish, French, German, Greek, Hungarian, Irish, Italian, Latvian, Lithuanian, Maltese, Polish, Portuguese, Romanian, Slovak, Slovenian, Spanish and Swedish languages, the texts in each of these languages being equally authentic, shall be deposited in the archives of the Government of the Italian Republic, which will transmit a certified copy to each of the governments of the other signatory States. 2. This Treaty may also be translated into any other languages as determined by Member States among those which, in accordance with their constitutional order, enjoy official status in all or part of their territory. A certified copy of such translations shall be provided by the Member States concerned to be deposited in the archives of the Council.').

'new' official language joins the EU, these treaties will be translated into this new language, and those translations will become authentic, as well.

3.2.3 *Official Texts and Official Translations*

As explained above, authentic texts must be distinguished from official texts and official translations. An example of a treaty where not all the official languages of the treaty were accepted as authentic is the 1947 peace treaty with Finland (one of the Paris Peace Treaties following World War Two).[34] Often states prepare official translations of treaties that are concluded in a different language than the official language of the state.[35] This translation is then submitted together with the authentic version of the treaty to parliamentary approval and published in the national gazette.[36] The main advantage of this practice is the broad accessibility to the treaty for the stakeholders of the contracting state so that they have access to their rights set forth in the treaty.

3.3 The Interpretation of Multilingual Treaties: Article 33 of the Vienna Convention

Many multilateral treaties have more than one authentic language and, in addition thereto, official texts and official translations may exist. Questions arise as to how such multilingual treaties are to be interpreted and how interpretation issues having their source in the different language versions are to be resolved. The main principles regarding the interpretation of multilingual treaties are set forth in Article 33 of the Vienna Convention, which provides as follows:

1. When a treaty has been authenticated in two or more languages, the text is equally authoritative in each language, unless the treaty provides or the parties agree that, in case of divergence, a particular text shall prevail.
2. A version of the treaty in a language other than one of those in which the text was authenticated shall be considered an authentic text only if the treaty so provides or the parties so agree.
3. The terms of the treaty are presumed to have the same meaning in each authentic text.
4. Except where a particular text prevails in accordance with paragraph 1, when a comparison of the authentic texts discloses a difference of meaning

34. Article 36 Treaty of Peace with Finland (1947) ('The present Treaty, of which the Russian and English texts are authentic, shall be ratified by the Allied and Associated Powers.'); Testimonium of the treaty ('Done in the city of Paris in the Russian, English, French and Finnish languages, this tenth day of February, One Thousand Nine Hundred Forty-Seven.').
35. For example, for Belgium, Art. 8 Act of 31 May 1961 on the use of languages in legislation, drafting, publication and entry into force of legislation and regulations (providing that a translation in French and Dutch of treaties concluded in other languages will be published in the Official Gazette).
36. J. Wouters & M. Vidal, *Non-tax Treaties: Domestic Courts and Treaty Interpretation*, in *Courts and Tax Treaty Law*, at 20 (G. Maisto ed., IBFD 2007).

> which the application of articles 31 and 32 does not remove, the meaning which best reconciles the texts, having regard to the object and purpose of the treaty, shall be adopted.

It is generally accepted that Article 33 of the Vienna Convention is part of customary international law and can therefore also be applied to states that are not participants to the Vienna Convention.[37] The interpretation of multilingual treaties is much debated in literature[38] and an in-depth analysis of this provision is beyond the scope of this chapter. Rather, the main principles are summarized below.[39]

First, unless the parties agree that one language version should prevail, all language versions are equally authentic and the terms of a treaty are presumed to have the same meaning in each authentic version. So each term (and thus the whole treaty) is presumed to have only one meaning. The presumption that the different language versions are all equal implies that, as a starting point, an interpreter can, for the purposes of routine interpretation, rely on one language version to interpret the treaty.[40] The Vienna Convention does not impose an obligation to consult several or all language versions. This does not mean, however, that the text is binding only in the national language.[41] The presumption that the different language texts are equal is a rebuttable presumption, and interpreters may prove there is a discrepancy between two or more language versions. According to Gardiner: 'The conclusion must be that the interpreter may legitimately use a single language for "routine" interpretation ..., but a prudent interpreter needs to be very aware of the possibility that language differences may be relevant'.[42]

Second, when a comparison of the authentic texts discloses a difference of meaning, the general interpretation rules of Articles 31 and 32 of the Vienna Convention must be applied. The general rules of interpretation require that a treaty be interpreted in good faith in accordance with the ordinary meaning to be given to the

37. Dörr & Schmalenbach, *supra* n. 12, at 588.
38. For example, M. Hilf, *Die Auslegung mehrsprachiger Verträge: Eine Untersuchung zum Völkerrecht und zum Staatsrecht der Bundesrepublik Deutschland*, Beiträge zum ausländischen öffentlichen Recht und Völkerrecht (Springer 1973); R.K. Gardiner, *Treaty Interpretation* (2nd ed., Oxford University Press 2015); P. Arginelli, *Multilingual Tax Treaties: Interpretation, Semantic Analysis and Legal Theory* (IBFD 2015).
39. *See also* G. Gaja, *The Perspective of International Law*, in *Multilingual Texts and Interpretation of Tax Treaties and EC Tax Law*, *supra* n. 18, at 91.
40. Dörr & Schmalenbach, *supra* n. 12, at 598; F.A. Engelen, *Interpretation of Tax Treaties under International Law: A Study of Articles 31, 32 and 33 of the Vienna Convention on the Law of Treaties and Their Application to Tax Treaties*, at 384 (IBFD 2004). The presumption of similar meaning is subject to criticism because it allows an interpreter to rely on one language version. If one looks at only one language, divergences between different language versions are not discovered and the treaty might be applied in a different way in different states. Several authors assert that there is a need to consult and compare several or all authentic language versions. *See* R.X. Resch, *Not in Good Faith: A Critique of the Vienna Convention Rule of Interpretation Concerning Its Application to Plurilingual (Tax) Treaties*, Brit. Tax Rev. 3, at 307–328 (2014); C.B. Kuner, *The Interpretation of Multilingual Treaties; Comparison of Texts Versus the Presumption of Similar Meaning*, 40 Int'l. Comp. L. Q., at 953–964 (1991).
41. Wouters & Vidal, *supra* n. 36, at 19.
42. Gardiner, *supra* n. 38, at 421.

terms of the treaty in their context and in light of the treaty's object and purpose.[43] When these general interpretation rules do not provide a solution, the interpreter must adopt the meaning which best reconciles the texts, having regard to the object and purpose of the treaty. According to several scholars, the application of the interpretation rules under Articles 31 and 32 of the Vienna Convention will clarify – in most cases – the divergence between authentic texts.[44] The Vienna Convention does not provide for the solution that in case of divergence, the language in which the treaty was negotiated is to prevail. However, this does not mean that the same weight must always be attributed to all authentic languages.[45] Most scholars assert that, in certain cases, more weight may be given to the language(s) in which the treaty is negotiated and drafted.[46]

If the general rules of interpretation do not resolve the interpretation issue, the interpreter must reconcile the texts in light of the object and purpose of the treaty. Both Articles 31(1) and 33(4) of the Vienna Convention refer to the object ant purpose of the treaty, and therefore the relevance of 33(4) is sometimes questioned. However, scholars have noted that under Article 33(4), the interpreter enjoys much greater freedom in reconciling the texts compared to the general rules of interpretation of Articles 31 and 32, as the interpreter must look at only the object and purpose of the treaty there, whereas Article 31(1) emphasizes the primacy of the text of the treaty.[47] Although the Vienna Convention does not state that in case of divergence, the more restrictive meaning is to prevail (the principle of restrictive interpretation), Wouters and Vidal conclude that 'the meaning which best reconciles the different versions, having regard to the object and purpose of the treaty, will prevail, and this will often – but not necessarily – be the lowest common denominator. In other words, if there is a version with a more restricted meaning, that version will have the upper hand unless it frustrates the object and purpose.'[48]

Furthermore, only the authentic languages of a treaty are authoritative. The authentic language versions form the starting point of the interpretation process. Official texts and official translations are not authoritative, and Article 33 of the Vienna Convention does not afford any relevance to these language versions.[49] Although official translations are not authoritative, their influence should not be underestimated

43. Article 31(1) Vienna Convention. For the application of Arts 31 and 32 of the Vienna Convention, *see* Chapter 2 of this book.
44. Engelen, *supra* n. 40, at 395; Linderfalk, *supra* n. 15, at 358; Arginelli, *supra* n. 38, at 351.
45. Dörr & Schmalenbach, *supra* n. 12, at 594. The classic example is the interpretation of the UN Charter by the International Court of Justice. That Court seems to place more importance on the French and English language texts, rather than the other authentic texts.
46. Aust, *supra* n. 21, at 252; Arginelli, *supra* n. 38, at 286.
47. Dörr & Schmalenbach, *supra* n. 12, at 600. For a discussion on the relevance of the reference to the object and purpose of the treaty in both Art. 31(1) and Art. 33(4) of the Vienna Convention, *see* Engelen, *supra* n. 40, at 402 et seq.
48. Wouters & Vidal, *supra* n. 36, at 20.
49. This does not mean that no value can be attributed to official translations in the interpretation process. Official translations can, in certain circumstances, qualify as supplementary means under Art. 32 of the Vienna Convention. *See* Engelen, *supra* n. 40, at 396; Arginelli, *supra* n. 38, at 287.

according to some authors.[50] Individuals and courts might wrongfully consult and rely on these official translations, rather than the authentic versions.

3.4 Conclusion

The authentic language of a treaty is a common issue in international public law, and treaty practice reveals a wide range of solutions. The contracting states are free to decide on the number of languages in which they conclude a treaty, as well as which languages will be authentic. The common practice these days is to conclude multilateral treaties in a limited number of authentic languages, although it is also possible to conclude a multilateral treaty in only one language or in all the official languages of the contracting parties. In other words, from an international law perspective, nothing prevented the participating states from concluding the MLI in only one language or in all official languages of the participating states. The choice of a limited number of authentic languages follows general treaty practice and is based on practical reasons.

The plurality of authentic languages adds a new element to the interpretation of a treaty,[51] namely the comparison of different language versions. Interpretation issues related to multilingual treaties have been discussed extensively in public international law, and Article 33 of the Vienna Convention contains the main rules regarding how treaties authenticated in two or more languages are to be interpreted. The basic assumption is that the terms of the treaty have the same meaning in each authentic text, and multilingual treaties should be interpreted in accordance with Articles 31 and 32 of the Vienna Convention. When a comparison of the authentic texts reveals a difference of meaning which the application of Articles 31 and 32 does not resolve, the meaning which best reconciles the texts, having regard to the object and purpose of the treaty, is to be adopted. Although a treaty might have several authentic language versions, the treaty has only one single meaning.

4 THE AUTHENTIC LANGUAGES OF THE MLI AND TAX TREATIES

An analysis is provided here of the choice of English and French as the authentic languages of the MLI, as well as the consequences of this choice for the interpretation of tax treaties modified by the MLI. Furthermore, potential interpretation issues are discussed. This section builds on the general interpretation rules described in section 3.3 above.

4.1 Overview of the Most Common Practices in Tax Treaties

Most tax treaties are concluded in the official languages of the contracting states. Like in other treaties, often the final clause or the testimonium of a tax treaty stipulates the authentic language(s). If the contracting states have the same official language, the

50. Wouters & Vidal, *supra* n. 36, at 21, *with reference to* Hilf, *supra* n. 38, at 200.
51. Yearbook of the Intl. Law Commission 1966-II, at 225, para. 6.

treaty will normally be concluded in only one language.[52] If the contracting states have different official languages - and this will often be the case, the tax treaty will usually be concluded in two or more authentic languages.[53] Sometimes states include, in addition to their official languages, also a neutral third language,[54] often English. Another practice is to include a provision that a certain language will prevail in case of divergence between the different authentic language versions of a treaty.[55] Yet another option is for states decide to conclude a tax treaty in only one language that is not an official language of either of the contracting states.[56] Thus, there are several options in practice.

It has been estimated that more than 80% of tax treaties have English as one of the authentic languages. Less than 10% of tax treaties have French as one of the authentic languages, and less than 10% use neither French nor English.[57] As a consequence, most states have experience with concluding tax treaties in more than one authentic language, and the use of English and/or French as an authentic language seems to be a common practice for most states. Several scholars have analysed the interpretation of tax treaties authenticated in two of more language.[58] Tax treaties are treaties under public international law[59] and they are subject to the interpretation rules of the Vienna Convention. As a consequence, Article 33 of the Vienna Convention applies to tax treaties authenticated in two or more languages, and they must be interpreted according to the principles set out under section 3.3 above.

52. For example, testimonium of the tax treaty between Germany and Austria (Concluded on 24 August 2000, entry into force on 18 August 2002) ('Done in duplicate in Berlin on 24 August 2000, both in the German language.').
53. For example, testimonium of the tax treaty between Belgium and Germany (Concluded on 11 April 1967, entry into force on 30 July 1969) ('Done in duplicate at Brussels, this 11th day of April 1967, in the French, Dutch and German languages, all three texts being equally authoritative.').
54. Often, this neutral third language is English. For example, testimonium of the tax treaty between Italy and Brazil (Concluded on 3 October 1978, entry into force on 24 April 1981) ('Done in duplicate at Rome the day of October 3rd 1978 in the Portuguese, Italian and English languages, all texts being equally authentic … .').
55. For example, testimonium of the tax treaty between Belgium and Croatia (Concluded on 31 October 2001, entry into force on 1 April 2004) ('Done in duplicate at Brussels, this 31st day of October 2001, in the English, French, Dutch and Croatian languages, all texts being equally authentic. In case of divergence between the texts, the English text shall prevail.').
56. For example, testimonium of the tax treaty concluded between the Netherlands and Turkey (Concluded on 27 March 1986, entry into force on 30 September 1988) ('Done at Ankara, this twenty-seventh day of March 1986 in duplicate in the English language.').
57. S. Austry et al., *The Proposed OECD Multilateral Instrument Amending Tax Treaties*, 70 Bull. Int'l. Taxn. 12, at 686 (2016). The OECD referred to the same numbers during the OECD Tax Talks webcast of 5 December 2016, available at http://video.oecd.org/3301/or/Webcast-OECD-Tax-Talks.html, accessed 14 July 2017.
58. For example, M. Lang, *The Interpretation of Tax Treaties and Authentic Languages*, in *Essays on Tax Treaties: A Tribute to David A. Ward* (G. Maisto, A. Nikolakakis & J.M. Ulmer eds., IBFD 2015); Arginelli, *supra* n. 38; Engelen, *supra* n. 40.
59. M. Lang & F. Brugger, *The Role of the OECD Commentary in Tax Treaty Interpretation*, 23 Austrl. Tax Forum, at 97 (2008), *citing* K. Vogel, *Introduction*, in *Klaus Vogel on Double Taxation Conventions*, para. 28 (Wolters Kluwer 1997).

4.2 The Authentic Languages of the MLI: French and English

French and English are the authentic languages of the MLI. Official translations in Arabic, German, Italian and Spanish are already available,[60] and official translations into other languages will follow.[61] The choice of French and English as the authentic languages is not a surprise, as also the OECD Model Convention and the Commentary thereon are drafted in French and English. French and English are also the official languages of the OECD,[62] and it is often the case that multilateral treaties are negotiated and authenticated in the official languages of the hosting organization.[63] Furthermore, one can see that English and - to a lesser extent - French are common tax treaty languages. From a practical perspective, it is positive that there are only two authentic languages. This should limit the risk of interpretation issues related to inconsistencies between authentic language versions. In addition, as mentioned under section 4.1, most states already have experience with English and/or French as an authentic language of (some of) their tax treaties.

It will be interesting to see whether the choice of English and French will influence the authentic languages of future tax treaties. Most parties to the MLI were willing to give up their official language, and it remains to be seen whether they will also be willing to do so in future. Will this lead to more tax treaties concluded in only English or French? For example, if an English-speaking state wants to conclude a new tax treaty with a state the official language of which is not English or French, and requests that the treaty be authentic only in English, would it not be a realistic option for the treaty to be concluded in English only if this country already gave up its official language for the MLI? The same question can be asked with regard to the conclusion of a new tax treaty with two states that both do not have French or English as an official language, and one state requests that the treaty be authentic only in English or French.[64]

4.3 Interpretation of Tax Treaties Modified by the MLI

The question arises as to how one should interpret tax treaties not concluded in English or French that are modified by the MLI. The Explanatory Statement to Accompany the Convention (hereinafter 'the Explanatory Statement') provides that 'where questions of interpretation arise in relation to Covered Tax Agreements concluded in other

60. The translations of the MLI into German, Italian and Spanish were prepared by the members of the ad hoc group. The translation into Arabic was prepared by the OECD Secretariat.
61. For example, translations into Dutch, Greek, Russian and Swedish.
62. Testimonium of the Convention on the Organisation for Economic Co-operation and Development (1960) ('Done in Paris, this fourteenth day of December, Nineteen Hundred and Sixty, in the English and French languages, both texts being equally authentic … .').
63. For example the treaties concluded under the framework of the United Nations are usually authentic in the six official languages of the United Nations. *Supra* n. 27.
64. In the past, several states that do not have English or French as an official language have concluded tax treaties only in English.

languages or in relation to translations of the Convention into other languages, it may be necessary to refer back to the English or French authentic texts of the Convention'.[65]

Indeed, tax treaties that are modified by the MLI can have complex language structures. The MLI will add provisions in French and English to tax treaties which have neither French nor English as an authentic language, or to tax treaties that already have French and/or English as an authentic language. The modifications by the MLI to tax treaties will be authentic in French and English only, even if the tax treaty concerned did not stipulate that (one of) these languages are authentic. This might leads to complex situations. For example authentic provisions in French and English will be inserted into the tax treaty between Germany and Austria which is authentic only in German, or authentic provisions in French and English will be inserted into the tax treaty between the Netherlands and Finland which is authentic only in English.[66] As a result, when consulting a provision of a tax treaty that is modified by the MLI, it might occur that the authentic language(s) of one paragraph are the authentic languages of the original tax treaty, and the authentic language of following paragraph as modified by the MLI are authentic in French and English. It could even be that the MLI inserts or replaces only a few words within a paragraph, so that only a few words are authentic only in French and English.[67]

Of course, the MLI is – just like tax treaty – a treaty under public international law and must be interpreted in accordance with the interpretation rules under the Vienna Convention.[68] The general interpretation rules of Articles 31 and 32 of the Vienna Convention apply, as does Article 33 of the Vienna Convention concerning the interpretation of treaties authenticated in two or more languages. Under Article 33, the official translations made by the participating states are not authoritative. Only the French and English versions of the provisions inserted through the MLI into bilateral tax treaties are authentic. From an international law perspective, no explicit value is given to official translations.[69] Therefore, interpreters are to rely on the French and English versions of the MLI and not on any official translations, and domestic courts must apply the authentic language versions when interpreting provisions of a tax treaty that are modified by the MLI.[70] However, as mentioned, some scholars have noted the

65. OECD, *Explanatory Statement to the Multilateral Convention to Implement Tax Treaty Related Measures to Prevent Base Erosion and Profit Shifting*, at 75, para. 317 (2016).
66. *See also* the example provided in the introduction. The authentic languages of the 1981 Austria-Italy tax treaty are German and Italian. As a consequence, when one wants to consult this treaty as modified by the MLI, the original provisions of the tax treaty are authentic in German and Italian, while the provisions 'inserted' by the MLI are authentic in French and English. As a result, it is possible that some paragraphs of a certain provision of the tax treaty could be authentic only in German and Italian, while some other paragraphs of that provision as modified by the MLI are authentic only in French and English.
67. M. Lang, *Die Auslegung des multilateralen Instruments*, Steuer und Wirtschaft International (SWI) 1, at 22 (2017).
68. Lang, *supra* n. 67, at 11.
69. Wouters & Vidal, *supra* n. 36, at 21.
70. The OECD states that 'The translations of the MLI in other languages are provided only for information purposes. Only the signed English and French MLI are the authentic MLI texts applicable.' *See* http://www.oecd.org/tax/treaties/multilateral-convention-to-implement-tax-treaty-related-measures-to-prevent-beps.htm (accessed 8 July 2017).

wrongful practice in other areas of international law where domestic courts consider only the official translations when interpreting a treaty. It remains to be seen whether this will also be the case regarding the interpretation of tax treaties modified by the MLI. If, for example, a tax treaty concluded only in Spanish is modified by the MLI and an official translation and a consolidated version in Spanish are available, there is a risk that a domestic judge could wrongly rely on the official Spanish version rather than on the authentic French and English provisions of the MLI.[71]

Thus, the provisions of a tax treaty that are modified by the MLI are authentic only in French and English and must be interpreted in these two languages. But what happens when there is an ambiguity or a divergence between the French and English version? In such case, the general interpretation rules of Articles 31 and 32 of the Vienna Convention must be applied, and the interpreter is obliged to attempt to resolve the issue based on the principles set forth in these provisions.[72] The consequences of these complex language structures should therefore not be overestimated.[73] The terms of the French and English language version are presumed to have the same meaning,[74] and if there is an inconsistency between the two language versions, the MLI should be interpreted - like any other treaty - in good faith in accordance with the ordinary meaning to be given to the terms of the treaty in their context and in light of its object and purpose.[75,76] Only when the general interpretation rules of Articles 31 and 32 of the Vienna Convention do not resolve the interpretation issue, must the interpreter adopt the meaning that best reconciles the texts having regard to the object and purpose of the treaty.[77]

Although the OECD noted in the in the BEPS Action 15 documents that there might be interpretation issues concerning the authentic languages of the MLI and the authentic languages of tax treaties authenticated in other languages, the Explanatory Statement neither provides more practical guidance than the paragraph quoted at the beginning of this subsection, nor concrete examples regarding how one should interpret tax treaties modified by the MLI. For some situations, clarifications would have been helpful in order to remove uncertainty. For example, what if the MLI were

71. This is just one example. Of course similar risks arise with respect to official translations into other languages. There is also a risk that for the interpretation of the Austria-Italy tax treaty as modified by the MLI, an Austrian judge could rely on the official German translation for the provisions amended by the MLI, and the risk an Italian judge could rely on the official Italian translation. This could lead to a different application of the provisions of the MLI in different countries, which also might differ from the English and French authentic language versions. This is against the general principle set forth in Art. 33 of the Vienna Convention that a treaty authentic in two or more languages is supposed to have only one single meaning.
72. Article 33(4) Vienna Convention.
73. *See also* Lang, *supra* n. 67, at 22–23.
74. Article 33(3) Vienna Convention.
75. For more on the application of Arts 31 and 32 of the Vienna Convention, *see* Chapter 2 of this book.
76. Several scholars have taken the view that official translations can – in certain circumstances – qualify as supplementary means under Art. 32 of the Vienna Convention. *Supra* n. 49.
77. Article 33(4) Vienna Convention.

to modify a tax treaty that is concluded in French or English, or a multilingual tax treaty which states that the English or French language prevails in case of divergence? In such situations, the modifications by the MLI should remain authentic in French and English, both languages being equally authentic. The modifications made by the MLI to the tax treaty are not subject to the language regulations of the original tax treaty, but only to the language provision of the MLI. Only in this way can a consistent interpretation of the MLI by the parties to the MLI be maintained. However, it is not unlikely that someone will argue that, in such case, the authentic language in which the tax treaty was concluded or the prevailing language of the tax treaty, should prevail. A clarification in the Explanatory Statement would have helped to clarify such situations.

4.4 Mutual Agreement and Conference of the Parties

If there is an interpretation issue related to an inconsistency between the French and English language versions of the MLI, the members to the MLI can address this issue to the Conference of the Parties.[78] This can be concluded from the wording of Article 32(2) of the MLI, which states that 'Any question arising as to the interpretation or implementation of this Convention may be addressed by a Conference of the Parties convened in accordance with paragraph 3 of Article 31 (Conference of the Parties)'. In the authors' opinion, an interpretation issue related to an inconsistency between the French and English language version falls under 'any question arising as to the interpretation or implementation of this Convention'. Furthermore, the Explanatory Statement refers specifically to the authentic languages of the MLI in its commentary on Article 32(2).[79] For details on the working of the Conference of the Parties, *see* Chapter 4 of this book.

An issue related to potential inconsistency between the French and English language versions could also fall under the scope of Article 32(1) of the MLI, which provides as follows:

> Any question arising as to the interpretation or implementation of provisions of a Covered Tax Agreement as they are modified by this Convention shall be determined in accordance with the provision(s) of the Covered Tax Agreement relating to the resolution by mutual agreement of questions of interpretation or application of the Covered Tax Agreement (as those provisions may be modified by this Convention).

An interpretation issue related to an inconsistency between the French and English languages can be a 'question arising as to the interpretation or implementation of provisions of a covered tax agreement as they are modified by the MLI', and therefore parties to the MLI may attempt to resolve the issue by mutual agreement.

78. For the working of the conference of the parties, *see* Chapter 3 of this book.
79. Explanatory Statement, *supra* n. 65, at 75, para. 317. *See also* Lang, *supra* n. 67, at 22.

4.5 Must an Interpreter Consult Both the French and English Language Versions?

The Vienna Convention does not impose an obligation to consult several or all authentic language versions for the interpretation of a multilingual treaty, and the prevailing opinion in public international law is that – according to the principles set forth in Article 33 of the Vienna Convention – an interpreter may rely on one language version to interpret the treaty for the purposes of routine interpretation.[80] This entails that the French and English language versions of the MLI are equally authoritative, and the terms in each language version are presumed to have the same meaning. An interpreter should therefore, in principle, be able to rely on one of the language versions when interpreting the provisions of the MLI, unless a discrepancy or ambiguity has been discovered.[81]

4.6 Must the Same Value Be Given to the French and English Versions If There Is a Divergence?

Under Article 33(3) of the Vienna Convention, the terms of the French and English versions are presumed to have the same meaning. This is a rebuttable presumption, and as soon as the presumption is rebutted the interpretation rules set forth in Article 33(4) will come into play.[82] Most authors agree that an interpreter is not always obliged to give the same weight to each authentic language version.[83] The Vienna Convention does not preclude one from giving more value to the language in which a multilingual treaty was drafted. As Aust has stated: 'If a treaty is drafted and negotiated in only one language, it is normal to place more reliance on that text'.[84] Therefore, the question should be raised as to whether more value can be given to the French or English language version of the MLI. In the authors' opinion, this would be the case if it can be proven that the MLI (or certain of the BEPS Actions) was (were) mainly negotiated and drafted in one language, and the other language version would be a mere translation.

There are indications that English was the main working language during the drafting process of the MLI. The MLI was adopted on 24 November 2016. The final version of the MLI is based on an English working document, and the French authentic language version is based on this working document.[85] Also, the French version of the Explanatory Statement was published at a later date on the website of the OECD than the English version, which might also be an indication that English was the dominant

80. For some criticism of the lack of an obligation to compare different language versions, *see* section 3.3 (The Interpretation of Multilingual Treaties: Article 33 of the Vienna Convention) and in particular *supra* n. 45.
81. The rule that there is no obligation to consult all authentic language has been criticized. *Supra* n. 40. *See also* Lang, *The Interpretation of Tax Treaties*, *supra* n. 58, at 21.
82. *See* section 3.3 (The Interpretation of Multilingual Treaties: Article 33 of the Vienna Convention).
83. For an overview, *see* Arginelli, *supra* n. 38, at 272 et seq.
84. Aust, *supra* n. 21.
85. E. Reimer, *Meilenstein des BEPS-Programmes: Das Multilaterale Übereinkommen zur Umsetzung der DBA-relevanten Maßnahmen*, Internationales Steuerrecht (IStR) 1, at 2 (2017).

working language, and the French version of the Explanatory Statement is a translation of the English version. Furthermore, some authors have already mentioned that the OECD tax work is mainly done in English, and that the French version is usually a translation.[86] However, an argument to defend that the MLI was negotiated and drafted in English *and* French is the clear statement in the Action 15 Discussion Draft.[87] So, although there are indications that English was the main negotiating and drafting language, an interpreter must be careful with placing more emphasis on the English language version. Lang notes that 'more weight could only be put to a specific language version if there is a clear indication that this language was the predominant working language during drafting. If other versions were carefully drawn by the negotiators having reference to all the texts, they were not mere translations'.[88]

It will be interesting to see how courts will rule in cases where this argument is raised. For example what if the tax authorities of a country raise the argument that more weight should be given to the English version? If the tax authorities were involved in the preparation of BEPS project documents, it might be difficult to counter this argument. And what if the taxpayer raises such an argument? It remains to be seen how courts will deal with such issues down the road.

4.7 Would a Single Authentic Language Have Been Better?

As seen above, the choice of French and English as the authentic languages of the MLI is not without consequences. Although most of the issues related to a divergence between the French and English languages can probably be resolved by the general interpretation rules under Articles 31 and 32 of the Vienna Convention, an extra language adds a new element to the interpretation process, and it is likely that courts in future will have to rule in cases that have their source in a divergence between the English and French language versions. The question therefore arises as to whether it would not have been better to conclude the MLI in only one language. Based on section 2 above, it seems that this option was considered[89] and that it would be consistent with the arguments set forth in the 2014 Deliverable and the 2015 Final Report. If there were only one authentic language, there would be no need to translate the MLI into another authentic language and, more significantly, there would be no risk of any divergence

86. J. Sasseville, *Multilingual Issues under the OECD Model Convention and Commentaries*, in *Multilingual Texts and Interpretation of Tax Treaties and EC Tax Law*, *supra* n. 18; Lang, *The Interpretation of Tax Treaties*, *supra* n. 58.
87. *Supra* n. 6 ('The multilateral instrument is being negotiated in English and French … .').
88. Lang, *The Interpretation of Tax Treaties*, *supra* n. 58, citing J.M. Mössner, *Die Auslegung mehrsprachiger Staatsvertrage*, 15 Archiv des Völkerrechts, at 273, 290 (1971/1972); Shelton, *supra* n. 12, at 637.
89. The single language would then most likely be English. If already more than 80% of tax treaties have English as an authentic language, it is clear that English is the dominant language. This is supported by the indications that the main language during the drafting process was English. A single language also does not sound unreasonable. Most of the parties to the MLI had to give up their official language, so at least in theory it could have been requested that the French-speaking states do the same.

between the authentic texts. The goal of a consistent application of the provisions of the MLI in the different states would have been easier to achieve.

Scholars already defended that a single 'tax treaty language' could resolve interpretation issues related to divergences between different authentic texts.[90] If there were to have been only one authentic language, that would certainly also have facilitated the interpretation of the MLI. There would be no need to consult and compare the English and French versions of the different provisions of the MLI. Although a single language would facilitate the interpretation of the MLI, it would not remove all interpretation issues. First, as mentioned, also when a treaty is concluded in only one language interpretation issues related to the language could arise, as not all states 'speak the same English' (e.g., British English, American English). An English word might have a different meaning in different states and be interpreted in a different way. Furthermore, terms evolve in time and space, which increases the risk of a different meaning. Second, sometimes comparing different language versions could clarify the meaning of a certain term. If a term is unclear or ambiguous in one language version, a comparison with another language could clarify the meaning of the term or resolve the ambiguity. This possibility is obviously not available if there is only one language version, and in such view having two or more authentic languages could be seen as an advantage. The conclusion is therefore that a single authentic language would certainly not have removed all language-related interpretation issues and that having two authentic languages also has advantages.

5 CONCLUSION

The MLI will insert provisions authentic in English and French in bilateral tax treaties which might have different authentic languages. This could lead to a complex language structure. For example authentic provisions in French and English will be inserted into the tax treaty between Germany and Austria which is authentic only in German, and as a consequence, some parts of a provision might be authentic only in German and others authentic in French and English. Article 33 of the Vienna Convention contains the interpretation rules for treaties authenticated in two or more languages, and the bilateral tax treaties amended by the MLI must be interpreted in light of these rules. Under Article 33 of the Vienna Convention, the English and French language versions are equally authoritative, and the terms of the treaty are presumed to have the same meaning in each language version. An interpreter should therefore, in principle, be able to rely on one of the authentic language versions for the interpretation of the provisions of the MLI, unless a divergence or ambiguity has been discovered. If a difference in meaning between the French and English versions of the MLI has been exposed, an interpreter should compare the authentic language versions and attempt to reconcile

90. A. Fantozzi, *Conclusions*, in *Multilingual Texts and Interpretation of Tax Treaties and EC Tax Law*, *supra* n. 18, at 342 ('the use of English as "the" single language, and the decision to draft tax treaties only in that official language, together with the adoption of a common set of binding legal definitions, might contribute to removing the majority of the inconveniences related to translation'). *See also* Resch, *supra* n. 40, at 327–328.

the versions in good faith in accordance with the ordinary meaning to be given to the terms of the treaty in their context and in light of its object and purpose. Only when the general interpretation rules of Articles 31 and 32 of the Vienna Convention do not resolve the interpretation issue, must the interpreter adopt the meaning that best reconciles the texts having regard to the object and purpose of the treaty.

Official translations into other language are prepared, and this will guarantee that more taxpayers have access to the MLI. However, these official translations do not have authentic value, and interpreters and courts must rely only on the authentic French and English versions of the MLI when they interpret provisions of a bilateral treaty modified by the MLI. It remains to be seen whether courts will effectively respect this rule, and if many issues related to a divergence between the French and English versions of the MLI will arise. It is remarkable that the Explanatory Statement does not provide clear guidance on how an interpreter is to apply the authentic languages and official translations of the MLI and tax treaties when interpreting a tax treaty modified by the MLI. This would certainly have helped to clarify issues related to the authentic languages and official translations of the MLI and of tax treaties that will almost certainly arise in future.

CHAPTER 5

The Legal Relevance of the Minimum Standard in the OECD/BEPS Project

Andreas Langer

1 GENERAL REMARKS

The OECD/G20 Base Erosion and Profit Shifting (BEPS) project has articulated fifteen Actions aimed at combating BEPS. Some of these BEPS Actions also contain suggestions that should be implemented through amendments to bilateral tax treaties. All the suggestions in the BEPS Actions – including the tax treaty-related ones – were classified as minimum-standard measures, common approaches or best practices.[1] Four 'minimum standards' have been articulated, meaning that countries have agreed on the implementation of these standards. These minimum-standard measures were established to tackle issues in cases where inaction by some countries would have created negative spillovers for other countries (including adverse impacts on competitiveness).[2] To ensure the implementation of these four minimum standards, monitoring mechanisms have been developed by the Inclusive Framework on BEPS, in order to supervise the jurisdictions' compliance with their commitments and the articulated standards, as well as to ensure a level playing field.[3]

Although there is a political commitment by the G20 and OECD member countries on the implementation of these four minimum standards, all minimum-standard suggestions in the BEPS final reports must be classified as soft law from a legal

1. OECD, *Explanatory Statement: 2015 Final Reports*, OECD/G20 Base Erosion and Profit Shifting Project (2015), para. 11.
2. OECD, *Explanatory Statement: 2015 Final Reports*, *supra* n. 1, para. 11. All G20 and OECD member countries have committed to consistent implementation of these four minimum standards in the areas of preventing treaty shopping (BEPS Action 6), country-by-country reporting (BEPS Action 13), combating harmful tax practices (BEPS Action 5) and improving dispute resolution (BEPS Action 14).
3. OECD, *Explanatory Statement: 2015 Final Reports*, *supra* n. 1, para. 14.

perspective. Describing some actions as soft law indicates that the minimum-standard suggestions of the BEPS Actions are not in fact law, but their importance within international society is such that it is worth paying attention to.[4] The OECD itself states that all BEPS outputs – including the minimum-standard suggestions – 'are not legally binding but there is an expectation that they will be implemented accordingly by countries that are part of the consensus'.[5]

Nevertheless, some tax treaty-related minimum-standard suggestions will gain legal effects through the Multilateral Instrument (MLI), which has been developed to modify existing bilateral tax treaties by direct implementation of the tax treaty measures developed in the course of the OECD/G20 BEPS project.[6] The MLI will enable all parties to meet at least the treaty-related minimum standards that were agreed as part of the final BEPS package, which are provisions for the prevention of treaty abuse under BEPS Action 6 and for the improvement of dispute resolution under BEPS Action 14.[7] The implementation of these minimum standards will be enabled on the basis of four articles under the MLI. These provisions deal with the purpose of a covered tax agreement (Article 6), prevention of treaty abuse (Article 7), mutual agreement procedures (Article 16) and corresponding adjustments (Article 17).

The term 'minimum standard' is explicitly used in two of these articles (Articles 7 and 16) as a legal term there. However, there is neither a definition of the term 'minimum standard' nor a description of the content of the minimum standard in the MLI. Inspired by the explanations in the Explanatory Statement to the MLI, 'It was agreed that a number of the BEPS measures are minimum standards, meaning that countries have agreed that the standard must be implemented',[8] the term 'minimum standard' can be therefore defined as a provision that must be applied by the contracting parties for the purposes of this article. Moreover, the term 'minimum standard' is used only in the last paragraphs dealing with the preconditions for reservations and as part of references to the OECD/G20 BEPS package. In Article 7 (Prevention of Treaty Abuse), the MLI refers to the 'minimum standard for preventing treaty abuse under the OECD/G20 BEPS package'. In addition, explicit references to the 'minimum standard for improving dispute resolution under the OECD/G20 BEPS package' are included in Article 16 (Mutual Agreement Procedures).

Set forth in the MLI, the minimum standard in the MLI not only became a legal term, but also gained some legal relevance: The minimum-standard measures in the MLI are part of the MLI as a multilateral contract. Parties are basically obliged to implement at least the minimum-standard measures of the MLI, wherefore these minimum standards become legally binding. The legal effect of the MLI's minimum standard results from the legal quality of the MLI as a multilateral contract and from the obligation for joining countries to implement the minimum-standard measures of the

4. John O'Brien, *International Law*, at 98 (Cavendish Publishing Ltd 2001).
5. OECD, *BEPS – Frequently Asked Questions*, http://www.oecd.org/ctp/beps-frequentlyaskedquestions.htm.
6. OECD, *Explanatory Statement to the Multilateral Convention to Implement Tax Treaty Related Measures to Prevent Base Erosion and Profit Shifting* (2016), para. 6.
7. OECD, *Explanatory Statement to the MLI* (2016), *supra* n. 6, para. 14.
8. OECD, *Explanatory Statement to the MLI* (2016), *supra* n. 6, para. 3.

MLI. It is therefore essential to underscore that it is not the minimum-standard suggestions set forth in the *BEPS final reports* that have gained some legal effects.[9] Instead, only the minimum-standard provisions *in the MLI* – although containing nearly the same content as those set forth in the BEPS final reports – have gained legal effects due to the legal quality of the MLI and the obligation of the participating parties to implement the minimum-standard measures of the MLI. As a consequence, it is necessary to distinguish between the minimum standards in the final BEPS reports and the minimum standards in the MLI itself.

Against this background, especially the content of the minimum standard in the MLI must be determined carefully. As such, this chapter will clarify the content of the minimum standard in the MLI. Although there are some references to the 'minimum standard ... under the OECD/G20 BEPS package', the minimum-standard suggestions articulated in BEPS Actions 6 and 14 are not necessarily needed to determine the content of the minimum standard in the MLI. Instead, the classification as a minimum-standard provision in the MLI is a result of the taxonomy of the MLI and its provisions, which will be shown in this chapter. In addition, it must be verified whether the references to the 'minimum standard ... under the OECD/G20 BEPS package' in the MLI may constitute a further interpretation rule for those two articles, where they are found. This article will also contemplate whether parties aiming to meet the minimum standard of the MLI through bilateral negotiations must first refer to the minimum standard as suggested by the BEPS final reports or as stated in the MLI itself instead.

2 THE CONTENT OF THE MINIMUM STANDARD IN THE MLI

2.1 The Minimum Standard in Article 7 of the MLI

Article 7 (Prevention of Treaty Abuse) is one of the articles under the MLI containing the term 'minimum standard for preventing treaty abuse under the OECD/G20 BEPS package' in its reservation paragraphs. Article 7 aims at the implementation of special provisions in tax treaties to combat treaty abuse, thereby reflecting a tax treaty-related minimum standard of BEPS Action 6.[10] BEPS Action 6 provides three alternative rules to address situations of treaty abuse. First, a general anti-abuse rule based on the principal purposes of transactions or arrangements (hereinafter 'the principal purposes test') is suggested. Alternatively, specific anti-abuse rules or a limitation-on-benefits provision are provided to fulfil the minimum standard of BEPS Action 6. As a second alternative to meet the minimum standard of BEPS Action 6, a principal purposes test and either a simplified or detailed limitation-on-benefits provision is to be implemented

9. OECD, *Explanatory Statement to the MLI* (2016), *supra* n. 6, para. 110 ('While [the MLI] refers to "the OECD/G20 BEPS package" in order to identify the minimum standard for preventing treaty abuse, the obligation imposed on the Contracting Jurisdictions is to use their best efforts to reach bilateral agreement on a provision that is consistent with the agreed minimum standard. It is not meant to suggest that any legal obligations are imposed by the BEPS package. ... ').

10. OECD, *Preventing the Granting of Treaty Benefits in Inappropriate Circumstances – Action 6: 2015 Final Report*, OECD/G20 Base Erosion and Profit Shifting Project (2015), para. 22.

in tax treaties. Finally, as a third possibility, a detailed limitation-on-benefits provision, supplemented by a mechanism that would deal with conduit arrangements not already dealt with in tax treaties, is suggested in order to meet the minimum standard of BEPS Action 6. At first glance, it seem as if the reference to the minimum standard of BEPS Action 6 could determine the minimum standard of Article 7 of the MLI, as well. However, as there are no legal effects arising from the BEPS final reports - although there might be political commitments for implementation - the content of the minimums standard of Article 7 must be determined on the basis of the wording and taxonomy of the MLI first, as only the MLI gains legal relevance as a multilateral contract.

Article 7(1) provides for the implementation of a general anti-abuse rule based on the principal purposes of transactions or arrangements as the default option. Parties are also allowed to supplement this principal purposes test by choosing to apply a simplified limitation-on-benefits provision (Article 7(6)). However, parties may reserve the right not to apply the principal purposes test as the default option under certain stated conditions, 'thereby meeting the minimum standard for preventing treaty abuse under the OECD/G20 BEPS package' (Article 7(15)(a)). If a party intents to adopt a combination of a detailed limitation-on-benefits provision and either rules to address conduit financing structures or a principal purposes test - thereby meeting the minimum standard, it may reserve the right not to apply the principal purposes test on the basis of Article 7(1). As a party *thereby* meets the minimum standard, it is obvious to classify the intention to adopt a combination of a detailed limitation-on-benefits provision and either rules to address conduit financing structures or a principal purposes test at least as one component of the 'minimum standard for preventing treaty abuse under the OECD/G20 BEPS package' within the MLI. Two further references to the 'minimum standard for preventing treaty abuse under the OECD/G20 BEPS package' cannot provide further results for determining the content of the minimum standard in the MLI, as it is in both cases only stated, 'Contracting Jurisdictions shall endeavour to reach a mutually satisfactory solution which meets the minimum standard', without any further indications as regards the determination of the minimum standard.

However, a determination of the content of minimum standard in Article 7 only on the basis of these references would be shortsighted. In order to identify the entire scope of the minimum standard of Article 7, it is also necessary to analyse Article 7 from a systematic perspective and in light of its object and purpose. The MLI's overall structure shows that the principal purposes test as the default option must be regarded as a component of the 'minimum standard for preventing treaty abuse under the OECD/G20 BEPS package' in the MLI, too. Usually, a party is given the flexibility to opt out of the provisions of the MLI entirely, in cases where a substantive provision does not reflect the minimum standard.[11] If a provision does so, opting out of that provision is possible only in limited circumstances, such as where the concerned tax treaties

11. OECD, *Explanatory Statement to the MLI* (2016), *supra* n. 6, para. 14.

already meet that standard.[12] In fact, most of the articles in the MLI enable the parties to opt out,[13] or the parties even have to opt in explicitly.[14] However, opting out of Article 7 is possible only in limited circumstances. A party may opt out of the default option only when a principal-purposes-test provision already exists under the tax treaties or when the party meets the minimum standard pursuant to Article 7(15)(a). Therefore, a party has the choice to implement either (i) the principal purposes test clause as the default option or (ii) the minimum standard as stated in the paragraphs dealing with the reservations due to Article 7(15)(a). It is for this reason that also the implementation of a general anti-abuse rule based on the principal purposes of transactions or arrangements must be classified as a further component of the minimum standard of Article 7 in the MLI. The minimum standard of Article 7 contains, therefore, at least either the implementation of the default option due to Article 7(1) or the obligation to follow the minimum standard under the regime on reservations envisaged by Article 7(15)(a).

In addition, it is questionable as to whether the supplement to apply a simplified limitation-on-benefits provision pursuant to Article 7(6) must be considered as a third component of the minimum standard in the MLI. Then, the minimum standard of Article 7 would be basically congruent with the minimum standard as suggested in the Action 6 Final Report.[15] Although the implementation and application of a simplified limitation-on-benefits provision would also fulfil the aim of a principal-purposes-test clause – and could therefore be classified as a minimum standard of the MLI, there are better grounds not to consider this supplement as a third part of the minimum standard of Article 7 from a formal systematic perspective. It is explicitly stated the parties 'may choose' this supplement. In addition, parties are also not obliged to apply an alternative provision instead, whereas there is no legal obligation to implement a simplified limitation-on-benefits provision on the basis of the MLI.

Consequently, the content of the minimum standard of Article 7 and that of the minimum standard of BEPS Action 6 vary slightly. However, the determination of the minimum standard of Article 7 based on its wording and structure is also in line with the MLI's purpose. Even if the contents of the minimum standards deviate, the aim of the MLI to implement at least the treaty-related minimum standards that were agreed as a part of the final BEPS package is served. By providing for the mandatory implementation of a principal-purposes-test clause or the intention to adopt a detailed

12. OECD, *Explanatory Statement to the MLI* (2016), *supra* n. 6, para. 14; Florian Haase, Das sog. Multilaterale Instrument (IWB 2017 Nr. 1 vom 13.01.2017), 20 et seq.
13. Reservation clauses in Art. 3(5)(a), Art. 4(3)(a), Art. 5(8), Art. 8(3)(a), Art. 9(6)(a), Art. 10(5)(a), Art. 11(3)(a), Art. 12(4), Art. 13(6)(a) and Art. 14(3)(a). In all these cases, opting out of the whole article is possible without any further requirements of explanations.
14. Part VI. (Arbitration): Art. 18(1) ('A Party may choose to apply this Part with respect to its Covered Tax Agreements and shall notify the Depositary accordingly … .').
15. Pursuant to the BEPS package, countries should, at a minimum, implement: (i) a principal purposes test only; (ii) a principal purposes test and either a simplified or detailed limitation-on-benefits provision; or (iii) a detailed limitation-on-benefits provision, supplemented by a mechanism that would deal with conduit arrangements not already dealt with in tax treaties. OECD, *Action 6 Final Report*, *supra* n. 10, para. 22; OECD, *Explanatory Statement to the MLI* (2016), *supra* n. 6, para. 89.

limitation-on-benefits provision, the MLI meets two of the three options to fulfil the minimum standard as suggested in BEPS Action 6. Although one alternative to the principal purposes test clause, namely the simplified limitation-on-benefits provision, is not part of the MLI's minimum standard, this formal deviation is not in contradiction to the purpose of the MLI. As each of the two minimum-standard alternatives would also fulfil the minimum standard of the Action 6 Final Report separately, the minimum standard of this BEPS Action will be implemented through the MLI, as countries joining the MLI are basically legally bound to implement one of these options. Additionally, the MLI also enables parties to choose the third option and implement the third minimum-standard suggestion of BEPS Action 6. This structure also reflects one intention of the MLI, namely not to not give preference to a particular way of meeting the minimum standard, in cases where a minimum standard - of the BEPS Actions - can be satisfied in multiple alternative ways.[16]

This analysis of Article 7 of the MLI shows that a fall-back to BEPS Action 6 is not necessary in order to determine the content of its minimum standard. The content of the minimum standard of Article 7 results from the wording and the structure of the MLI. Therefore, the references to the 'minimum standard for preventing treaty abuse under the OECD/G20 BEPS package' in Article 7 are merely declarative and would not have been necessary to determine the content of the minimum standard in Article 7.

2.2 The Minimum Standard in Article 14 of the MLI

Besides the references to the 'minimum standard for preventing treaty abuse under the OECD/G20 BEPS package' in Article 7, the term 'minimum standard' is also used in Article 16, with aims at the implementation of provisions regarding mutual agreement procedures and thereby meeting one tax treaty-related minimum standard of BEPS Action 14 (Mutual Agreement Procedures).[17] Some provisions dealing with preconditions for reservations to Article 16 refer to the 'minimum standard for improving dispute resolution under the OECD/G20 BEPS'. Again, the question arises as to whether the references to the minimum standard of BEPS Action 14 could constitute the content of the minimum standard in Article 16, or whether the content can be read out of the MLI and Article 16 themselves.

Article 16(1) through (3) provides for the implementation of Article 25(1) through (3) of the OECD Model Tax Convention (hereinafter 'the OECD Model'), which already incorporates the changes made to Article 25 under the work of BEPS Action 14. However, Article 16 opens the possibility for parties to opt out of some parts of these provisions by meeting the 'minimum standard for improving dispute resolution under the OECD/G20 BEPS package'. First, a party may reserve the right for the first sentence of Article 16(1)[18] not to apply on the grounds that it intends to meet the minimum

16. OECD, *Explanatory Statement to the MLI* (2016), *supra* n. 6, para. 14.
17. OECD, *Explanatory Statement to the MLI* (2016), *supra* n. 6, para. 193.
18. Article 16(1), 1st sentence ('Where a person considers that the actions of one or both of the Contracting Jurisdictions result or will result for that person in taxation not in accordance with the provisions of the Covered Tax Agreement, that person may, irrespective of the remedies

standard for improving dispute resolution under the OECD/G20 BEPS package: Opting out by meeting the minimum standard is then possible if the contracting jurisdiction ensures that – irrespective of the remedies provided under domestic law – a taxpayer that considers taxation not to be in accordance with the tax treaty, may present the case to the competent authorities. Additionally, contracting jurisdictions must ensure the implementation of a bilateral notification or consultation process for cases in which the competent authority does not consider the taxpayer's objection to be justified. As it is stated 'meet the minimum standard for improving dispute resolution under the OECD/G20 BEPS package *by ensuring* ...', this assurance can be classified as one of the components of the minimum standard of Article 16.

In addition, a party may also reserve the right for the second sentence of Article 16(1)[19] not to apply on the grounds that the party intends to meet the minimum standard for improving dispute resolution under the OECD/G20 BEPS package by ensuring that a taxpayer may present the case within a period of at least three years from the first notification of the action resulting in taxation not in accordance with the provisions of the tax treaty. As it is explicitly stated 'meet the minimum standard ... *by ensuring* ...', this assurance also must be classified as a further part of the 'minimum standard for improving dispute resolution under the OECD/G20 BEPS package' in Article 16.

Third, there is also the possibility that a party need not apply the second sentence of Article 16(2)[20] on the grounds that any agreement reached via the mutual agreement procedure is to be implemented notwithstanding any time limits under domestic laws or on the grounds that the party accept a treaty provision 'intending to meet the minimum standard for improving dispute resolution under the OECD/G20 BEPS package' in its bilateral treaty negotiations. Such a treaty provision must provide for two elements: First, the treaty provision must clarify that there may not be any adjustments after a mutually agreed period of time. Second, the treaty provision must ensure that the contracting jurisdictions do not include profits that would have accrued to the enterprise, but then – by reason of the conditions referred to a provision in the tax treaty relating to associated enterprises – have not so accrued after a mutually agreed period of time. As it is also stated in Article 16(5)(c)(ii) that by accepting such a treaty provision, the 'minimum standard for improving dispute resolution under the OECD/G20 BEPS package' would be met, the content of this treaty provision must be classified as a third component of the 'minimum standard for improving dispute resolution under the OECD/G20 BEPS package' in Article 16 of the MLI. Thus, the minimum standard of Article 16 in the MLI contains at least these three elements.

However, in order to determine the whole content of the minimum standard of Article 16, it is necessary to analyse the design of Article 16 in more depth. Against this

provided by the domestic law of those Contracting Jurisdictions, present the case to the competent authority of either Contracting Jurisdiction.').

19. Article 16(1), 2nd sentence ('The case must be presented within three years from the first notification of the action resulting in taxation not in accordance with the provisions of the Covered Tax Agreement.').
20. Article 16(2), 2nd sentence ('Any agreement reached shall be implemented notwithstanding any time limits in the domestic law of the Contracting Jurisdictions.').

background, it is questionable as to whether also the default options in Article 16(1) through (3) must be classified as a minimum standard of Article 16 from a systematic perspective. If there is only a restricted possibility for parties to opt out of the default provisions, there are solid grounds to classify provisions as minimum standards of the MLI.[21]

Article 16 opens the possibility to opt out of the default option as set forth in Article 16(1) through (3) only in limited ways. A party may opt out of the first and second sentences of Article 16(1) and the second sentence of Article 16(2) only by meeting the minimum standard of Article 16 as set forth in the regime on reservations. In all other cases - regarding the first sentence of Article 16(2) and the first and second sentences of Article 16(3) - there are even no reservations foreseen. As a party therefore either needs to (already) fulfil the provisions under Article 16(1) through (3) or must implement a minimum standard, also the default option of Article 16(1) through (3) specifying provisions for the mutual agreement procedure must be classified as a minimum standard of the MLI from a systematic perspective. In sum, also the default provisions of Article 16(1) through (3) must be classified as minimum-standard measures in the MLI.

In addition to the references to the minimum standard under the OECD/G20 BEPS package in Article 16(3), the Explanatory Statement to the MLI also contains some explicit references to certain elements of BEPS Action 14. There it is stated that Article 16(1) through (3) 'reflect[s] the treaty obligation under element 3.1 of the Action 14 minimum standard to allow a taxpayer to present a case to the competent authority of either Contracting Jurisdiction'.[22] Element 3.1 of the BEPS Action 14 minimum standard basically requires the permission for a request for MAP assistance to be made to the competent authority of either contracting state,[23] whereby the minimum standard of Article 16 corresponds with the minimum standard as suggested in BEPS Action 14. The classification of Article 16 as a minimum-standard measure in the MLI is also in line with one of the MLI's purposes, namely to ensure the implementation of the tax treaty-related minimum-standard measures of the BEPS final reports.

In sum, the content of the minimum standard of Article 16 results from the wording and the structure of the MLI and Article 16, as well. There is no need for a fall-back to BEPS Action 14 to determine the content of the minimum standard in Article 16. The references to the 'minimum standard for improving dispute resolution under the OECD/G20 BEPS package' are not needed to determine the content of the minimum standard in Article 16, and for that reason these references are merely declarative on these matters. The content of the minimum standard of Article 16 is congruent with the corresponding aspects of the minimum standard of BEPS Action 14, and for that reason also one intention of the MLI - the implementation of the tax treaty-related minimum standards - is fulfilled.

21. OECD, *Explanatory Statement to the MLI* (2016), *supra* n. 6, para. 14: Where a substantive provision does not reflect a minimum standard, a party is basically allowed to opt out of these provisions of the MLI entirely.
22. OECD, *Explanatory Statement to the MLI* (2016), *supra* n. 6, para. 192.
23. OECD, *Making Dispute Resolution Mechanisms More Effective – Action 14: 2015 Final Report* (2015), para. 9.

2.3 The Minimum Standard in Article 6 of the MLI

In addition to the provisions of the MLI which – at least in the paragraphs dealing with the preconditions for a reservation – explicitly refer to a certain minimum standard under the OECD/BEPS package, there are two further articles in the MLI reflecting a minimum standard that are neither termed as such nor contain any references to a minimum standard of the OECD/G20 BEPS package. One of these minimum-standard provisions can be found in Article 6 (Purpose of a Covered Tax Agreement), which requires the implementation of a preamble text, thereby reflecting one minimum standard of BEPS Action 6.[24] The preamble must clarify that a treaty benefit will not be granted if obtaining that benefit was one of the principal purposes of any arrangement, which would be not in accordance with the object and purpose of the relevant provisions.[25]

Although there are no references to a minimum standard under the OECD/G20 BEPS package, Article 6(1) (the implementation of a preamble) must be classified as a minimum-standard measure in the MLI due to the MLI's taxonomy. As the MLI usually allows a party to opt out of all provisions unless they reflect minimum-standard provisions,[26] the classification of Article 6(1) as a minimum-standard measure results from the regime on reservations. Pursuant to Article 6(4), opting out of Article 6(1) is possible only if a covered tax agreement already contains such preamble language describing the intention of the contracting jurisdictions to eliminate double taxation without creating opportunities for non-taxation or reduced taxation. Consequently, a party may not opt out of the provision under Article 6(1) as long as the preamble language is not already implemented in the party's tax treaties. Therefore, Article 6(1) must also be seen as a minimum-standard provision under the MLI from a systematic perspective. Additionally, Article 6(3) enables parties to implement a supplement to the preamble text. However, besides the explicit wording of the MLI ('Parties may also choose'), there is no obligation for the implementation of an alternative provision instead of this supplement. Therefore, this provision cannot be classified as a minimum standard under the MLI.

The classification of Article 6(1) – the inclusion of a preamble text – as a minimum-standard provision in the MLI is also in line with the purpose of the MLI. Unlike Article 6, the Explanatory Statement explicitly states that Article 6 is a minimum-standard measure. The Explanatory statement refers to BEPS Action 6, when it is stated:

> The minimum standard for protection against the abuse of tax treaties under Action 6 (Preventing the Granting of Treaty Benefits in Inappropriate Circumstances) requires countries to include in their tax treaties an express statement that their common intention is to eliminate double taxation without creating

24. OECD, *Action 6 Final Report*, *supra* n. 10, para. 72.
25. In addition, there would be a supplement for the preamble text. As there is no obligation for implementation, it is not part of the minimum standard in Article 6.
26. OECD, *Explanatory Statement to the MLI* (2016), *supra* n. 6, para. 14.

opportunities for non-taxation or reduced taxation through tax evasion or avoidance, including through treaty-shopping arrangements.[27]

As Article 6(1) will implement the minimum-standard suggestions of BEPS Action 6, it is perfectly reasonable to classify Article 6(1) as a minimum-standard measure under the MLI due to its taxonomy, although there are no references to the minimum standard of the OECD/BEPS package.

Although the term 'minimum standard' is not used in Article 6, nor is there any reference to a minimum standard under the OECD/G20 BEPS package, Article 6(1) must be classified as a minimum-standard measure under the MLI. This classification of Article 6(1) as a minimum-standard provision results from the design of the provision and the MLI only.

2.4 The Minimum Standard in Article 17 of the MLI

Finally, Article 17 (Corresponding Adjustments) also reflects a tax treaty-related minimum standard of the OECD/G20 BEPS package and must be classified as a minimum-standard provision of the MLI, as well, although there are also no references to a minimum standard in Article 17. Instead, the classification as a minimum-standard measure results from the structure of Article 17 and form the regime on reservations that deviates from the general structure of the MLI. Other than the single paragraphs in Article 17, the Explanatory Statement explicitly refers to some tax treaty-related measures of BEPS Action 14: On the basis of Article 17, one minimum standard of BEPS Action 14 (Element 1.1.; access to the mutual agreement procedures) must be ensured.[28] In addition, Article 17 will also enable parties to meet Best Practice 1 (inclusion of Article 9(2) of the OECD Model) of BEPS Action 14.[29] Nevertheless, as the content of a minimum standard in the MLI may result only through the MLI and its wording and structure, the content of the minimum standard of Article 17 must be determined through a precise analysis of Article 17.

Article 17 requires the implementation of provisions dealing with corresponding adjustments based on Article 9(2) of the OECD Model, and must thereby meet one tax treaty-related best practice of BEPS Action 14 as a default option.[30] However, there are some possibilities for parties to opt out of this implementation. First, opting out is possible if - in the absence of a provision referred to in Article 17(1) or (2), the party must make the appropriate adjustment referred to in Article 17(1) or if the party's competent authorities endeavour to resolve the case under a MAP (Article 17(3)(b)). In addition, opting out is also possible if a party has already notified a reservation under Article 16(5)(c)(ii) and accepted a special treaty provision there.[31] Due to the special

27. OECD, *Explanatory Statement to the MLI* (2016), *supra* n. 6, para. 75.
28. OECD, *Action 14 Final Report*, *supra* n. 23, para. 43. The inclusion of Art. 9(2) of the OECD Model is classified as a best practice only under para. 9 of BEPS Action 14.
29. OECD, *Action 14 Final Report*, *supra* n. 23, para. 43; OECD, *Explanatory Statement to the MLI* (2016), *supra* n. 6, para. 209.
30. OECD, *Explanatory Statement to the MLI* (2016), *supra* n. 6, para. 210.
31. *See* section 2.2.

structure of Article 17, a party must either (i) implement either the default option under Article 17(1) and implement provisions dealing with corresponding adjustments or (ii) fulfil the conditions set out under the reservation provisions in Article 17(3). It is also clarified that a party may opt out – as a third possibility – of the entire article only if the tax treaties concluded earlier by this party already contain a provision that provides for corresponding adjustments based on Article 9(2) of the OECD Model (Article 17(3)(a)). As there is no possibility to opt out of the implementation of either Article 17(1) or (3) – unless there is already such a provision in the tax treaty – the entire Article 17 can be seen as a minimum-standard provision from a systematic perspective. The default options and the conditions set out for a potential reservation must be treated as equivalent as two alternatives to meet the minimum standard of Article 17. Therefore, the minimum standard of Article 17 consists of the choice between these two alternatives:[32] Countries are obliged to implement either the default option of Article 17(1) – the implementation of Article 9(2) of the OECD Model and thereby meeting Best Practice 1 of BEPS Action 14, or the alternative provisions enabling taxpayer access to MAPs in transfer pricing cases under Article 17(3), which reflects a tax treaty-related minimum standard of BEPS Action 14.

The content of the minimum standard of Article 17 goes then beyond the minimum standard as under BEPS Action 14, as Best Practice 1 must also be classified as one aspect of the minimum standard in Article 17. However, this deviation does not contradict the MLI's purpose. In any case, there is no legal obligation for parties to go beyond the minimum standard under BEPS Action 14 on the basis of the MLI as long as the second alternative is chosen: If a party fulfils the requirements under the regime on reservations, the party meets at least the minimum standard articulated in element 1.1. of BEPS Action 14. However, if a party chooses the default option and implements provision on the basis of Article 9(2) OECD Model, the party meets Best Practice 1 and even goes beyond the minimum standard under BEPS Action 14 on a purely voluntary basis.

As a result, the minimum standard of Article 17, which formally deviates from the minimum standard in BEPS Action 14, can be determined through an analysis of Article 17 itself. There is no need for the use of the term 'minimum standard' to characterize the provisions in Article 17 as a minimum-standard provision in the MLI. There is also no need for reference to a minimum standard under the OECD/G20 BEPS package in Article 17 in order to constitute a minimum standard of the MLI there.

2.5 Intermediate Results and Limitation on the Implementation of the MLI's Minimum Standard

The analyses of the minimum standard articles under the MLI show that the content of the MLI's minimum standard results from the structure of the MLI and its (minimum standard) provisions. If a provision of the MLI denies the possibility to opt out (unless

32. The minimum standard of Art. 17 would contain two alternatives, comparable to the minimum standard of BEPS Action 6, which even provides for three alternatives as a minimum standard.

there are already some corresponding provisions implemented in tax treaties), this provision must be classified as a minimum-standard provision. The use of the term 'minimum standard' and the references to a minimum standard under the final BEPS package do not determine the minimum standard's content. In addition, these references are found in only two of four articles under the MLI reflecting a minimum standard. Furthermore, it would be doubtful as to whether these references - if they were to be necessary to constitute the content of a minimum standard - would be sufficiently specified to determine a minimum standard. Instead, the references to a minimum standard under the final BEPS package are merely declarative with regard to the determination of the content of the minimum standard.

As the minimum standard of the MLI arises only from the convention itself, there are even some - at least formal - deviations from the minimum standard in the BEPS final reports. However, these deviations do not contradict the MLI's intention (the implementation of the tax treaty-related minimum-standard measures), as by meeting the minimum standard of the MLI also the minimum standard of the BEPS final reports is usually met. The analyses of the four minimum standard articles in the MLI proves that the term 'minimum standard' or the terms 'minimum standard for preventing treaty abuse under the OECD/G20 BEPS package' or 'minimum standard for improving dispute resolution under the OECD/G20 BEPS package' must be seen as independent legal terms of the MLI, although they might have nearly the same contents at first glance.

Although it is the intention of the MLI to ensure at least the implementation of the tax treaty-related minimum-standard measures of the final OECD/G20 BEPS package, there are some limitations on their mandatory implementation on the basis of the MLI. First, the implementation of the tax treaty-related minimum standards through the MLI is limited to the countries joining the MLI. Countries that do not join the MLI are not legally obliged to implement the tax treaty-related minimum standards as suggested by the BEPS Actions or provided for in the MLI,[33] as long as there are no other legal instruments providing for a mandatory implementation of these minimum standards. In addition, all parties joining the MLI may choose the tax treaties that will be changed by the MLI: The Explanatory Statement points out that:

> there may be circumstances in which a Party prefers not to include a specific agreement in the scope of application of the Convention, because, for example, the agreement has been recently renegotiated to implement the outcomes of the BEPS Project, or is currently under renegotiation with the intent of implementing those outcomes in the renegotiated agreement. This is accomplished by ensuring that the Convention will apply only to an agreement specifically listed by the Parties ... to that agreement.[34]

Therefore, there is also no legal obligation to implement the tax treaty-related minimum-standard measures on the basis of the MLI into all tax treaties that have not

33. L.E. Schoueri & R.A. Galendi Jr., *Interpretative and Policy Challenges Following the OECD Multilateral Instrument (2016) from a Brazilian Perspective*, 71 Bull. Int'l. Taxn. 6, at 342 (2017).
34. OECD, *Explanatory Statement to the MLI* (2016), *supra* n. 6, para. 14.

been listed by the parties.[35] In these cases, the MLI would not be applicable and there would be no mandatory implementation of the minimum-standard measures of the MLI. Furthermore, there are some provisions under the MLI reflecting a minimum standard that open the opportunity for bilateral negotiations outside of the MLI to meet the minimum standard of the MLI. In such cases, however, there is no guarantee for the implementation of any tax treaty-related minimum-standard measure. For example Article 7(15)(b) requires only the intention to meet the minimum standard and to 'endeavour to reach a mutually satisfactory solution, which meets the minimum standard'. As the MLI merely requires that the parties endeavour to reach consensus, there would be no legal consequences if there were a failure of negotiations. Although the MLI will certainly ensure the implementation of the tax treaty-related minimum-standard measures in many cases, even the MLI is not able to ensure a global implementation of the tax treaty-related minimum-standard measures as a legal obligation.

3 REFERENCES TO THE MINIMUM STANDARD AS INTERPRETATION AID?

3.1 Legal Relevance of the OECD/G20 BEPS Package When Interpreting the Minimum Standard of the MLI

Some provisions in Articles 7 and 16 explicitly refer to a minimum standard under the OECD/G20 BEPS package. Additionally, there are some more precise references to the minimum-standard suggestions of BEPS Actions 6 and 14 in the Explanatory Statement regarding all four minimum standard articles under the MLI. Against this background, it is questionable as to whether these references could create a further interpretation rule for – at least – the two minimum standard articles of the MLI, where these references to the minimum standard in the OECD/G20 BEPS package are used.

This issue is significant not only when interpreting these provisions under the MLI, but also when interpreting the treaty provisions that will be changed on the basis of the MLI. Therefore, finally, taxpayers are also directly affected by the interpretation of these provisions if the relevant articles are applicable to them. To answer the question as to whether the references to the 'minimum standard for preventing treaty abuse under the OECD/G20 BEPS package' and to the 'minimum standard for improving dispute resolution under the OECD/G20 BEPS package' in Articles 7 and 16 create an additional interpretation rule for these both articles, it is first necessary to analyse the relevance of the tax treaty-related minimum-standard suggestions in the final BEPS package and their explanations when interpreting the MLI provisions independent of explicit references to the minimum standard under the OECD/G20 BEPS package.

35. Schoueri & Galendi Jr., *supra* n. 33, at 342 et seq.

3.2 The BEPS Final Reports as Interpretation Aids under Article 31(2) of the Vienna Convention

In addition to the interpretation rules in the MLI itself,[36] the provisions of the MLI must be interpreted in line with the principles of interpretation under the Vienna Convention on the Las of Treaties (hereinafter Vienna Convention).[37] As the Vienna Convention codifies international customary law, these interpretation rules are also relevant for all those countries that have not joined the Vienna Convention.[38] Pursuant to Article 31(1) of the Vienna Convention, a treaty must be interpreted in good faith and in accordance with the ordinary meaning to be given to the terms of the treaty in their context and in light of its object and purpose. The term 'context' is specified in more detail in Article 31(2) of the Vienna Convention: The context comprises – in addition to the wording, including its preamble and annexes – any agreement relating to the treaty which was made between all the parties in connection with the conclusion of the treaty and any instrument which was made by one or more parties in connection with the conclusion of the treaty and accepted by the other parties as an instrument related to the treaty.

Against this background, one must verify whether the BEPS Actions including some tax treaty-related suggestions and explanations could be classified as an agreement relating to the treaty pursuant to Article 31(2)(a) of the Vienna Convention. If so, all of these BEPS Actions and the further explanations therein would have to be included when interpreting the provisions of the MLI. Nevertheless, the BEPS final reports were crafted by bodies of an international organization and government representatives there, but not by the parties joining the MLI themselves.[39] Therefore, the BEPS Actions cannot be regarded as an agreement that was made between all the parties in terms of the Vienna Convention, as there is no identity of parties. Furthermore, the BEPS final reports were already published in 2015. Thus, those BEPS final reports cannot be classified as agreements that were made in connection with the conclusion of the treaty (i.e., the MLI). Instead, the MLI was designed and concluded as a reaction to, and as a consequence of these BEPS final reports. Consequently, the BEPS final reports cannot be classified as an agreement relating to the treaty pursuant to Article 31(2)(a) of the Vienna Convention.

It is also questionable as to whether the BEPS final reports could be classified as instruments under Article 31(2)(b) of the Vienna Convention, meaning any instrument related to the treaty which was made by one or more of the parties in connexion with the conclusion of the treaty and accepted by the other parties. One could argue, for example, that the parties joining the MLI have implicitly accepted the BEPS final

36. M. Lang, *The Interpretation of the Multilateral Instrument*, Skattepolitisk Oversigt (2017), forthcoming; M. Lang, *Die Auslegung des multilateralen Instruments*, Steuer und Wirtschaft International (SWI), at 12 et seq. (2017).
37. Lang, *Die Auslegung des multilateralen Instruments*, *supra* n. 36, at 11 et seq.
38. M. Lang, *The Interpretation of Tax Treaties and Authentic Languages*, in *Essays on Tax Treaties: A Tribute to David A. Ward*, at 18 (G. Maisto et al. eds., IBFD 2013); A. Aust, *Modern Treaty Law and Practice*, at 12 et seq. (Cambridge University Press 2007).
39. M. Lang, *Die Bedeutung des Musterabkommens und des Kommentars des OECD-Steuerausschusses für die Auslegung von Doppelbesteuerungsabkommen*, in *Aktuelle Entwicklungen im Internationalen Steuerrecht*, at 17 (W. Gassner et al. eds., Linde 1994).

reports as a further instrument for the interpretation, as the MLI will implement in tax treaties the new tax treaty-related suggestions to combat BEPS based on the BEPS final reports. However, a precondition for the classification as an instrument under Article 31(2)(b) is that such an instrument have been agreed in connection with the conclusion of the treaty. As the BEPS final reports were already published before the issuance of the MLI, this cannot the case. As a consequence, the BEPS final reports may not be subsumed under Article 31(2)(a) of the Vienna Convention, such that they cannot be deemed to be an interpretation aid for the provisions of the MLI on this legal basis.

3.3 The BEPS Final Reports as Special Meaning

Although the BEPS final reports cannot be classified as interpretation tools pursuant to Article 31(2) of the Vienna Convention, there are solid grounds to consider some suggestions of the BEPS final reports as special meaning due to Article 31(4) of the Vienna Convention. Consequently, these suggestions would be also relevant when interpreting the MLI. In accordance with Article 31(4) of the Vienna Convention, a special meaning is to be given to a term if it is established that the parties so intend. This interpretation rule is especially critical as a legal basis for the interpretation of tax treaties, in particular when dealing with the relevance of the OECD Model and the Commentary thereon when interpreting tax treaties.[40] It is said that terms in tax treaties that use an identical wording as the OECD Model are meant to have the same meaning as those terms have in the OECD Model if there are no signs that the parties wanted to deviate from this meaning.[41] Therefore, the OECD Model and Commentary can be regarded as an interpretation tools for the corresponding provisions of concluded tax treaties due to Article 31 of the Vienna Convention.[42]

This approach is also transferable to the suggestions made by the BEPS final reports and the articles under the MLI: There are good reasons to use the BEPS final reports when interpreting the articles in the MLI, as the MLI will implement tax treaty-related anti-BEPS measures based on the final BEPS package, as long as if it is established that the parties so intend. Where parties do not opt out of provisions under the MLI, it can be taken for granted that they accept the meaning of these provisions as they are articulated in the MLI, as long as there are no other signs that the parties wanted some deviations to the meaning as suggested in the BEPS final reports. The MLI usually does not give the possibility to opt out of minimum-standard provisions, as these provisions will basically be implemented into bilateral tax treaties. Therefore, it

40. Lang, *The Interpretation of Tax Treaties and Authentic Languages*, *supra* n. 38, at 28; Lang, *Die Bedeutung des Musterabkommens und des Kommentars des OECD-Steuerausschusses für die Auslegung von Doppelbesteuerungsabkommen*, *supra* n. 39, at 17 et seq.

41. H. Ault, *The Role of the OECD Commentaries in the Interpretation of Tax Treaties*, in *Essays on International Taxation: To Sidney I. Roberts with Esteem and Affection from the Participating Authors and the Partners of Roberts & Holland*, at 61 et seq. (K. van Raad & H. Alpert eds., Kluwer Law Int'l. 1993); Lang, *The Interpretation of Tax Treaties and Authentic Languages*, *supra* n. 38, at 28.

42. Lang, *Die Bedeutung des Musterabkommens und des Kommentars des OECD-Steuerausschusses für die Auslegung von Doppelbesteuerungsabkommen*, *supra* n. 39, at 19.

can be argued that parties basically intend to accept the special meaning of the BEPS final reports. It is for this reason that the minimum standards set forth in the BEPS final reports may also be relevant when interpreting the minimum-standard provisions of the MLI on the basis of Article 31(4) of the Vienna Convention.

Furthermore, there are also good reasons to consider the tax treaty-related BEPS final reports as circumstances of the MLI's conclusion in terms of Article 32 of the Vienna Convention. As the MLI will implement tax treaty-related anti-BEPS measures, the BEPS final reports are the only reason for the existence of the MLI and therefore a significant part of the 'circumstances of the treaty's conclusion' pursuant to Article 32 of the Vienna Convention. However, the supplementary means of interpretation under Article 32 are relevant when interpreting tax treaties only in limited ways.[43] As the BEPS final reports may already be taken into account when interpreting the MLI, there is no need for recourse to the subsidiarily applicable Article 32 of the Vienna Convention.

As a result, the passages of the BEPS Actions 6 and 14 final reports that deal with minimum-standard measures normally may be used for interpretation of the minimum standard articles in the MLI, as long as there are no other indicators that the parties wanted to deviate from the meaning as set forth in the BEPS final reports. Thus, the references to the minimum standard under the OECD/G20 BEPS package in the MLI and the explicit references to certain passages of the BEPS Actions 6 and 14 final reports in the Explanatory Statement would not have been necessary to underscore the relevance of the BEPS final reports as an interpretation aid.[44] The references to the OECD/G20 BEPS package are therefore merely declarative in this area.

3.4 Legal Relevance of a Revised Minimum Standard in the OECD/BEPS Package When Interpreting the MLI

The references to the minimum standard of the OECD/G20 BEPS package in the MLI do not create a further interpretation rule for the minimum-standard provisions of the MLI. Instead, the BEPS final reports may be used as an interpretation aid of the (minimum standard) articles of the MLI on the basis of general interpretation principles. However, it is necessary to analyse the issue as to whether the explicit references to the 'minimum standard ... under the OECD/G20 BEPS package' in the MLI allow a dynamic approach to interpretation after a possible amendment or even

43. Lang, *Die Bedeutung des Musterabkommens und des Kommentars des OECD-Steuerausschusses für die Auslegung von Doppelbesteuerungsabkommen*, *supra* n. 39, at 16.
44. However, this does not say anything about the real importance of the text of the BEPS final reports when interpreting the MLI. The BEPS Actions may easily be displaced within the process of interpretation by the wording, the structure or the purpose of a provision within the MLI. As there may be slight deviations from the minimum standard within the BEPS Actions, these deviations must also be taken into account by involving the BEPS Actions in the interpretation of provisions within the MLI. Lang, *Die Bedeutung des Musterabkommens und des Kommentars des OECD-Steuerausschusses für die Auslegung von Doppelbesteuerungsabkommen*, *supra* n. 39, at 19 et seq.

after a possible extension of the minimum standard and its explanations in the BEPS final reports and should serve as 'dynamic references'.

Against this background, it is questionable as to whether changes in the content of the minimum standard under the OECD/G20 BEPS package could affect the interpretation of the minimum-standard provisions in the MLI. Such changes within the content of the minimum standard under the OECD/G20 BEPS package would involve a potential extension of the minimum standard of BEPS Action 6 or 14 in future.[45] Furthermore, the explanations and examples that are set forth in the BEPS final reports to determine the minimum standard there could be revised or even completely changed. The question then arises as to whether the latest content and the latest explanations of the minimum standard under the OECD/G20 BEPS package may be relevant when interpreting the minimum-standard provisions in the MLI. A follow-up question arises as to whether provisions in tax treaties that have been changed on the basis of some minimum standard articles of the MLI, should then be interpreted in accordance with new minimum standards and their explanations.

There is a similar discussion regarding a number of references in tax treaties to the Commentary on the OECD Model. One reason for the insertion of such interpretation references to the Commentary in tax treaties might be – besides a common basis for interpreting the tax treaty and the intention to achieve some legal certainty – to force the judiciary to follow the Commentary in its judgments by elevating the weight of the Commentary as a means of interpretation.[46] Therefore, one reason to insert a reference to the Commentary in a tax treaty might be an effort to ensure consistent interpretation of the treaty and to provide legislative encouragement for the courts to adopt an ambulatory interpretation of the treaty using the Commentary. Such references could therefore serve to anchor a dynamic interpretation of tax treaties.[47] However, such an intention to anchor a dynamic interpretation is subject to pointed criticism. As such references are often unclear and ambiguous, they could also support a static interpretation.[48] In addition, constitutional issues might arise that contradict a dynamic approach. As the OECD Committee on Fiscal Affairs consists of only government representatives, the tax administrations would then have it completely within their power to amend the contents of a tax treaty without any determination. As in many states, not the tax administration, but rather the legislature has the authority to agree to tax treaties, this would be in contradiction of some constitutional law requirements.[49]

It is questionable as to whether the references in the MLI to a minimum standard under the OECD/G20 BEPS package could be compared to so-called partial

45. Additionally, it is possible that suggestions within other tax treaty-related BEPS Actions could be declared as a minimum standard in the future too. However, in such cases, there would be no references to these BEPS final reports as references are to be found only in Arts 7 and 16.
46. C. West, *References to the OECD Commentaries in Tax Treaties: A Steady March from 'Soft' Law to 'Hard' Law*, 9 World Tax J. 1, at 150 (2016).
47. West, *supra* n. 46, at 152.
48. M. Lang, *Later Commentaries of the OECD Committee on Fiscal Affairs, Not to Affect the Interpretation of Previously Concluded Tax Treaties*, Intertax, at 7, 8 (1997).
49. Lang, *Later Commentaries of the OECD Committee on Fiscal Affairs*, *supra* n. 48.

interpretation rules, which restrict the interpretation to which the contracting states are bound to particular paragraphs of the Commentary on the OECD Model.[50] Against this background, one could argue that changes to the minimum standards under the OECD/G20 BEPS package or further explanations must be taken into account when interpreting the minimum standard articles of the MLI. However, the same reasons articulated for the relevance of references to the Commentary on the OECD Model, speak against a dynamic approach by the reference to the minimum standard of the OECD/G20 BEPS package. First, the references to the minimum standard under the OECD/G20 BEPS package are unclear and ambiguous, as they do not refer to certain paragraphs of the BEPS final reports. Furthermore, these references are to be found exclusively in the paragraphs dealing with reservations. In addition, not all four minimum standard articles contain references to the minimum standard. Furthermore, such dynamic references would be problematic from the perspective of national constitutional law.[51] As changes to the minimum standard's content and explanations would be decided by bodies of the OECD, they would be then allowed to amend the content of the MLI, although they are not parties to the MLI.[52]

Finally, there are some indications in the Explanatory Statement that exclude a dynamic interpretation of the minimum-standard provisions of the MLI. The Annex to the MLI contains references to all BEPS final reports that will be implemented through the MLI.[53] As the Annex refers to the 2015 final reports (published on 5 October 2015), there is little leeway for dynamic interpretation after a possible amendment of the minimum standard under the OECD/G20 BEPS package.

In sum, the references to the OECD/G20 BEPS package therefore cannot be used as a legal basis for a potential dynamic interpretation of the minimum-standard provisions in the MLI or in changed tax treaties, as they would not be accordingly specified and would be constitutionally doubtful. In addition - referring to the static references in the Annex to the Explanatory Statement, it seems that it was not even the intention of the MLI to create some dynamic references. Consequently, the references to the OECD/G20 BEPS package in the MLI also do not create a further (dynamic) interpretation rule.

4 LEGAL RELEVANCE OF THE MINIMUM STANDARD OF THE OECD/G20 BEPS PACKAGE FOR BILATERAL NEGOTIATIONS

There are alternative means of satisfying some articles under the MLI that reflect the minimum standard. To ensure that the minimum standard can be met in such circumstances, the MLI provides for bilateral negotiations. In cases where the parties adopt different approaches to meet the minimum standard that requires the inclusion of a specific type of treaty provision, those jurisdictions must endeavour to reach a

50. West, *supra* n. 46, at 141 et seq.
51. Lang, *Later Commentaries of the OECD Committee on Fiscal Affairs*, *supra* n. 48.
52. Lang, *Die Bedeutung des Musterabkommens und des Kommentars des OECD-Steuerausschusses für die Auslegung von Doppelbesteuerungsabkommen*, *supra* n. 39, at 28.
53. OECD, *Explanatory Statement to the MLI* (2016), *supra* n. 6, Annex, 84.

mutually satisfactory solution consistent with the minimum standard.[54] These obligations to engage in bilateral negotiations in order to meet the minimum standard can be found in Articles 7 and 16. The reservation paragraphs of these provisions contain explicit references to the minimum standard to improve dispute resolution under the OECD/G20 BEPS package and to prevent treaty abuse under the OECD/G20 BEPS package which should be met by a mutually satisfactory solution. Against this background, it is questionable as to whether the parties are bound to the minimum standard set forth in the BEPS final reports in their bilateral negotiations, or whether they must be guided by the minimum standard in the MLI.

Article 7 (Prevention of Treaty Abuse) enables a party to meet the minimum standard based on the party's intention to adopt a detailed limitation-on-benefits provision, supplemented by a mechanism that would deal with conduit arrangements, which also reflects a minimum-standard measure set forth in BEPS Action 6. As a detailed limitation-on-benefits provision would require substantial bilateral customization, which would be challenging in the context of the MLI, the MLI does not include such a detailed limitation-on-benefits provision itself. Parties 'that prefer to address treaty abuse by adopting a detailed limitation-on-benefits provision are permitted to opt out of the PPT and must endeavour to reach a bilateral agreement that satisfies the minimum standard'.[55] Article 7(15)(a) allows parties that intend to satisfy the minimum standard by adopting a combination of a detailed limitation-on-benefits provision and either rules to address conduit financing structures or a principal purposes test, to opt out of including in their tax treaties the principal purposes test as set forth in Article 7(1). It is then required that the contracting jurisdictions endeavour to reach a mutually satisfactory solution which is in line with this alternative in order to meet the 'minimum standard ... under the OECD/G20 BEPS package'.

In this regard, the Explanatory Statement states:

> The term 'a detailed limitation on benefits provision' in paragraph 15(a) refers to a detailed provision of the type appearing in paragraphs 1 through 6 of Article X (Entitlement to Benefits) of the OECD Model Tax Convention produced in paragraph 25 (page 21) of the Action 6 Report, which will be further developed in the course of the follow-up work on BEPS. The term 'a principal purpose test' means a provision of the type described in paragraph 1.[56]

The Explanatory Statement further states as follows:

> [this reference] was included to identify the minimum standard for preventing treaty abuse, the obligation imposed on the Contracting Jurisdictions is to use their best efforts to reach bilateral agreement on a provision that is consistent with the agreed minimum standard. It is not meant to suggest that any legal obligations are imposed by the BEPS package.[57]

54. OECD, *Explanatory Statement to the MLI* (2016), *supra* n. 6, at 14.
55. OECD, *Explanatory Statement to the MLI* (2016), *supra* n. 6, at 90.
56. OECD, *Explanatory Statement to the MLI* (2016), *supra* n. 6, at 110.
57. OECD, *Explanatory Statement to the MLI* (2016), *supra* n. 6, at 110.

However, these references to Article X (1) through (6) of the OECD Model and to the follow-up work on BEPS must be seen critically. As only the MLI will gain legal effects as a multilateral contract, it should be sufficient to reach a mutual solution that reflects the minimum standard as set forth in the MLI and Article 7(15)(a), which may slightly deviate from the suggestions in the Action 6 Final Report. Therefore, the suggestions in the Action 6 Final Report are not binding for the contracting jurisdictions in their bilateral negotiations. Nevertheless, Article X (1) through (6) of the OECD Model as articulated in the Action 6 Final Report may be taken into consideration in the process of interpreting Article 7(15)(a) if these provisions can be classified as interpretation tools pursuant to Article 31(4) of the Vienna Convention.

Additional bilateral negotiations are required pursuant to Article 7(16). The reservation clause in Article 7(16) will ensure that the minimum standard can be also met in the cases where contracting jurisdictions each adopt a different approach to meet the minimum standard. Therefore, this paragraph requires the parties to endeavour to reach a mutually satisfactory solution which would be in line with the minimum standard for preventing treaty abuse under the OECD/G20 BEPS package. The meaning of this reference is not clear. It is questionable as to whether the parties must meet the minimum standard set forth in the MLI or whether they must fulfil the minimum-standard suggestions set forth in the Action 14 Final Report. Only the minimum standard that arises in Article 7 can be meant, as the content of the minimum standard for preventing treaty abuse under the OECD/G20 BEPS package directly arises from the MLI and only the MLI gains legal effects. However, the Action 14 Final Report may be also used as one factor when interpreting Article 7. In any case, there is no obligation to actually come to a solution and to meet the minimum standard, as Article 16 requires merely to 'endeavour to reach a mutually satisfactory solution, which meets the minimum standard'.

Further bilateral negotiations may also be necessary to meet the minimum standard of Article 16. Parties may submit a reservation on the application of the second sentence of Article 16(2) and thus not require the implementation of all agreements reached via mutual agreement procedure notwithstanding any time limits in the domestic law of the contracting jurisdictions (Article 16(5)(c)). However, such a reservation is allowed only in accordance with Article 16(5)(c) on the grounds that, for the purposes of all of its covered tax agreements, either: (i) all agreements reached via mutual agreement procedure must be implemented notwithstanding any time limits in the domestic law of the contracting jurisdictions; or (ii) it intends to meet the minimum standard by accepting, in its bilateral treaty negotiations, alternative treaty provisions that limit the time during which a contracting jurisdiction may make an adjustment pursuant to provisions modelled after Article 9(1) or 7(2) of the OECD Model, in order to avoid late adjustments with respect to which mutual agreement procedure relief will not be available.[58] However, this reference to the minimum standard under the

58. OECD, *Explanatory Statement to the MLI* (2016), *supra* n. 6, at 202.

OECD/G20 BEPS package in Article 16(5)(c) has only subordinated relevance for the bilateral negotiations. The treaty provision that must be accepted in bilateral negotiations is already defined in Article 16(5)(c)(ii)(A) and (B). Therefore, the parties are first bound to this aspect of the minimum standard as it is set forth in the MLI as a multilateral treaty. As the provision that is to be negotiated is described in detail, a reference to the OECD/G20 BEPS package and to the Action 14 Final Report would not have been necessary and is merely declarative.

5 CONCLUSION

The MLI was designed to modify existing bilateral tax treaties by direct implementation of the tax treaty measures developed in the course of the OECD/G20 BEPS Project, as well as to ensure the implementation of the tax treaty-related minimum-standard measures there. This implementation will be enabled on the basis of four articles in the MLI that reflect a minimum standard, namely Article 6 (Purpose of a Covered Tax Agreement), Article 7 (Preventing Treaty Abuse), Article 16 (Mutual Agreement Procedure) and Article 17 (Corresponding Adjustments).

The minimum standard in the MLI also gains legal effects, as the minimum-standard measures in the MLI are part of the MLI as a multilateral contract. Parties are basically obliged to implement the minimum-standard measures of the MLI, as a result of which these minimum standards become legally binding. The legal effect of the MLI's minimum standard results from the legal quality of the MLI as a multilateral contract and from the obligation for joining countries to implement the minimum-standard measures. It is essential to bear in mind that not the minimum-standard suggestions set forth in the BEPS final reports or these parts of the BEPS final reports that have gained some legal effects, but instead, only the minimum-standard provisions in the MLI – containing nearly the same content as set forth in the BEPS final reports – have gained legal effects due to the legal quality of the MLI and the obligation of the participating parties to implement the minimum-standard measures on the basis of the MLI.

As there are some references to the 'minimum standard … under the OECD/G20 BEPS package', these minimum-standard suggestions set forth in the BEPS Actions 6 and 14 final reports could be used to determine the content of the minimum standard in the MLI. However, the content of the minimum standard of the MLI results directly from the wording and the structure of the provisions that reflect a minimum standard. Therefore, there is no need to have recourse to the BEPS final reports. As one consequence, the content of the minimum standard of the MLI may even vary from the treaty-related minimum standards as suggested in BEPS Actions 6 and 14 final reports.

The references to the 'minimum standard … under the OECD/G20 BEPS package' in the MLI also do not create a further interpretation rule for the minimum standard articles in the MLI, where they are used, as the BEPS final reports may already be taken into account when interpreting the MLI on the basis of Article 31(4) of the Vienna

Convention. In addition, these references are not capable of constituting some dynamic references to a future changed content of the minimum standard under the OECD/G20 BEPS package. There are also no binding effects of the minimum standards set forth in the BEPS final reports for bilateral negotiations meeting the minimum standard, as binding effects result only from the MLI - as a multilateral contract - itself.

CHAPTER 6

The Relationship Between Tax Treaties and the Multilateral Instrument: Compatibility Clauses in the Multilateral Instrument

Sriram Govind & Pasquale Pistone[*]

1 INTRODUCTION

Double taxation avoidance agreements (tax treaties) are bilateral in nature and allocate taxing rights between two states so as to avoid double taxation. However, in modern times, double non-taxation has also been a concern ever since multinationals began to use loopholes in domestic tax law and tax treaty rules to obtain unintended, skewed consequences, and to exploit cross-border tax disparities to obtain unintended tax advantages. Consequently, the OECD and G20 launched the Base Erosion and Profit Shifting (BEPS) project which, in turn, has led to unprecedented support to tackle aggressive tax planning. In October 2015, the final reports on the BEPS Actions were released, setting forth, among other things, some minimum standards as regards tax treaty rules, some optional tax treaty rules and some best practices/framework rules for domestic anti-avoidance practices.

Implementation of those treaty-based changes in over 3,000 treaties[1] through bilateral renegotiations would be very difficult and time-consuming. Therefore, the treaty-based changes have been implemented through a multilateral instrument (MLI). Action 15 of the BEPS Project envisaged the creation of a multilateral treaty, executed

* The authors would like to thank Dr Panos Merkouris and Nathalie Bravo for their valuable input. The authors would also like to thank the participants of the Round Table chaired by Prof. Pasquale Pistone at the Vienna University of Economics and Business (WU), on 24 May 2017 for their input. This study is funded by the Austrian Science Fund (FWF).

1. According to the IBFD database, there are 3,115 tax treaties in force and available in the English language as of September 2017.

by multiple countries, modifying the application of each tax treaty that involves the parties to the instrument. Accordingly, the text of the MLI was adopted on 24–25 November 2016 and since the first signing ceremony on 7 June 2017, as of 1 August 2017, seventy jurisdictions have signed the MLI and have already begun the ratification process.

Although the MLI is a multilateral treaty under public international law with its own direct effect, it is unique to the extent that it stands to modify only the application of bilateral treaties between the parties to the MLI. Even though general rules of conflict exist under public international law, the instrument has included specific 'compatibility clauses' in each provision to specify how each tax treaty provision is to be modified. This is largely unchartered territory in public international law – especially so in international taxation. Therefore, it is critical to analyse the public international law aspects of how the MLI will interact with tax treaties.

In this context, this chapter will analyse the relationship between the MLI and tax treaties and whether the proposed option of specific compatibility clauses is the optimum solution.

2 THE MLI AND TAX TREATIES

Apart from the main proposal for the MLI, BEPS Action 15 also contains a toolbox for the MLI which deals with the various public international law concerns as regards the instrument (hereinafter the 'Toolbox'). The Toolbox looks at the interaction between the MLI and tax treaties, and discusses options for how potential conflicts should be dealt with. Although it considers the use of the general interpretive rule of *lex posterior*, the Toolbox recommends the use of compatibility or conflict clauses to ensure that there is no difficulty in applying the MLI in relation to tax treaties. In this context, it is critical to analyse how the MLI can create a situation of conflict with tax treaties.

There are various types of treaty conflicts involving tax treaties, including:[2]

- conflicts between two tax treaties;[3]
- conflicts between tax treaties and other international tax treaties (such as the 1979 Multilateral Convention for the Avoidance of Double Taxation of Copyright Royalties);[4]
- conflicts between tax treaties and other treaties that contain specific tax provisions (such as bilateral investment treaties or trade treaties);

2. The first four items of this classification are adopted from *On Conflicts and Other Interactions Between Double Taxation Agreements and Non-Tax Treaties*, Ch. 3, available at: http://www.dfdl.com/wp-content/uploads/2010/09/Conflicts_and_Other_Interactions_Between_DTAs_and_Non-Tax_Treaties_Above_and_Beyond_Treaty_2004.pdf (Treaty Paper).
3. In triangular tax cases, conflicts may arise in terms of two different tax treaties being applicable, resulting in different consequences.
4. Notably, this Convention only allows negotiation of bilateral agreements based on its format and does not discuss conflicts with tax treaties. However, this convention was never in force, as the minimum signatory requirement was not met.

- conflicts between tax treaties and other treaties with no tax focus (such as human rights treaties); and
- conflicts between tax treaties and supranational law (such as European Union law).[5]

Resolution of these conflicts is generally a matter of concern, as there are no prescribed hierarchy rules among treaties, and all treaties are equally ranked according to international law[6] (except if a treaty merely codifies *jus cogens*).[7] However, treaties amending or modifying existing treaties are generally considered subordinate to the basic instrument unless the parties intend them to be autonomous.[8]

The Vienna Convention on Law of Treaties[9] (hereinafter the 'Vienna Convention') is generally referred to in situations involving two or more treaties. Articles 39 and 40 of the Vienna Convention deal with the amendment of treaties by subsequent treaties; Article 59 deals with the case of a subsequent treaty terminating an earlier treaty; and Article 30 is usually used in case of conflicts between two successive treaties.[10] As the MLI will interact and co-exist with existing treaties by modifying their application (and not by amending them), Article 30 of the Vienna Convention needs to be analysed.[11]

Article 30(1) provides that the provision deals with 'successive treaties dealing with the same subject matter'.[12] Per Article 30(2), if a treaty provides that it is subject to a previous treaty, the previous treaty governs on any issue of compatibility. Further, per Article 30(3), if parties to one treaty become parties to a second treaty, the second

5. Under *Costa v. E.N.E.L.*, European Union law has supremacy over both domestic law and other international agreements, thereby creating conflicts between measures of EU law and tax treaties that are not in line with them. IT: ECJ, 15 July 1964, Case 6/64, *Flaminio Costa v. E.N.E.L.*
6. I. Seidl-Hohenveldern, *Hierarchy of Treaties*, in *Essays on the Law of Treaties: A Collection of Essays in Honour of Bert Vierdag*, at 7–8 (Klabbers & Lefeber eds., M. Nijhoff 1998); N. Matz-Lück, *Treaties, Conflicts Between*, in *Max Planck Encyclopaedia of Public International Law* (Oxford University Press 2015).
7. A treaty in conflict with *jus cogens* is void under Art. 53 of the Vienna Convention on the Law of Treaties.
8. Seidl-Hohenveldern, *supra* n. 6, at 9; P. Reuter, *Introduction to the Law of Treaties*, at 26 (Continuum International Publishing 1989).
9. United Nations Convention on the Law of Treaties, signed at Vienna 23 May 1969, entry into force on 27 January 1980.
10. A. Sadat-Akhavi, *Methods of Resolving Conflicts Between Treaties*, at 47–59 (M. Nijhoff 2003). The Vienna Convention also contains specific modification provisions where parties to a multilateral convention wish to enter into a later *inter se* agreement – but this is not relevant for the present discussion.
11. J. Malherbe, *The Issues of Dispute Resolution and Introduction of a Multilateral Treaty*, 43 Intertax 1, at 94 (2015); N. Bravo, *The Multilateral Tax Instrument and Its Relationship with Tax Treaties*, 8 World Tax J. 3 (2016). Even if the modification is formally considered an 'amendment', nothing in Art. 39 prevents an amendment of bilateral treaties through a subsequent multilateral instrument. *See* C. Innamorato, *Expeditious Amendments to Double Tax Treaties based on the OECD Model*, 36 Intertax 3, at 121 (2008).
12. There is much discussion on how the Vienna Convention is not equipped to deal with conflicts in treaties concerning different subject matters. However, as the MLI and tax treaties deal with the same subject matter, this will not be discussed in detail. But *see generally* A. Ali Ghouri, *Is Characterization of Treaties a Solution to Treaty Conflicts?*, 11 Chinese J. Intl. L. at 247, 249–252 (2012).

treaty governs the relationship between the parties as regards any point where it is incompatible with the first. Finally, per Article 30(4), if any party to the first treaty is not a party to the second treaty, and vice versa, only the treaty that it is party to will apply.

Therefore, Article 30(2) deals only with conflict clauses where priority of the previous treaty is retained. In all other cases with identical parties for both treaties, the residual clause in Article 30(3), i.e., the *lex posterior* rule, will apply.[13] Article 30(2) and (3) each use the term 'compatibility'. This term is not defined in the Vienna Convention and scholars have maintained differing views as regards the scope of the term. The traditional definition laid down by Jenks restricts the term only to cases where parties cannot simultaneously comply with obligations under both treaties.[14] This definition was followed and defended by some other scholars, as well.[15] However, later scholars, including Vranes, Pauwelyn and Borgen have adopted a much broader definition that includes conflicts arising from conflicting permissive and prescriptive norms.[16]

If the Vienna Convention is to be applied to conflicts between the MLI and tax treaties, a broader definition may be necessary, as the MLI may, in cases of abuse, allow something that is not permissible under a tax treaty. For instance would Jenks consider it 'incompatible' that a particular permanent establishment non-discrimination provision is affected by the third jurisdiction permanent establishment situation as envisaged in Article 10 of the MLI? As there is ambiguity in this position, relying on the Vienna Convention alone may create a bit of uncertainty.

Further, prior to the Vienna Convention, there were several cases where the *lex prior* doctrine was considered more appropriate in a treaty conflict situation than the *lex posterior* doctrine.[17] In this regard, a noteworthy view is asserted by

13. C.J. Borgen, *Resolving Treaty Conflicts*, 37 Geo. Wash. Int'l. L.Rev., at 573, 577 (2005).
14. C.W. Jenks, *Conflict of Law-Making Treaties*, 30 Brit. Y.B Int'l. L., at 426 (1953).
15. For scholars who have followed this position, *see* E. Vranes, *The Definition of 'Norm Conflict' in International Law and Legal Theory*, 17 Eur. J. Int'l. L. 2, at 395, 402 (2006), *citing* W. Karl, *Conflicts Between Treaties*, in *Encyclopaedia of Public International Law*, vii, at 467, 468 (R. Bernhardt ed., North Holland 1984); W. Czapliński & G. Danilenko, *Conflicts of Norms in International Law*, 21 Neth. Y.B Int'l. L. 3, at 12–13 (1990); R. Wolfrum & N. Matz, *Conflicts in International Environmental Law*, at 4 (Springer Verlag 2003). *See also* J. Pauwelyn, *Conflict of Norms in Public International Law: How WTO Law Relates to other Rules of International Law* (Cambridge University Press 2003), (citing Klein, Wilting and Kelsen (in his earlier works) as having followed this definition). Vranes also mentions that this earlier view of Kelsen is in contradiction to his later view in H. Kelsen, *Allgemeine Theorie der Normen*, at 79 (Manz Verlag Wien 1979).
16. E. Vranes, *supra* n. 15; J. Pauwelyn, *supra* n. 15; C.J. Borgen, *supra* n. 13.
17. Central American Court of Justice, 30 September 1915, *Costa Rica v. Nicaragua*, AJIL 11 (1917), 181–229; Central American Court of Justice, 9 March 1917, *El Salvador v. Nicaragua*, AJIL 11 (1917): 674–730; Permanent Court of Intl. Justice, 5 September 1931, *Customs Regime Between Germany and Austria*, Advisory Opinion, PCIJ Series A/B 41, at 42; Permanent Court of Intl. Justice, 12 December 1934, Oscar Chinn case (*United Kingdom v. Belgium*), PCIJ Series A/B 63; Eur. Ct. Human Rights, 21 November 2001, *Al-Adsani v. The United Kingdom* [GC] - 35763/97, para. 61, Separate Opinion of Judge Eysinga, 131 and Separate Opinion of Judge Schücking, 148. All of these are referred to in *Principles of Conflict Resolution within the Interpretative Process of Article 31(3)(c)*, in P. Merkouris, *Article 31(3)(c) VCLT and the Principle of Systemic Integration: Normative Shadows in Plato's Cave* (Brill 2015). *See also* UN Int'l. Law Commission, Report of the Study Group of the Int'l. Law Commission, *Fragmentation of International Law*, U.N. GAOR,

Schulz[18] and relied on by Borgen[19] under which it is doubted whether *lex posterior* as laid out in Article 30(3) is a customary international law principle as in the case of much of the Vienna Convention.[20] If this rule is not considered customary international law, Article 30(3) would be binding only on signatories to the Vienna Convention. Some important signatories to the MLI have not ratified the Vienna Convention (e.g., India). This could create an issue if Courts in these jurisdictions prefer a politically favoured interpretation that leads to cherry-picking between the original tax treaty and the MLI provisions. Moreover, as suggested by Seidl-Hohenveldern and Reuter,[21] treaties amending or modifying existing treaties (such as the MLI) may be considered subordinate to the basic instrument unless the parties intend them to be autonomous i.e., the *lex prior* rule, which may affect uniformity in interpretation.

In the absence of the *lex posterior* rule being mandatory, an interpretation using Articles 31 and 32 based on 'object and purpose' may have to be followed.[22] Furthermore, the *lex specialis* rule may be applied in certain cases where the MLI rule is considered more specific than the tax treaty provision. However, this exercise may lead to subjective determinations by various Courts and ultimately, disharmony. Further, even if the *lex posterior* rule is relied on, since the MLI itself provides a lot of flexibility to States and the operation of some provisions are subject to the choice or exercise of options, the *lex posterior* rule may not be precise enough to meet the objects of the MLI. So, specific clauses within the MLI dealing with a conflict between the MLI and tax treaties would be the most ideal solution.[23]

3 CONFLICT AND COMPATIBILITY CLAUSES

According to the International Law Commission (ILC), a conflict clause is 'a clause in a treaty intended to regulate the relation between the provisions of the treaty and those of another treaty or of any other treaty relating to the matters with which the treaty

54th Sess., at 2 (13 April 2006), U.N. Doc. A/CN.4/L.628 (2002) (noting that both *lex prior* and *lex posterior* are used as interpretive tools for treaty conflicts based on circumstances).

18. Borgen, *supra* n. 13, at 588, *citing* A. Schulz, *The Relationship Between the Judgments Project and other International Instruments*, at 14 (Hague Conference on Private International Law, Prel. Doc. 24, 2003).
19. Borgen, *supra* n. 13, at 587, 602.
20. As mentioned in Merkouris, *supra* n. 17, at 175, the *lex posterior* doctrine has been considered a general principle, a principle of interpretation or conflict resolution, a maxim, a doctrine, a subordinate interpretive criteria, guidelines, presumptions, system rules, principles of legal logic and tools of conflict resolution by various authors and courts, thereby creating confusion as to the general nature. However, Merkouris concludes that *lex posterior* and *lex specialis* are considered accepted as 'customary international law' or as general principles.
21. *Supra* nn. 6 and 8.
22. Treaty Paper, *supra* n. 2.
23. Bravo, *supra* n. 11, arrived at the same conclusion to accommodate cases where original tax treaty provisions meeting BEPS standards are intended to be retained. Merkouris, *supra* n. 17, noted that the major weakness of a conflict clause is dealing with situations where all parties to the subsequent treaty are not the same as in the earlier treaty. As this is not a matter of concern either in the MLI, the case for conflict clauses is strengthened.

deals.'[24] Further, according to the ILC report on the fragmentation of international law,[25] there are seven types of conflict clauses:

- clauses that prohibit the conclusion of incompatible subsequent treaties (such as the North Atlantic Treaty Organization (NATO) treaty);[26]
- clauses that expressly permit subsequent 'compatible' treaties (e.g., the UN Convention on the Law of the Sea);[27]
- clauses in the subsequent treaty providing that it 'shall not affect' the earlier treaty (e.g., the Geneva Convention on High Seas);[28]
- clauses in the subsequent treaty that provide that among the parties, it overrides the earlier treaty (e.g., the extradition treaty between the EU and the United States);[29]
- clauses in the subsequent treaty that expressly abrogate the earlier treaty (e.g., the UN Convention on the Law of the Sea);
- clauses in the subsequent treaty that expressly maintain earlier compatible treaties (e.g., the UN Convention on the Law of the Sea); and
- clauses that promise that future agreements will abrogate earlier treaties (e.g., Article 307 of the Treaty of the European Union).

Borgen[30] also refers to The Treaty Maker's Handbook,[31] which lays down the following varieties of conflict clauses:[32]

- clauses where the present treaty prevails over all other treaties;
- clauses where the present treaty prevails over all earlier treaties;

24. Treaty Paper, *supra* n. 2, at 63, *citing* Reports of the Intl. Law Commission, Yearbook Intl. Law Commission, vol. II, at 214 (1966).
25. Intl. Law Commission, *supra* n. 17, at 138.
26. Article 8 reads as follows: 'Each Party declares that none of the international engagements now in force between it and any other of the Parties or any third State is in conflict with the provisions of this Treaty, *and undertakes not to enter into any international engagement in conflict with this Treaty*' (emphasis added).
27. Article 311(3) reads as follows: 'Two or more States Parties may conclude agreements modifying or suspending the operation of provisions of this Convention, applicable solely to the relations between them, provided that such agreements do not relate to a provision derogation from which is incompatible with the effective execution of the object and purpose of this Convention, and provided further that such agreements shall not affect the application of the basic principles embodied herein, and that the provisions of such agreements do not affect the enjoyment by other States Parties of their rights or the performance of their obligations under this Convention.'
28. Article 30 reads as follows: 'The provisions of this Convention shall not affect conventions or other international agreements already in force, as between States parties to them.'
29. Article 18 reads as follows: 'This Agreement shall not preclude the conclusion, after its entry into force, of bilateral Agreements between a Member State and the United States of America consistent with this Agreement.'
30. *Supra* n. 13.
31. *The Treaty Maker's Handbook*, at 210–212 (H. Blix & J.H. Emerson eds., Oceana Publications 1973).
32. Merkouris, *supra* n. 17, refers to Sadat-Akhavi, *supra* n. 10, while proposing two categories with three sub-categories each focusing on the priority element; Pauwelyn, *supra* n. 15, proposes three categories, referring to prior treaties, future treaties and intra-treaty conflicts; Czapliński and Danilenko, *supra* n. 15, refer to four categories.

- clauses where the present treaty prevails over earlier treaties for parties to the present treaty;
- clauses where the parties to the present treaty undertake an obligation not to enter into later treaties inconsistent with the present one;
- clauses where supplementary agreements are permitted only if they are compatible with the present treaty; and
- clauses where the parties to the present treaty undertake an obligation to modify existing treaties that they may have with third parties.

Common conflict clauses in the tax context include[33] Article 28 of the OECD Model Convention,[34] Article 27(2) of the OECD-Council of Europe Multilateral Convention on Mutual Administrative Assistance in Tax Matters,[35] Article 2103(2) of the North American Free Trade Agreement[36] and Article 1(2) of United Kingdom-United States tax treaty (2001).[37]

However, in the case of the MLI, the clause would seek to modify the application of existing bilateral agreements between parties and in most cases, resolve inconsistencies in favour of the MLI while both instruments remain active. A typical 'conflict' clause would generally lead to the overriding of one treaty in favour of another. In a situation such as the MLI where both treaties remain in force, the term 'compatibility clause' or 'interaction clause' as suggested in environmental law research would be more appropriate.[38]

The exact wording used in the compatibility clause is critical. Some clauses are worded in particularly vague terms and rather than help in interpreting a conflict, create more confusion.[39] In such cases, the intention of the parties has been sought through the *travaux préparatoires*, leading to more confusion.[40] To avoid this, these

33. Examples derived from Treaty Paper, *supra* n. 2.
34. Article 28 provides that nothing in the Convention shall affect the fiscal privileges of members of diplomatic missions or consular posts under customary international law or special agreements on that subject matter.
35. This provision gives priority to the EU, EEC treaties for member countries as against the convention.
36. This provision gives priority to tax treaty rules as against the North American Free Trade Agreement on conflict.
37. This provision states that the treaty does not affect benefits under any other treaty between the parties.
38. H. van Asselt, F. Sindico & M.A. Mehling, *Global Climate Change and The Fragmentation of International Law*, 30 L. & Policy 3, at 423, 431 (2008).
39. Bravo refers to the conflict clause in the Cartagena Protocol on Biosafety to the Convention on Biological Diversity as being particularly loosely worded in Bravo, *supra* n. 11. The International Law Commission also refers to Art. 22 of the 1992 Biodiversity Convention as containing a loosely worded, vague conflict clause. *See* Intl. Law Commission, *supra* n. 17, at 137. While the above examples are referred to in Merkouris, *supra* n. 17, at 188, the 2001 International Treaty on Plant Genetic Resources for Food and Agriculture and the 1989 Basel Convention on the Control of Transboundary Movements of Hazardous Wastes and their Disposal are also mentioned.
40. Merkouris, *supra* n. 17, citing Sadat-Akhavi, *supra* n. 10, at 206–207. Sadat-Akhavi mentions three cases where this was done: the 1961 Single Convention on Narcotic Drugs, the 1951 Universal Copyright Convention and the 1974 Convention of the Unification of Certain Rules relating to the Carriage by Sea of Passengers and their Luggage.

compatibility clauses must be drafted precisely and clearly without leaving room for ambiguity. There are several compatibility clauses in multilateral conventions which seek to modify bilateral conventions and which are drafted precisely with a reference to the clauses that are sought to be modified.[41]

Moreover, the MLI would require one compatibility clause per provision, as the interaction of each provision with existing tax treaties and the proposed modification would be different.[42] However, as mentioned in the Toolbox, reference to the exact provision, the application of which is being modified, in each bilateral treaty would be impossible in the MLI, as (i) several clauses dealing with the same subject matter are worded differently in tax treaties and (ii) the numbering of clauses is not uniform across the vast worldwide tax treaty network.

Therefore, while modifying the application of existing provisions, precise language relating to the subject matter of each provision should be used such that the application of the corresponding provision in each covered tax treaty is modified.

4 COMPATIBILITY CLAUSES IN THE MLI

4.1 The Format of Compatibility Clauses in the MLI

The MLI follows the format recommended above by using one compatibility clause for each provision. However, the arbitration part contains a single compatibility provision,[43] as the provisions in Part VI are to be applied cumulatively, unlike the rest of the MLI. As provided in the Explanatory Statement,[44] the following language schemes have been used for the compatibility clauses in the MLI, depending on the context:

41. The best example of a well-drafted compatibility clause in a similar situation is Art. 16(3) of the UN Convention against Transnational Organized Crime (15 November 2000) which provides that 'Each of the offences to which this article applies shall be deemed to be included as an extraditable offence in any extradition treaty existing between States Parties. States Parties undertake to include such offences as extraditable offences in every extradition treaty to be concluded between them' (thus modifying all bilateral extradition treaties between two signatories). Bravo, *supra* n. 11, refers to the following clauses in multilateral conventions that modify bilateral treaties, similar to the MLI, and are worded precisely: International Convention for the Suppression of the Financing of Terrorism, Art. 11 (9 December 1999); Convention for the Suppression of the Illicit Traffic of Dangerous Drugs, Art. 9 (26 June 1936), Convention for the Suppression of Unlawful Seizure of Aircraft, Art. 8 (16 December 1970); International Convention against the Taking of Hostages, Art. 10 (17 December 1979); International Convention against the Recruitment, Use, Financing and Training of Mercenaries, Art. 15 (4 December 1989); International Convention for the Suppression of Terrorist Bombings, Art. 9 (12 January 1998); Agreement on Extradition between the European Union and the United States of America, Art. 3 (25 June 2003); Agreement on Mutual Legal Assistance between the European Union and the United States of America, Art. 3 (25 June 2003); International Convention for the Suppression of Acts of Nuclear Terrorism, Art. 13 (14 September 2005); and International Convention for the Protection of all Persons from Enforced Disappearance, Art. 13 (20 December 2006).
42. C. Silberztein & J. Baptiste Tristram, *OECD: Multilateral Instrument to Implement BEPS*, 23 Int'l. Transfer Pricing J. 5 (2016).
43. Article 26 MLI.
44. Explanatory Statement to the MLI, para. 15, pages 5, 6.

MLI provision applies 'in place of' existing provision

Where such language is used, the corresponding tax treaty provision would be replaced by the MLI provision. Here, it is not envisaged that the MLI provision be added to tax treaties that do not contain a corresponding provision.

MLI provision 'applies to' or 'modifies' an existing provision

Where such language is used, the corresponding tax treaty provision would be modified by the MLI provision without replacing it. In this case, as well, it is not envisaged that the MLI provision be added to tax treaties that do not contain a corresponding provision.

MLI provision applies 'in the absence of' existing provision

Where such language is used, if the concerned tax treaties do not contain the corresponding provision, the MLI provision will be added to the tax treaty.

MLI provision applies 'in place of or in the absence of' existing provision

Where such language is used, the MLI provision will replace an existing corresponding tax treaty provision; if the tax treaty does not contain the provision, the MLI provision will be added to the tax treaty. This is the broadest possible scenario where the MLI provision should be applicable in all cases, except where an authorized reservation is exercised.

The compatibility clauses for the substantive provisions in the MLI are ordered into the above four categories as follows:

'In Place Of'	*'Applies to/Modifies'*	*'In the Absence Of'*
Article 5(7) providing Option *C* in the methods for elimination of double taxation provision where exemption provisions will be replaced by modified credit provisions, but only in treaties that contain exemption provisions	Article 5(3) and (4) providing Options *A* and *B* dealing with the switch from exemption to credit in case of no or low taxation at source or deduction claimed at source along with dividend exemption in the residence state	Article 16(4)(b) and (c) regarding provisions added to the mutual agreement procedure only if they are not present in existing tax treaties
Article 12(3) dealing with commissionaire arrangements that apply only to tax treaties with dependent agent permanent establishment clauses		-

'In Place Of'	*'Applies to/Modifies'*	*'In the Absence Of'*
Article 13(5)(a) dealing with activities that do not constitute permanent establishments, replacing existing lists	Article 7(5) dealing with the extension of discretionary relief to existing principal purpose test clauses	-
-	Article 13(5)(b) regarding Option *B* dealing with insertion of a provision excluding fragmentation possibilities in the list of activities that do not constitute a permanent establishment	-

'In Place of or In Absence Of'
Article 3(4) dealing with income earned by or through transparent entities
Article 4(2) dealing with the tie-breaker clause for entities other than individuals that are dual resident
Article 6(2) dealing with the addition of the anti-BEPS objectives in the preamble
Article 7(2) dealing with the principal purpose test and 7(14) dealing with the simplified limitation-on-benefits clause
Article 8(2) dealing with the minimum holding period for the reduced intercorporate dividend rate
Article 9(2) dealing with the time threshold and expansion of covered capital assets to partnership/trust interests in the case of capital gains on indirect alienation of real property
Article 9(5) option dealing with the same conditions as in Article 9(2), but also prescribing a 50% threshold
Article 10(4) dealing with third jurisdiction permanent establishment-related avoidance
Article 11(2) dealing with the savings clause
Article 14(2) dealing with splitting of contracts-based additions to the building/installation project permanent establishment provision
Article 16(4)(a)(i) and (ii) dealing with revised language for the mutual agreement procedure allowing access to competent authority of either jurisdiction, revising the three-year threshold
Article 17(2) dealing with corresponding adjustments in the case of transfer pricing
Article 26(1) dealing with the arbitration part of the MLI

However, the application of the MLI provision is also linked to the notification of the relevant provisions in tax treaties to the depositary by each contracting jurisdiction. In cases where the relevant compatibility clause uses the terminology 'in place of', 'applies to/modifies' or 'in the absence of', the MLI provision would generally not be applicable where even one country has not notified the treaty provisions covered by the

MLI provision.[45] However, subject to there being no reservation on the application of the MLI provision as a whole by either State, where the compatibility clause uses the terminology 'in place of or in the absence of', tax treaty provisions notified by both States would be replaced by the MLI provision; where they are not notified, both provisions would co-exist and the MLI provision would 'supersede' the provisions of the tax treaty only in case of incompatibility.[46]

The general scheme of how the compatibility clauses work in sync with the notification provisions is set forth in the table below:[47]

Compatibility Clause	*Notification by Both Countries*	*Notification Mismatch (Notification by One Country)*	*Notification by Neither Country*	*Reservation by One of the Countries, Where Allowed*
'in place of'	Tax treaty provision replaced by MLI provision	MLI provision does not apply	MLI provision does not apply	MLI provision does not apply
'applies to' or 'modifies'	Tax treaty provision modified by MLI provision without replacement	MLI provision does not apply	MLI provision does not apply	
'in the absence of'	MLI provision is added to tax treaty	MLI provision does not apply	MLI provision does not apply	
'in place or in the absence of'	Tax treaty provision replaced by MLI provision	MLI provision applies and supersedes provisions in tax treaty to the extent of incompatibility	MLI provision applies and supersedes provisions in tax treaty to the extent of incompatibility	

45. For example Art. 5 dealing with methods for elimination of double taxation contains several options, and notification of the choice and tax treaty provisions dealing with the option is necessary for the MLI provision to apply.
46. For example Art. 3 dealing with transparent entities would lead to the MLI provision replacing tax treaty provisions, as in the compatibility clause, only where existing tax treaty provisions dealing with such issues are notified. If the provisions are not notified, both provisions are understood to co-exist, where the MLI provision would 'supersede' the tax treaty provision in case of incompatibility. However, there are exceptions. For example, Article 9(5) is subject to a notification requiring a 'choice' to be made by the Parties, even though the compatibility clause used is 'in place of or in the absence of'. For more on the notification provisions, *see* C. Zöhrer, Chapter 9 of this book.
47. Chart adopted from OECD, *Applying the Multilateral Instrument Step-by-Step*, available at: https://www.oecd.org/tax/treaties/step-by-step-tool-on-the-application-of-the-MLI.pdf.

Therefore, it can be concluded from the above that in most cases, as long as (i) two jurisdictions have ratified the MLI and have notified an existing tax treaty between them as covered by the MLI and (ii) either of these jurisdictions has not placed a reservation on the application of the provision as a whole as provided under the MLI, provisions containing the compatibility clause 'in place of or in the absence of' are meant to apply in precedence over the provisions in the tax treaty, irrespective of notification of an existing provision dealing with the same subject. A detailed illustration depicting the functioning of compatibility clauses and the notification provisions in the MLI *in toto* is provided as an Annexe to this chapter.

The drafting of compatibility clauses in the MLI has largely been an extremely precise exercise and ticks most of the boxes in terms of adequately defining compatibility between the MLI and tax treaties. In most cases, the wording adopted by the MLI seems to achieve the intended results, as well. However, there are certain issues that also need to be considered.

4.2 Issues with Regard to Compatibility Clauses in the MLI

The following issues may arise and need to be dealt with in the text of compatibility clauses in the MLI.

4.2.1 Issues with Regard to the Minimum Standards

As indicated in section 1 of this chapter, the BEPS Project was undertaken with the aim of enhancing international tax coordination in a way that could effectively counter unintended cross-border tax advantages in the form of international tax avoidance and aggressive tax planning.[48] However, in order to achieve political agreement, certain measures were considered more important than others, and the final BEPS reports set forth measures on the basis of 'minimum standards' and 'best practices'. While the minimum standards are considered mandatory for the states that participated in the project, best practices would be merely recommendations for further action. The minimum level of action envisaged under the minimum standards was required in order for the overall project to remain coordinated in terms of approach.[49] The OECD's BEPS monitoring process would continue to assess whether states are complying with the minimum standards, which may result in political consequences for those that do

48. The concept of tax avoidance is broader than aggressive tax planning, as the latter is confined to a cross-border situation where differences between tax systems are exploited by a taxpayer to create a tax advantage, whereas any circumvention of tax rules may create tax avoidance. *See* P. Pistone, *The Meaning of Tax Avoidance and Aggressive Tax Planning in European Union Tax Law: Some Thoughts in Connection with the Reaction to Such Practices by the European Union*, in *Tax Avoidance Revisited in the EU BEPS Context* (A.P. Dourado ed.), IBFD, October 2017.
49. P. Pistone, R. Julien & F. Cannas, *Can the Derivative Benefits Provision and the Competent Authority Discretionary Relief Provision Render the OECD-Proposed Limitation on Benefits Clause Compatible with EU Fundamental Freedoms*, in *Base Erosion and Profit Shifting (BEPS)*, at 212 (M. Lang, P. Pistone, A. Rust, J. Schuch & C. Staringer eds., Linde 2016).

not comply in the future. However, the BEPS final reports continue to remain soft law and – in the absence of sanctions – would be hardly enforceable from a legal perspective.

However, as discussed, the MLI, under Action 15, has been created so as to multilaterally implement the tax treaty-related changes envisaged in the BEPS Project into various bilateral tax treaties. Through the reservation process in the MLI, legal sanction has been given to the tax treaty-related minimum standards, as states are free to place a reservation against applying such provisions only if the minimum standards are otherwise complied with. Notably, as the term 'minimum standard' has been referred to in the MLI as an obligation,[50] one could even question whether the soft law nature of the term has been transformed into hard law.[51]

Under the BEPS Action 6 final report, the minimum standard that countries need to adhere to is to include either a principal purpose test (combined with a simplified limitation-on-benefits clause or not) or a detailed limitation-on-benefits clause coupled with domestic anti-conduit rules.[52] However, Article 7(2) of the MLI – the compatibility clause for the principal purpose test – only allows replacement of an existing principal purpose test clause with the MLI principal purpose test clause or the addition of the MLI principal purpose test clause to a treaty where such test is absent.

As the minimum standard only requires two states to have either a principal purpose test alone or coupled with a limitation-on-benefits test, some pairs of states may wish to replace their existing, loosely or too narrowly worded limitation-on-benefits provisions with the broad principal purpose test clause in the MLI.[53] Although the MLI could have allowed such flexibility by expanding the compatibility clause provided in Article 7(2), allowing the MLI principal purpose test clause to replace existing treaty-level general or specific anti-avoidance rules, the present provision does not allow this.[54]

---

50. Article 7 of the MLI especially contains the term 'minimum standard' and allows reservations against applying the principal purpose test contained therein if the 'minimum standard' is otherwise met through a detailed limitation-on-benefits clause.
51. For the legal relevance of minimum standards and an analysis of this point, *see* A. Langer in Chapter 5 of this book, where it has been concluded that this is not the case
52. There is scope to argue that mandatory minimum standards that provide alternatives should be equivalent in terms of scope and effect. However, it is clear that the limitation-on-benefits and principal purpose test are not equivalent as minimum standards, and this would create bias and two blocks of countries. *See* Pistone, Julien & Cannas, *supra* n. 49, at 212.
53. This is especially so for EU countries, as limitation-on-benefits clauses are being questioned by the European Commission as restrictive of the fundamental freedoms. Separately, some countries may even wish to have uniform treaty practice by establishing identical clauses for all of its tax treaties and thus, to shift from the limitation-on-benefits approach to a principal purpose test approach.
54. Article 7(6) and 7(17) provide that the simplified limitation-on-benefits clause would be applicable only to states that have made a choice by notification for the same. However, Art. 7(17)(e) also provides that the MLI simplified limitation-on-benefits clause would be given precedence in case of inconsistencies even if not notified. Although this wording may allow modification of existing limitation on benefits provisions even where no choice is made for the same, it is clear that there is still no option provided to replace an existing limitation-on-benefits clause with a principal purpose test clause.

As the purpose of creating such a framework within the MLI was to give legal sanction to the tax treaty-related minimum standards, the provisions of the MLI should ideally be equivalent in scope to such minimum standards. In light of this, the compatibility clause attached to the principal purpose test, i.e., Article 7(2), should have allowed the replacement of all existing treaty-wide anti-avoidance provisions (which should be sufficient as long as it meets the minimum standard).

4.2.2 Issues in the Positioning of Provisions

Issues could arise in the compatibility clauses depending on how the scope of the MLI is interpreted as well. The OECD, in its legal note on the functioning of the MLI,[55] has clarified that the MLI modifies only the application of the tax treaty using the *lex posterior* principle, and does not modify the language of the tax treaty itself, as in the case of an amendment. However, as the MLI uses language such as 'in place of' and 'replaced' in the compatibility clauses, which in turn are specific provisions meant to avoid a subjective *lex posterior* approach, and the notification provisions, the legal effect of the MLI may be unclear in the hands of tax authorities or courts. It remains plausible that a court would consider that the MLI provision actually modifies the provisions of a bilateral tax treaty and not just their application. This would particularly be so if States choose to create consolidated versions where MLI provisions are inserted within the tax treaty. If this approach were to be followed, there are several issues in relation to how a particular provision would be positioned in the tax treaty.

First, Article 13(2) or (3) of the MLI, which seek to modify the list of activities in a tax treaty that will not constitute a permanent establishment, are to apply in place of 'relevant parts' of existing provisions under the compatibility clause contained in Article 13(5)(a) of the MLI.[56] However, if the latter approach as regards the scope of MLI is adopted, as Articles 13(2) and 13(3) refer directly to the existing list provided in the tax treaty and propose modifications, without providing text that would replace such provisions, applying these provisions may become difficult. This may have the legal consequence that there is no substantive text provided in the MLI that can be added in place of the 'relevant parts' of such provisions, even if this expression is defined by two states.[57]

55. OECD Directorate of Legal Affairs, Multilateral Convention to Implement Tax Treaty Related Measures to Prevent Base Erosion and Profit Shifting: Functioning under Public International Law, available at: https://www.oecd.org/tax/treaties/legal-note-on-the-functioning-of-the-MLI-under-public-international-law.pdf, paras 14–18.
56. A noteworthy question that can also be considered here concerns whether this provision would be compatible with all sorts of existing permanent establishment provisions, as permanent establishment provisions are diverse in nature and contain distinct differences (such as the 'service permanent establishment' provision, 'supervisory services' in the building site/assembly project permanent establishment provision, inclusion of warehouses as a permanent establishment as in the UN Model, etc.).
57. Two states may also define 'relevant parts' differently, leading to disagreement on the mechanics of a concept that they agree on. This may lead them to not choose the MLI option, but to bilaterally agree on text to modify their tax treaty.

For example if the existing tax treaty contains Article 5(4) as contained in the OECD Model and the states wish to modify the provision under the recommendations in BEPS Action 7, the compatibility clause contained in Article 13(5)(a) allows only a direct replacement of 'relevant parts' of the present article with Article 13(2) or 13(3).[58] However, Article 13(2)(a) and 13(3)(a), the first sub-part of both provisions, is worded to include 'the activities specifically listed in the Covered Tax Agreement (prior to modification by this Convention) as activities deemed not to constitute a permanent establishment…'. This would lead to the consequence that, if this approach is followed as regards the scope of the MLI, subsequent to modification, the text of the tax treaty may now contain a reference to the old text of the tax treaty as regards the primary list of activities that do not constitute a permanent establishment (if the latter approach as regards the scope of the MLI is adopted).

It is clear that the OECD has devised this mechanism considering the OECD vision as regards the scope of the MLI and because the provisions corresponding to Article 5(4) may be differently worded in several tax treaties, especially because the OECD and UN Models use different language for this provision. It is also evident that interpretation of the new provision using Article 31 of the Vienna Convention,[59] would lead to the implication that the text prior to modification is retained in the tax treaty, as intended by the OECD. However, as the MLI has direct legal effect, the text that may be construed by authorities to 'replace' existing text should ideally not have contained further references to previous text in the interest of clarity, and should have contained a concrete and well-defined list.

Therefore, the compatibility clause in this provision could have used the 'applies to or modifies' language so that – irrespective of how the scope of the MLI is interpreted – it could modify the existing list without replacing it entirely.

Second, similar to the above concern, several provisions in the MLI that could be seen as replacing existing tax treaty provisions contain references to 'covered tax agreements' and paragraphs within the MLI. For example Article 12(1) of the MLI dealing with revisions to the dependant agent permanent establishment provision, refers to 'covered tax agreements' and the following paragraph 2 of the MLI provision. If the language is directly imported, the term 'covered tax agreement' would not be defined in the tax treaty and paragraph 2 of the MLI provision may not correspond to paragraph 2 of the tax treaty provision, giving rise to concerns.

As in the above case, this issue may not arise except in exceptional cases and may be resolved by interpretation under Article 31, reading the MLI in the context of the tax

58. As indicated, the Explanatory Statement details that the language 'in place of' in a compatibility clause refers to a direct replacement of the previous provision with a new provision. Furthermore, although notification by states is mandatory for this provision to become applicable and there is no 'replacement' rule in the notification provision attached to this provision, the language of the compatibility clause should still take precedence.

59. Referring primarily to the ordinary meaning in good faith with regard to the context and object and purpose of the provision. Furthermore, the authors believe that the Explanatory Statement would have great interpretive relevance as an agreement or instrument executed along with the treaty, providing 'context' as defined in Art. 31(1)(b) of the Vienna Convention.

treaty provision. However, a revision of the principal provision that is to be added to a tax treaty to refer to itself and its own paragraphs, might have been better for legal certainty.

Third, by this interpretation, problems in positioning may also arise where provisions are to be added 'in the absence of' existing provisions, as no clarity has been provided as to where these provisions would be added in the tax treaty.

For example the provision on 'corresponding adjustments' in Article 17 of the MLI could be added in the absence of such provisions in a tax treaty – but states may disagree as to whether this provision should be a continuation to Article 9(1) of the tax treaty; a new paragraph; and some countries could even assert that this could be an explanation clarifying the scope of Article 9(1). Furthermore, the location of a provision in a new article, paragraph or a sub-paragraph may mean different things for interpretation. For example the addition of the 'savings clause' as a new provision in a tax treaty would mean something completely different to adding a 'savings clause' within an existing anti-avoidance provision in the tax treaty.[60]

Where such language is used, considering possible interpretation difficulties in the future where various States may interpret the scope of the MLI differently, it would have been more ideal to specify whether the newly added provision would be a new paragraph or add to an existing sub-paragraph in the tax treaty so as to prevent these issues in interpretation. However, the authors believe that this should not be a concern if there is a broad acceptance as regards the scope of the MLI, i.e., that it only stands to modify the application of a tax treaty and not to modify the language of the tax treaty itself.

4.2.3 Issues in Articles with Options

In general, where articles allow the contracting jurisdiction the discretion to choose between various provisions in relation to one subject matter, the corresponding compatibility clauses need to be tightly worded in order to ensure that it applies only in cases where the relevant option has been selected by the jurisdiction.

For example Article 5(3), (4) and (7) of the MLI are worded in such a way that they seem applicable irrespective of the choice made under Article 5(1). Although Article 5(1) allows the jurisdiction a choice between these compatibility clauses, as well, and the exercise of the options is dictated by the notification provision in Article 5(10), as the compatibility clauses are separate provisions contained in the tax treaty, from a legal standpoint, such option may not render the other options inactive

60. In such cases, one would again have to use interpretation techniques under Art. 31 of the Vienna Convention. Even though the wording of the MLI and the Explanatory Statement along with the background of each revision in the BEPS reports may provide enough context to point one towards the consequences intended by the OECD, a language revision would definitely have been preferable in the interest of legal certainty, to ensure that different states do not interpret these provisions differently.

automatically unless there is forceful wording to that extent in Article 5(1) or in each of these compatibility clauses (making them subject to the choice of the respective substantive provision).

This confusion is even more apparent in Article 7 of the MLI dealing with the methods to combat treaty abuse as laid out in the BEPS Action 6 final report. While Article 7(1)-(5) deal with the principal purpose test and provide for their compatibility - allowing their application in place of, or in absence of existing principal purpose test clauses, Article 7(6) allows for the option of a simplified limitation-on-benefits clause in addition to this. Article 7(14) is the prescribed compatibility clause for the simplified limitation-on-benefits clause that makes it applicable in place of, or in absence of other limitation-on-benefits clauses. However, without a qualifier in Article 7(6) that Article 7(14) is part of the option of the jurisdiction, there could be a legal interpretation that all existing limitation-on-benefits provisions are to be replaced by the provision in Article 7(14).

Although the notification provisions[61] read with the Explanatory Statement[62] would provide a definite solution here and resolve this uncertainty in favour of the intention of the drafters while interpreting the provision under Article 31 of the Vienna Convention, it would have definitely been easier and more in line with clarity in drafting for a specific reference to be added to Article 7(14) that it is applicable subject to choice under Article 7(6). This drafting style has already been used in Article 26, i.e., the compatibility clause for Part VI (the arbitration provisions).[63]

4.2.4 *Conflict in Conflict Clauses*

Research in the field of treaty conflicts also looks at the interaction of conflict clauses with each other. As tax treaties are customized to a large extent, it may be impossible to rule out tax treaties containing language retaining supremacy in dealing with a subject. In case of a 'conflict in conflict clauses', general rules of interpretation may need to be referred to again.[64]

In order to avoid this, it might have been better to specify that the provision of the MLI would supersede the tax treaty provision in terms of compatibility or conflict clauses in the tax treaty that exclude future agreements on a subject matter. However, it could be argued that the notification mismatch related provisions in the MLI provisions that contain the compatibility clause 'in place of or in the absence of' which provide that the MLI provision would supersede the tax treaty provisions in case of incompatibility, may be considered to provide clarity in such situations.

61. Each party that is to use the simplified limitation-on-benefits provisions is to notify the depository of such choice and disclose agreements containing similar provisions, as well.
62. The Explanatory Statement on the compatibility clause, however, provides that it is intended to apply in place of all existing limitation-on-benefits clauses.
63. The compatibility clause is subject to Art. 18, which provides for the choice to accept the arbitration option.
64. Merkouris, *supra* n. 17, at 191, refers to the conflict in conflict clauses in Art. 311 of the UN Convention on the Law of Sea and Art. 22 of the Convention on Biodiversity; *Vienna Convention on the Law of Treaties: A Commentary*, at 513 (Dörr & Schmalenbach eds., Springer 2012).

5 RELATIONSHIP WITH OTHER TREATIES AND FUTURE TREATIES

5.1 Relationship with Other Treaties

Although the relationship of the MLI with existing tax treaties has been discussed, it is also critical to discuss its relationship with other treaties between the states that are party to it.

The MLI can interact with other international agreements that are not directly linked to taxation, but can have an indirect impact on taxation as well. The most significant agreements to consider here are the treaties of the European Union; bilateral or multilateral investment treaties; and multilateral trade agreements.

5.1.1 Interaction with EU Law

European law is settled to the extent that Member States have the right to enter into tax treaties for the allocation of taxing rights, subject to the fact that the exercise of taxing rights once allocated should be subject to EU law.[65] Therefore, the Court of Justice of the European Union (CJEU) has traditionally not applied EU law to undo effects of double taxation created by a tax treaty.[66] However, certain provisions added to tax treaties by the MLI go beyond double taxation and – if applied by Member States – may be in conflict with EU law.[67] The following issues can be noted:

- limitation-on-benefits clauses may be in conflict with the fundamental freedoms;[68]

65. DE: ECJ, 21 September 1999, Case C-307/97, *Compagnie de Saint-Gobain, Zweigniederlassung Deutschland v. Finanzamt Aachen-Innenstadt*, para. 56.
66. FR: ECJ, 12 May 1998, Case C-336/96, *Gilly v. Directeur des services fiscaux du Bas-Rhin*, (1998) ECR I-02793; NL: ECJ, 5 July 2005, Case C-376/03, *D. v. Inspecteur van de Belastingdienst/ Particulieren/Ondernemingen buitenland te Heerlen*, (2005) ECR I-5821. For the interaction of tax treaties with EU law, *see also* e.g., BE: ECJ, 14 November 2006, Case C-513/04, *Mark Kerckhaert and Bernadette Morres v. Belgische Staat*, (2006) ECR I-10967; BE: ECJ, 16 July 2009, Case C-128/08, *Jacques Damseaux v. État Belge*, (2009) ECR I-06823; DE: ECJ, 17 October 1996, Joined Cases C-283/94, C-291/94 and C-292/94, *Denkavit Internationaal BV, VITIC Amsterdam BV and Voormeer BV v. Bundesamt für Finanzen*; FI: ECJ, 18 June 2009, Case C-303/07, *Aberdeen Property Fininvest Alpha Oy v. Uudenmaan verovirasto and Helsingin kaupunki*, (2009) ECR I-5145; FR: ECJ, 28 January 1986, *Commission v. France (Avoir Fiscal)*, Case 270/83, ECLI:EU:C:1986:37; UK: ECJ, 12 December 2006, Case C-374/04, *Test Claimants in Class IV of the ACT Group Litigation*, (2006) ECR I-11673; NL: ECJ, 11 August 1995, Case C-80/94, *G.H.E.J. Wielockx v. Inspecteur der Directe Belastingen*, ECR 1995 I-02493; UK: ECJ, 22 December 2010, Case C-277/09, *Commissioners for Her Majesty's Revenue & Customs v. RBS Deutschland Holdings GmbH*, (2010) ECR I-13805; SE: ECJ, 19 January 2006, Case C-265/04, *Margaretha Bouanich v. Skatteverket*, (2006) ECR I-923; NL: ECJ, 8 November 2007, Case C-379/05, *Amurta SGPS v. Inspecteur van de Belastingdienst/Amsterdam*, (2007) ECR I-9569.
67. According to C.H.J.I. Panayi, *The Compatibility of the OECD/G20 Base Erosion and Profit Shifting Proposals with EU Law*, 70 Bull. Int'l. Taxn. 1/2 (2016), broadly two-thirds of the action items in the BEPS project (many of them translated in the MLI) relate to the allocation of taxing rights and, thus, should not be subject to scrutiny under EU law as such.
68. *Open Skies* found a violation in a principally 'similar' provision in air transport agreements, while *ACT GLO* upheld a unique limitation-on-benefits clause contained in the dividend article

- the qualified person tests/discretionary relief provision in the limitation-on-benefits clause or the discretionary relief provision in the principal purpose test clause may be in conflict with EU State aid rules;[69]
- the principal purpose test may be in conflict with the fundamental freedoms;[70] and
- the dispute resolution mechanism used in the MLI may be in conflict with the mechanism in the EU dispute resolution directive.[71]

In a situation where the application of any or all of the above provisions are found to be in violation of EU law, the MLI may need to be modified with regard to tax treaties

in the UK-Netherlands tax treaty. UK: ECJ, 5 November 2002, Case C- 466/98, *Comm'n v. United Kingdom*, (2002) ECR I-09427; Case C-467/98, *Comm'n v. Denmark*, (2002) ECR I-09519; Case C-468/98, *Comm'n v. Sweden*, (2002) ECR I-09575; Case C-469/98, *Comm'n v. Finland*, (2002) ECR I-09627; Case C-471/98, *Comm'n v. Belgium*, (2002) ECR I-09681; Case C-472/98, *Comm'n v. Luxembourg*, 2002 ECR I- 09741; Case C-475/98, *Comm'n v. Austria*, 2002 ECR I-09797; Case C-476/98, *Comm'n v. Germany*, 2002 ECR I-09855.; UK: ECJ, 12 December 2006, Case C-374/04, *Test Claimants in Class IV of the ACT Group Litigation*, (2006) ECR I-11673. *See* P. Pistone, *Test Claimants in Class IV of the Act Group Litigation: Limitation on Benefits Clauses Are Clearly Different from Most-Favoured Nation Clauses*, Brit. Tax Rev. 4, at 363–365 (2008). Several other authors have criticized the ACT IV decision, as well. Panayi, *supra* n. 67; T. Lyons, *Class IV Act: Limited Benefits for All*, Brit. Tax Rev. 2 (2007), P. Plansky & H. Schneeweiss, *Limitation on Benefits: From the US Model 2006 to the ACT Group Litigation*, 35 Intertax 8/9 (2007). Although the derivative benefits and discretionary relief provisions have been suggested as additions to undo the EU law restriction involved, authors have claimed this to be an unsatisfactory solution, as well. For a detailed analysis of this question, *see* Pistone, Julien & Cannas, *supra* n. 49. The EC is presently investigating the EU law compliance of limitation-on-benefits clause in the Netherlands-Japan tax treaty as well.

69. Multiple chapters refer to this discussion in *Base Erosion and Profit Shifting (BEPS)*, *supra* n. 50 and in Brit. Tax Rev. 3, at 315–362 (2015).
70. The 'purpose'-based test may be in violation of the 'wholly artificial arrangement' requirement laid down by the ECJ in *Cadbury Schweppes*. UK: ECJ, 12 September 2006, Case C-196/04, *Cadbury Schweppes v. Commissioners of Inland Revenue*, (2006) ECR I-07995 *See* Panayi, *supra* n. 68; O. Koriak, *The Principal Purpose Test under BEPS Action 6: Is the OECD Proposal Compliant with EU Law?*, 56 Eur. Taxn. 12 (2016). The principal purpose test clause contains a discretionary relief provision. It is worth discussing whether this would align it with the *Cadbury Schweppes* rule.
71. Council Directive (EU) 2017/1852 of 10 October 2017 on tax dispute resolution mechanisms in the European Union, Official Journal of the European Union L 265/1. This conflict may arise because the EU dispute resolution directive prescribes different procedural rules for the mutual agreement procedure and subsequent arbitration. As regards the choice of procedure, this issue may be a lesser concern, as the choice is in the hands of the taxpayer and both instruments require previous procedures to be terminated prior to initiation. Furthermore, in the final Directive text, the scope of the Directive is linked to tax treaties and/or the EU Arbitration Convention preventing most cases of conflict. Finally, as regards arbitration, this issue is resolved since more effective arbitration provisions are specifically allowed by the MLI in Article 26. However, the issue may become more complicated if the proposed Common Consolidated Corporate Tax Base (CCCTB) Directive also comes into effect, which prescribes a different profit attribution technique than what is contained in a tax treaty. *See also* S.P. Govind & L. Turcan, *The Changing Contours of Dispute Resolution in the International Tax World: Comparing the OECD Multilateral Instrument and the Proposed EU Arbitration Directive*, 71 Bull. Intl. Taxn. 3/4 (2017).

involving EU Member States.[72] As these issues would apply to treaties involving third countries as well, this may turn out to be a cumbersome exercise for the EU Member States.

Another noteworthy issue regarding EU law concerns whether the EU can negotiate an amendment to the MLI as a party to ensure homogeneity in application by all of its Member States and in order to prevent conflict with EU law owing to differing application. Under Article 3(2) of the Treaty on the Functioning of the European Union (TFEU), the EU has exclusive competence for the conclusion of an international agreement when, among other things, its conclusion may affect common rules or alter their scope. Furthermore, Article 216 of the TFEU grants the EU competency to conclude international agreements with third countries where it is necessary to achieve the objectives of the treaties or likely to affect common rules or alter their scope.

Although 'direct taxation' has not been listed as either an exclusive competence or a shared competence in the treaties, as direct taxation affects the common market by way of intra-EU cross-border trade, investment, the provision of services and employment, the EU has competency in the area of direct taxation under Article 4(2) of the TFEU.[73] Direct taxation is therefore, generally, an area where competences are shared by the EU with the Member States. This may lead to a view that any international agreement on direct taxation that affects the scope of exercise of EU law is an exclusive competence of the EU. Furthermore, according to the ECJ decision in *ERTA*,[74] the EU has 'implied powers' in respect of agreements with third parties so long as they fall within the broad objectives of the EU.[75] Therefore, even if the competence to conclude agreements on direct taxation may also be considered to be shared with pre-emption (as in the case of Article 115 of the TFEU),[76] the Member States may lose their competence wherever the EU chooses to exercise its powers.[77]

The scope of the external competence of the EU has been decided by the ECJ recently in relation to the EU-Singapore free trade agreement, and it was held that trade and investment generally fall within the exclusive competence of the EU, except for non-direct investment and the investor-State dispute settlement mechanism.[78] This

72. Although international agreements in violation of EU law are not invalidated, Member States may be bound to terminate/modify them under the *Open Skies* decision. *See* C.H.J.I. Panayi, *Exploring the Open Skies: EC-Incompatible Treaties Between Member States and Third Countries*, Y.B Eur. L., at 315 (2006).
73. *See* S. Leible & M. Schröder, *Art 115 AEUV*, in *EUV/AEUV*, para. 4 (R. Streinz ed., C.H. Beck 2012).
74. ECJ, 31 Mar. 1970, Case 22/70, *Commission v. Council* (ERTA), [1971] ECR 263 (giving rise to the *ERTA* doctrine).
75. This should be read along with Art. 21 of the Treaty of the European Union which requires the Union to pursue actions that 'promote an international system based on stronger multilateral cooperation and good global governance'.
76. B.J.M. Terra & P.J. Wattel, *European Tax Law*, at 9 (Wolters Kluwer 2012); arguments of the Commission in *Commission v. Belgium*, 6 June 2013, Case C-383/10, ECLI:EU:C:2013:364, para. 10.
77. P. Pistone, *The Impact of European Law on the Relations with Third Countries in the Field of Direct Taxation*, 34 Intertax 5, at 244 (2006); T. O'Shea, *Double Tax Conventions and the European Union*, 10 EC Tax J. 3, at 77–78 (2010).
78. ECJ, 16 May 2017, Opinion 2/2015, *Re: Free Trade Agreement Between the European Union and the Republic of Singapore*, ECLI:EU:C:2017:376.

decision is of great importance to the interaction between EU law and tax treaties in general, as the general competence of the EU over matters in investment and trade could pave the way for harmonization of tax treaties across Europe at the EU level going forward.[79] If this is the case, it remains to be seen whether, if parts of the MLI as discussed above are found to be in violation of EU law, the EU itself may enter into a protocol amending the MLI as regards EU Member States.[80]

5.1.2 Interaction with International Investment Treaties

Investment treaties, which can either be bilateral investment treaties or multilateral treaties regarding investment, establish standards of protection for investors in respect of their investment in the host state, such as guarantee of fair and equitable treatment, guarantee of full protection and security, guarantee against arbitrary and discriminatory treatment, guarantee for national treatment and most-favoured nation treatment, guarantee against expropriation and guarantee concerning the free transfer of capital.[81]

Although tax measures are considered to be included in the standards governed by investment treaties,[82] several investment treaties contain tax carve-out provisions that remove taxation matters from the ambit of the treaty, ranging from exclusion of all taxation matters from all guarantees, to exclusions except in cases of expropriations or limited exclusions only as regards extension of tax treaty benefits under the most-favoured nation guarantee.[83]

79. O'Shea, *supra* n. 77. The areas of tax law presently covered by directives are the Parent-Subsidiary-Directive (Council Directive 2011/96/EU, [2011] OJ L345/8, as amended by Directive 2014/86/EU, [2014] OJ L219/40, and Directive (EU) 2015/121, [2015] OJ L21/1), the Interest-Royalties-Directive (Directive 2003/49/EC, [2003] OJ L157/49), the Merger Directive (Directive 2009/133/EC, [2009] OJ L310/34), the Directive on Mutual Assistance (Directive 2011/16/EU, [2011] L 64/1, as amended by Directive 2014/107/EU, [2014] OJ L359/1, the Savings Directive (Directive 2003/48/EC, [2003] OJ L157/38, as amended by Directive 2014/48/EU, [2014] OJ 111/50) (proposed to be repealed), the Directive on Recovery of Tax Claims (Directive 2010/24/EU, [2010] OJ L84/1) and most recently, the Anti-Tax Avoidance Directive (Directive 2016/1164/EU, [2016] OJ L193/1) and the Dispute Resolution Directive, *supra*, n. 71. Most of these directives have already influenced the impact of tax treaties within the EU, as EU law takes primacy over tax treaties and more restrictive provisions of tax treaties have been broadened owing to these directives. *See* Innamorato, *supra* n. 11, at 121.
80. Such a protocol could also include conflicts in form rather than substance with EU law. For example Art. 12 of the MLI dealing with commissionaire arrangements is dealt with in EU law under the category of abuse and, thus, could lead to different results. Therefore, an EU-level harmonized approach to this provision may be desirable.
81. *See* C. Schreuer, *Investments, International Protection*, in *Max Planck Encyclopedia of Public International Law* (OUP 2010).
82. For a detailed discussion of tax carve-out clauses in investment treaties and how to interpret them, *see* Y. Brauner & G. Kofler, *The Interaction of Tax Treaties with International Economic Laws: Global Tax Treaty Commentaries*, Global Tax Treaty Commentaries, section 3.3.2.; P. Pistone, *General Report*, in *The Relationship Between Taxation and Bilateral Investment Agreements* (M. Lang et al. eds., IBFD), forthcoming.
83. M. Davie, *Taxation-Based Investment Treaty Claims*, 6 J. Int'l. Dis. Settlement 1, at 202(2015), at 210–219.

In the absence of such carve-outs, some jurisdictions grant priority to the standards in investment treaties,[84] while others grant priority to tax treaty provisions as a more special provision in case of conflict.[85] In the latter situation, although the MLI should ordinarily prevail, as *lex specialis* or *lex superior* principles are subjective in nature, it may be difficult to arrive at a clear solution. However, in a jurisdiction where the investment treaty standards are granted priority, as the MLI is similar in nature to tax treaties, the investment treaty may take priority over the MLI, and anti-avoidance measures added to only a few specified tax treaties under the MLI may be affected by the standards in the investment treaties. This is especially so if the anti-avoidance measures are implemented without safeguards such as grandfathering of existing investments. In such a case, MLI provisions such as the principal purpose test, limitation-on-benefits or other specific anti-avoidance measures may violate standards in investment treaties, ranging from fair and equitable treatment in the case of unfair taxation in violation of legitimate expectations,[86] most-favoured nation and national treatment measures in case of discriminatory application of anti-avoidance rules towards certain jurisdictions or expropriation where the economic value of an investment is ruined by the unfair tax measures.[87]

5.1.3 Interaction with Trade Agreements

Agreements on trade law may be affected by the MLI only to the extent that the discriminatory use of anti-abuse provisions under the MLI may be considered an infraction of the most-favoured nation and national treatment requirements under the General Agreement on Tariffs and Trade (GATT) or the General Agreement on Trade in Services (GATS).[88] Furthermore, the measures introduced through the MLI could also

84. The Netherlands and Serbia take this approach. P. Pistone (*General Report*), D. Smit (*Netherlands*) & S. Kostic, M. Jovanovic & G. Ilic Popov (*Serbia*), in *The Relationship Between Taxation and Bilateral Investment Agreements*, *supra* n. 82.
85. *Supra* n. 84. *See also Australia, Canada, Germany & Russia*, in *The Relationship Between Taxation and Bilateral Investment Agreements*, *supra* n. 82 (citing the usage of the *lex specialis* or *lex superior* rule to give priority to the more specific tax treaty provision).
86. *See* the *Vodafone* dispute in India where Vodafone challenged the retrospective application of the indirect transfer tax rules by India in respect of its purchase of Hutchinson-Essar's Indian business. The decision of the arbitral tribunal in the *Vodafone* case could be key in laying down a path for investment treaty-related claims as regards unfair anti-avoidance measures.
87. T. Walde & A. Kolo, *Investor-State Disputes: The Interface Between Treaty-Based International Investment Protection and Fiscal Sovereignty*, 35 Intertax 8/9 (2007). For a detailed analysis on this topic, *see also* S.P. Govind & L. Turcan, *Cross-Border Tax Dispute Resolution in the 21st Century: A Comparative Study of Existing Bilateral and Multilateral Remedies*, Deriv. & Fin. Instruments, 5 (September/October), Volume 19.
88. The GATS specifically provides for a carve-out for tax treaty provisions. However, there is discussion as to whether this carve-out is only as regards provisions that concern 'double taxation' or not, leaving room open for scrutiny of anti-avoidance provisions. Authors have generally been conservative about extending the requirements in GATT to tax treaties, as they generally do not relate to trade in goods, and it would be difficult to identify where the export or import of goods is involved in a discriminatory tax rule. Some authors believe the carve-out in GATS should be extended to GATT, as well. Another possible view is that the negotiation of a bilaterally accepted tax treaty would result in the waiver of a claim on grounds of the GATT and/or GATS. The carve-outs in GATS for national treatment are also addressed in the OECD

be considered a 'subsidy' under the Subsidies and Countervailing Measures Agreement under the GATT (similar to the EU State aid issue mentioned above).[89] Similar measures would also be available (more along the lines of the EU State aid rules) under the EEA Agreement, the EU-Swiss Agreement and various stabilization and association agreements/interim trade agreements with non-EU European countries.[90]

However, unlike in the case of State aid within the EU and EEA, the GATT and GATS do not have direct affect and would require a state-initiated action to move towards the dispute resolution mechanism at the World Trade Organization (WTO Panel) level which would be more difficult. Moreover, to date, very few tax cases have been taken up by the WTO Panel.

5.2 Interaction with Future Treaties

Another issue that deserves discussion concerns the relationship between the MLI and future treaties. As the subsequent modification of existing tax treaties is dealt with extensively in Chapter 11 of this book, the authors will deal with the relationship with future treaties only briefly, with emphasis on conflicts between the MLI and such treaties.

Article 41 of the Vienna Convention deals with *inter se* bilateral or multilateral agreements modifying a multilateral convention. Article 41(1)(a) allows subsequent modification of a multilateral convention if the convention itself allows the same. Furthermore, Article 41(1)(b) allows subsequent modification of a multilateral convention if the convention itself does not prohibit the same and (i) the modification does not affect the rights/obligations of other parties and (ii) the modification does not relate to a provision the derogation from which would affect the object and purpose of the convention. Article 41(2) also provides that in cases falling under Article 41(1)(a), unless the treaty provides otherwise, the parties seeking to modify their obligations must notify the other parties to the convention.

Article 30 of the MLI provides that the parties to the MLI are free to modify the covered tax agreements subsequent to entry into force of the MLI.[91] Therefore, it is clear that even if the modification of covered tax agreements is considered an *inter se* agreement as under Article 41, Article 30 qualifies as a permission under Article

Model: Commentary on Art. 25. *See* S. van Thiel, *General Report*, in *WTO and Direct Taxation*, at 23, 24, 41, 42 (M. Lang, J. Herdin-Winter & I. Hofbauer-Steffel eds., Linde 2005); J.E. Farrell, section 4.6.3. Non-Discrimination (Art. 24) and National Treatment, in *The Interface of International Trade Law and Taxation: Defining the role of the WTO* (IBFD 2013).

89. However, a 'subsidy' that is actionable would, among other things, require it to be export- or import-contingent and as in the case of GATT, it would be difficult to characterize discretionary relief under an anti-abuse measure as falling under these brackets.
90. M. Blauberger & R.U. Kramer, *European Competition vs. Global Competitiveness: Transferring EU Rules on State Aid and Public Procurement beyond Europe*, 13(1) J. Industry, Competition and Trade, 171–186 at 176–177 (March 2013).
91. The Explanatory Statement in para. 310 clarifies that this provision allows revisions to bilateral tax treaties subsequent to modification by the MLI. Moreover, the OECD has clarified this further in OECD Directorate of Legal Affairs, Multilateral Convention to Implement Tax Treaty Related Measures to Prevent Base Erosion and Profit Shifting: Functioning under Public International Law, *supra* n. 55.

41(1)(a) allowing such modification. However, the authors believe that the notification requirement under Article 41(2) may be activated, as Article 30 of the MLI does not expressly waive such requirement.[92]

Although there is no provision governing the relationship of the MLI with new tax treaties entered into subsequent to the entry of force of the MLI, under Article 1 of the MLI, the MLI should apply only to existing tax treaties that are notified. Thus, new tax treaties should not be covered within the scope of the MLI as 'subsequent' treaties.

From a policy perspective, unrestricted possibility for subsequent modifications to tax treaties may work against the spirit of the MLI, as changes to clauses such as the limitation-on-benefits / principal purpose test clauses may result in treaty shopping favouring those few jurisdictions. The Toolbox had suggested possible obedience clauses in the MLI, which may have been lost in the course of the diplomatic exercise of finalizing the MLI. However, a watered down obedience clause requiring the object and purpose of the MLI to be maintained in subsequent treaties, at least as regards the clauses enshrining minimum standards, might have been desirable.[93]

Furthermore, even if the ratification of tax treaties in the future is allowed without restrictions under Article 41, the MLI continues to have legal effect as a treaty entered into by the states where the concerned tax treaty has been notified and the MLI provision is made applicable. This creates a conflict between the newly created tax treaty and the MLI in the form of a conflict between two successive norms. Here, guidance provided by Article 30 of the Vienna Convention would be relied on and generally, *lex posterior* as contained in Article 30(3) would give preference to the later bilateral tax treaty. However, as noted in section 2 of this chapter, the *lex posterior* rule is not considered conclusive as regards conflict between two co-existing treaties, and the prior treaty may be given priority in certain cases.[94] Generally, an interpretation under Article 31 of a provision of the future treaty could also result in the retention of the MLI provision, at least as regards the minimum standards, being considered as part of the context or object and purpose, resulting in an interpretation favouring the continued application of the MLI unless the MLI rule is expressly withdrawn in the future treaty.[95]

92. For a detailed analysis of the requirement of notification, *see* N. Bravo in Chapter 11 of this book.
93. This was done in Art. 311(2) of the UN Convention on the Law of the Sea, referred to in Intl. Law Commission, *supra* n. 17, at 159.
94. *See* Merkouris, *supra* n. 17, for cases where the *lex prior* principle has been used to resolve treaty conflicts. Furthermore, if the MLI is considered a 'special rule' as regards anti-avoidance, the *lex specialis* principle may be used to give priority to the MLI over the later tax treaty. As noted in *Merkouris, supra* n. 17, H. Grotius, *The Rights of War and Peace* (2005 ed.) vol. 2 (Book II) [1625], Chapter XVI, section XXIX refers to the *lex specialis* principle having priority over the *lex posterior* principle in case of conflicts, and this view has been followed by several authors such as N. Kontou, *The Termination of Treaties in Light of New Customary International Law*, at 143-144 (Clarendon Press 1994), at 143-144; H. Aufricht, *Supersession of Treaties in International Law*, 37 Cornell L.Rev., at 698 (1952). Furthermore, Art. 31 of the Vienna Convention, which provides general principles for interpretation of a treaty provision, also contains a paragraph, namely para. 4, allowing a special meaning to a term to be adopted where appropriate, allowing such 'special meaning' to be extracted from the MLI.
95. This position has also been considered by N. Bravo in Chapter 11 of this book. This position could be further bolstered by the notification provisions in the MLI in case of provisions where the compatibility clause includes the wording 'in place of or the absence of'. As discussed, in

An interesting point to consider at this juncture is whether parties may withdraw from or terminate the MLI as regards all or some of their tax treaties.[96] The MLI provides for a withdrawal process by notification under Article 37 where future obligations under the MLI would be avoided but existing notified tax treaties would remain as modified by the MLI even after withdrawal. Surprisingly, there is no formal provision providing for termination. However, the right to termination may be implied from the nature of the treaty itself,[97] allowing termination under Article 56 of the Vienna Convention. Under Article 70 of the Convention, the termination of a treaty releases parties from further obligations to apply the treaty, but does not affect legal situations created by the treaty prior to termination. This is similar to the withdrawal mechanism set out in Article 37, as well. Therefore, a termination of, or withdrawal from the MLI under this process, may allow parties to enter into future treaties without the issue of conflict with the MLI.

Another question that may give rise to issues is whether future non-tax treaties having tax implications may interact with the MLI. Although the *lex specialis* rule should allow priority to the MLI in most cases, there may be a situation where, for example, a future investment treaty that contains no tax carve-out provision may be considered to overrule the obligation created under the MLI on the basis of the *lex posterior* principle as well. As discussed in detail above, as there is no single solution to such interpretive questions, a case-by-case approach would have to be adopted, which in turn could lead to issues.

6 CONCLUSION

It is clear that as ambitious as the proposal was, the OECD has lived up to its promise by delivering an almost entirely watertight instrument through the MLI. The involvement of experts on public international law, unlike in several previous projects, has paid dividends and the provisions largely have legal consequences similar to intended

such provisions, if the tax treaty provision is not notified by either jurisdiction, the MLI provision would 'supersede' the tax treaty provision to the extent of incompatibility. In a situation where the MLI provision is expressly modified by a renegotiation of the bilateral tax treaty, this provision could still be considered a 'conflict clause' that overrides *lex posterior*, giving precedence to the MLI provision. Another noteworthy argument that could be raised in the future is also under Art. 31(3)(c) of the Vienna Convention where relevant international law rules between the parties may be used to interpret an agreement. If the 'minimum standard' concept arising from the BEPS Actions and endorsed by the MLI is to be considered a 'rule of international law' in the future, priority may be given to the minimum standards even while interpreting a future treaty. Furthermore, owing to continued state practice in a coordinated manner, if the minimum standards in the MLI evolve to be considered *jus cogens*, a future treaty in conflict with the MLI may not be allowed under international law. For a discussion on the legal relevance of the concept of minimum standards, *see* A. Langer, Chapter 5 of this book.

96. For in-depth consideration of these issues, *see* B. Hörtenhuber, Chapter 10 of this book.
97. L.R. Helfer, *Terminating Treaties*, in *The Oxford Guide to Treaties* 634, 637–639 (D. Hollis ed., Oxford University Press 2012) (referring to the International Law Commission Reports where this situation was held applicable if the treaty is clearly 'temporary' in nature).

consequences. This can be seen also in how they have approached the compatibility of the MLI with tax treaties where comprehensive compatibility clauses have been drawn up.

As the MLI follows a rather novel approach of modifying the application of existing tax treaties without nullifying or amending them, the interaction of the MLI with tax treaties will be of great significance in the future. The authors have concluded from their research in this chapter that rather than follow general rules of public international law such as *lex posterior* or *lex specialis* which lead to heterogeneous application, the approach adopted in the MLI of using express and specific compatibility clauses in each provision is the correct way forward for dealing with conflicts with tax treaties.

However, as the compatibility clauses require extreme precision in wording, there are a few issues that have been noted here that could create interpretation issues in future. Further, the authors conclude that the MLI could also interact with future tax treaties or with other treaties, such as supranational treaties having primacy, such as the treaties of the EU, or bilateral investment or trade treaties having impact on tax matters, leading to significant consequences that have been noted. The authors have also noted that such conflicts with supranational law which are impermissible may lead to a possible EU-level protocol to the MLI to adjust the provisions accordingly.

While the MLI is legally well tailored, the level of political compromise in the instrument is still disappointing. Even though the MLI has finally provided the much-awaited and much-needed multilateral approach to international taxation, it fails to achieve uniformity in international tax rules, owing to the granting of too much flexibility to the adopting states. Although this may be owing to political compromises made in order to achieve consensus, one can only implore the OECD to work with other international organizations such as the UN to understand concerns of the larger bloc of countries so as to try and give more of a say to developing countries and emerging economies through follow-up work on the BEPS Project to achieve more consensus on the MLI without its being overly flexible.

7 ANNEXE

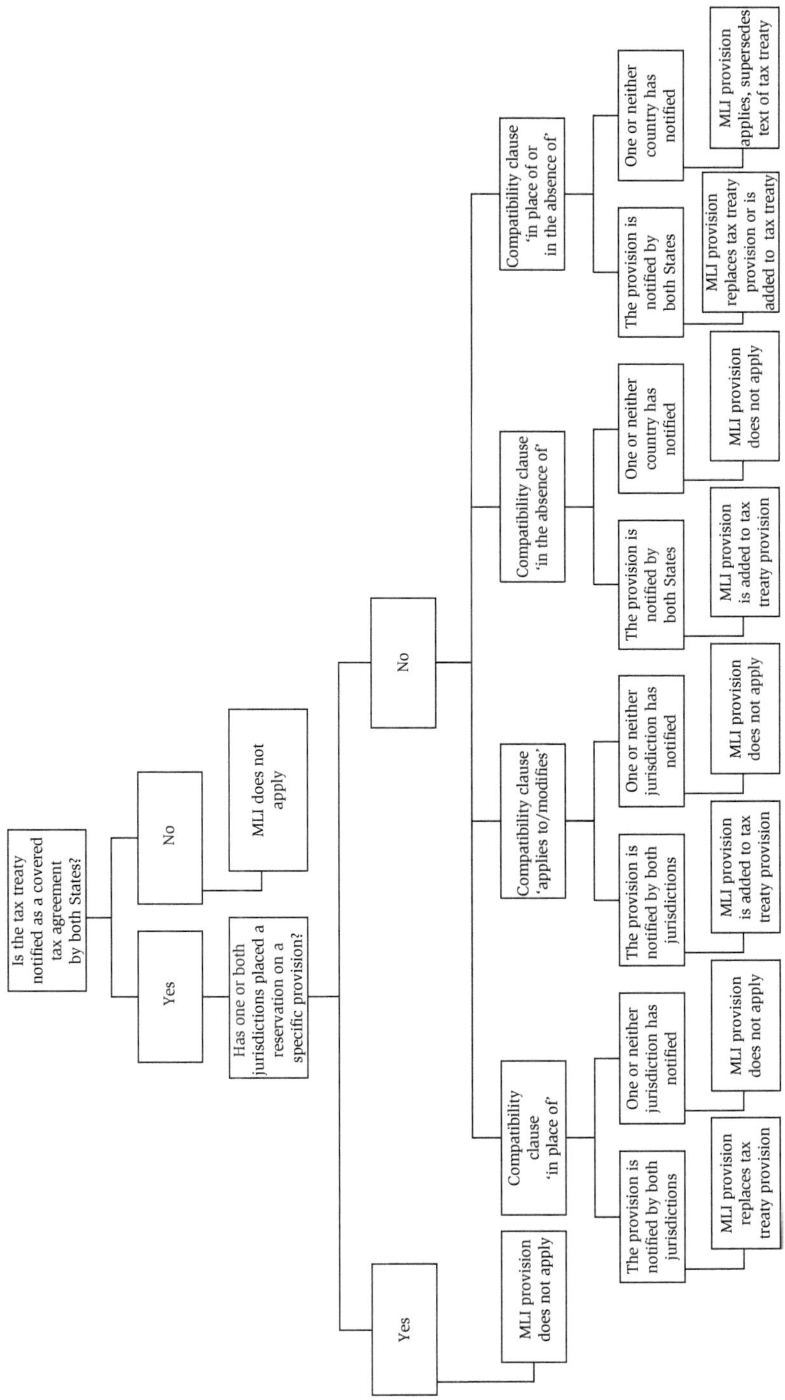
Is the tax treaty notified as a covered tax agreement by both States?
Yes
No
MLI does not apply
Has one or both jurisdictions placed a reservation on a specific provision?
Yes
No
MLI provision does not apply
Compatibility clause 'in place of'
Compatibility clause 'applies to/modifies'
Compatibility clause 'in the absence of'
Compatibility clause 'in place of or in the absence of'
The provision is notified by both jurisdictions
One or neither jurisdiction has notified
The provision is notified by both jurisdictions
One or neither jurisdiction has notified
The provision is notified by both States
One or neither country has notified
The provision is notified by both States
One or neither country has notified
MLI provision replaces tax treaty provision
MLI provision does not apply
MLI provision is added to tax treaty provision
MLI provision does not apply
MLI provision is added to tax treaty provision
MLI provision does not apply
MLI provision replaces tax treaty provision or is added to tax treaty
MLI provision applies, supersedes text of tax treaty

CHAPTER 7

Options under the Multilateral Instrument

Alexandra Miladinovic & Alexander Rust

1 INTRODUCTION

Bilateral treaties are negotiated between the contracting states in accordance with the needs and desires of each contracting state. However, in the case of a multilateral treaty, it is generally not possible to take the wishes of all parties into account. Once the text of a multilateral treaty is finalized, each country must decide whether joining the treaty is worthwhile in the long term. However, in a multilateral context, an absolute 'take it or leave it' approach would greatly diminish the chance of achieving a high number of countries as signatories of the treaty. Without the possibility for unilateral adjustment, it would be almost impossible to agree on the text of a multilateral treaty.[1] According to the leading principles of public international law, parties to a multilateral treaty are therefore not hindered: (i) to exclude or modify the legal effect of particular treaty provisions;[2] or (ii) to choose among a set of provisions[3] to bring the treaty into a form that suits the parties' requirements and individual preferences to the extent possible. The multilateral instrument (MLI) provides this kind of flexibility by incorporating options, thereby enabling the parties to shape the MLI according to their wishes.[4]

Section 2 of this chapter analyses the different types of options under the MLI and examines the options included from various perspectives. Starting with an examination of the functioning of options from a technical perspective, this section also focuses on

1. F. Hoffmeister, *Article 17*, in *Vienna Convention on the Law of Treaties: A Commentary*, para. 4 (O. Dörr & K. Schmalenbach eds., Springer-Verlag 2012).
2. Especially on reservations, *see Vienna Convention on the Law of Treaties* (hereinafter 'the Vienna Convention'], Arts 19–23 (23 May 1969).
3. Article 17 of the Vienna Convention in particular deals with the choice of differing provisions.
4. OECD, *Explanatory Statement to the Multilateral Convention to Implement Tax Treaty Related Measures to Prevent Base Erosion and Profit Shifting* (2016), para. 14.

the purpose of the implementation of options and the legal consequences that are triggered. Section 3 is devoted to the formal requirements in order to exercise these options. This section discusses notifications and reservations, which are the two forms of exercising options,[5] the timing and the reversibility of options in the MLI.

2 DIFFERENT TYPES OF OPTIONS

2.1 Types of Options According to the BEPS Action 15 Final Report

2.1.1 BEPS Action 15 Final Report

Before the MLI was drafted, the OECD had introduced, in its base erosion and profit shifting (BEPS) Action 15 Final Report, the mechanisms to provide flexibility for the MLI.[6] Even at that time, it was clear that the various parties were not prepared to agree on all BEPS proposals. Some parties were willing to implement most of the proposals, while other parties were much more hesitant. As a consequence, it was necessary to provide several alternatives to achieve the most important BEPS goals by means of only one uniform instrument.[7]

In the Action 15 Final Report, the OECD made a distinction between two types of mechanisms that grant flexibility with regard to the level of commitment.[8] On the one hand, the level of commitment can vary with respect to certain parties. It is not unusual that a party – for various reasons – is willing to accept a higher level of commitment vis-à-vis specific parties and a lower level towards other parties. Therefore, flexibility should be provided to adapt the degree of commitment depending on the partner jurisdiction in question.[9] On the other hand, there could be different degrees of commitment relating to the substance of specific provisions in general with effect towards all the parties to the multilateral treaty. The situation may arise where a party is ready to fulfil the most essential requirements only, whereas other parties want to go beyond what is necessary and implement additional commitments. This is why the parties should have the possibility to choose their own degree of substantive commitment towards the other treaty parties.[10]

However, the OECD decided not to provide the possibility for the contracting states to choose a different level of commitment towards different partner jurisdictions within the MLI because the achievement of the BEPS goals is meant to be a policy decision which could not be perfectly achieved if they were to be applied differently among specific partners within the MLI network. Nevertheless, the OECD recognized that in particular cases where special provisions are in place in the parties' tax treaties, the contracting states could prefer to keep specific provisions as agreed, and, thus,

5. OECD, *Explanatory Statement to the MLI* (2016), *supra* n. 4, para. 15.
6. OECD, *Developing a Multilateral Instrument to Modify Bilateral Tax Treaties – Action 15: 2015 Final Report*, OECD/G20 Base Erosion and Profit Shifting Project (2015), paras 41–47.
7. OECD, *Action 15 Final Report*, *supra* n. 6, para. 41.
8. OECD, *Action 15 Final Report*, *supra* n. 6, para. 42.
9. Hoffmeister, *supra* n. 1, para. 4.
10. OECD, *Action 15 Final Report*, *supra* n. 6, para. 42.

exceptions were included that allow parties to reserve the right not to apply an MLI provision with regard to a certain subset of tax treaties in special circumstances.[11] It must be emphasized that by this means, the MLI does not allow a choice of a different application towards particular treaty partners, but only permits an exceptional application for certain provisions contained in the parties' tax treaties. If the parties still want to undertake a different level of commitment vis-à-vis respective parties, there always remains the possibility to amend the relevant tax treaty with the parties concerned after entering into the MLI. This solution is also in line with Article 30 of the MLI which allows for a subsequent modification of bilateral tax treaties by the various parties.

Regarding the flexibility in substantive commitment, by contrast, the OECD developed modalities to effectively introduce flexible elements into the MLI, which can be exercised solely towards all treaty parties to the MLI.[12] After taking into consideration other already existing international treaties concluded multilaterally in non-tax related fields and the techniques used therein,[13] the OECD proposed three tools to fulfil this task.[14] According to the OECD proposal, a high level of flexibility can be achieved if a core set of provisions is accompanied by the possibility to *opt out* of measures that are considered to be too expansive, to voluntarily *opt in* for additional commitments and to *choose among alternative solutions* of equal value to select the most appropriate one. These devices, so-called opt-out clauses, opt-in clauses and alternative provisions are discussed below.

2.1.2 Opt-Out Clauses

Through opt-out mechanisms, parties are explicitly permitted either to expressly exclude the application of a specific provision as a whole or to express the intention to opt out of certain parts of a provision, both to a clearly defined extent.[15] Thus, to avoid too many discrepancies, the treaty may contain explicit opt-out clauses stating the possibility for the parties to declare non-acceptance within a particular framework.[16]

If a treaty party prefers to make use of the possibility to opt out of treaty provisions, an official act is required to inform the other parties of the deviation.[17] Although the exclusion of provisions may be decided unilaterally, the decision also has effect towards the other parties when applying the MLI.[18] One common method to officially declare the non-application of certain clauses is the formulation of reservations. Thereby, the party reserving the right makes a unilateral statement at a particular

11. OECD, *Explanatory Statement to the MLI* (2016), *supra* n. 4, para. 14.
12. OECD, *Action 15 Final Report, supra* n. 6, para. 43.
13. For example, International Labour Convention No. 63 (1938) or the Statute of the International Criminal Court (1998).
14. OECD, *Action 15 Final Report, supra* n. 6, para. 43.
15. International Law Commission (ILC), Report of the ILC, 63. Session, Supplement No. 10, Commentary to Guideline 1.1.6., para. 1 (2011).
16. OECD, *Action 15 Final Report, supra* n. 6, para. 44.
17. *See also* Art. 23 of the Vienna Convention, which provides that a reservation must be formulated in writing and communicated to the contracting states.
18. *See also* Art. 21 Vienna Convention (on the legal effects of reservations).

point in time.[19] For example, Article 19 of the Vienna Convention on the Law of Treaties (hereinafter 'the Vienna Convention') stipulates that a reservation must be made when signing, ratifying, accepting, approving or acceding to a treaty. In accordance with international law, the formulation of reservations is permissible unless the treaty specifies the contrary or the reservation is contradictory to the object and purpose of the treaty.[20] In treaty practice, exhaustive lists of permitted reservations may be introduced to preserve uniformity and prevent the opt-out from the most essential provisions.[21]

In literature, the distinction between explicit opt-out clauses and reservations is highly debated.[22] Although the OECD distinguishes explicit opt-out clauses from reservations in the BEPS Action 15 Final Report,[23] it must be admitted that no clear dividing line can be drawn between those two mechanisms.[24] However, irrespective of whether the exclusive provisions used in a multilateral treaty fall under one or the other category, there is consensus that both are opt-out mechanisms pursuing the same purpose.[25]

The final proposal of the MLI incorporates several provisions explicitly allowing for an opt-out throughout the treaty text.[26] In addition, Article 28 of the MLI sets out an exhaustive list of authorized reservations by reference to the specific treaty provisions providing for the opting-out.[27] By this means, the possibility to deviate from the MLI is limited in two ways. First, the treaty includes explicit opt-out clauses. In addition, Article 28 on reservations ensures that the possible deviations from the MLI are restricted, as no other reservations than those expressly permitted by the opt-out provisions in the treaty may be made.[28] As some opt-out clauses do not permit a complete exclusion, but allow the exclusion of the application of certain MLI provisions only to a limited extent, the minimum standard is realized.

2.1.3 Opt-In Clauses

In contrast to opt-out clauses, opt-in mechanisms are provisions under which a party may voluntarily accept additional obligations that are not necessarily required by the MLI.[29] As opt-in clauses are not mandatory, they are not automatically applicable when entering into the MLI. For this reason, the contracting parties willing to undertake

19. Article 2(1)(d) Vienna Convention, under which the term 'reservation' means a unilateral statement, however phrased or named, made by a state, when signing, ratifying, accepting, approving or acceding to a treaty, whereby it purports to exclude or to modify the legal effect of certain provisions of the treaty in their application to that state.
20. Article 19 Vienna Convention.
21. This mechanism is used e.g., in Art. 30 of the Convention on Mutual Administrative Assistance in Tax Matters (1988).
22. ILC, *supra* n. 15, Commentary to Guideline 1.5.3., para. 5.
23. OECD, *Action 15 Final Report*, *supra* n. 6, paras 43 et seq.
24. *See also* ILC, *supra* n. 15, Commentary to Guideline 1.5.3., para. 5.
25. For example, ILC, *supra* n. 15, Commentary to Guideline 1.5.3., para. 11.
26. For example, Arts 14(3), 15(2) or 16(5) MLI.
27. Exception in Art. 28(2) MLI for arbitration.
28. Benjamin Walker, Reservations to the Multilateral Instrument.
29. For example, ILC, *supra* n. 15, Commentary to Guideline 1.5.3., para. 3.

further commitment must explicitly accept the application of those clauses by means of a declaration or any other official manifestation specified by the MLI.[30] Opt-in clauses may appear in various forms. To commit further actions in pursuit of the treaty objectives, the treaty may, for instance, offer the parties explicit opt-in provisions clearly providing for the specific possibility for additional commitment.[31]

The conclusion of optional protocols to a multilateral treaty would be another example of a way to voluntarily opt in and thereby to be bound by more provisions than required.[32] Even though alternative provisions are considered to be their own category of optional mechanisms,[33] they can show similarities to opt-in clauses under certain circumstances.[34] Thus, these provisions can be construed in a way that allows a choice among different alternatives, including the possibility to apply none of the alternatives offered. Thus, whenever a treaty party decides to apply one of the alternatives, that party technically opts in to the provision if there is a possibility not to opt for any of the alternative clauses. Therefore, alternative measures (which are dealt with more in depth in the following section) can have elements of opt-in clauses as well.

The proposed MLI contains several concrete opt-in clauses. One example of such a clause is Article 6(3) of the MLI, which permits the parties to include an optional addition to the preamble text proposed in Article 6(1) of the MLI. Accordingly, a party may choose to add a sentence referring to a desire to further develop the economic relationship and to enhance cooperation in tax matters.[35] As the preamble text plays a major role in treaty interpretation, the additional sentence is also to be taken into consideration when interpreting tax treaties.[36] Furthermore, the MLI also includes alternative provisions that theoretically are comparable to opt-in clauses to the extent that they offer the possibility not to opt for any of the alternative provisions. To name but one, Article 5 of the MLI (on the application of methods for the elimination of double taxation) is a prominent example, as the parties to the MLI have the choice to apply either Option A, Option B or Option C, or may choose to apply none of the options. As soon as the parties opt for one of those three options, they actually opt in to the provision, as none of the options would be applicable without express consent.[37] In order to make their choice official and for the opt-in to be effective, the MLI stipulates that the parties must notify their decision under Article 29 of the MLI.

Most opt-in clauses used in the MLI are introduced to supplement other provisions that are mandatory to extend the application range of a respective provision. As mentioned, the opt-in mechanism in Article 6(3) of the MLI is supplementary to Article 6(1) of the MLI. Both provisions are related to the same content, namely to the

30. As is also the case with opt-out clauses pursuant to Art. 23 of the Vienna Convention and alternative provisions under Art. 17 of the Vienna Convention.
31. For example, Art. 41(1) *International Covenant on Civil and Political Rights* (1966).
32. *See* e.g., *European Convention for the Protection of Human Rights and Fundamental Freedoms* (1950).
33. ILC, *supra* n. 15, Commentary to Guideline 1.5.3., para. 12.
34. OECD, *Action 15 Final Report*, *supra* n. 6, para. 44.
35. OECD, *Explanatory Statement to the MLI* (2016), *supra* n. 4, para. 83.
36. OECD, *Explanatory Statement to the MLI* (2016), *supra* n. 4, para. 23.
37. OECD, *Action 15 Final Report*, *supra* n. 6, para. 44.

preamble of the underlying tax treaties.[38] Apart from that, the MLI not only contains opt-in clauses that are included together with other mandatory provisions of the treaty to expand their scope, but also includes one entire optional part that is self-standing and includes a set of provisions.[39] Article 18 of the MLI stipulates that a party is free to choose to apply Part VI of the MLI on arbitration. The optional Part VI of the MLI was developed to introduce provisions on mandatory binding arbitration in case the competent authorities do not reach a mutual agreement within a certain period of time.[40] Contrary to the other opt-in clauses of the MLI, Part VI aims to operate as one single cohesive arbitration provision, although it consists of a couple of provisions.[41]

2.1.4 Alternative Provisions

In general, alternative provisions may be inserted in a multilateral treaty if more than one solution enables the achievement of the overall purposes of the treaty or if various options have almost the same or a similar effect concerning the fulfilment of treaty objectives and lead to a comparable result. If the purpose of a treaty can effectively be achieved by different means, it is possible for a multilateral treaty to offer the contracting parties the chance to select the most appropriate one or the one that most perfectly fits into their respective tax policy system.[42] Through alternative provisions, flexibility is provided if the ultimate goal can be reached in multiple ways because it offers the parties the possibility to tailor the application of the MLI according to their preferences.

In the MLI, there are two types of alternative provisions. One mechanism used would be alternative provisions with a default option.[43] The clauses falling under this category can be described as follows: Within one article of the MLI, there is a general rule that – in principle – is mandatory. This clause applies when the contracting parties enter into the agreement. However, the treaty offers an alternative solution and contains clauses that may be chosen instead of the general rule. Thus, the parties may decide whether they want to stay with the general rule or deviate from that predetermined provision and to opt for the alternative instead. If none of the alternatives is opted for or the parties do no react, the general rule will still continue to apply as it is the 'default option'.

To illustrate this a bit, the functioning is explained here by using a specific example. Article 9(1) of the MLI contains a model provision on capital gains from the

38. Other examples for options that are introduced to supplement other provisions include Art. 7(3) and (4) of the MLI providing for a provision supplementary to the principal purpose test which is set out in Art. 7(1) of the MLI.
39. OECD, *Explanatory Statement to the MLI* (2016), *supra* n. 4, para. 20.
40. OECD, *Explanatory Statement to the MLI* (2016), *supra* n. 4, para. 19. The optional part was established on the basis of the findings of OECD, *Making Dispute Resolution Mechanisms More Effective – Action 14: 2015 Final Report* (2015).
41. OECD, *Explanatory Statement to the MLI* (2016), *supra* n. 4, para. 20.
42. C. Hilling, *Article 17*, in *The Vienna Conventions on the Law of Treaties: A Commentary*, para. 16 (O. Corten & P. Klein eds., Oxford Univ. Press 2011).
43. The term 'default option' is used in the Explanatory Statement on Art. 7 of the MLI. OECD, *Explanatory Statement to the MLI* (2016), *supra* n. 4, para. 90.

alienation of shares or other interests deriving their value from immovable property. This provision is the general provision and aims to update and standardize the wording of the already existing tax treaty provisions on capital gains contained in Article 13(4) of the OECD Model.[44] The general provision is drafted in a way that it allows to leave the specifications of the value thresholds relevant for the application of the provision on capital gains already contained in the parties' tax treaties.[45] However, the general rule may be applied only if a similar clause on capital gains has already been included in the respective tax treaty. Therefore, Article 9(3) and (4) of the MLI grants the parties the possibility to alternatively choose the provision as produced in the BEPS Action 6 Final Report[46] instead. In contrast to the general provision, the alternative sets out concrete value thresholds and allows a party to introduce a provision on capital gains into a treaty that does not have such a rule.[47] Thus, if a party wants to apply the alternative rather than the general rule, it must make a notification to the depositary to officially opt for the other provision.[48] In sum, alternative provisions with a default option are mechanisms comprising more than one option, provided that one of the options applies as a general rule. Only if the treaty party reacts and explicitly opts for another alternative, will the alternative option apply. If no reactions follow, the general provision will be applicable and obligatory.[49]

Another type of alternative mechanism that appears in the MLI is alternative provisions without a default option. Compared to the first mentioned type, this kind of alternative provision is slightly different, as it can be characterized by the fact that two or more alternatives are offered by the treaty whereby none of those alternatives or any general rule is applicable if the contracting party does not explicitly opt for it. In other words, the treaty grants the treaty parties the possibility to choose one out of a few alternatives, and if none is applied, then no predetermined general provision or default option is applicable, and the provision simply does not apply. This is why, as indicated above, those clauses reflect similarities to opt-in clauses. For, as any party does not explicitly opt for one of the alternatives, the provision is not applicable. An example for such an alternative provision without a default option is, as mentioned, Article 5 of the MLI, describing three alternative ways to address problems arising from the application of the methods articles of tax treaties.[50] Another example is Article 13(1) of the MLI,

44. OECD, *Explanatory Statement to the MLI* (2016), *supra* n. 4, para. 128.
45. OECD, *Explanatory Statement to the MLI* (2016), *supra* n. 4, para. 131.
46. OECD, *Preventing the Granting of Treaty Benefits in Inappropriate Circumstances – Action 6: 2015 Final Report*, OECD/G20 Base Erosion and Profit Shifting Project (2015), para. 44.
47. OECD, *Explanatory Statement to the MLI* (2016), *supra* n. 4, para. 133.
48. Article 9(8) MLI.
49. Article 7 on the prevention of treaty abuse is another example of alternative provisions with a default option. According to the explanations to Art. 7 of the MLI (*see* OECD, *Explanatory Statement to the MLI* (2016), *supra* n. 4), the principal-purpose-test clause can satisfy the minimum standard on its own and therefore it is presented as a default option in para. 1.
50. OECD, *Explanatory Statement to the MLI* (2016), *supra* n. 4, para. 60.

which includes two possible ways to tackle the artificial avoidance of permanent establishment status through specific activity exemptions as proposed in the BEPS Action 7 Final Report.[51]

2.1.5 Analysis and Suitability of These Categories

In the BEPS Action 15 Final Report, the OECD proposed tools most commonly utilized when flexibility needs to be introduced to multilateral treaties. The core set of mechanisms elaborated and suggested by the OECD consists of opt-in clauses, opt-out clauses and alternative provisions.[52] Each type has its typical field of application that had to be considered when incorporating the various BEPS measures into the MLI and drafting its text.[53] Even though the introduction of flexible mechanisms was required to some extent in order to facilitate the conclusion of the MLI, the utilization had to be carefully considered for each clause individually, as a multitude of optional measures would eventually bring more complexity into the system than necessary and affect the application of the treaty in practice.[54] However, neither the BEPS Action 15 Final Report nor the other BEPS final reports provided any concrete substantive instructions on which (flexible) BEPS measures are to be included by which type of option.[55]

The recommendation of the OECD in Action 15 was actually purely focused on giving advice on the functioning of the different optional measures, and refers to examples of how options are typically technically implemented in common international practice.[56] The task to transfer the results of the relevant BEPS final reports into the MLI, however, was assigned to the OECD group of experts.[57] The group not only had to decide what substantive provisions would require some degree of flexibility on the basis of the final BEPS report package, but also had to select the most appropriate technical form to provide flexibility in a following step. The situation was aggravated by the fact that the MLI was to be the first multilateral instrument on substantive tax provisions. In the past, no comparable tax treaty of this size had been concluded multilaterally that could have been taken as an example.[58]

When drafting the proposal for the MLI, however, the group of experts came to the solution to insert all three types of options and thereby use a mix of optional mechanisms.[59] To fully analyse the actual fields of application of options, their functioning and the effect in the MLI, a closer look needs to be taken at the material rather than a technical categorization, as the types of mechanisms represent only the

51. The alternatives reflect the work as produced by OECD, *Preventing the Artificial Avoidance of Permanent Establishment Status – Action 7: 2015 Final Report*, OECD/G20 Base Erosion and Profit Shifting Project (2015) pp 28–29 and 38.
52. OECD, *Action 15 Final Report*, *supra* n. 6, para. 42.
53. OECD, *Explanatory Statement to the MLI* (2016), *supra* n. 4, para. 6.
54. *See also* N. Bravo, *The Multilateral Tax Instrument and Its Relationship with Tax Treaties*, 8 World Tax J. 3, at 295 (2016).
55. OECD, *Explanatory Statement to the MLI* (2016), *supra* n. 4, para. 8.
56. OECD, *Explanatory Statement to the MLI* (2016), *supra* n. 4, para. 5.
57. OECD, *Explanatory Statement to the MLI* (2016), *supra* n. 4, para. 6.
58. OECD, *Action 15 Final Report*, *supra* n. 6, para. 9; Bravo, *supra* n. 54, at 280 et seq.
59. OECD, *Explanatory Statement to the MLI* (2016), *supra* n. 4, para. 14.

means of how to put an idea properly into a most suitable (legal) form. Thus, to gain a better understanding of their relation to the articles of the OECD Model that they materially concern, it is necessary to scrutinize the purpose of the particular options and the legal consequences depending on different consent requirements.

2.2 Classification of the Options According to the Articles of the OECD Model Convention

The OECD Model consists of several parts that can loosely be summarized as follows. As is the case with almost any convention, in the beginning there is the preamble, followed by the personal and material scope.[60] Next, Chapter II of the OECD Model sets forth a series of definitions.[61] In the subsequent section, Articles 6–8 and 10–22 of the OECD Model contain the allocation rules. The last part of the OECD Model contains the method article[62] and other special provisions.

As general principle, the MLI is not intended to represent a completely independent instrument replacing the numerous existing tax treaties concluded by the contracting parties, but rather to operate as a complementary tool that must be read in conjunction with those treaties that still remain valid.[63] Against this background, it is worthwhile to elaborate on the particular parts or provisions of the OECD Model that will be matched by the optional provisions of the MLI. As opt-out clauses and reservations have been inserted in almost every provision of the MLI, they are not taken into account at this point. Thus, more attention is devoted to the categorization of the alternative provisions and opt-in clauses foreseen by the MLI according to the structure of the OECD Model and to the parts they concern.

When applying existing tax treaties along with the MLI, the first option that could have a major influence on the application and interpretation of the treaties is set out in Article 6 of the MLI and offers the possibility to voluntarily opt-in to a supplementary sentence in the preamble of tax treaties.[64] Furthermore, Article 7 of the MLI targets the official definition of permanent establishments and enacts changes to prevent the artificial avoidance of PE status through specific activity exemptions. This provision corresponds to Article 5 of the OECD Model.[65] As concerns the influence of the MLI options on the allocation rules, only Article 13 of the OECD Model on capital gains is affected. In that regard, Article 9 of the MLI incorporates certain adjustments relating to capital gains from shares in immovable property proposed by the BEPS Action 6 Final Report. With a view to the exemption and credit method provided by Article 23A and 23B of the OECD Model, options are inserted by Article 5 of the MLI to adapt those

60. Articles 1 and 2 OECD Model Convention on Income and Capital (hereinafter 'OECD Model').
61. Articles 3–6 OECD Model.
62. Article 23A and 23B OECD Model.
63. OECD, *Explanatory Statement to the MLI* (2016), *supra* n. 4, para. 13.
64. As proposed by OECD, *Action 6 Final Report, supra* n. 46.
65. This provision addresses BEPS measures as proposed by OECD, *Action 7 Final Report, supra* n. 51.

provisions and thereby tackle potential issues arising from their application.[66] The option regarding arbitration corresponds to Article 25(5) of the OECD Model.[67] However, the principal-purpose-test rule (or simplified limitation-on-benefits clause serving as a substitute) does not fit into the existing structure of the OECD Model.[68] As no comparable provisions existed before, the optional provisions regarding the principal-purpose-test rule are to be applied with respect to most tax treaties for the first time.

It is thus clear that the optional mechanisms in the MLI have an impact on all relevant parts of the OECD Model.

2.3 Classification of the Options According to Their Purpose

The MLI was initiated to implement measures to prevent BEPS based on the findings presented in the BEPS final reports. Although the OECD aimed to harmonize as many measures as possible to counter BEPS most effectively, it was clear from the outset that a complete harmonization would be a very ambitious goal that was not likely be achieved.[69] When drafting the MLI, the OECD group of experts thus had to figure out to what extent modifications to the MLI should be permitted. As also has been briefly touched upon, before the concrete form of the mechanism to effect individual adjustments could be selected, careful consideration had to be given to the necessity and purpose of the use of options in a particular place.

In order to group the options identified in the MLI according to their purpose, a more detailed assessment of the optional mechanisms and their content had to be carried out. In essence, five categories can be observed.[70] First, there are several options deployed to implement the minimum standard. Second, some options are primarily introduced to update bilateral treaties that do not follow the newest version of the OECD Model or do not follow the OECD Model at all. The third group comprises options introduced purely to provide flexibility to the parties by offering a choice between a selection from various measures all leading to one and the same goal. Forth, options can be employed to show consideration for particular states in cases where no common consensus could be reached among all or most of the OECD member countries when preparing the BEPS final reports. Finally, options are inserted to adjust formal requirements with respect to the MLI itself.

---

66. The proposal for this treaty provision was produced by OECD, *Countering Harmful Tax Practices More Effectively, Taking into Account Transparency and Substance – Action 5: 2015 Final Report*, OECD/G20 Base Erosion and Profit Shifting Project (2015).
67. The proposal for inserting an arbitration clause stems from OECD, *Action 14 Final Report*, *supra* n. 40.
68. The rules aimed at preventing the granting of treaty benefits in inappropriate circumstances were proposed by OECD, *Action 6 Final Report*, *supra* n. 46.
69. OECD, *Action 15 Final Report*, *supra* n. 6, para. 41.
70. However, it must be admitted that the categorization is not clear-cut, and a definite distinction is not possible in each scenario, as there might be options that could fall under more than one category.

The first set of options to be discussed are optional mechanisms introduced for the purpose of implementing the minimum standard.[71] Although the notion of 'minimum standard' goes back to the BEPS final reports,[72] it is not expressly defined therein. Basically, the term describes a minimum level of commitment which definitely must be undertaken when entering into the MLI and which cannot be deviated from by the parties. The legal norms that are considered to represent the minimum standard are characterized by the fact that the exclusion of the application of said provisions is not possible.[73] The provisions forming the minimum standard are considered to be absolutely essential to the MLI and symbolize the key points of the treaty concerned. Provisions building the minimum standard are compulsory for the parties to the MLI. In the MLI, minimum standard provisions are easily identifiable, as the possibility to opt out is restricted. Opt-out clauses and reservations, respectively, were inserted in almost every (substantive) provision of the MLI and most of them - save for a few particular exceptions - allow a party to reserve the right not to apply the entirety of a certain article. Only in four provisions of the MLI[74] is the exclusion permissible only if the underlying tax treaty already (i) contains a clause with at least a comparable wording or content or (ii) provides a solution that is considered to be equivalent.[75] By not granting the possibility to exclude the application of certain contents, opt-out clauses or reservations are employed in the MLI to establish the framework of provisions most essential and absolutely necessary to fulfil the treaty objectives, and thereby simultaneously define and form the minimum standard.[76]

Moreover, there is another group of options that are inserted to modernize very old tax treaties, to standardize treaties that do not follow the OECD Model or merely to update treaties not following the latest version of the OECD Model.[77] Many bilateral treaties are in place that were concluded years or even decades ago when BEPS concerns on such a scale could not have been anticipated. Other treaties were formerly negotiated without taking the OECD Model into account, but rather some other existing model that did not provide for such anti-BEPS measures.[78] Furthermore, there are treaties that were concluded rather recently following a previous version of the OECD Model and need comparably fewer adaptations to comply with the newest BEPS

71. OECD, *Explanatory Statement to the MLI* (2016), *supra* n. 4, para. 14.
72. In the executive summary of the findings of OECD, *Action 6 Final Report, supra* n. 46, for example, the term 'minimum standard' is referred to when describing that the countries have committed to ensure a minimum level of protection against treaty shopping.
73. OECD, *Explanatory Statement to the MLI* (2016), *supra* n. 4, para. 14.
74. The four provisions reflecting the minimum standard are Art. 6 concerning the preamble, Art. 7 on principal purpose test and simplified limitation on benefits, Art. 16 and Art. 17 of the MLI.
75. For example, Art. 6(4) MLI stating that '[a] Party may reserve the right for paragraph 1 not to apply to its Covered Tax Agreements that already contain preamble language describing the intent of the Contracting Jurisdictions to eliminate double taxation without creating opportunities for non-taxation or reduced taxation, whether that language is limited to cases of tax evasion or avoidance [...] or applies more broadly'.
76. *See also* Andreas Langer, The Legal Relevance of the Minimum Standard in the OECD/BEPS Project.
77. OECD, *Explanatory Statement to the MLI* (2016), *supra* n. 4, para. 15.
78. Many tax treaties follow the structure of other model tax conventions, such as the UN or US Model Tax Convention.

standards. For all those treaties that no longer satisfy current requirements, provisions are foreseen by the MLI to bring the entirety of bilaterally concluded treaties up to date.[79]

However, in certain cases there may be a different degree of adjustment that is needed with regard to treaties which have been entered into more recently where the OECD Model served as a basis in the contractual negotiations, compared to more exotic treaties or treaties dating back several years. To take account of the distinct level of adaptation needed, options were introduced into the MLI. By offering the parties the possibility to choose between alternatives to opt for the clause most suitable for a party's existing treaty network, the options enable the treaty parties to bring the relevant treaty provision of all treaties available to the same status, irrespective of the time of conclusion or of the model convention used.[80] Again, Article 9 of the MLI can be taken as a perfect example for options aimed at providing alternative solutions to update the tax treaties covered by the MLI. The provision on capital gains from shares in immovable property contains one version to update bilateral treaties that already have a corresponding clause, but also offers the treaties where such a clause was not negotiated for whatever reason the possibility to alternatively opt for the version of initial inclusion of a provision on capital gains (resembling Article 13(4) of the OECD Model as proposed by the BEPS Action 6 Final Report).[81]

Furthermore, there is a third category when considering the purpose and the reason for the insertion of options, namely the provision of flexibility to a contracting party to enable choices of solutions most in line with its individual taxation policy.[82] Most optional mechanisms used in the MLI fall under this group of options. Article 7 of the MLI is a typical example of inserting an option so that a treaty party can select a measure from a pool of different alternatives which most appropriately fits into its fiscal policies and strategies. Whereas Article 7(1) of the MLI sets forth a principal-purpose-test rule, under which any benefit is to be denied if obtaining that benefit was one of the principal purposes of an arrangement, Article 7(3) and (4) of the MLI permits the choice to include an additional provision that is to be applied together with the principal-purpose-test rule and, in exceptional cases, allows the tax authorities to still grant the benefit that would otherwise have to be denied. Alternatively, if a contracting party is not convinced to apply a principal-purpose-test rule alone, the MLI offers the chance to opt for a simplified limitation-on-benefits provision to supplement the principal purpose test.[83] For treaty parties that do not prefer any option and therefore do not want to opt for either the principal-purpose-test rule or the supplementary simplified limitation-on-benefits clause, there is the possibility to rely on other measures as long as the minimum standard is fulfilled.[84] As set forth in Article 7(15) of the MLI, treaty abuse can also be addressed properly by using, for example, a detailed limitation-on-benefits provision in combination with a general anti-abuse rule. Due to

79. OECD, *Action 15 Final Report*, *supra* n. 6, para. 26.
80. OECD, *Explanatory Statement to the MLI* (2016), *supra* n. 4, paras 133 and 135.
81. OECD, *Explanatory Statement to the MLI* (2016), *supra* n. 4, para. 133.
82. OECD, *Explanatory Statement to the MLI* (2016), *supra* n. 4, para. 14.
83. Article 7(6) MLI.
84. OECD, *Explanatory Statement to the MLI* (2016), *supra* n. 4, para. 90.

this wide range of offers of different variations and combinations, a choice is facilitated that most perfectly complies with the contracting parties' tax policy approach.[85] Through flexible mechanisms, the parties to the treaty are able to adapt the BEPS measures individually in a most preferred manner corresponding to their willingness and level of commitment.

What is more, the MLI utilizes options to give the contracting parties the opportunity to adopt additional measures on a voluntary basis.[86] Anti-BEPS measures that go beyond what is commonly agreed or considered to be absolutely necessary by the OECD and G20 countries are not obligatory and should therefore not be automatically included in a treaty text upon conclusion. Rather than an automatic inclusion, the possibility to freely decide whether or not to go for further commitment should be available for the treaty parties. Therefore, some MLI options serve the purpose of voluntarily broadening the intensity of application of the MLI. The set of provisions of Part VI on arbitration is one optional mechanism introduced to fulfil such a function.[87] The arbitration clause was introduced in the form of an option because no consensus could be reached among the OECD and G20 countries regarding the adoption of arbitration as a tool to resolve MAP cases.[88] As no common agreement could be achieved, such actions cannot be expected to be undertaken by all parties to the MLI. That is why the clauses had to be drafted in a manner such that this optional part may be applied only upon express consent of the contracting party.[89] This way, all parties willing to commit are able to apply the clauses on arbitration set forth in Articles 18–26 of the MLI, whereas all parties that did not express an interest in doing so are not forced to adopt the provisions on MAP arbitration.[90]

The last group that can be observed comprises optional clauses allowing the parties to the MLI to deviate from, and to replace certain references pursuant to Article 35 of the MLI relating to the entry into force of the MLI itself. The options are not concerned with any substantive provisions and do not cause any material changes to the MLI when applied, but are aimed at providing flexibility to the formal application of the MLI.[91]

There are different motives and reasons for the introduction of options. Options were drafted by the group of experts to define the minimum standard, to update treaties with different preconditions or to provide more than one solution to enact certain BEPS measures based on the preferences of the contracting parties. The differing purpose

85. OECD, *Explanatory Statement to the MLI* (2016), *supra* n. 4, para. 14.
86. OECD, *Explanatory Statement to the MLI* (2016), *supra* n. 4, para. 14.
87. The substance and modalities of implementation of the arbitration provision had to be developed as part of the negotiation of the MLI. *See also* OECD, *Explanatory Statement to the MLI* (2016), *supra* n. 4, para. 9.
88. OECD, *Action 14 Final Report*, *supra* n. 40, paras 62 et seq.
89. OECD, *Explanatory Statement to the MLI* (2016), *supra* n. 4, para. 9; OECD, *Action 14 Final Report*, *supra* n. 40, para. 63.
90. Article 18 of the MLI provides that the part on arbitration 'shall apply to two Contracting Jurisdictions with respect to a Covered Tax Agreement only where both Contracting Jurisdictions have made such a notification'.
91. Choices regarding the formal application may be made in Art. 35(1), (2), (3), (5) and (7) of the MLI.

that is pursued by the MLI options had to be taken into account especially when considering the technical implementation thereof. Options that are used to delimit the minimum standard usually are opt-out clauses, as they impose limitations on the exclusion of provisions through the permission of opting-out of the application of a specific provision only to a certain extent.[92] Regarding clauses aimed at equalizing the standards of atypical and old treaties, as well as treaties that follow the OECD Model in principle (although not the latest version) by means of two pertinent concepts, alternative provision mechanisms are regularly employed. The same is true with provisions aimed at providing possibilities of choice between various solutions to select one most favourable measure. Flexibility in the level of additional, voluntary commitment is mainly established through opt-in mechanisms within the MLI.[93]

2.4 Classification of the Options According to Legal Consequences

The conclusion of both bilateral and multilateral treaties is conditional upon agreement between two or more parties. To reach a consensus between the parties to a treaty, it is inevitably required to find a compromise that is satisfactory to all parties concerned. In the majority of cases, a party will be willing to accept certain commitments in the negotiating process only if the other potential party is also ready to undertake at least a similar level of commitment. Thus, one of the main principles of international law is the principle of reciprocity.[94] In other terms, the notion of reciprocity can be described as the relation between states that grant each other a comparable or even the same treatment. Thus, as a general rule of public international law, one treaty party can expect to be treated in a certain manner by the other contracting party only to the extent that it is prepared to offer such treatment equally to the other party.[95] As a consequence, only in exceptional cases will a treaty party approve unilateral adjustments by other parties, especially if it results in implications for all parties to the treaty.[96] It has been emphasized several times that the optional measures are offered by the MLI to take into account the parties' individual preferences. Thus, the focus in this section is on the realization of the principle of reciprocity in the MLI.

As a rule, optional mechanisms, by definition, are applicable and therefore trigger legal consequences upon express consent by the parties.[97] For this reason, each option in the MLI reveals both the requirement of consent and depending on that, its legal effect.[98] The principle of reciprocity is realized when the same legal consequence

92. *See* OECD, *Explanatory Statement to the MLI* (2016), *supra* n. 4, para. 14.
93. *See* OECD, *Explanatory Statement to the MLI* (2016), *supra* n. 4, para. 14.
94. C. Walter, *Article 21*, in *Vienna Convention on the Law of Treaties: A Commentary*, *supra* n. 1, para. 19.
95. Walter, *supra* n. 94, para. 19.
96. Walter, *supra* n. 94, para. 20.
97. *See* definitions provided in sections 2.2, 2.3 and 2.4.
98. For example, Art. 9(8) of the MLI stipulates that the option in 'Paragraph 4 shall apply to a Covered Tax Agreement only where all Contracting Jurisdictions have made such a notification'. Therefore, the provision requires that all contracting parties give consent to the application of the option (i.e., consent requirement) for the choice to apply (i.e., legal consequence).

of an option applies for both parties.[99] In the MLI, there are clauses where the same legal effect is triggered only in the event that all parties to the treaty choose to apply exactly the same option or, expressed differently, if all treaty parties make an equal choice of an option. In consequence, if the parties' choices deviate from each other – either because one party wants to apply a particular option and the other party does not, or the contracting parties both opt for differing provisions, the legal effect will not be produced.[100] Most optional mechanisms used in the MLI are dependent on such unanimous decision of the contracting parties. The provision on artificial avoidance of PE status pursuant to Article 13 of the MLI, for instance, clarifies that the choice for one of the alternative provisions will apply with respect to the provisions of the parties' tax treaty and therefore be legally effective 'only where *all* Contracting Jurisdictions have chosen to apply the same option' (emphasis added). Similarly, unanimity is required by Article 18 of the MLI to trigger legal consequences, as the optional Part VI on arbitration will apply in relation to two contracting parties 'only where *both* Contracting Jurisdictions' (emphasis added) have chosen to opt for it.

Notwithstanding the principle of reciprocity that is undoubtedly fulfilled in both examples,[101] the difference in wording of the approval requirements inevitably gives rise to the question as to whether the requirements of consent actually are different. Fundamentally, the MLI does not replace existing tax treaties, but is intended to coexist and to be read and applied together with the treaties covered.[102] However, a party's treaty network does not necessarily consist of only bilateral treaties. Even though tax treaties are entered into most commonly by two contracting parties, some treaties, such as the Nordic Multilateral Double Taxation Convention,[103] are concluded between more than two parties. For this reason, the differing wording may imply that in all cases the triggering of legal consequences depends on identical decisions of all treaty parties, such that each party to the underlying tax treaty that is covered by the MLI must give its consent. With regard to bilateral treaties, this would mean that both parties must choose the same option, while in the case of multilateral treaties, the entire group must agree with the option. The use of two different words and, in this context, the application of distinct approval requirements of options can plausibly be assumed if the distinction were intended for a particular reason.

Unfortunately, the Explanatory Statement to the MLI does not indicate the reasoning for inserting two different conditions for consent which legitimately needs to

99. Walter, *supra* n. 94, para. 19.
100. In case of divergent choices, Art. 7(7) of the MLI provides special rules that can be applied if the parties agree to such exceptional application.
101. The clauses are reciprocal because the legal consequence is triggered in the same way for all or both parties respectively.
102. OECD, *Explanatory Statement to the MLI* (2016), *supra* n. 4, para. 13.
103. Convention between the Nordic Countries for the Avoidance of Double Taxation with respect to Taxes on Income and on Capital (23 September 1996). The six signatory states are Denmark, the Faroe Islands, Finland, Iceland, Norway and Sweden.

be questioned.[104] Indeed, one possible explanation could be the fact that the application of some reciprocal options depends on the condition that all parties have opted for the same solution, whereas the optional part on arbitration requires only the consent of two parties to be legally effective. As noted above, only a limited number of countries expressed the intention to adopt and implement mandatory binding arbitration to ensure the resolution of disputes.[105] Norway and Sweden, two of the six parties to the Nordic Multilateral Double Taxation Convention, are among those states that were interested in the implementation of an arbitration clause to the MLI.[106] However, the other four current signatory states to the Nordic Convention did not declare such interest. For this reason, it would not make sense if the optional part on arbitration triggers legal consequences only if actually *all* contracting parties choose to apply, as it would be impossible for the two parties to the Nordic Convention that are in favour of the arbitration clause to incorporate it in relation to each other unless the other parties respond to the insertion of the part accordingly. This is why the requirement of consent of *both* parties could be required, as it is one way to prevent the parties to multilateral tax treaties willing to pursue a higher level of commitment than the others from being blocked by the remaining treaty parties.

As soon as the respective requirement of consent set out in the reciprocal optional provision in addition to other formal requirements (*see* Part III. Exercise of Options) is properly met, the option applies and the same legal consequence is triggered with regard to the parties concerned. The compatibility clauses included in the MLI itself clarify how to apply the relevant option in relation to existing provisions of the parties' tax treaties and how the concrete option interacts with the other corresponding provisions of the MLI.[107]

However, the principle of reciprocity is fulfilled not only if the condition of unanimity is met. When considering reservations, it suffices that only one party reserves the right not to apply (parts of) a certain provision of the MLI to trigger the same legal consequence for the other party, as well.[108] More precisely, whenever one party makes a reservation, the clause will generally not be applicable for both parties (or all parties in the case of treaties concluded with more than two parties) to the extent that the reservation has been exercised, irrespective of the choice of the other party (or parties in the case of multilateral tax treaties). This principle is also explicitly pointed out by Article 28(3) of the MLI, under which a reservation made will modify the provision to which the reservation relates to the same extent for both the reserving and the other party unless explicitly provided otherwise.[109] Another example which shows

104. There is no explanation for using a different consent requirement of 'both' instead of 'all' in the Explanatory Statement on Art. 18 of the MLI. The same is true with Art. 24 of the MLI, the other optional provision within the optional Part VI which also requires such bilateral consent.
105. OECD, *Action 14 Final Report*, *supra* n. 40, paras 62 et seq.
106. OECD, *Action 14 Final Report*, *supra* n. 40, paras 62 et seq.
107. OECD, *Explanatory Statement to the MLI* (2016), *supra* n. 4, para. 15. *See also* Pasquale Pistone & Sriram Govind, The Relationship Between Tax Treaties and the Multilateral Instrument: Compatibility Clauses in the Multilateral Instrument.
108. Walter, *supra* n. 94, para. 19.
109. *See also* OECD, *Explanatory Statement to the MLI* (2016), *supra* n. 4, para. 270.

that unanimous consent is not necessarily required to trigger an equal legal effect for both parties is the option set out in Article 23(4) and (5) of the MLI providing that the competent authorities of both parties must ensure that any information received from either competent authority is not disclosed by means of an agreement with the taxpayer involved in an arbitration proceeding. This provision, which is an optional provision within the optional Part VI on arbitration, applies for both contracting parties if either party chooses to apply it.[110] To conclude, even though there is no unanimous decision among the parties, there are provisions that are compliant with the principle of reciprocity because the legal consequence remains the same for the parties involved.

By contrast, some options in the MLI do not comply with the principle of reciprocity. Accordingly, non-reciprocal optional mechanisms have unilateral effect and apply independent of the choice of the other contracting party.[111] This means that, unlike reciprocal provisions, the legal effect of these provisions is not necessarily the same for both parties. For example, if both parties opt for the same option, the provision will be applicable for both. Therefore, even though the clause is effective unilaterally, the legal effect will still be the same for both parties, as both opted for the same provision. However, if one party decides to opt for one alternative and the other party chooses another alternative, each party will apply the option that it has chosen, irrespective of what the other party opted for due to the unilateral effect. In such case, different options will be applicable and will, thus, trigger different legal consequences for each treaty party.[112]

Article 5 of the MLI on the application of methods for elimination of double taxation is a clause which should be paid attention to and which is not in accordance with the principle of reciprocity. Under this provision, the parties are permitted to choose either Option A, B or C, or to apply none of the options. Where each contracting party chooses a different option, i.e., one party opts for A and the other prefers B, or one party applies one of the options and the other treaty party does not select any of the options, Article 5(1) of the MLI stipulates that 'the Option chosen by each Contracting Jurisdiction shall apply with respect to its own residents'.[113] In fact, this MLI provision corresponds to the method provisions set forth in Article 23A and Article 23B of the OECD Model and provides three possibilities to adapt them.[114] As has already been the case with the provisions of the OECD Model providing for the exemption method and the credit method, the selection of one of these three options has only unilateral effects and establishes certain obligations only to that contracting party that has opted for one

110. OECD, *Explanatory Statement to the MLI* (2016), *supra* n. 4, para. 250.
111. On exceptions to the principle of reciprocity in general, *see also* Walter, *supra* n. 94, para. 19.
112. In the Explanatory Statement, the term 'asymmetrical' application is used to describe the triggering of different legal consequences. OECD, *Explanatory Statement to the MLI* (2016), *supra* n. 4, paras 60 and 102.
113. OECD, *Explanatory Statement to the MLI* (2016), *supra* n. 4, para. 60.
114. OECD, *Explanatory Statement to the MLI* (2016), *supra* n. 4, paras 61, 64 and 68.

of the alternatives.[115] This example shows a derogation from the principle of reciprocity,[116] as the choice of one party is effective irrespective of the preference of the other contracting party.

Another example of a non-reciprocal application of options can be found in Article 7 of the MLI. Under Article 7(6) of the MLI, the simplified limitation-on-benefits provision is applicable and therefore will replace the predetermined principal-purpose-test clause of Article 7(1) of the MLI only where all contracting parties have chosen to apply it. However, Article 7(7)(b) of the MLI allows those parties that decide to apply the principal purpose test alone to allow the other party to apply the simplified limitation on benefits asymmetrically.[117] Such an agreement between the parties to deviate from the general rule in Article 7(6) of the MLI requiring unanimous choice for the application of the simplified limitation on benefits, leads to two different legal consequences and consequently to a deviation from the principle of reciprocity.

To conclude, throughout the MLI the principle of reciprocity is predominantly adhered to, particularly with regard to options. According to this, most optional provisions included trigger legal effects only if both or all parties decide to choose the same option and thereby are prepared to grant the same treatment to each other. Nevertheless, there are a few exceptions where a deviation from reciprocity can be observed. Among those options, the alternative provision to adjust the OECD methods to eliminate double taxation is found in the MLI. In view of the fact that the exemption method and the credit method have been used in OECD model conventions all along, the application – in practice – of one method by one party and the other method by the other party shows that this non-reciprocal provision is commonplace and has indeed already been accepted in the past.[118]

3 EXERCISE OF OPTIONS

3.1 Notifications and Reservations

The discussion here focuses on the formal prerequisites regarding the exercise of options.

Basically, the MLI is meant to be one single agreement with one uniform text concluded by a multitude of parties.[119] Particularly, this uniform MLI text includes provisions that may be deviated from, provisions that offer the parties different alternatives that may be selected and clauses that may be voluntarily applied. As each

115. OECD, *Explanatory Statement to the MLI* (2016), *supra* n. 4, para. 60.
116. However, there is an exception foreseen in Art. 5(9) of the MLI. Under this clause, a party that does not opt for Option C may reserve the right not to permit the other party to apply Option C, as well. Thus, by means of a reservation, one treaty party may preclude the application of Option C for both parties. As the legal effect (i.e., the non-application of this particular option) will be the same for both treaty parties if either party decides to make the reservation, this exceptional provision shows elements of reciprocity.
117. OECD, *Explanatory Statement to the MLI* (2016), *supra* n. 4, para. 102.
118. OECD, *Explanatory Statement to the MLI* (2016), *supra* n. 4, para. 60.
119. OECD, *Action 15 Final Report*, *supra* n. 6, para. 19.

party has its own preferences due to its tax policy pursued or for any reason whatsoever, it is unlikely that the choice for one option will be identical for all contracting parties. The inclusion of all the preferences for each option of each party into one instrument would make the MLI more complex than it already is.[120] In addition, including all the choices the parties make in one instrument would not be feasible, considering the fact that the text of the entire MLI must be amended whenever a jurisdiction decides to join the convention at a later stage to become a party to the treaty or every time an option needs to be reversed. For the reason of flexibility and to reduce complexity, the parties' choices and deviations from the uniform text of the MLI thus should not change the treaty text itself. Instead of expanding the sufficiently sophisticated MLI text, the exercise of options by the treaty parties should not take place within the treaty itself, but in a separate form. That is why exercising options is pursued on the basis of a notification process, which seems to be a more practicable solution.[121]

A reference to the means by which an option is to be exercised is provided for each MLI provision containing an optional mechanism. For example, Article 9(8) of the MLI stipulates that 'each party that chooses to apply paragraph 4 [determining the option on capital gains] shall notify the Depositary of its choice'. Thus, for each optional provision, the MLI indicates that a notification is required to formally exercise the option in order to gain the status of legal relevance. In addition, an exhaustive list of options subject to notification is specified by Article 29(1) of the MLI.[122] Reservations, by contrast, are conclusively listed in a separate provision.[123] In particular, the procedure and requirements of reservations with regard to opt-out clauses or reservations are provided in Article 28 of the MLI.

In this context, one should bear in mind that notifications and reservations made by a treaty party will apply to all its tax treaties covered by the MLI.[124] Thus, it is not possible for a party to name only particular parties or jurisdictions in relation to which an option should be exercised. The MLI options are namely not meant to be notified towards specific parties individually, but to a party's whole set of covered tax treaties altogether.[125] Consequently, the parties are generally not permitted to choose different options for different covered tax agreements, i.e., a contracting party may not apply, for example, one alternative in relation to certain treaties and another alternative with regard to the others.[126] However, in several opt-out clauses the possibility was included to exceptionally reserve the right not to apply a certain provision with respect to a

120. OECD, *Action 15 Final Report, supra* n. 6, para. 19.
121. OECD, *Explanatory Statement to the MLI* (2016), *supra* n. 4, para. 15. For more details on notifications, *see also* Christiane Zöhrer, Notifications According to the Multilateral Instrument and Consolidated Versions of Tax Treaties.
122. OECD, *Explanatory Statement to the MLI* (2016), *supra* n. 4, para. 294.
123. With the exception of reservations in relation to Part VI of the MLI, *see also* OECD, *supra* n. 4, para. 264.
124. OECD, *Explanatory Statement to the MLI* (2016), *supra* n. 4, para. 14.
125. The only exception to this rule exists within the optional Part VI of the MLI where parties that choose to apply the optional part on arbitration are also permitted to formulate reservations under Art. 28(2) of the MLI with regard to the scope of cases that may be eligible for arbitration.
126. OECD, *Explanatory Statement to the MLI* (2016), *supra* n. 4, para. 14.

subset of tax agreements.[127] The reason behind the inclusion of such a partial opt-out was to permit the parties to preserve the application of special provisions with objectively defined characteristics contained in existing tax treaties in exceptional cases in order to take into account relevant tax policy strategies.[128]

To make use of an option according to the formal requirements, the notification must be made to the OECD, which holds the official function of depositary.[129] The idea behind this concept is that the OECD is exclusively in charge and thus responsible for administering and centrally managing the total number of notifications submitted by the contracting parties. The information on what kind of options are notified exactly and applied respectively by which contracting jurisdictions must be gathered by the depositary.[130] If a reciprocal optional provision needs both parties to have made the same choice in order to trigger legal consequences, the current status of whether each contracting party actually has made its choice accordingly can be easily ascertained due to the notification process.[131]

3.2 Timing of the Exercise of the Option

In this context, one major issue concerns the timing of exercising the options provided by the MLI. With regard to the question as to the point in time at which options may be exercised, Article 29(1) of the MLI stipulates that the parties shall notify a list of their choices 'at the time of signature or when depositing the instrument of ratification, acceptance or approval'. More clarification on this point is brought by the following paragraphs of Article 29. Thus, Article 29(4) of the MLI provides that if a party does not make its notifications at the time of signature, it must submit at least a provisional list of expected notifications at that time. In such case, the list of notifications must be completed upon deposit of the relevant instruments.[132] According to Article 29(3) of the MLI, notifications made at the time of signature are not considered to be definitive and must be confirmed upon deposit of either the instrument of ratification, acceptance or approval. The same is true for reservations, as Article 28(5)-(7) of the MLI mirror the cited provisions related to the timing of submitting notifications to the depositary and therefore apply for the notification of reservations accordingly. In light of these provisions, one can conclude that the latest possible time of exercising an option would be the moment of deposit of the instrument of ratification, acceptance or approval.[133]

127. For example, Art. 8(3) or 13(6)(b) of the MLI which specifically sets forth the requirements that a treaty provision of a covered tax treaty must contain in order to be excludable by the parties.
128. OECD, *Explanatory Statement to the MLI* (2016), *supra* n. 4, para. 14.
129. OECD, *Explanatory Statement to the MLI* (2016), *supra* n. 4, para. 15.
130. OECD, *Action 15 Final Report*, *supra* n. 6, para. 50.
131. OECD, *Explanatory Statement to the MLI* (2016), *supra* n. 4, para. 15.
132. OECD, *Explanatory Statement to the MLI* (2016), *supra* n. 4, paras 300 et seq.
133. OECD, *Explanatory Statement to the MLI* (2016), *supra* n. 4, paras 267 and 292.

3.3 Reversibility of Options

3.3.1 Legitimate Interests to Reverse Options

Reversibility is another issue that needs to be emphasized in the context of the exercise of options. As has been noted, the parties are invited to submit a list of notifications when depositing the final documents required in order to enter into the MLI at the latest.[134] However, the situation could arise where, after a certain time has passed since becoming party to the MLI, a party is reconsidering its decision for one or the other option, either because it experienced difficulties in connection with the application in practice or it would prefer another solution because it seems to be a more reasonable choice in retrospect. Another reason could be, for example, that the parties decide not to exercise the option immediately when entering into the MLI, but want to wait and see how its implementation will succeed with other contracting parties. Particularly the optional Part VI on arbitration could be one of those candidates in practice, where the majority of the parties to the MLI most probably intend to await the experiences of other parties first before considering opting in to such clause themselves.

Based on this, the question arises as to whether the MLI permits the contracting parties to reverse their decisions made without necessarily considering a withdrawal from and re-entering into the MLI or subsequent amendment of all underlying tax treaties simply by means of notification or reservation at a later point in time. Thus, it is questionable as to whether the MLI allows the parties directly through the exercise of options to subsequently declare the choice to opt for certain provisions for the first time, to choose another option in place of an option previously chosen at a later point in time or even to withdraw an optional provision again retrospectively that was opted-in when the party entered into the MLI.

In this connection, the MLI does not provide any general statement as to the reversibility of options.[135] As there are significant differences in reversibility between reservations or opt-out clauses on the one hand and opt-in and alternative provisions on the other, and no generalized answer can be given, the different means of reversing options that are of major practical relevance must be examined separately.

3.3.2 First-Time Exercise of Options after Conclusion

The examination begins with options that the contracting parties plan to exercise for the first time after the moment of entering into the MLI upon deposit of the instrument of ratification, acceptance or approval. The relevant provision concerning opt-in clauses and alternative provisions can be found in Article 29(6) of the MLI, which stipulates that '[a] Party may make additional notifications [to the exhaustive list of options] pursuant to subparagraphs b) through s) of paragraph 1 by means of a

134. According to Art. 29 of the MLI.
135. The possibility of reversibility of options was actually also not emphasized as such within the introductory chapters to the Explanatory Statement. For example, OECD, *Explanatory Statement to the MLI* (2016), *supra* n. 4, para. 15.

notification addressed to the Depositary'. Unfortunately, the MLI itself does not provide an indication as to what exactly is meant by the words 'additional notification' or the time at which such a notification may be made. However, some further clarification is provided by the Explanatory Statement, which provides that 'Paragraph 6 allows Parties to make additional notifications [...] after becoming a Party to the Convention by means of a notification addressed to the Depositary'.[136] After reading the explanations, it becomes clear that 'additional notifications' can be understood as notifications that are made subsequently to the conclusion of the MLI. The exercise of options is therefore not completely excluded after entering into the MLI. On the contrary, the MLI explicitly authorizes the parties to notify their choice of options even at a not expressly specified point in time after becoming party to the MLI. Even though not further clarified, the words 'additional notification' unambiguously suggest that notifications that are made in addition to the notifications already submitted to the depositary should be definitely covered by the authorization.[137]

Compared to notifications of opt-in clauses and alternative provisions, the permissibility of a first-time exercise of opt-out clauses or reservations after entering into the MLI does not seem to be quite clear. Article 28(5) of the MLI provides that '[r]eservations shall be made at the time of signature or when depositing the instrument of ratification, acceptance or approval, subject to the provisions of paragraphs 2, 6 and 9 of this Article, and paragraph 5 of Article 29 (Notifications)'. Thus, the provision on the timing of reservations stipulates, similar to its counterpart in Article 29(1) of the MLI, that – subject to the provisions explicitly enumerated – the latest point in time for submitting a reservation is the time of deposit of the instruments necessary to conclude the treaty.[138] Thus, reference is made to Article 29(5) of the MLI, which foresees the additional notification if the list of agreements falling under the scope of the MLI is expanded, i.e., if new parties join the MLI.[139] This means that each time a new party enters into the MLI, all the other parties are exceptionally permitted to make notifications towards this new party even though the general timing limit in Article 28(5) of the MLI may have elapsed some time ago.[140] Furthermore, there is another reference to Article 28(2) and (6) of the MLI which allows the parties to submit additional reservations relating to Part VI to the depositary towards the tax treaties of already existing treaty parties at the time that it chooses to apply this optional part on arbitration.

What is more, Article 28 of the MLI on reservations contains one more exception permitting the contracting parties to notify reservations for the first time after concluding the MLI. Article 28(9) of the MLI (which will be subsequently touched upon below in the context of the withdrawal or replacement of reservations) provides that '[a]ny Party which has made a reservation in accordance with paragraph 1 or 2 may at any time withdraw it or replace it with a more limited reservation by means of a notification

136. OECD, *Explanatory Statement to the MLI* (2016), *supra* n. 4, para. 307.
137. Article 29(6) of the MLI further specifies the time when additional notifications are to take effect.
138. OECD, *Explanatory Statement to the MLI* (2016), *supra* n. 4, para. 277.
139. OECD, *Explanatory Statement to the MLI* (2016), *supra* n. 4, paras 303–305.
140. OECD, *Explanatory Statement to the MLI* (2016), *supra* n. 4, para. 305.

addressed to the Depositary'. Its second sentence further provides that '[s]uch Party shall make any additional *notifications* pursuant to paragraph 6 of Article 29 (Notifications) which may be required as a result of the withdrawal or replacement of the reservation' (emphasis added).

It follows from this provision that a reservation that has already been made, may be withdrawn completely or exchanged only for a provision that is more limited in scope. If it therefore apparently seems to be intended by the drafters of MLI to allow parties that have made use of a reservation to lift only the limitations previously set by reservations,[141] it would be contradictory if parties that have not made use of reservations to a certain provision ever before were to be permitted to place new restrictions. This view is supported by the second sentence of Article 28(9) of the MLI allowing additional *notifications* with reference to Article 29(6) of the MLI required after withdrawing or replacing reservations. Due to this provision, the parties are expressly authorized to opt for one alternative provided by Article 13 of the MLI, for example, after withdrawing the reservation that was made for that entire provision at the time of concluding the MLI. As this provision was apparently included to clarify that additional *notifications* for opt-in clauses and alternative provisions are always possible,[142] even in case of the withdrawal of reservations, no provision expressly permitting additional *reservations* in general was introduced into Article 28 of the MLI. *E contrario* one can therefore conclude that the intention of the drafters was to exclude the general possibility of making additional *reservations* after entering into the MLI.[143] Apart from the exceptions explicitly set out by Article 28(6) of the MLI, one can conclude that reservations that are not made at the time of entering into the MLI should not be permissible.

In sum, whereas it could be derived that it should be in line with Article 29(6) of the MLI for the parties to the MLI to be allowed to add opt-in clauses and alternative provisions not previously exercised to the list of notifications being at the disposal of the depositary, it is not permitted to subsequently notify further reservations or opt-out clauses. One plausible reason for the different treatment of first-time exercise of opt-in clauses as well as alternative provisions on the one hand, and opt-out clauses or reservations on the other, could possibly lie in the promotion of the objective of the MLI.[144] Whenever parties voluntarily opt-in into an obligation within the MLI, be it at the time of conclusion of the treaty or at any later moment, the additional commitment is considered to be in pursuit of the treaty objective. The same is true for alternative provisions that offer the possibility not to choose any of the alternatives provided by

141. OECD, *Explanatory Statement to the MLI* (2016), *supra* n. 4, para. 282.
142. OECD, *Explanatory Statement to the MLI* (2016), *supra* n. 4, para. 304.
143. In addition, the Explanatory Statement emphasizes that the possibility of replacement of a reservation cannot be used to place new restrictions on the modifications of a party's covered tax treaties. This explanation could also imply that the establishment of 'new restrictions' in general is not permitted by the MLI as well. OECD, *Explanatory Statement to the MLI* (2016), *supra* n. 4, para. 282.
144. OECD, *Explanatory Statement to the MLI* (2016), *supra* n. 4, para. 1.

the MLI. If a party decides to opt for one of the alternatives provided at a later point in time, it makes perfect sense that this choice should be accepted by the MLI.

By contrast, reservations generally pursue a different aim, namely to minimize the scope of the application of the MLI.[145] If additional reservations were to be made at any time, this would run counter to the treaty objective of targeting BEPS and would thereby move the parties further away from achieving the treaty purpose. As reservations typically reduce the overall commitment, the parties are not absolutely free to add as many reservations as they want after entering into the MLI. The only reservations that may be made after becoming a treaty party are limited. Obviously, it would be reasonable, for instance, to leave the parties the right to choose the level of commitment that they are prepared to undertake towards each party and especially vis-à-vis new parties.[146] Therefore, those reservations are permitted that allow a party to reserve the rights not to apply provisions towards new parties.

3.3.3 *Change or Replacement of Options after Conclusion*

The discussion here will investigate how a change in options is governed by the MLI. Under Article 28(9) of the MLI, the replacement of reservations or opt-out clauses is allowed as long as the replaced reservation is less strict than the reservation exercised before. The Explanatory Statement gives further guidance on the interpretation and application of the conditions for the replacement of reservations.[147] Thus, a party that initially reserved the right not to apply the entirety of an article within the MLI would be allowed to reduce the scope of that reservation and its field of application to a certain provision of the same article concerned. By means of an example, it is explained in the Explanatory Statement that the opposite scenario would be prohibited due to the limitation on replacing reservations.[148] Thus, a situation in which a more limited reservation was previously made and the party subsequently prefers the expansion of the scope of the reservation to the entire provision would not be covered by the authorization.

At any time after entering into the MLI, a party could change its point of view and prefer another alternative over the alternative that was exercised before. For this reason, it is necessary to examine whether the replacement of an alternative option that has already been exercised by a contracting party may fall within the meaning of an 'additional notification' under Article 29(6) of the MLI. As stated, the term 'additional' basically implies that the notification is made in addition to another. Put simply, the replacement of a provision, however, actually means nothing other than the withdrawal of one option combined with the exercise of a different one.

145. This is clear, as it, by definition (Art. 2(1)(d) Vienna Convention), excludes or modifies the legal effect of treaty provisions.
146. OECD, *Action 15 Final Report*, *supra* n. 6, para. 42.
147. OECD, *Explanatory Statement to the MLI* (2016), *supra* n. 4, para. 282.
148. OECD, *Explanatory Statement to the MLI* (2016), *supra* n. 4, para. 282.

Of course, one could argue that exercising a different option instead of the previous one can be interpreted as being an additional component of the list of notifications as it was, as a matter of fact, not included prior to the replacement. However, such an interpretation would not correspond to the true meaning of the word. Another argument speaking against the permissibility of a change in options can again be based on Article 28(9) of the MLI, which explicitly permits the withdrawal or replacement of reservations. Conversely, it could therefore be construed as implying that the replacement of (alternative) options by means of notifications is prohibited because, as would be the opposite case with reservations, it is not expressly allowed by the MLI.[149] In conclusion, the better arguments speak in favour of the view that an exchange of one alternative that was already exercised, with another alternative, is not permitted.

While the exchange of alternative provisions after entering into the MLI does not seem to be intended within the MLI, the replacement of reservations with others is allowed, although restricted to reservations more limited in scope. The reason for prohibiting a permanent possibility to switch between alternatives could be the intentional avoidance of frequent modifications which would make the application of the MLI even more difficult in practice.[150] Moreover, continuous changes would not only be complicated, but would also be contrary to the principle of legal certainty. This is why, in principle, the parties to the MLI should be bound by their decisions and should not change the applicable provisions on a case-by-case basis. However, with regard to reservations, there is an exception to this rationale. On the grounds that a switch from strict reservations to more limited ones generally contributes to the objectives of the MLI, those kinds of amendments seem to be exceptionally accepted even though the principle of legal certainty is not adhered to. This is probably the reason why solely reservations aiming to ease restrictions previously made by the parties are permitted by the MLI.

3.3.4 Withdrawal of Options after Conclusion

Eventually, parties may have a legitimate interest to withdraw their choice of option completely. Again, Article 29 of the MLI on notifications does not provide an answer to the question as to whether opt-in clauses or alternative provisions exercised at the time of concluding the MLI may simply be withdrawn at a later point in time.[151] As no provision explicitly regulates the notifications of the withdrawal of an option, one should assume that such an action is not permitted by the MLI. Contrarily, as regards the withdrawal of reservations, Article 28(9) of the MLI serves as a legal basis which allows the parties to cancel a reservation to a provision that was notified earlier.[152]

149. Neither Art. 29(5) of the MLI nor the Explanatory Statement indicates that a replacement is permissible. OECD, *Explanatory Statement to the MLI* (2016), *supra* n. 4, paras 303–306.
150. OECD, *Action 15 Final Report*, *supra* n. 6, para. 50.
151. There is also no answer to this question in the Explanatory Statement. OECD, *Explanatory Statement to the MLI* (2016), *supra* n. 4, paras 292–309.
152. OECD, *Explanatory Statement to the MLI* (2016), *supra* n. 4, para. 282.

The justification for expressly permitting the withdrawal of reservations could be based on the fact that the cancellation of reservations means a step forward with regard to fulfilling the objective of the MLI. Fewer reservations inevitably lead to an increase in commitment. On the other hand, the non-inclusion of such possibility with relation to notifications could be substantiated by the fact that the withdrawal of opt-in clauses or alternative provisions previously chosen and applied does not represent progress, but rather a step backwards considering the treaty objectives.

4 CONCLUSION

In the MLI opt-in clauses, opt-out clauses and alternative provisions are included so as to provide flexibility to the treaty parties. Those three mechanisms are exercised by the parties by means of notifications and reservations made to the depositary when entering into the MLI. One issue that could play a major role in practice concerns the possibility of reversing options previously exercised. As a general rule, notifications with regard to opt-in clauses and alternative provisions are permissible as long as further commitment in fulfilment of the objectives of the MLI is pursued. Thus, only (additional) notifications for options not notified at the time of conclusion of the treaty are later permitted. However, the application of opt-out clauses or reservations shows an effect in the opposite direction. Thus, it is not the inclusion of reservations that advances the purpose of the treaty, but rather the exclusion or reduction thereof. As the withdrawal or replacement of reservations with less restrictive reservations favours the achievement of the treaty objectives, it is expressly permitted by the MLI.

The reversal of options by which the purpose of the MLI is contradicted is generally not possible within the MLI. Treaty parties still wanting to reduce their level of commitment by means of reversing the options exercised earlier will need to do so indirectly. Article 30 of the MLI, for example, enshrines the possibility to subsequently modify underlying bilateral tax treaties by way of individual agreement of new provisions or conditions with the other contracting party.[153] To avoid the re-negotiation of numerous bilateral tax treaties to modify the options exercised once, the parties concerned could also consider withdrawing from the MLI under Article 37 thereof and subsequently re-entering into the MLI.[154]

153. *See also* OECD, *Explanatory Statement to the MLI* (2016), *supra* n. 4, para. 310.
154. *See also* OECD, *Explanatory Statement to the MLI* (2016), *supra* n. 4, para. 351.

CHAPTER 8

Reservations to the Multilateral Instrument

Benjamin Walker

1 INTRODUCTION

This chapter is dedicated to reservations to the multilateral instrument (MLI). The reservation mechanism is a key feature of the MLI, and stakeholders need to carefully consider its full implications. Section 2 provides a brief discussion of the history of reservations in international law and some key debates that have shaped the development of reservations. Section 3, the largest section of this chapter, comprehensively analyses Article 28 ('Reservation article') and covers the four major categories of reservations under the MLI, namely minimum standard reservations, non-minimum standard reservations, arbitration reservations and other reservations. A technical analysis of Article 28 reveals how the drafters have placed a strong emphasis on certainty through their use of long and complex reservation provisions. Furthermore, this section considers some potential legal issues arising from the MLI. While the author advocates good faith from the parties, reservations under the MLI provide parties with several different policy options, and the potential for mischievous strategies against the intent of the MLI is quite high.

2 BACKGROUND

2.1 Generally

The MLI easily represents the single greatest change to the business of concluding double taxation conventions (hereinafter 'tax treaties') since the first tax treaty signed by Prussia and the Austrian-Hungarian Empire in 1899. The MLI has fundamentally altered the landscape of tax treaties between countries around the world. By late July 2017, sixty-eight jurisdictions had signed the MLI, encompassing over 1,000 tax treaties. Although there have been multilateral instruments for tax matters in the past,[1] the overwhelming majority of agreements occur bilaterally between countries. The MLI project is nothing short of a spectacular achievement in determination, irrespective of the validity of the approach.

Reservations are known by tax scholars, although only in the context of the OECD Model Tax Convention (OECD Model) and the commentary thereon (hereinafter 'the Commentary on the OECD Model'). Reservations are usually made by countries in the process of drafting the OECD Model and its commentary. Countries usually make reservations to reflect a position that is contrary to the final text or where they adopt a different approach. In any case, they are regarded as exceptional. Furthermore, the OECD Model and its commentary are not considered hard law. However, reservations under the MLI are a key and fundamental part of the MLI. They are considered as opt-out provisions and standard under international law. Therefore, tax scholars will need to grasp the scope of reservations and their implications for tax treaties.

Reservations under the MLI are a key component and without such reservations, the MLI would fall apart as countries could not sign on to such sweeping changes where there is a lack of political will or their own agreements are simply different. Hence, the reservations permit political agreement and allow countries to at least come to the table. They allow countries to commit to certain minimum standards which are generally accepted, while opting-out of enhanced measures. It is clear that the OECD invested heavily in the reservations section as reflected in the so-called speed-dating sessions where countries came together and attempted to agree on specific applicable provisions. Before analysing the MLI, however, it is necessary to briefly consider how a reservation is defined and how reservations have been used under international law.

2.2 What Constitutes a Reservation?

The Vienna Convention on the Law of Treaties (hereinafter 'the Vienna Convention'), defines a reservation as 'a unilateral statement, however phrased or named, made by a State, when signing, ratifying, accepting, approving or acceding to a treaty, whereby it purports to exclude or to modify the legal effect of certain provisions of the treaty in their application to that State'.[2]

A reservation is used in international treaties as a tool to include as many parties as possible (i.e., universality of parties). As states will seldom agree on every article, a reservation allows a party to choose its obligations and still sign the underlying agreement. At the same time, reservations should not fundamentally erode the terms of the agreement (i.e., integrity of terms). Whenever reservations are used, there is a balancing act between universality of the parties and integrity of terms.[3] Drafting an

1. Nordic Double Taxation Convention (1983); South-East European Multilateral Double Taxation Agreement (1922); Double Taxation Convention of the ANDEAN Group (1971).
2. Article 2.1(d).
3. C. Walter, *Art. 19: Formulation of Reservations*, in *Vienna Convention on the Law of Treaties: A Commentary*, at 240 (O. Dörr & K. Schmalenbach eds., Springer-Verlag Berlin Heidelberg 2012).

international agreement that carefully balances these two factors is a difficult task, and the use of reservations in previous international treaties illustrates this difficult balancing act.

2.3 History

The first reservation made in an international treaty was between Sweden and Norway in the Final Act of the Vienna Congress in 1815.[4] The doctrine of unanimity was prevalent in the nineteenth century, whereby all parties to the treaty had to agree to the reservation; otherwise the party that made the reservation must remove the reservation or withdraw from the treaty altogether. The integrity of terms was more important than universality of the parties (drafting an agreement acceptable to the largest number of parties). This approach was followed in the twentieth century by the League of Nations. However, the Pan-American Union used a different approach, namely that objections to a reservation did not exclude the contracting state, but rather that objection affected only that clause.[5]

The International Court of Justice opinion adopted a new approach which advocated an object and purpose test.[6] If a reservation is against the object and purpose of the international treaty and parties object, the reservation is not part of the treaty. This approach ultimately found its way into the Vienna Convention on the Law of Treaties concluded in 1969.

2.4 Vienna Convention on the Law of Treaties

Articles 19–23 under section 2 of the Vienna Convention provide the interpretation of reservations under international law. Given that the MLI is a multilateral treaty under international law, a brief summary of the key points is necessary.

Section 2 of the Vienna Convention establishes that the text of the treaty is paramount. However, in certain cases where the text does not provide, the object and purpose of the treaty are relevant. Article 19 sets forth how reservations are formulated. A reservation is allowed no later than when acceding to a treaty if the text of the treaty allows for such a reservation (Article 19(a) and (b)) or if Article 19(a) and (b) are not applicable, the reservation is not incompatible with the object and purpose of the treaty. Article 20 covers acceptance of, and objection to reservations. Acceptance of a reservation is generally not required unless (i) expressly provided or (ii) the object and purpose of the treaty requires acceptance. Article 21 outlines the legal effects of reservations and of obligations to reservations. The effect is relatively simple: the reservation is applicable only to the specific provision in question and it applies

4. Walter, *supra* n. 3, at 242.
5. Walter, *supra* n. 3, at 243.
6. ICJ, *Reservation to the Convention on the Prevention and Punishment of the Crime of Genocide* (Advisory Opinion) [1951] ICJ Rep. 15 et seq.

between the reserving state and the other relevant states. Article 22 covers withdrawal of reservations and of objections to reservations. A state may generally withdraw a reservation or objection unless the text of the treaty provides otherwise. Article 23 covers the procedure regarding reservations, under which any reservation must generally be in writing and communicated to the other parties.

Another significant source of law is the International Law Commission (ILC). Since 1993, the ILC has produced many reports covering various issues under the Vienna Convention. A 1995 report stated that the ILC should act as a guide to the Vienna Convention.[7] Thus, any serious discussions about the interpretation of the Vienna Convention must involve the ILC reports. The reader will later discover that the MLI has taken some elements of the Vienna Convention and incorporated them into the MLI.[8]

3 RESERVATION ARTICLE

3.1 Rationale of the MLI

There have been efforts in the past to conclude multilateral double taxation conventions (hereinafter 'multilateral tax treaties') with some success.[9] Furthermore, the European Union has concluded a number of tax-related treaties.[10] However, the vast majority of tax treaties are concluded bilaterally, and efforts to conclude a multilateral tax treaty have failed.[11] There are a number of obstacles to multilateral tax treaties, including substantial work input, divergent tax systems and economic relations.[12] The perceived abuse of tax systems by large multinational enterprises has spurred efforts to counter such behaviour by governments across the world, culminating in the 15 Actions of the OECD/G20 Base Erosion and Profit Shifting (BEPS) project. Action 15 was initiated to develop a MLI to allow countries to swiftly implement the Actions without the burdensome task of renegotiating all tax treaties. After two years of work, the final MLI was released, along with an Explanatory Statement, on 24 November 2016.[13]

7. Walter, *supra* n. 3, at 244.
8. For example, Art. 28(3).
9. Nordic Double Taxation Convention (1983); South-East European Multilateral Double Taxation Agreement (1922); Double Taxation Convention of the ANDEAN Group (1971).
10. European Convention on Mutual Assistance (1988); Parent-Subsidiary Directive of the European Community (1990); The Arbitration Convention (1990).
11. For example, the League of Nations, European Economic Community and European Free Trade Association.
12. H. Loukota, *Multilateral Tax Treaty Versus Bilateral Treaty Network*, in *Multilateral Tax Treaties: New Developments in International Tax Law*, Series on International Taxation, at 95 (M. Lang, H. Loukota & J. Schuch eds., Kluwer Law International 1998).
13. OECD, *Multilateral Convention to Implement Tax Treaty Related Measures to Prevent Base Erosion And Profit Shifting* (2016); OECD, *Explanatory Statement to the Multilateral Convention to Implement Tax Treaty Related Measures to Prevent Base Erosion and Profit Shifting* (2016).

3.2 Reservations under the MLI

The MLI contains a wide range of reservations in nearly all articles and it can be somewhat overwhelming for the reader. The drafters of the MLI have clearly favoured the use of reservations as a tool to increase the universality of the parties. The carefully pre-defined reservations ensure a high degree of certainty. Article 28 deals exclusively with how reservations function under the MLI. Therefore, it is necessary to analyse Article 28 and the four major categories of reservations.

3.3 Scope

Article 28(1) provides that no reservations may be made to the MLI unless expressly permitted in Article 28(1)(a) through (u). Article 28(1)(a) through (u) cover various articles in the MLI which contain a specific reservation clause. The reservations allowed under the various articles relate to minimum standard provisions (i.e., where a party must meet the minimum standard of the provision) and non-minimum standard provisions (i.e., where a party is not required to meet the minimum standard of the provision). Thus, the MLI is explicitly clear about what reservations may be made, and the corollary is a high degree of certainty. The downside of this approach is a relatively technical MLI, which parties will need to read carefully in order to fully comprehend. Parties need to read every reservation provision contained in Article 28(1)(a) through (u) and assess their reservation options. Reservations are not subject to acceptance. If one party makes a reservation under the MLI, the old provision between the reserving party and all other parties remains applicable. Article 28(1) does not apply to reservations under Part VI (Arbitration).

Part VI is an optional provision for parties covering mandatory binding arbitration of mutual agreement procedures. It contains a comprehensive section for arbitration between two states where competent authorities are unable to reach an agreement within a fixed period of time. Parties must notify the depositary that they are opting in to the provision. Article 28(2) provides a specific rule for a party opting to apply Part VI (Arbitration). A party may formulate one or more reservations in respect of 'scope of cases' eligible for arbitration under the provisions of Part VI, which the author categorizes as arbitration reservations. Furthermore, there are specific reservations allowed in Part VI which also constitute arbitration reservations.[14] However, such reservations are subject to acceptance.[15] A reservation is 'accepted by a party if it has not notified the depositary that it objects to the reservations by the end of a period of twelve months beginning on the date of notification of the reservation by the depositary or by the date on which it deposits its instrument of ratification, acceptance, or approval, whichever is later'.[16]

All parties, therefore, must be observant of all reservations made in relation to Part VI and carefully consider their response to any reservations. The Sub-Group had

14. Article 28(2)(a).
15. Article 28(2)(b).
16. Article 28(2)(b).

considered using a list of defined reservations with regard to scope of cases; however it was unlikely that a consensus could be reached on such a list and, therefore, parties are given the opportunity to tailor their scope of cases.[17]

Article 28(2)(a) also provides that a party may choose to apply Part VI after it becomes a party to the MLI and that reservations must be made at the same time as the party's notification to the depositary. Thus, a party could choose note to opt in to Part VI, assess how other parties react to Part VI, and then act accordingly.[18]

3.4 Categories of Reservations

Before further analysing Article 28, it is necessary to categorize the different reservations applicable under the MLI, as they have different legal effects. As stated above, the MLI contains four major categories of reservations, namely minimum standard reservations, non-minimum standard reservations, arbitration reservations and other reservations.

3.4.1 Minimum Standard Reservations

Minimum standard reservations are reservations relating to articles which form part of the minimum standard for BEPS, i.e., standards that must be followed by parties as part of the BEPS project. These articles include: Purpose of a Covered Tax Agreement (Article 6), Prevention of Treaty Abuse (Article 7), Mutual Agreement Procedure (Article 16) and Corresponding Adjustments (Article 17). These are where parties may not reserve the entire article, but may make other reservations where existing provisions already meet the minimum standard or parties intend to meet the standard. Thus, parties need to carefully consider their existing agreements and assess whether the standard is already met. While this chapter does not provide a comprehensive analysis of the underlying measures, it is necessary to describe briefly the relevant measures and how the reservations relate thereto.

Article 6: Purpose of a Covered Tax Agreement

Article 6 concerns the purpose of a covered tax agreement. It reflects a minimum standard for protection against the abuse of treaties under Action 6. Article 6 modifies the preamble text of each covered tax agreement to include:

> Intending to eliminate double taxation with respect to the taxes covered by this agreement without creating opportunities for non-taxation or reduced taxation through tax evasion or avoidance (including through treaty-shopping arrangements aimed at obtaining reliefs provided in this agreement for the indirect benefit of residents of third jurisdictions).[19]

17. OECD, *Explanatory Statement*, *supra* n. 13, Art. 28, para. 2.
18. For a policy discussion, *see* section 4.
19. MLI, Art. 6(1).

Article 6(4) provides that a party may, however, reserve the right not to apply Article 6(1) where the covered tax agreement already contains such preamble language describing the intent of the contracting jurisdictions to eliminate double taxation without creating opportunities for non-taxation or reduced taxation, whether that language is limited to cases of tax evasion or avoidance (including through treaty-shopping arrangements aimed at obtaining relief under the covered tax agreement for the indirect benefit of residents of third jurisdictions) or applies more broadly. As the Explanatory Statement is silent on what exactly constitutes 'preamble language', parties need to carefully consider whether existing agreements already meet this standard. However, the existing language must at least mention tax evasion or avoidance.

Article 7: Prevention of Treaty Abuse

Article 7 deals with prevention of treaty abuse. The minimum standard is that parties must include:[20]

- a principal-purpose test only;
- a principal-purpose test *and* either a simplified or detailed limitation-on-benefits provision; or
- a detailed limitation-on-benefits provision including a mechanism dealing with conduit arrangements.

Article 7(1) contains the principal-purpose test. Action 6 provides three alternative rules to address treaty abuse, namely the principal-purpose test, a simplified limitation-on-benefits or a detailed limitation-on-benefits provision. Article 7(3) simply allows parties that have not opted out of the principal-purpose test under Article 7(15)(a), to choose to include Article 7(4) in its covered tax agreements. Article 7(4) reflects the additional provision with some minor changes and is an optional provision; it will apply only where all contracting jurisdictions have chosen to apply it by making a notification under Article 7(17)(b).

Article 7(15) defines the main reservations allowed under Article 7. Article 7(15)(a) allows parties to reserve Article 7(1) (principal-purpose test) where they intend to adopt a combination of a detailed limitation-on-benefits and either rules to address conduit financing structures or a principal-purpose-test provision. Article 7(15)(b) allows parties to reserve Article 7(1) and (4) with respect to covered tax agreements that already contain a principal-purpose test. Article 7(15)(c) allows parties to reserve a simplified limitation-on-benefits in respect of covered tax agreements that already contain a limitation-on-benefits provision described in Article 7(14).

Article 16: Mutual Agreement Procedure

Article 16 outlines the mutual agreement procedure and reflects Action 14. Article 16(1) through (3) are based on the text of Article 25(1) of the OECD Model. Article 16(1) allows a person to present a case to a competent authority of either contracting

20. MLI, Art. 7(1).

jurisdiction where that person considers that the covered tax agreement has not been followed. Article 16(2) provides that the competent authority shall endeavour to resolve the case by mutual agreement with the other competent authority where the objection is satisfied and they cannot reach a satisfactory solution.

Article 16(5) defines the reservations allowed under Article 16. It is intended to reflect variations in the way the minimum standard can be implemented. Article 16(5)(a) allows a party to reserve the first sentence of Article 16(1) where it intends to meet the minimum standard by allowing a taxpayer to present a case to the competent authority of the contracting jurisdiction of which it is a resident and that contracting jurisdiction will implement a bilateral notification or consultation process with the competent authority of the other contracting jurisdiction for cases presented by the taxpayers to its competent authority in which its competent authority does not consider the taxpayer's objection to be justified.[21]

Article 16(5)(b) allows a party to reserve the second sentence of Article 16(1) where it intends to meet the minimum standard by ensuring that for purposes of all such covered tax agreements, the taxpayer referred to in Article 16(1) may present the case within a period of at least three years from the first notification of the action resulting in taxation not in accordance with the provisions of the covered tax agreement.

Article 16(5)(c) allows a party to reserve the second sentence of Article 16(2). This is allowed where, for purposes of all of its covered tax agreements, either: (i) all agreements reached via mutual agreement procedure shall be implemented notwithstanding any time limits in the domestic law of the contracting jurisdiction; or (ii) it intends to meet the minimum standard by accepting, in its bilateral treaty negotiations, alternative treaty provisions that limit the time during which a contracting jurisdiction may make an adjustment pursuant to provisions modelled after Article 9(1) or Article 7(2) of the OECD Model, in order to avoid late adjustments with regard to which mutual agreement procedure relief will not be available.[22]

Article 17: Corresponding Adjustments

Article 17 provides for the possibility of jurisdictions to use corresponding adjustments unilaterally in cases where a taxpayer objects under the mutual agreement procedure in transfer pricing cases. Article 17(1) is based on Article 9(2) of the OECD Model. Article 17(2) provides a compatibility clause that Article 17(1) shall apply in place of or in the absence of a provision requiring that a contracting jurisdiction shall make a corresponding adjustment where the other contracting jurisdiction makes an adjustment that reflects the arm's length profits of an enterprise.

Article 17(3) defines the reservations allowed under Article 17. Article 17(1) is not required as part of the Action 14 minimum standard, although jurisdictions are required to (i) provide access to the mutual agreement procedure in transfer pricing cases and (ii) implement the resulting mutual agreement. Article 17(3) provides for a number of reservation options. Parties may reserve the entire article where its covered

21. OECD, *Explanatory Statement*, *supra* n. 13, Art. 7, para. 5.
22. OECD, *Explanatory Statement*, *supra* n. 13, Art. 16, para. 5.

tax agreement already contains such a provision described in Article 17(2). To reflect this, parties shall make the appropriate adjustments referred to in Article 17(1) or its competent authority shall endeavour to resolve the case under the mutual agreement procedure. Furthermore, where a party has made a reservation under Article 16(5)(c)(ii) to reserve the right for Article 17 not to apply to its covered tax agreements on the basis that in its bilateral treaty negotiations, it shall accept a treaty provision of the type contained in Article 17(1). A party may also reserve the right for Article 17 not to apply to its covered tax agreements that already contain a provision of the same type.

3.4.2 Non-minimum Standard Reservations

Unlike the minimum standard reservations, non-minimum standard reservations are applicable to articles which do not form part of the minimum standard that must be implemented by parties. Therefore, parties are able to reserve the right to not apply the entire article.

Article 3: Transparent Entities

Article 3 covers income earned through transparent entities. Article 3(4) is the compatibility clause which provides that Article 3(1):

> shall apply in place of or in the absence of provisions of a Covered Tax Agreement to the extent that they address whether income derived by or through entities or arrangements that are treated as fiscally transparent under the tax law of either Contracting Jurisdiction (whether through a general rule or by identifying in detail the treatment of specific fact patterns and types of entities or arrangement) shall be treated as income of a resident of a Contracting Jurisdiction.

Article 3(5) defines the reservations allowed under Article 3. Article 3(5)(a) provides that a party can reserve the entirety of the article. Article 3(5)(b) allows a party to reserve Article 3(1) to covered tax agreements that already contain a provision described in Article 3(4). A party may also to reserve Article 3(1) to covered tax agreements that already contains a provision described in Article 3(4): which denies treaty benefits in the case of income derived by or through an entity or arrangement established in third jurisdictions (Article 3(5)(c)); which identifies in detail the treatment of specific fact patterns and types of entities or arrangements (Article 3(5)(d)); which identifies in detail the treatment of specific fact patterns and types of entities or arrangements and denies treaty benefits in the case of income derived by or through an entity or arrangement established in a third jurisdiction (Article 3(5)(e)); which identifies in detail the treatment of specific fact patterns and type of entities or arrangements (Article 3(5)(g)). Article 3(5)(f) allows a party to reserve Article 3(2).

Article 4: Dual-Resident Entities

Article 4 provides the rules for determining the treaty residence of a person other than an individual that is resident of more than one contracting state. The contracting states shall endeavour by mutual agreement to determine which state the person is a resident. If there is no agreement between the states, such person is not entitled to any relief.

Article 4(3) defines the reservations allowed under Article 4. Article 4(3)(a) allows a party to reserve the entirety of Article 4, and Article 4(3)(b) through (d) allow a party to reserve the right not to apply the entirety of Article 4 to covered tax agreements that contain provisions with specific, objectively defined characteristics. Article 4(3)(e) allows to a party to replace the text of Article 4(1) with a separate text. Article 4(3)(f) allows a party to reserve the entirety of Article 4 with parties that have made the reservation in Article 4(3)(e).

Article 5: Application of Methods for Elimination of Double Taxation

Article 5 provides three alternative means to address problems arising from the inclusion of the exemption method in treaties with respect to items of income that are not taxed in the state of source. Article 5(8) and (9) define the reservations allowed under Article 5. Article 5(8) allows a party to reserve the right not to apply the entire article with respect to one or more identified covered tax agreements if they do not choose one of the three alternative options. This provision is unique for the MLI, as in all other provisions that allow a party to reserve the right not to apply an entire article, there is no requirement to identify which agreements are applicable. Parties will need to carefully consider which agreements they wish to identify.

Article 5(9) allows a party that does not choose Option C (one of the three alternatives) to reserve the right not to permit the other contracting jurisdiction to apply Option C. The party must also identify which covered tax agreement is applicable.

Article 8: Dividend Transfer Transactions

Article 8 provides for a minimum shareholding period for a company to be entitled to a reduced rate of taxation on dividends from a subsidiary. Article 8(3) defines the reservations allowed under Article 8. Article 8(3)(a) allows a party to reserve the entirety of Article 8. Article 8(3)(b) allows a party to reserve the right not to apply the entirety of Article 8 to covered tax agreements that contain a minimum holding period. Covered tax agreements often contain two different rates, namely a reduced rate for a minimum shareholding period and a higher rate where the period is not met. Article 8(1) adds a minimum shareholding period for the latter rate. Article 8(3)(b)(ii) and (iii) allow a party to choose to preserve a minimum shareholding period included in provisions of a covered tax agreement that is shorter or longer than 365 days.

Article 9: Capital Gains from Alienation of Shares or Interests of Entities Deriving their Value Principally from Immovable Property

Article 9 deals with situations where assets are contributed to an entity shortly before the sale of shares or comparable interests in that entity in order to dilute the proportion of the value of the entity that is derived from immovable property.[23]

Article 9(6) defines the reservations allowed under Article 9. Article 9(6)(a) allows a party to reserve the right not to apply the entirety of Article 9. Article 9(6)(b)

23. OECD, *Explanatory Statement*, *supra* n. 13, Art. 9, para. 1.

and (c) allow parties to opt out of either Article 9(1)(a) or (b) separately. Article 9(5)(d) and (e) allow parties to opt out of Article 9(1)(a) where a covered tax agreement already contains a provision that includes a testing period or a provision that applies to alienation of interests other than shares, respectively. Article 9(6)(f) allows parties to opt out of Article 9(4) where a covered tax agreement already contains provisions described in Article 9(5).

Article 10: Anti-Abuse Rule of Permanent Establishments Situated in Third Jurisdictions

Article 10 provides an anti-abuse rule for permanent establishments situated in third jurisdictions. The article provides that the benefits of a treaty will not apply to any item of income on which the tax rate in the third jurisdiction in which an exempt permanent establishment is located is less than 60% of the tax that would be imposed in the contracting jurisdiction of an enterprise.

Article 10(5) defines the reservations allowed under Article 10. Article 10(5)(a) allows a party to reserve the right not to apply the entirety of Article 10. Article 10(5)(b) allows a party to opt out of Article 10 where a covered tax agreement already contains the provisions described in Article 10(4). Article 10(5)(c) allows parties to apply Article 10 only to its covered tax agreement that already contain the provisions described in Article 10(4).

Article 11: Application of Tax Agreements to Restrict a Party's Right to Tax Its Own Residents

Article 11 deals with the so-called saving clause which preserves the right of a contracting jurisdiction to tax its own residents.

Article 11(3) defines the reservations allowed under Article 11. Article 11(3)(a) allows a party to reserve the entirety of Article 11. Article 11(3)(b) allows a party to opt out of Article 11 where a covered tax agreement already contains a provision described in Article 11(2).

Article 12: Artificial Avoidance of Permanent Establishment Status through Commissionaire Arrangements and Similar Strategies

Article 12 deals with the changes to Article 5(5) and (6) of the OECD Model. The changes were made to prevent commissionaire and similar strategies from falling outside the agency PE classification.

Article 12(4) defines the reservations allowed under Article 12. Article 12(4) allows a party to reserve the right not to apply the entirety of Article 12. There are no other reservations allowed. This is because the previous agency PE classification is so widely used by contracting parties that there are no real other provisions which could be considered as equivalent. Thus, the decision as to whether to reserve under Article 12 is relatively straight-forward.

Article 13: Artificial Avoidance of Permanent Establishment Status Through the Specific Activity Exemptions

Article 13 deals with changes to Article 5(4) of the OECD Model. Article 5(4) includes a list of exceptions to permanent establishment status. The changes are intended to make it more difficult to fall under the paragraph and prevent the deemed existence of a permanent establishment. A party may choose to apply Article 5(2) (Option A) or Article 5(3) (Option B), or to apply neither option.

Article 13(6) defines the reservations allowed under Article 13. Article 13(6)(a) allows a party to reserve the right not to apply the entirety of Article 13. Article 13(6)(b) allows a party that chooses to apply Option A to also reserve the right for Option A not to apply to provisions of a covered tax agreement that already explicitly state that the activities listed therein shall be deemed not to constitute a permanent establishment only if they are of a preparatory or auxiliary character. Article 13(6)(c) allows a party to reserve the right not to apply Article 13(4).

Article 14: Splitting up of Contracts

Article 14 deals with the prevention of PE status under Article 5(3) of the OECD Model (construction site permanent establishment) by the splitting up of contracts. Article 14(3) defines the reservations allowed under Article 14. Article 14(3)(a) allows a party to reserve the right not to apply the entirety of Article 14. Article 14(3)(b) allows a party to reserve the entirety of Article 14 with respect to covered tax agreements relating to the exploration of natural resources.

Article 15: Definition of a Person Closely Related to an Enterprise

Article 15 covers the definition of a 'person closely related to an Enterprise' as it relates to the various changes made under Articles 12–14 of the MLI. Article 15(2) defines the reservations allowed under Article 15. Parties may reserve the right not to apply the entirety of Article 15 where a reservation has been made Article 12(4), Article 13(6)(a) or (c) and Article 14(3)(a).

3.4.3 *Arbitration Reservations*

As mentioned, Part VI is an opt-in provision. Furthermore, parties may reserve the scope of cases under Part VI. However, there are also defined reservations allowed within Part VI which are important to note. Given that Part IV is an opt-in provision, the author has presented these reservations as a separate category; however the reservations operate similar to the minimum standard reservations as articles in Part VI may not be entirely reserved not to apply.

Article 19: Mandatory Binding Arbitration

Article 19 deals with issues submitted by the taxpayer for arbitration where contracting states are unable to reach an agreement under the mutual agreement procedure.

Article 19(11) and (12) define the reservations allowed under Article 19. Article 19(11) allows a party to reserve the right to replace the two-year period contained in Article 19(1)(b) with a three-year period. Article 19(12) gives priority to decisions by a court or administrative tribunal. Article 19(12)(a) allows a party to make a reservation for arbitration issues to which a decision on this issue has already been rendered by a court or administrative tribunal of either contracting state. Article 19(12)(b) allows a party to make a reservation in instances where a decision has been rendered by a court or administrative tribunal of one of the contracting jurisdictions after a request for arbitration has been made. In that case, the arbitration process shall terminate.

Article 23: Type of Arbitration Process

Article 23 deals with the default rules with respect to the type of arbitration process. Article 23(2), (3), (6) and (7) define the reservations allowed under Article 23. Article 23(2) allows a party to reserve the right not to apply Article 23(1). In such cases, the competent authorities may mutually agree on different rules. Otherwise, Article 23(1)(a) through (c) provide procedural rules known as the 'independent opinion' approach.

Article 23(3) allows a party that has not made a reservation under Article 23(2) to reserve the right to not apply Article 23(1) and (2) to covered tax agreements with parties that have made such a reservation. In such a case, competent authorities of the contracting jurisdictions should attempt to reach an agreement in relation to those covered tax agreements. Where there is no agreement, Article 19 (Mandatory Binding Arbitration) will not apply to those covered tax agreements.

Article 23(6) allows a party, other than a party that has chosen to apply Article 23(5), to reserve the right not to apply Article 23(5) with respect to one or more identified covered tax agreements. However, Article 23(7) allows a party that has chosen to apply Article 23(5), to reserve the right for Part VI not to apply with respect to any covered tax agreement for which the other contracting jurisdiction has made the reservation pursuant to Article 23(6).

Article 24: Agreement on a Different Resolution

Article 24 allows parties to agree on a different resolution within three calendar months after an arbitration decision has been made. Article 24(3) defines the reservations under Article 24. Article 24(3) allows a party that chooses to apply Article 24(2), to reserve the right for Article 24(2) to apply only with respect to its covered tax agreements for which Article 23(2) ('independent opinion' approach) applies.

Article 26: Compatibility

Article 26 deals with the interaction between the provisions of Part VI and the provision of covered tax agreements that provide for arbitration of mutual agreement procedure. Although other parts of the MLI include a compatibility clause, Article 26 consolidates the rules for compatibility into one provision. Article 26(4) defines the reservations allowed under Article 26. Article 26(4) allows a party to reserve the right not to apply Part VI to one or more identified covered tax agreements that already provide for mandatory arbitration of unresolved issues arising from a mutual agreement procedure case. 'Mandatory binding arbitration' is defined as 'if, under specific circumstances (such as a request by a person who presented the case), the competent authorities are required to submit issues arising in a mutual agreement procedure case that are not resolved after a specific amount of time to arbitration, and the outcome of that arbitration is binding on the competent authorities'.[24]

3.4.4 *Other Reservations*

There are also reservations in relation to Articles 35 (Entry into Effect) and 36 (Entry into Effect of Part VI). Article 35(6) and (7) define the reservations allowed under Article 35. Article 35(6) allows a party to reserve the right not to apply Article 35(4). Article 35(4) provides that Article 16 (Mutual Agreement Procedure) shall have effect with respect to a covered tax agreement for a case presented to the competent authority of a contracting jurisdiction on or after the latest of the dates on which the Convention enters into force, except for certain cases. Article 35(7) allows a number of reservations in relation to the entry into force of various provisions. It allows parties to change references to suit their own time commitments.

Article 36(2) defines the reservations allowed under Article 36. Article 36(2) allows a party to reserve the right for Part VI (Arbitration) to apply to a case presented to the competent authority of a contracting jurisdiction prior to the later of the dates on which the Convention enters into force for each of the contracting jurisdictions to the covered tax agreement only to the extent that the competent authorities of both contracting jurisdictions agree that it will apply to that specific case.

3.4.5 *Summary of Reservations*

A brief review of the various reservations under the MLI illustrates the complex nature of the various reservations. The author has distinguished the reservations into four clearly defined categories: minimum standard reservations, non-minimum standard reservations, arbitration reservations and other reservations. One clear problem is the likely difficulty for readers attempting to understand and interpret the MLI. However, it is necessary to further analyse the provisions of Article 28. The reader should have a good understanding of the different categories of reservations. Nevertheless, there are still a number of key areas which must be addressed here, namely legal effect of a reservation, timing of a reservation, notification of a reservation and later withdrawal.

3.5 Legal Effect of a Reservation

Article 28(3) provides for the legal effect of a reservation:

> Unless explicitly provided otherwise in the relevant provisions of this Convention, a reservation made in accordance with paragraph 1 or 2 shall:
>
> a) modify for the reserving Party in its relations with another Party the provisions of this Convention to which the reservation relates to the extent of the reservation; and

24. OECD, *Explanatory Statement*, *supra* n. 13, Art. 26, para. 4.

> b) modify those provisions to the same extent for the other Party in its relations with the reserving Party.

Article 28(3) simply confirms the effect of reservations made under Article 28(1) and (2). It mirrors Article 21(1) of the Vienna Convention. Article 28(3)(a) provides that the legal relations between the reserving state and those states which have not objected to the reservation are determined by the reservation. Article 28(3)(b) expresses the principle of reciprocity. Reciprocity, unlike other areas of international law,[25] is an important feature for international tax law. A reservation does not work only one way, but works both ways, providing symmetry. A clear inference is that only reservations made in accordance with Article 28(1) and (2) have the effect of modifying legal obligations. Reservations made under Article 28(1) are not subject to acceptance. Thus, the legal effect applies once a reservation has been made. However, as reservations under Article 28(2) are subject to acceptance, the legal effect applies only if the other parties do not object to the reservation.

The Explanatory Statement provides that:

> unless a provision of a Convention explicitly provides otherwise, a reservation will modify the relevant provisions of the Convention as between the reserving Party and *all other Parties to the Convention*, i.e. for the reserving Party in its relations with the other Parties and for those other Parties in their relations with the reserving Party. In other words, reservations will apply symmetrically, unless provided otherwise.[26]

This is a very significant point. When a party makes a reservation, unless otherwise provided, the reservation will apply to all other parties. Therefore, parties cannot simply pick and choose the countries to which it wishes to apply a reservation and others to which it does not. This is particularly relevant for the reservation of the scope of cases under Part VI. Party *X* cannot reserve a scope of cases for Party *Y* but not Party *Z*. However, parties may pick and choose a particular subset of reservations under Article 28(8).[27]

3.5.1 *Legal Consequences of Impermissible Reservations*

It is possible for a contracting party to make a reservation in contravention of the MLI. For example, a party could make a reservation expressly prohibited by the MLI or make a unilateral statement creating a reservation expressly allowed under the MLI, but not in accordance with the procedure laid down in the MLI. It may seem obvious to the reader that such a reservation is not valid, namely on account of the 'permissibility' theory.[28] This theory holds that validity of a reservation is determined solely on treaty

25. For example, international human rights law.
26. OECD, *Explanatory Statement*, *supra* n. 13, Art. 28, para. 3 (emphasis added).
27. *See* section 3.7 Notification of a reservation.
28. Walter, *supra* n. 3, at 255.

interpretation.[29] However, there is another theory, namely the 'opposability' doctrine. This theory holds that the validity of a reservation 'depends solely on the acceptance of the reservation by another contracting State'.[30] Thus, a reservation made in contravention of the MLI may be valid between the reserving state and all other contracting parties that accept the reservation.

As stated in section 2, Article 19 of the Vienna Convention provides for a three-tier test for the formulation of reservations. Article 19(b) allows reservations to be made where 'the treaty provides that only specified reservations...may be made'. The MLI, therefore, could fall under Article 19(b). The MLI reservations are reservations to specific provisions.[31] Therefore, an impermissible reservation has no legal effect.

Article 19(c) also provides the residual object and purpose test, which needs to be considered. It serves as a means to balance the interests of states to act in their national interest and the integrity of the terms. The test has been described as an 'enigma'[32] due to the difficulty of defining the object and purpose and applying it to real-world cases.

The ILC used the principle of Article 31 of the Vienna Convention to apply to define the object and purpose of a treaty:

> The object and purpose of the treaty is to be determined in good faith, taking account of the terms of the treaty in their context. Recourse may also be had in particular to the title of the treaty, preparatory work of the treaty and the circumstances of its conclusion and, where appropriate, the subsequent practice agreed upon by parties.[33]

The terms of the MLI and good faith between parties, therefore, are essential. The reservation article (Article 28) of the MLI is extremely complex and detailed compared to other international agreements. The drafters certainly favoured certainty over broad, flexible provisions. Good faith is an inherently difficult term to define and implement. However, implicit in good faith is that contracting parties act transparently and act in accordance with the terms of any agreements. Both strains of reasoning support the 'permissibility' theory, thus, only a reservation made in accordance to the MLI is valid for international legal purposes.

However, there is a significant caveat which developed known as the 'collective acceptance of all other contracting parties'.[34] A reservation which is prohibited or one which is incompatible with its object and purpose, is valid where all parties to an agreement do not object to a reservation which is prohibited or one which is

29. This view is supported by *Guide to Practice on Reservations to Treaties, sixty-third session*, UN, 2011 para. 4.5.3. and S.R. Pellet: 'A reservation formulated in spite of the express or implicit prohibition from the provisions of the treaty or from its incompatibility with the object and purpose of the treaty is not valid, without there being any need to distinguish between these two ground for invalidity.' 10th Report, Addendum 2 (n. 178), para. 187.
30. Walter, *supra* n. 3, at 255.
31. For example, the 1958 Geneva Convention on the Continental Shelf.
32. I. Buffard & K. Zemanek, *The 'Object and Purpose' of a Treaty: An Enigma?*, 3 Austrl. Rev. Int'l. & Eur. L., at 311, 342 (1998).
33. *Guide to Practice on Reservations to Treaties, supra* n. 29, para. 3.1.6.
34. Walter, *supra* n. 3, at 278.

incompatible with its object and purpose.[35] This amounts to an amendment of the treaty itself. The particular peculiarity of the MLI – in that it seeks to modify almost 2,000 bilateral tax treaties – however, needs to be considered. One deals, on the one hand, with a MLI and its components. On the other hand, it is the terms of the underlying covered tax agreements that are being modified. Any subsequent amendment is covered under the MLI. Article 30 addresses any subsequent modification of a covered tax agreement between contracting parties. This would apply to reservations to any underlying agreement. Article 33 provides for an amendment where a party makes a proposal by submission to the depositary. This would apply to reservations to the MLI itself. Therefore, given that Article 33 explicitly covers amendments to the MLI, an impermissible reservation would not be valid even if another party accepts the impermissible reservation, as it would amount to an amendment, which is explicitly covered under Article 33.

3.6 Timing of a Reservation

The timing of reservations is essential for the operation of a treaty. States need to know when to make reservations. Article 28(5) through (7) of the MLI set out the timing of making reservations. Article 28(5) provides as follows (emphasis added):

> Reservations shall be made *at the time of signature or when depositing the instrument of ratification, acceptance or approval,* subject to the provisions of paragraphs 2, 6 and 9 of this Article, and paragraph 5 of Article 29 (Notifications). However, for a Party which chooses under Article 18 (Choice to Apply Part VI) to apply Part VI (Arbitration) after it has become a Party to this Convention, reservations described in subparagraphs p), q), r) and s) of paragraph 1 of this Article shall be made at the same time as that Party's notification to the Depositary pursuant to Article 18 (Choice to Apply Part VI).

A reserving party must make a reservation at the time of signature or when depositing the instrument of ratification, acceptance or approval. However, this general rule is subject to a number of provisions. Article 28(2), as discussed above, covers reservations under Part VI. In particular, a party that chooses to apply Part VI after it has become a party, must make reservations at the time of that party's notification to the depositary pursuant to Article 18 that it chooses to apply Part VI. The reservations apply to all other parties. Thus, a party cannot simply adopt a pick-and-choose approach. Article 28(6) allows the possibility to withdraw or replace reservations, and Article 29(5) provides for the possibility to make new reservations if an agreement added to the list notified under Article 2(1)(a)(ii) is the first to fall within the scope of a reservation listed in Article 28(8) or if a newly added agreement is the first inclusion in the list of a tax agreement entered into by or on behalf of a jurisdiction or territory the international relations of which the party is responsible.

35. *Guide to Practice on Reservations to Treaties supra* n. 29, para. 3.3.3.

Article 28(6) of the MLI provides as follows:

> If reservations are made at the time of signature, they shall be confirmed upon deposit of the instrument of ratification, acceptance or approval, unless the document containing the reservations explicitly specifies that it is to be considered definitive, subject to the provisions of paragraphs 2, 5 and 9 of this Article, and paragraph 5 of Article 29 (Notifications).

This provides an exception to the general rule where a signatory explicitly specifies that the list of reservations it makes at the time of signature is to be considered definitive. In this case, no confirmation of the reservations is required upon deposit of the instrument of ratification, acceptance or approval. However, this is subject to the provisions of Article 28(2), (5) and (9) and Article 29(5). Article 28(2) and (5) allow a party which chooses to apply Part VI after it has become a party to the Convention to make the reservations permitted under Part VI at the time it chooses to apply Part VI. Article 28(9) allows a party to withdraw or replace a reservation (discussed below). Article 29(5) allows a party to make a new reservation if an agreement listed in Article 28(8) or if a newly added agreement is the first inclusion in the list of a tax agreements entered into by or on behalf of a jurisdiction or territory for the international relations for which the party is responsible. Thus, only in this context is a later reservation allowed. It seems unlikely that parties would provide a definitive reservation as they remove the advantage of assessing notifications and reservations made by other parties. However, if parties are acting in good faith and have already concluded that they are not willing to apply may of the articles, definitive reservations are likely.

Article 28(7) provides as follows: 'If reservations are not made at the time of signature, a provisional list of expected reservations shall be provided to the Depositary at that time'. Article 28(7) is a critical provision. This ensures a certain degree of transparency and certainty for other parties. The Explanatory Statement provides that 'provisional indications of intended positions are important to allow an understanding of the likely changes to an existing tax agreement and to facilitate domestic ratification procedures as well as to prepare for the implementation of the modifications made by the Convention'.[36]

Article 28(5) already provides that reservations may be made when depositing the instrument. Thus, a party could provide a provisional list at the time of signature and then subsequently provide extra reservations to than the provisional list. This is confirmed by the Explanatory Statement: 'The procedural list of expected reservations under Article 28(7) does not restrict the ability of that Signatory to submit a modified list of reservations upon deposit of the instrument of ratification, acceptance or approval.'[37]

However, this would counter efforts to provide transparency and certainty under Article 28(7). This will again depend on how parties react to the MLI and whether good faith is adopted.

36. OECD, *Explanatory Statement*, *supra* n. 13, Art. 28, para. 7.
37. OECD, *Explanatory Statement*, *supra* n. 13, Art. 28, para. 7.

3.7 Notification of a Reservation

Before discussing the notification of reservations, it is important to consider notifications more generally under the MLI. Article 1 provides that the MLI modifies all covered tax agreements as defined in Article 2(1)(a). Article 2 provides as follows:

> For the purpose of this Convention, the following definitions apply:
>
> a) The term 'Covered Tax Agreement' means an agreement for the avoidance of double taxation with respect to taxes on income (whether or not other taxes are also covered):
>   i) that is in force between two or more:
>   A) Parties; and/or
>   B) jurisdictions or territories which are parties to an agreement described above and for whose international relations a Party is responsible; and
>   ii) with respect to which each such Party has made a notification to the Depositary listing the agreement as well as any amending or accompanying instruments thereto (identified by title, names of the parties, date of signature, and, if applicable at the time of the notification, date of entry into force) as an agreement which it wishes to be covered by this Convention.

Therefore, a party must actively notify whether an agreement is applicable to the MLI. Parties may have a number of reasons for not notifying an agreement. 'For example, a Party may wish not to include an agreement in the scope of application of the Convention based on the fact that the agreement has been recently renegotiated to implement the outcomes of the BEPS Project, or is currently under renegotiation with the intent of implementing those outcomes in the renegotiated agreement.'[38] Thus, reservations are relevant only for agreements which have been explicitly listed.

Another significant component of the MLI is the compatibility clauses. Parties are generally required to make notifications specifying which covered tax agreement contains a certain provision that is to be superseded or modified by a provision of the MLI. The effect of notifications varies depending on the type of compatibility clause that applies to that provision. For example, where a provision of the MLI applies 'in place or in the absence of' an existing provision of a covered tax agreement, even where a party does not notify an existing provision, the MLI will prevail over the existing provision, superseding it to the extent that it is incompatible with the relevant provision of the MLI. Therefore, parties need to be particularly aware of their own provisions when they do not make reservations under certain articles.

Specific Notifications under Article 28

Article 28(8) provides that when reservations are made by a party under the listed provisions of Article 28(8)(a) through (o), an exhaustive list of the covered tax agreements (including the article and paragraph number of each provision) which are within the scope of the reservation as defined in the relevant provision, must be

38. OECD, *Explanatory Statement*, *supra* n. 13, Art. 2, para. 1.

provided. The listed provisions defined in Article 28(8)(a) through (o) relate *only* to reservations that apply to a subset of covered tax agreements based on objective criteria. They *do not* relate to reservations that allow a party to fully reserve an entire article of the MLI.

An illustrative example is helpful to demonstrate the full impact of the paragraph. Article 8(h) refers to Article 10(5)(b) and (c) (Anti-Abuse Rule for Permanent Establishments Situated in Third Jurisdictions). Article 10(5) provides as follows:

> A Party may reserve the right:
>
> (a) For the entirety of this Article not to apply to its Covered Tax Agreements;
> (b) For the entirety of this Article not to apply to its Covered Tax Agreements that already contain the provisions described in paragraph 4;
> (c) For this Article to apply only to its Covered Tax Agreements that already contain the provisions described in paragraph 5.

Therefore, where a party makes a reservations under Article 10(5)(a), there is no requirement under Article 28(8) to provide a list of agreements. This is consistent with the MLI's general principle that reservations will apply universally and the conformity of provisions. This is reflected in the Explanatory Statement: 'Where a Party uses a reservation to opt out of a provision of the Convention, that provision will not apply as between the reserving Party and all other Parties to the Convention.'[39]

Thus, where a party wishes to reserve the right not to apply Article 10, it must make such a reservation subject to Article 28(5) through (7).

However, where a party wishes to make a reservation under Article 10(5)(b) and (c), it must provide a list of the covered tax agreements which are within the scope of the reservation, including a list of the article and paragraph number of each relevant provision.[40] Thus, where a party believes that a covered tax agreement already contains the provisions under either Article 10(4) or (5), it must provide the relevant covered tax agreement with article and paragraph number.

There is, however, one key caveat. The last sentence of Article 28 provides that the reservations described in Article 28(a) through (o) 'shall not apply to any covered tax agreement that is not included on the list described in this paragraph'. Therefore, where a party does not list the covered tax agreement, it is not covered as a reservation. Furthermore, there is no compatibility clause under Article 28. Thus, a party could, whether deliberately or otherwise, not list a relevant provision. This is explicitly mentioned in the Explanatory Statement. This appears to be at odds with the intent of the paragraph. Furthermore, without a list of covered tax agreements, there would be a high degree of uncertainty in relation to whether certain provisions already contained in covered tax agreements are covered. It seems that the drafters made a deliberate policy decision to favour certainty over universality.

For example, Party *A* decides to make a reservation under Article 10(5)(b). Without Article 10(8), there would be a large degree of uncertainty as to which existing

39. OECD, *Explanatory Statement*, *supra* n. 13, Art. 28, para. 14.
40. OECD, *Explanatory Statement*, *supra* n. 13, Art. 28, para. 8.

provisions are covered by the reservations. The last sentence of Article 10(8) simply clarifies a logical inference from Article 10(8), that the reservation does not apply unless specifically listed. The parties have total authority to decide which covered tax agreements are covered by the reservation and which are not.

However, the strategic pick-and-choose approach would ultimately be fruitless. For example, Party *A* has ten covered tax agreements with various other parties containing the same provisions described in Article 10(4). It decides to list only five of the covered tax agreements. The non-listed covered tax agreements that do not have a reservation simply use Article 10(1) through (3). The listed covered tax agreements that do have a reservation simply adopt the existing provision in their covered tax agreements which already contain the provisions described in Article 10(4).

Providing a list

Article 28(8) provides that parties must provide a list. Therefore, where a party does not provide such list, one could argue that a breach of the MLI has occurred. Where a party does not undertake MLI actions in good faith, there are potential consequences that need to be considered. Article 60 of the Vienna Convention provides for the termination or suspension of the operation of a treaty as a consequence of a 'material breach'. A material breach is defined as '(a) a repudiation of the treaty not sanctioned by the present Convention' or '(b) the violation of a provision essential to the accomplishment of the object or purpose of the treaty'. It is clear that it would not constitute a repudiation of the treaty under (a). The question, therefore, arises as to whether Article 28(8) of the MLI is essential to the accomplishment of the object or purpose of the treaty.

As noted, the intention to the MLI is to include the greatest number of agreements as possible, but to allow parties to exclude certain provisions or agreements where there are reasonable policy reasons. If the above-mentioned avenues for disputes are met with resistance, parties could consider whether a material breach has occurred. However, this is certainly an extreme case, and hopefully only a hypothetical situation that does not occur in the real world. Although it is not within the scope of this chapter to discuss breaches under the MLI, parties should be aware of the relevant international law when they undertake a certain approach.

May a Party Make a Late Reservation?

The MLI explicitly provides that reservations must generally be made at the time of signature or when depositing the instrument of ratification, acceptance or approval.[41] A contracting party may formulate a late reservation before this time. If a party makes a reservation after the permitted time has expired, what are the consequences? One view is that late reservations are valid where none of the other contracting parties object to the reservation.[42] This is reflected in state practice and in the Guidelines of the

41. MLI, Art. 28(5).
42. Walter, *supra* n. 3, at 257.

ILC.[43] Therefore, any late reservation is valid between the reserving states and all other states that do not object to the reservation.

The author argues, however, that late reservations should not be permitted. First, the OECD has invested a large amount of resources in formulating the complex reservation articles. The reservation article (Article 28) is likely the most sophisticated and technical reservation article under international law. So-called speed dating between parties, whereby parties attempted to identify the relevant provisions applicable, provided a platform for clarifying and understanding the underlying covered tax agreement. Therefore, a late reservation would clearly be against the object and purpose of the MLI. Parties have a long period within which to consider the relevant reservations. Allowing late reservations from sixty-eight different jurisdictions would create chaos, and a subsequent breakdown of the MLI would follow.

3.8 Later Withdrawal

Article 28(9) allows a party which has made a reservation in accordance with Article 28(1) or (2), to, at any time, withdraw it or replace it with a more limited reservation by means of a notification addressed to the depositary. The provision, therefore, is intended to allow parties to reduce their reservations in future, but not to assert more reservations. The policy goal is to provide increased integrity for the MLI provisions. Although reservations under the MLI are an important tool to provide initial universality, the integrity of terms is another key policy factor. Thus, Article 28(9) is intended to allow greater integrity of terms with reduced reservations.

Article 28(9)(a) applies to all contracting jurisdictions that are parties to the MLI on the date of receipt by the depositary of the notification of withdrawal or replacement of the reservation under two categories of reservations, namely: (i) reservations to provisions relating to taxes withheld at source; and (ii) reservations to all other provisions.

Category (i) provides that the first taxes in relation to which the withdrawal or replacement of a reservation will have effect, are those for which the event giving rise to the taxes occurs on or after 1 January of the next year following the expiration of a period of six calendar months beginning on the date of the communication by the depositary of the notification of the withdrawal or replacement to all parties and signatories.[44]

Category (ii) provides that the first taxes in relation to which the withdrawal of the reservation will have effect are those which are levied with respect to periods beginning on or after 1 January of the next year following the expiration of a period of six calendar months beginning on the date of the communication by the depositary of the notification of the withdrawal or replacement of the reservation.[45] Article 28(9)(b) applies with respect to a covered tax agreement for which one or more contracting jurisdictions becomes a party to the MLI after the date of receipt by the depositary of the

43. *Guide to Practice on Reservations to Treaties supra* n. 29, paras 2.3.1 and 2.3.2.
44. OECD, *Explanatory Statement, supra* n. 13, Art. 28, para. 9.
45. OECD, *Explanatory Statement, supra* n. 13, Art. 28, para. 9.

notification of withdrawal or replacement: on the latest of the dates on which the MLI enters into force for those contracting jurisdictions.

A critical implication is that parties may simply withdraw a reservation if they seek to change their covered tax agreements. Previously, parties had to renegotiate or withdraw their tax treaties if they were not content with the status quo. Where both parties make a reservation withdrawal, or where one party makes a withdrawal and the other party had originally made no reservation, the underlying covered tax agreement is modified. Thus, covered tax agreements will change at a greater speed in future, which will enhance the underlying goals of the BEPS project. Stakeholders will need to monitor reservations made to the depositary.

Is a Withdrawal Legally Permitted?

If State *A* unilaterally withdraws a reservation to the MLI, this has the effect of changing the relevant covered tax agreements with other states. It is unclear whether this is legal from a domestic perspective. A national constitution may preclude the alteration of an international agreement without the consent of the national legislature. Some have argued that acceptance of a reservation creates a contractual obligation between the parties which precludes the unilateral withdrawal of a reservation.[46] Therefore, consent of the other party is required.

The MLI contains reservations that do not require acceptance and MAP reservations that do require acceptance. Thus, one could argue that only the withdrawal of MAP reservations require acceptance by the other party. On the other hand, all other reservation withdrawals do not require acceptance.

Article 22(1) of the Vienna Convention expressly allows the withdrawal of a reservation without the consent of the state which accepted the reservation. The MLI, in contrast, is silent as to whether acceptance by the other states is required. One could argue the MLI deliberately ignored the Vienna Convention and, therefore, acceptance is required. However, this is a false argument for two reasons. First, the reservation article is extremely detailed and ensures flexibility for countries. Second, Article 28(9) requires only a notification to the depositary and outlines the effect of the withdrawal based on the notification. The drafters of the MLI would have explicitly stated that acceptance is required if that had been the intent.

The ILC has also never questioned the unilateral withdrawal of a reservation: 'Unless the treaty otherwise provides, a reservation may be withdrawn at any time and the consent of a state or of an international organization which has accepted the reservation is not required for its withdrawal.'[47] The ILC reports are only soft law and, as such, not authoritative. The formulation of reservations under Article 19 is silent with regard to the requirement of acceptance by the other parties. Thus, one could argue that Article 22 of the Vienna Convention relates only to reservations that do not

46. J.M. Ruda, *Reservations to Treaties (Volume 146)*, in *Collected Courses of the Hague Academy of International Law*, 146 Recueil des cours de l'Academie de Droit international de la Haye 95, at 201 (Hague Academy of International Law 1975).
47. Report of the International Law Commission, fifty-fifth session, Supplement No. 10 (A/58/10) 2003, at para. 2.5.1.

require acceptance. The MLI reservations are distinguishable by reservations that require acceptance (MAP reservations) and those that do not require acceptance. Therefore, as the MAP reservations require acceptance, one could argue that they should also require acceptance by the other states to withdraw the reservations. It would be asymmetrical to require acceptance of MAP reservations, but not require acceptance of the withdrawal of reservations. Furthermore, given the significance of the MAP provision, it would be a grave infringement of the rights of State *B*.

For example, State *A* makes a reservation to certain cases that State *B* accepts. The MAP provision is applicable except for the reserved cases. After two years, State *A* withdraws the reservation. If acceptance is not required, all the scope of cases would apply. However, it is hardly harmful to State *B*, as it did not originally reserve the scope of cases. If acceptance is required, State *B* would have the option of maintaining the status quo or switching to its original wishes under the MLI. State *B* may have policy reasons to maintain the status quo.

If State *C* did not accept the reservation made by State *A*, the whole MAP provision would not apply. Once the reservation is withdrawn, if acceptance is not required, the entire MAP provision would apply. This particular case represents a significant change in the relationship between State *A* and State *C*. Again, one could argue that State *C* originally intended to apply the scope of cases; thus it is hardly harmful to State *C*. However, again, State *C* may have policy reasons to maintain the status quo.

Overall, the author asserts that acceptance is not required, as Article 28 clearly does not require acceptance and any consideration about an asymmetrical application of the reservations article is perhaps a fair criticism, but not legally valid. The Explanatory Statement does not provide further guidance. The author acknowledges the future problems that could arise in this area. Furthermore, the constitution of a country may forbid a change to an international agreement without the consent of the legislature. This must be considered on a country-by-country basis.

Partial withdrawal

The subsequent logical deduction is that a partial reservation also requires no acceptance from the other parties, given that it is less significant than a full reservation. The ILC report confirms this interpretation: 'The partial withdrawal of a reservation is subject to the same formal and procedural rules as a total withdrawal and takes effect on the same conditions'.[48]

Therefore, a partial withdrawal must be subjected to the same legal regime as a total withdrawal.[49] The underlying argument is again a battle between flexibility and integrity of the MLI: on the one hand, flexibility of the party to decide its obligations more freely, on the other hand, upholding and promoting the articles of the MLI. The author asserts that acceptance is not required. First, it is established international law under the Vienna Convention and the ILC reports that require no acceptance. Second, it promotes the integrity of the terms without greatly reducing flexibility. If a country

48. *Ibid.*, at 2.5.10.
49. Supported by Walter, *supra* n. 3, at 324.

had originally withheld a reservation, it would not be not a serious limitation to hold that country to its decision. Furthermore, any national legislature that approves the MLI is agreeing to be constrained by the inability to accept the withdrawal of reservations.

4 CONCLUSION

Reservations are a key feature of the MLI. Parties must have a deep understanding of reservations in order to implement their policy objectives, as the provisions are extremely detailed and complicated. Only expressly permitted reservations contained in the provisions of the MLI are expressly allowed. There are four categories of reservations. First, minimum standard reservations, where reservations are allowed only to the extent that the party intends to meet the minimum standard contained in the article. Parties need to seriously consider their own policy objectives in relation to these minimum standards. As the MLI applies only to listed agreements, a party can choose which agreements it wishes to list. Thus, countries need to consider non-minimum standard reservations before they notify an existing agreement. Furthermore, they also need to consider whether provisions contained in existing provisions meet the minimum standards. As noted, the compatibility clause can have the effect of superseding an existing provision even where the provision is not notified. As there will be much political pressure on parties to meet these standards, there should be many listed agreements notified. If a party does not wish to have these standards in its existing agreements with certain countries, it should not list the existing agreements.

Second, there are non-minimum standard reservations, where parties are not required to meet the minimum standard, such that parties can reserve the right not to apply the entire article. Once a party has decided to list an existing agreement, it must consider whether to fully reserve an article or whether existing provisions meet the standard. Again, parties need to be aware of the compatibility clauses. Third, there are arbitration reservations, where a party that has opted in to Part VI, may reserve the scope of cases. Furthermore, there are particular reservations that may be made in Part VI, although these reservations are only where the parties will meet a certain standard in a different manner. Lastly, other reservations relate to the entry into force of the MLI. Parties need to carefully consider these provisions for timing purposes.

The legal effect of a reservation is a critical point to consider. Where a party reserves the right for the entirety of an article not to apply, this applies to all agreements notified to the depositary.[50] Where a party reserves the right to limit the scope of cases under Part VI, this applies to all other parties. Where a party reserve the right to apply its own provisions under a set of objectively defined characteristics, it must list the provisions; otherwise the reservation is not applicable. Furthermore, unlike all other reservations, this is subject to acceptance by parties. Where a party accepts the reservation, the reservation applies. Where a party objects to a reservation, the entire

50. Except for Art. 5 where a party must list the provision.

Part VI does not apply. The author has argued that an impermissible reservation is not permitted under the MLI, given the complexity of the undertaking.

The timing of reservations is extremely important. A reservation may occur either at the time of signature or when depositing the instrument of ratification, acceptance or approval. A later reservation is not allowed. However, a later withdrawal of a reservation is allowed, which will increase the speed of change for underlying covered tax agreements in future. Therefore, based on the signatures of other parties, parties will be able to assess the other parties' commitments and tailor their final commitments in the instrument of ratification. This period will be crucial to determine how parties react to various reservations. However, parties are not bound by reservations made at the time of signature. Therefore, parties that make a reservation at the time of signature, may add or delete reservations by the time of the deposit of instrument of ratification, acceptance or approval. As a consequence, there is a potential for political gamesmanship by the different parties – something that parties which operate in good faith should consider. However, the author argues that all parties should approach the MLI in good faith and take this opportunity to improve the operation of tax treaties. Ultimately, cooperation between all parties will ensure that every party benefits from the MLI.

CHAPTER 9

Notifications According to the Multilateral Instrument and Consolidated Versions of Tax Treaties

Christiane Zöhrer

1 ENSURING LEGAL CERTAINTY

The multilateral instrument (MLI) - in creating a system of opt-outs, opt-ins and choices - provides for a considerable amount of flexibility. This flexible approach is necessary in order to reflect variations in different tax treaties and country preferences, and it not only allows a maximum number of countries to join the MLI, but also helps to achieve the goals set out by it. However, at the same time, it must be ensured that the modifications resulting from the application of the MLI are clearly understood by the relevant stakeholders in order to ensure the instrument's effectiveness. Thus, modifications resulting from the application of the MLI and the level of commitment undertaken by the parties involved need to be clear and transparent. Therefore, striking the appropriate balance between meeting the need for clarity and transparency on the one hand and ensuring a high degree of flexibility to the participants on the other, was one of the major challenges faced in developing the instrument.

Possible means of effectively addressing this sensitive issue and ensuring the highest degree of legal certainty possible include implementing a system of notifications and developing a mechanism of producing consolidated versions. This chapter presents a comprehensive overview of notifications and consolidated versions in both international law and in the context of the MLI. It will assess the timing of notifications and the content that they must display, and will analyse their effects. A possible incongruence of notifications is another crucial issue that will be discussed in great detail here.

Another tool that can be used to address the challenges that result from the flexible approach provided for in the MLI is the preparation of consolidated versions of treaties as modified by the MLI. Even though such versions contain numerous advantages when drafted carefully, multiple aspects need to be considered when developing consolidated versions of treaties as modified by the MLI. Furthermore, consolidated versions could also contain a considerable potential for conflict and give rise to interpretation issues. The third part of this chapter discusses this issue and carefully analyses the various aspects related to this topic.

2 NOTIFICATIONS

2.1 Scope

Whenever an international treaty is concluded, notifications play an important role, as they inform others of the various operations related to a specific treaty.[1] Formally, a notification is defined as 'the action to officially inform a third party of a fact, a situation, an action, a document in order to ensure that the object of the notification becomes henceforward legally known by the State to which it is addressed'.[2] A notification therefore serves the purpose to 'inform the contracting States of a fact implying that they adapt their behaviour in a manner consistent with their rights and obligations under the treaty'.[3] Several provisions in the Vienna Convention on the Law of Treaties (hereinafter 'the Vienna Convention') deal with notifications.[4] However, as the rules contained therein may be regarded as default rules, i.e., they apply unless the treaty otherwise provides, the MLI must be analysed carefully in order to assess the legal nature of notifications.

Each substantive provision of the MLI is structured alike and provides for one or more notification clause(s), requiring parties to notify certain circumstances to the depositary.[5] Article 29(1) of the MLI sets forth an exhaustive list of necessary notifications by reference to the provisions in which they are set out, and effectively requires the parties to make a notification to the depositary informing the depositary about the treaties to which they wish to apply the MLI, about the options they choose and about existing provisions that are within the scope of the compatibility clauses.[6]

Article 2(1)(a)(ii) of the MLI stipulates that only those treaties are covered with respect to which each party has made a notification to the depositary listing the agreement as well as any amending or accompanying instrument thereto as an

1. R. Daoudi, *Article 78: Notifications and Communication*, in *The Vienna Conventions on the Law of Treaties: A Commentary*, vol. II, para. 1, at 1758 (O. Corten & P. Klein eds., Oxford 2011).
2. Daoudi, *supra* n. 1, para. 2.
3. Daoudi, *supra* n. 1, para. 34.
4. In fact, thirteen of a total of eighty-five articles, namely Arts 16, 20, 25, 40, 41, 47, 58, 65, 67, 68, 77, 78 and 79 of the Vienna Convention, deal with this issue.
5. Articles 3 through 26 of the MLI are considered to be substantive provisions.
6. OECD, *Explanatory Statement to the Multilateral Convention to implement Tax Treaty Related Measures to Prevent Base Erosion and Profit Shifting* (2016), para. 294.

agreement which it wishes to be covered by the MLI.[7] Therefore, the parties can specify the tax treaties to which the instrument applies. A notification is required in order to avoid confusion or uncertainty about the scope of agreements covered and ensures that the MLI modifies only those agreements that have been specifically notified to the depositary. This approach provides for flexibility in the level of commitment and ensures that the instrument applies only in relation to agreements listed by the parties.[8] Choosing this approach allows a large number of countries to participate, even when certain tax policies cannot be harmonized amongst each other, considering that the level of commitment that the parties are prepared to undertake depends on the partner jurisdictions.[9] Therefore, the approach under the MLI affords maximum flexibility, and a state may decide that some of its treaties are covered by the MLI while others are excluded from its scope altogether. Possible reasons for not applying the MLI to certain treaties include the fact that the agreement was recently renegotiated to implement the outcomes of the OECD Base Erosion and Profit Shifting (BEPS) project or is currently under renegotiation with the intent of implementing them.[10] While it is perfectly acceptable for a state to decide which of its treaties should be modified by the MLI, the depositary must be informed of its choice. Conversely, those treaties that are not notified to the depositary are not subject to modification and remain unchanged.

While Article 29(1)(a) requires states to notify the depositary as to which treaties are to be covered by the scope of the MLI, Article 29(1)(b)-(t) requires states to make notifications related to the choice of optional provisions and notifications regarding which treaties are within the scope of the compatibility clause. A notification's precise scope is not uniform and its content is specified in the respective notification clause.[11] Some of the MLI's provisions offer multiple options and allow the parties to choose among them. Article 5 of the MLI, for instance, provides for three alternative ways for countries to address problems arising from the inclusion of the exemption method in treaties with respect to items of income that are not taxed in the source state. In this case, the states are free to choose option A, option B, or option C, or they may even choose to apply none of the specified options.[12] Therefore, whenever a state chooses one of the options under the MLI, it must notify the depositary of various facts, including its choice of option, each treaty containing a provision within the scope of the compatibility clause for that option and the article and paragraph number of each such provision.[13]

In some cases the work on the BEPS project produced a main provision that could be supplemented with an additional provision. This allows parties to commit to further action in pursuit of the MLI's objectives and go beyond the defined minimum number

7. Articles 29(1) and 2(1)(a)(ii) MLI.
8. OECD, *Explanatory Statement*, *supra* n. 6, para. 26.
9. OECD, *Developing a Multilateral Instrument to Modify Bilateral Tax Treaties – Action 15: 2015 Final Report*, OECD/G20 Base Erosion and Profit Shifting Project (2015), para. 42.
10. OECD, *Explanatory Statement*, *supra* n. 6, para. 26.
11. OECD, *Explanatory Statement*, *supra* n. 6, para. 15.
12. Article 5 MLI.
13. Article 5(10) MLI.

of commitments.[14] An example for such a provision is Article 6(3), which enables parties to include the full preamble language produced in the Action 6 Final Report instead of adopting only the portion related to the elimination of double taxation without creating the opportunities for non-taxation or reduced taxation through tax evasion or avoidance.[15] Parties that choose to apply the aforementioned provision must notify the depositary of their choice.[16]

2.2 Dispatch and Receipt of Notifications

2.2.1 Dispatch of Notifications

Matters of timing of the dispatch of a notification are extensively dealt with in the MLI. The timing of notifications is a crucial issue. This is reflected in the fact that three out of six paragraphs of Article 29 of the MLI deal with this complex and sensitive issue. Regarding the timing for making notifications, Article 29(1) of the MLI requires notifications to be made either at the time of signature or when depositing the instrument of ratification, acceptance or approval.[17] Essentially, a provisional list of notifications must be submitted at the time of signature, while a final list of notifications, which is subject to subsequent changes, must be provided at the time of the deposit of the instrument of ratification, acceptance or approval.[18] If notifications are not made at the time of signature, at least a provisional list of expected notifications must be provided to the depositary at that time.[19]

These provisional lists are subject to subsequent amendments and will therefore not restrict a state's ability to submit a modified list of notifications when depositing the instrument of ratification, acceptance or approval.[20] Instead, signatories will have the opportunity to discuss any mismatches in notifications and correct them prior to finalization of those lists. Therefore, provisional lists solely serve transparency purposes and intend to facilitate bilateral negotiations between treaty partners, as they enable them to discuss their respective lists and to evaluate the way their treaty would be modified. Furthermore, from a practical perspective, a provisional list will facilitate domestic ratification procedures and will prepare for the implementation of the modifications made by the MLI.[21]

If notifications are made at the time of signature, they will be confirmed upon deposit of the instrument of ratification, acceptance or approval, as this is the moment at which consent to be bound by the MLI is expressed following the completion of domestic procedures. A party that has provided the depositary with a list of notifications already at the time of signature may subsequently amend that list and add

14. OECD, *Action 15 Final Report, supra* n. 9, para. 53.
15. Article 6(3) MLI.
16. Article 6(6) MLI.
17. Article 29(1) MLI.
18. OECD, *Explanatory Statement, supra* n. 6, para. 292.
19. Article 29(4) MLI.
20. OECD, *Explanatory Statement, supra* n. 6, para. 302.
21. OECD, *Explanatory Statement, supra* n. 6, para. 302.

additional notifications or delete some of them.[22] Article 29(3) of the MLI allows for the possibility to provide the depositary with a final list of notifications already at the time of signature.[23] In this case, the document containing the notifications must explicitly specify that it is considered to be definitive and no confirmation is required. However, the definitive nature is subject to the provisions discussed in the subsequent paragraphs.[24]

The general rule that notifications must be made either at the time of signature or when depositing the instrument of ratification, acceptance or approval applies subject to Article 29(5), Article 29(6) and Article 35(7) of the MLI. The additional notifications permitted by Article 29(5) relate to the subsequent extension of the list of covered tax agreements, and allow parties to extend the list of agreements at any time by simply making a notification to the depositary after having provided the depositary with a final list of notifications. This provision requires the parties to specify whether or not the agreement falls within the scope of any of the reservations made thus far. If the newly added agreement is the first to fall within the scope of a specific reservation, the party may make a new reservation. Furthermore, the party is required to make any additional notifications in order to accurately reflect the agreement's first inclusion, meaning that where a provision supersedes or modifies specific types of existing provisions, parties must specify any provisions of that type contained in the treaty by means of a notification addressed to the depositary.[25]

While paragraph 5 deals with tax agreements that have thus far not been covered by the MLI, paragraph 6 allows for the possibility to make certain additional notifications in respect of the agreements that have already been included in the list of notified tax agreements and specifies the date on which notifications will take effect.[26] Finally Article 35(7) of the MLI provides that a party may reserve the right to delay the entry into effect of the provisions of the MLI and thus the modification of covered tax agreements until it has completed its internal procedure for this purpose.[27]

If a state fails to submit a notification in due time, its flexibility is reduced. The restriction as to the amount of flexibility afforded to the states can be attributed to the fact that a state's ability to amend its notifications after having deposited the instrument of ratification, acceptance or approval, is limited by the MLI and allowed only if explicitly authorized by the provisions discussed in the previous paragraphs. Therefore, while reservations can be replaced with more limited reservations, the opposite scenario is not possible.[28] Furthermore, the latest possible time to exercise an option would be the moment of deposit of the instrument of ratification, acceptance or approval. A subsequent change to the choice of option is thus prohibited.[29]

22. OECD, *Explanatory Statement*, *supra* n. 6, para. 300.
23. Article 29(3) MLI.
24. OECD, *Explanatory Statement*, *supra* n. 6, para. 301.
25. Article 29(5) MLI.
26. For further information, *see* Art. 25(6) MLI.
27. For further information, *see* Art. 35(7) MLI.
28. Article 28(9) MLI; OECD, *Explanatory Statement*, *supra* n. 6, para. 282.
29. For more in-depth treatment of these issues, *see* Chapters 7 and 8 of this book.

2.2.2 *Receipt of Notifications*

Another noteworthy aspect concerns the determination of the moment that notifications acquire legal relevance. Unlike in most bilateral situations where notifications are generally made directly to the other party, the fact that notifications are frequently made through a depositary in a multilateral context results in a delay between the time of dispatch of a notification and the time of its receipt by the addressee, leaving the assessment of the precise moment that notifications become legally operative to be quite challenging at times.[30] In principle, two options are possible: Notifications could attain legal relevance either once received by the depositary, or – alternatively – at the time they are received by the other parties to the MLI. The answer to this question depends largely on the classification of the role of the depositary, as – in order to protect the good faith of the receiving state – a notification must be brought to the attention of the state(s) to which it is addressed in order for it to be considered as being operative.[31] This approach aims at ensuring the security of conventional relations, considering that states continue to act in accordance with the current legal situation.[32]

While an early view in international law regarded the depositary as acting in the parties' name and therefore asserted that a notification was received by the states as soon as it was received by the depositary, a more modern view seems to favour a rather different approach. Pursuant to this view, the depositary has an independent function with its own rights and duties, and can therefore be considered as a trustee and instrument of the parties to the treaty, rather than as their agent or representative. Currently, the predominant view seems to suggest that the depositary assumes the role of notary for signatories or parties.[33] In light of these considerations, a notification received by the depositary cannot automatically be regarded as being simultaneously received by the states for which it is intended.[34] Instead, the depositary will have to inform the parties in order for the notification to attain legal relevance.[35] Therefore, the good faith of the receiving state(s) is protected as long as they have not been informed of the notification by the depositary. The latter approach was codified in Article 78(c) of the Vienna Convention, which states that 'except as the treaty or the present Convention otherwise provide, any notification or communication to be made by any State under the present Convention shall: (c) if transmitted to a depositary, be considered as received by the State for which it was intended only when the latter State has been informed by the depositary … '.[36]

The issue of determining the precise moment at which a notification acquires legal relevance is not explicitly addressed in the MLI. Therefore, the rules provided for

30. Daoudi, *supra* n. 1, para. 11.
31. Daoudi, *supra* n. 1, para. 1; M.E. Villiger, *Article 78: Notifications and Communications*, in *Commentary on the 1969 Vienna Convention on the Law of Treaties* (Martinus Nijhoff Publishers 2009), para. 9.
32. Daoudi, *supra* n. 1, para. 25.
33. Daoudi, *supra* n. 1, para. 21.
34. Villiger, *supra* n. 31, *Art. 76*, para. 3.
35. Villiger, *supra* n. 31, *Art. 78*, para. 10; Daoudi, *supra* n. 1, para. 6.
36. Article 78(c) Vienna Convention.

in Article 78 of the Vienna Convention apply, and notifications become legally relevant only after having been transmitted to the parties. In other words, notifications produce no legal effects for the state to which it is addressed upon their receipt by the depositary, i.e., before the state is aware of their existence. This is consistent with the approach foreseen in the MLI, as Article 39(2) of the MLI requires the depositary to inform the parties within one month about any notifications it has received.[37] If the depositary does not forward the notification in due time, the bilateral or multilateral agreement remains unaffected, as international law protects the good faith of the recipient.[38] As a considerable time span may pass between the dispatch and the receipt of a notification, the intended recipients may – unaware of any notification underway – take action which they would not have done otherwise. However, this period of time is governed by good faith and the position of the receiving state is protected.[39]

As notifications may not trigger any legal consequences prior to their receipt by the addressee(s), a state that wishes to withdraw a reservation or replace it with a more limited reservation must inform the depositary by way of a notification. This notification may not be afforded any legal relevance, and no amendment will occur before the other parties are informed of the notification. Considering the various means of transmission that are available, notifications may be received on different dates by the states. Corresponding to the different moments of a notification's receipt, its effects are produced at different dates vis-à-vis the other parties.[40] In this context, Daoudi calls on the drafters of international treaties to provide solutions in the provisions of the treaties themselves in order to remedy this shortcoming.[41] In the case of the MLI, a special regime is provided as to the time a withdrawal or replacement of a reservation by means of a notification takes effect.[42] Under this regime, a situation such as that described above is not possible unless the depositary lacks diligence and fails to inform certain states of the content of a notification that the depositary has received.[43]

2.3 Form and Content of Notifications

2.3.1 Form of Notifications

The provisions of the Vienna Convention do not generally specify in which form notifications must be made, as only notifications relating to situations in which a party 'invokes either a defect in its consent to be bound by a treaty or a ground for impeaching the validity of a treaty, terminating it, withdrawing from it or suspending its operation'[44] must be made in writing;[45] no specific formal requirement is prescribed

37. Article 39(2) MLI.
38. Villiger, *supra* n. 31, *Art. 78*, para. 10.
39. Villiger, *supra* n. 31, *Art. 78*, para. 11.
40. Daoudi, *supra* n. 1, para. 23.
41. Daoudi, *supra* n. 1, para. 37.
42. For more detailed information on this issue, *see* Art. 28(9) MLI.
43. For further information, *see* OECD, *Explanatory Statement*, *supra* n. 6, paras 286 et seq.
44. Article 65(1) Vienna Convention.
45. Article 67(1) Vienna Convention.

for notifications dealing with any other topic. This allows one to draw the conclusion that the instrument leaves open which form is to be employed, and that oral notifications may be feasible. As this approach would, however, put transparency and legal certainty in jeopardy, notifications are – in practice – mainly made in writing, especially in a multilateral context.[46]

The MLI also does not explicitly specify which form must be employed when submitting a notification, and therefore one could conclude that no formal requirements must be met and that notifications may be made both in writing and orally. This approach – while granting a considerable amount of flexibility – would, however, be clearly at odds with the requirement of transparency that is intrinsic to the MLI. Furthermore, despite the fact that the instrument does not contain an express requirement to submit notifications in writing, states are required to submit both a provisional and a final list of notifications.[47] The term 'list' clearly expresses the intention of the drafters, namely that notifications necessarily must be made in writing. Furthermore, Article 29(3) of the MLI refers to 'a document containing the notifications',[48] and additionally the depositary is required to maintain publicly available a list of notifications made by the parties.[49] The references to lists and documents allow for no other conclusion than that notifications must be made in writing. This approach also ensures the necessary transparency and allows for clarity.

2.3.2 Content of Notifications

International law does not require that a notification displays a specific content, and in the context of the MLI the content of a notification is not uniform, as it primarily depends on the type of notification that is made. Notifications aimed at amending an agreement must identify both the agreement and the amending or accompanying instrument by title, names of the parties, date of signature, and the date of entry into force.[50] Therefore, when providing its list of agreements, a party should include a reference to not only the original agreement, but also any instruments that have subsequently amended it. Again, including these will help ensure clarity and transparency.

Thus, the parties are requested to provide the depositary with all the relevant information set forth in Article 2(1)(a)(ii) of the MLI. However, situations of diverging notifications may occur despite this requirement, as the jurisdictions involved may submit diverging information with regard to, for example, the date of entry into force of a treaty or of an amending or accompanying instrument. The issue of incongruence in notifications and the effects stemming therefrom are not explicitly dealt with in the MLI, and international law is also silent on this sensitive issue.

46. Villiger, *supra* n. 31, *Art. 78*, para. 4.
47. Articles 29(3) and 29(4) MLI.
48. Article 29(3) MLI.
49. Article 39(3)(c) MLI.
50. Article 2(1)(a)(ii) MLI.

Therefore it is highly debatable how to proceed when faced with diverging notifications. One could argue that – due to the mismatch – the MLI does not apply to an agreement or to any amending or accompanying instrument thereto unless all the relevant information submitted to the depositary is fully consistent. Under such a formalistic approach, however, even the slightest deviation in the parties' notifications would render the instrument inapplicable to either the treaty as a whole or to one or more of its amendment(s). This approach would therefore be contrary to the instrument's express objective, i.e., the simultaneous amendment of a maximum number of treaties. Considering the object and purpose of the MLI, the better argument suggests adopting a more lenient approach. This consideration is backed by the possibility of analogously applying to the issue at hand, the guidelines contained in the Explanatory Statement describing possible ways to deal with a mismatch if a party fails to identify a relevant existing provision.[51]

Notification clauses relating to provisions that are within the scope of the compatibility clause frequently require that notifications include the article and paragraph number of each provision of an underlying agreement containing a provision described in one of the other paragraphs of the article. This is especially true if a provision in the MLI supersedes or modifies specific types of existing provisions of the underlying agreements. In such a case, the parties are generally urged to specify in their notification which of their treaties contain provisions of that type, and to identify these by providing their article and paragraph number.[52] A noteworthy question concerns the issue as to how to classify notifications that identify a specific treaty but fail to provide the necessary information regarding the precise article and paragraph number. If a jurisdiction submits an incomplete notification, e.g., it fails to provide the depositary with the full information stipulated in the provision's notification clause, it remains unclear whether such a notification triggers any legal consequences. As no answer to this specific question is provided for in the MLI and international law remains silent on this issue, particular attention must be paid to the nature and the classification of these criteria.

When examining the MLI's structure, it becomes clear that increased attention was afforded to ensuring transparency. It is therefore perfectly feasible that the requirement to provide the depositary with the article and paragraph number of a provision of the underlying bilateral or multilateral agreement containing a specified content was included in the notification clauses in order to facilitate the instrument's implementation and to further enhance clarity as to its application. An argument that supports this understanding is the fact that the Explanatory Statement states that specifying which treaties contain a provision of a certain type aims at ensuring clarity and transparency about the application of the MLI. This consideration suggests that while it might be safe to say that the requirement to transmit certain specified information regarding the precise article and paragraph number of an agreement serves

51. For further information on how to proceed in such a situation *see* OECD, *Explanatory Statement*, *supra* n. 6, para. 18.
52. OECD, *Explanatory Statement*, *supra* n. 6, para. 15.

transparency purposes, claiming that these requirements represent a constitutive element for the notification's legal relevance may be too far-reaching.

This view is compatible with the understanding provided for in the Explanatory Statement which deals with this issue in greater detail and requires that parties use their best effort in order to identify which of their treaties contain a specific type of provision. The Explanatory Statement further notes that 'it is expected that Parties would use their best efforts to identify all provisions ...',[53] but it also acknowledges that - despite this proclamation - situations in which a state fails to identify all relevant provisions may still occur.[54] In order to further decrease such a risk, the MLI requires the parties to provide the depositary with a provisional list of notifications already at the time of signature.[55] This approach gives the parties the opportunity to discuss any mismatches prior to finalizing their lists of notifications.[56] In the case of any disagreement between the parties to a specific treaty, the Explanatory Statement provides for quite a number of possible remedies to such conflicts and suggests, for example, settling the dispute by means of a mutual agreement procedure provided for in the underlying treaty. Alternatively, possible conflicts may also be resolved through a conference of the parties.[57] The issue of a party inadvertently omitting an existing provision could be addressed by making an additional notification.[58]

Thus, arguing that notifications gain no legal relevance unless all the requirements laid down in the respective notification clauses are fully complied with may be regarded as being too far-fetched. Should such a rigorous approach be adopted, states that have transmitted incomplete notifications should be informed about this fact accordingly in order to be given the opportunity to complete their notifications. Without the possibility of improvement, the compatibility of such an approach with the MLI's object and purpose might be called into question. Therefore, denying the legal relevance of incomplete notifications a priori may appear to be disproportionate. Rather than denying a notification's legal relevance up front, the depositary should - although not being legally required to do so - actively approach countries that fail to fully comply with the requirements set forth in the notification clauses. This approach is in line with the role of the depositary as provided for in the MLI, considering that the depositary is exclusively in charge of administering the notifications received by the various stakeholders.[59] Taking into consideration the requirement's purpose, it may not even seem proportionate to deny a notification's legal relevance if the parties refuse to provide the information requested by the depositary. This approach considers that the formal criteria set forth in the notification clauses undisputedly increase the level of transparency, while at the same time taking into account that no constitutive element is afforded to them.

53. OECD, *Explanatory Statement*, *supra* n. 6, para. 18.
54. OECD, *Explanatory Statement*, *supra* n. 6, para. 18.
55. Article 29(4) MLI.
56. OECD, *Explanatory Statement*, *supra* n. 6, para. 18.
57. Article 31(1) MLI.
58. Article 29(6) MLI; OECD, *Explanatory Statement*, *supra* n. 6, para. 18.
59. Article 76(2) Vienna Convention; Villiger, *supra* n. 31, *Art. 78*, para. 6.

2.4 Role of the Depositary

Pursuant to Article 76 of the Vienna Convention, 'the designation of the depositary of a treaty may be made by the negotiating States, either in the treaty itself or in some other manner. The depositary may be one or more states, an international organization or the chief administrative officer of the organization'.[60] There is no requirement under international law to designate a depositary, and the role is mainly provided for in a multilateral context where a large number of parties is involved.[61] In the case of the MLI, it specifies that the depositary is the Secretary-General of the OECD.[62] Although choosing the Secretary-General of the OECD as the depositary may not - prima facie - appear obvious, this approach is in line with the usual practice in international law of designating the international organization, its chief administrative officer or a body of the international organization as a treaty's depositary, considering that the treaty was adopted at a conference convened under the auspices of the OECD.[63]

From an international law perspective, the depositary assumes a significant key position and plays an essential procedural role in the smooth operation of a multilateral treaty, as the depositary is in charge of 'receiving and keeping custody of any instruments, notifications and communications'[64] relating to the treaty, as well as 'informing the parties and the states entitled to become parties to the treaty of acts, notifications and communications relating to the treaty'.[65] The depositary is exclusively responsible for administrating the notifications that were submitted, and is obliged to inform the other states of the notifications.[66] For transparency purposes, the depositary is required to maintain publicly available lists of both covered tax agreements and reservations and notifications made by the parties after having received them from one of the parties or signatories of the MLI.[67]

Furthermore, Article 39(2) of the MLI provides for a non-exhaustive list of acts, notifications and communications of which the depositary will notify all parties and signatories within one month. The depositary is required to notify the parties and signatories of any signature; the deposit of any instrument of ratification, acceptance of approval; and any reservation, notification, proposed amendment to, or withdrawal from the MLI.[68] Furthermore, any other communication related to the MLI must be notified.[69] This provision is essential in ensuring clarity and transparency to the greatest possible extent. That way, in order to remain up-to-date, contracting states will not be required to actively request information.

In accordance with the depositary's obligations under public international law, the depositary must inform the other parties to the MLI of all notifications that it has

60. Article 76(1) Vienna Convention.
61. Villiger, *supra* n. 31, *Art. 76*, para. 5.
62. Article 39(1) MLI.
63. Villiger, *supra* n. 31, *Art. 76*, para. 10.
64. Article 77(1)(c) Vienna Convention.
65. Article 77(1)(e) Vienna Convention.
66. Article 76(2) Vienna Convention; Villiger, *supra* n. 31, *Art. 78*, para. 6.
67. Article 39(3) MLI.
68. Article 39(2)(a)-(f) MLI.
69. Article 39(2)(g) MLI.

received.[70] This obligation relates only to the various parties to the MLI and does not extend to other relevant stakeholders. To further enhance transparency, other stakeholders should be given the possibility to subscribe to an automatic notification system to ensure that they receive the information as soon as it is notified by the depositary.[71] In order to provide all stakeholders with easy access to information regarding notifications, a publicly accessible electronic database or website and a system of subscriptions to electronic alerts when new notifications are added could be established.[72]

To sum up, the depositary is of paramount importance for the internal administration of a multilateral treaty as the depositary is responsible for ensuring compliance with the necessary formalities and procedures.[73]

3 CONSOLIDATED VERSION

3.1 Classification of Consolidated Versions

A consolidated version consists of the content of an amendment, or amendments if more than one, being incorporated in the content of the base publication.[74] A consolidated version would reflect the precise changes made to an existing bilateral agreement and furthermore would, where appropriate, reflect the level of commitment undertaken by the parties in cases where the MLI provides for flexibility.[75] Generally, consolidated versions benefit both taxpayers and tax administrators, and are developed for convenience purposes. Consolidated versions allow taxpayers to have the contents of multiple instruments – in this case a treaty, any existing amendments thereto and the provisions of the MLI – merged into one single document, and the legal situation as modified by the MLI could be recognized more easily. At the same time, the preparation of consolidated versions may help to facilitate the implementation of treaties as modified by the MLI by domestic tax administrators.

Neither the MLI nor international law requires the production of consolidated versions. This is reflected in the fact that the term 'consolidated version' is not mentioned at all in the MLI itself. Even the Explanatory Statement mentions the term only once, stating that '...while for internal purposes, some Parties may develop consolidated versions of their covered tax agreements as modified by the MLI, doing so is not a prerequisite for the application of the MLI'.[76] This paragraph clearly sets out that the production of consolidated versions is not a necessity under the MLI. They may, however, be produced on a voluntary basis, meaning that the MLI does not prohibit their production. The existence or non-existence of a consolidated version,

70. OECD, *Developing a Multilateral Instrument to Modify Bilateral Tax Treaties – Action 15: 2014 Deliverable*, OECD/G20 Base Erosion and Profit Shifting Project (2014), at p. 60.
71. OECD, *Action 15 Deliverable*, *supra* n. 70, at 60.
72. OECD, *Action 15 Deliverable*, *supra* n. 70, at 60.
73. Villiger, *supra* n. 31, *Article 76*, para. 3.
74. *See* http://www.iec.ch/mnet/media_resources/products/consolidated_versions.htm.
75. OECD, *Action 15 Final Report*, *supra* n. 9, para. 62.
76. OECD, *Explanatory Statement*, *supra* n. 6, para. 13.

however, does not have any influence on the instrument's validity, and the MLI will therefore be applicable even in the absence of a consolidated version.

The production of consolidated versions is neither a prerequisite for the application of the MLI nor necessary to ensure its validity. Furthermore, there is no uniform approach with regard to consolidated versions in the different countries, meaning that while some states legally require the production of consolidated versions, others may produce them only voluntarily and a considerable number of states does not produce such versions at all. Those states that are, pursuant to domestic law provisions, obliged to produce consolidated versions must prepare them in order to comply with national law. If, despite being legally required to do so, no such version is produced, the effects depend on the national law of the state concerned, and the lack of the preparation of a consolidated version does not result in the ineffectiveness of the instrument. Rather, the modification will nevertheless take effect on the date on which the MLI enters into force for the parties to a bilateral agreement.

The principle of *pacta sunt servanda*, which is enshrined in Article 26 of the Vienna Convention and which can be regarded as a pillar of treaty law, states that every treaty in force is binding upon the parties to it and that it must be performed in good faith.[77] Article 26 of the Vienna Convention merely emphasizes the duty of states under international law to fulfil a treaty that has been entered into, irrespective of its domestic legal system.[78] Thus, a party to the MLI may not deny its application based on the fact that a domestic law requirement, namely the preparation of a consolidated version, has not been fulfilled. The argument that its application will contradict the state's internal laws is not a valid one and will not render the MLI inapplicable. Therefore, the preparation of a consolidated version is for transparency reasons only and does not affect the legal relevance of the MLI.[79]

3.2 Benefits of Consolidated Versions

In future, after having ratified the MLI, both taxpayers and national tax administrations could possibly have to consider a multitude of legal provisions when assessing a cross-border situation. Both the text of the original treaty and the text of the MLI will require in-depth analysis in order to be able to properly evaluate the legal situation. Due regard will have to be given not only to the instrument's text and – although not as relevant as the text – its Explanatory Statement, but also to the options chosen and the reservations made. This could give rise to challenges when applying a treaty as modified by the MLI. Therefore, legal certainty may be jeopardized, and the risk of both misinterpretation and misapplication of modified treaty provisions could increase significantly. Thus, it is absolutely essential to ensure that the parties' rights and

77. Article 26 Vienna Convention.
78. Article 27 Vienna Convention.
79. OECD, *Action 15 Final Report, supra* n. 9, para. 63.

obligations are clearly understood by all the stakeholders involved. The modifications of existing treaties and the level of commitment undertaken need to be clear and transparent.[80]

In order to avoid putting legal certainty at risk and to ensure both transparency and clarity, seeing existing tax treaties replaced with versions that contain the MLI provisions might, for two major reasons, be useful, even for countries that normally do not produce such versions.[81] First, identifying which provisions of an existing treaty were modified by the MLI will be burdensome for taxpayers, as doing so would require a taxpayer to know about not only the position adopted by their country, but also about the position adopted by the other country. Therefore, in order to know which modifications occurred and to properly evaluate the valid legal position, taxpayers, who are often trained in neither tax nor in legal matters, will now have to carefully examine the options chosen by each of the treaty partners. The complexity thus created poses a serious threat to legal certainty and could significantly increase the risk of misinterpretation and misapplication of the MLI.

Second, in the past, bilateral tax treaties were exclusively modified by amending protocols and it was possible to refer to the specific articles and paragraph numbers that were amended, meaning that the amending protocols clearly spelled out the changes. This enormously facilitated – for both the tax authorities and the taxpayers – the application of the treaty as amended by the protocol. However, in the context of the MLI, these just mentioned cross-references to specific articles and paragraphs are not possible, as many bilateral treaties are simultaneously affected by the modification and treaties contain variations in both numbering and wording. Despite the fact that most treaties follow either the OECD or UN Model Tax Convention, the provisions contained therein frequently use different terminology and differ in the wording and enumeration used.[82,83] Therefore, using numerical cross-references to the provisions of the model conventions would not make sense, as these cross-references do not align precisely with the numbering of actual treaties.[84] The differences in wording, enumeration style and scope do not, for instance, allow the provision's compatibility clause modifying the definition of an agency permanent establishment to refer to Article 5(5) of the OECD Model or to Article 5 of existing tax treaties.[85]

Therefore, instead of cross-references to specified articles and paragraph numbers, the MLI makes use of descriptive language where a reference to provisions of existing tax treaties is needed. Therefore, the MLI's provisions can only describe the changes made to the treaties without identifying specific articles and paragraphs that

80. OECD, *Action 15 Final Report*, *supra* n. 9, paras 57 et seq.
81. For further information on consolidated versions and legal certainty, *see* S. Bendlinger, *Multilaterales Instrument zur automatischen Anpassung bestehender Doppelbesteuerungsabkommen*, Steuer und Wirtschaft International (SWI), at 2, 9 (2017).
82. N. Bravo, *The Proposal for a Multilateral Tax Instrument for Updating Tax Treaties*, in *Base Erosion and Profit Shifting (BEPS)*, at 328, 346 (M. Lang et al. eds., Linde 2015).
83. N. Bravo, *The Multilateral Tax Instrument and Its Relationship with Tax Treaties*, 8 World Tax J. 3, at 279, 281 (October 2016).
84. OECD, *Action 15 Final Report*, *supra* n. 9, para. 23.
85. Bravo, *supra* n. 82, at 297.

will require modification.[86] By clearly cross-referencing the relevant subject matter of bilateral treaties with appropriate language, a reference to articles of existing bilateral treaties will not be necessary.[87] Therefore, a precise description of the provisions that require modification will replace the reference to the articles and paragraphs that need to be amended. Not knowing which specific articles and paragraphs were modified by the MLI and to what extent the modification happened, may present a formidable challenge for all parties involved, and in order to avoid infringements of the existing treaty must be absolutely clear.[88]

Furthermore, another benefit of preparing a consolidated version is the increased usability.[89] Instead of analysing the MLI and any accompanying instrument, as well as the text of the original instrument and any amending protocol thereto, both the taxpayer and the tax administration will be required to look at only the consolidated version. Moreover, producing consolidated versions of treaties as modified by the MLI may help to facilitate the effective implementation of the provisions of the MLI by national tax administrations.

3.3 Challenges Associated with Developing Consolidated Versions

Considering the arguments mentioned above, the preparation of consolidated versions may appear useful for various reasons. The versions of treaties as modified by the MLI will, however, have to be prepared carefully. Numerous considerations need to be taken into account in order to ensure that they properly serve their purpose. As discussed, not all parties to the MLI have a domestic law obligation to prepare consolidated versions, and not all of them produce them voluntarily. Therefore, no uniform approach to the preparation of a consolidated version is available. However, if a different approach is applied in various countries, the preparation of consolidated versions may not result in an increase in the level of legal certainty. Thus, in order to ensure the greatest possible degree of legal certainty, the OECD should be involved in the process of preparing consolidated versions. The Action 15 Final Report also suggests including the depositary in the process of drafting a consolidated version.[90] The inclusion of the OECD is especially essential considering that the MLI constitutes an innovative approach with no exact precedent in the tax world, that bilateral treaties are highly varied in their details and that there are limited precedents for modifying bilateral treaties with a multilateral instrument.[91] Furthermore, the majority of states are inexperienced regarding the peculiarities of a multilateral treaty such as the MLI, and a considerable number of states are not familiar with producing consolidated versions of treaties. Therefore the role of the OECD and especially of the depositary should transcend a mere consultation of the countries involved. Instead, detailed

86. OECD, *Explanatory Statement*, *supra* n. 6, para. 15.
87. OECD, *Action 15 Final Report*, *supra* n. 9, para. 23.
88. Bravo, *supra* n. 82, at 348 et seq.
89. S. Schmidjell-Dommes, *Wie BEPSt Österreich?*, Transfer Pricing Int'l. 1, at 36, 39 et seq. (2017).
90. OECD, *Action 15 Final Report*, *supra* n. 9, para. 61.
91. OECD, *Action 15 Final Report*, *supra* n. 9, at Executive Summary.

guidelines should be provided by the OECD, and consolidated versions of treaties as amended by the MLI should be prepared by parties in collaboration with the depositary of the instrument.[92]

The guidelines provided for by the depositary could serve as a reference point for the parties and signatories, and they are especially valuable for countries that have thus far not created consolidated versions. When drafting a consolidated version, a state should, as a first step, identify the provisions of the MLI that will apply to its treaties. In order to be able to assess the extent of the amendment resulting from the MLI, a state will have to carefully analyse the options it chose and the reservations it made, and it will have to ascertain whether the other party has chosen the same options and whether the same or different reservations were made. After having identified the applicable provisions, the states will have to decide on the modality of incorporation. This step may, for various reasons, be challenging for the countries involved, as they might find it difficult to assess certain circumstances, i.e., the precise position of a newly added provision such as a principal purpose test clause. Countries may not know exactly how to incorporate such a provision into their existing treaties, or where to add and position it. In order to ensure consistency in the results, they should be able to turn to the OECD when experiencing such difficulties and receive information on the issue requested. This way, the OECD can provide more targeted assistance. When specific questions arise regularly, the OECD could actively approach countries in order to inform them about possible remedies and in order to provide for support when needed. Alternatively, the questions posed to the depositary and the answers thereto could be made publicly available. That way, consistency between different tax treaties with similar provisions could be ensured.

In preparing a consolidated version, the parties to the MLI should collaborate. This will effectively help to decrease the risk of misinterpretation and misapplication of the provisions of the MLI, and will most likely help to prevent future disputes between the parties to a specific bilateral or multilateral treaty. Furthermore, the consolidated version produced following the ratification of the MLI should also incorporate and reflect any prior amendments.

Moreover, the Explanatory Statement must be considered when drafting a consolidated version, as it provides detailed guidance on which provisions of bilateral treaties are intended to be modified by the MLI and also gives information on how the modifications will occur. In this regard, a provision's compatibility clause is also of utmost importance, as it defines the relationship between the provisions of the MLI and existing tax treaties in objective terms. The overlap of provisions of the MLI with provisions contained in existing bilateral agreements may result in a conflict which is addressed through a compatibility clause aimed at resolving it.[93]

Furthermore, in order to attain their objective, public availability of consolidated versions is crucial, as this approach will increase legal certainty. As such, taxpayers would have easy access to them and could quickly find out about the legal situation

92. OECD, *Action 15 Final Report*, *supra* n. 9, para. 61.
93. OECD, *Explanatory Statement*, *supra* n. 6, para. 15. For an in-depth consideration of these issues, *see* Chapter 6 of this book.

they are subject to. Thus, states preparing consolidated versions should make them publicly available. From the perspective of international law, there is no obligation to submit a consolidated version to the depositary. However, in practice, the transmission of such a version may be feasible, as in that case the depositary could then ensure that all consolidated versions are made publicly available. In order to provide the necessary information to all relevant stakeholders, including national tax administrations, domestic judges, taxpayers and civil society, consolidated versions of existing bilateral treaties should be included in a publicly accessible database.[94] This database could be administered by the depositary.

Additionally, the matter of the timing of producing consolidated versions should not be disregarded, and an early conclusion of the production of the consolidated versions should be ensured. In order to attain its objective, a consolidated version should ideally be available by the time of entry into effect of the provisions of the tax treaties as modified by the MLI.

3.4 Potential Legal and Practical Difficulties

One must bear in mind that consolidated versions may contain a considerable potential for conflict, particularly in situations where the content of the consolidated version deviates from the content that can be derived from the MLI and the underlying bilateral or multilateral agreement, as only the latter is authoritative from the perspective of public international law and consolidated versions are never afforded any legal relevance. It is critical to keep in mind that a consolidated version may not always accurately reflect the amendments that were intended to result from the application of the MLI. Such deviations in the content could be attributed to various reasons, including inadequate drafting or inconsistencies in the interpretation of the agreements.

While, as mentioned, consolidated versions are not afforded any legal relevance in international law, their classification in national law depends on the domestic law of each country. Thus, while some countries might attribute legal relevance to consolidated versions, others develop them solely for convenience purposes. Assuming that consolidated versions are not afforded any legal relevance, national tax administrations relying on the accuracy of a consolidated version may find themselves in a situation where it is successfully challenged in court by a taxpayer. Furthermore, a state may be faced with questions of state liability, as the MLI was not correctly implemented and it could therefore be fully liable for the infringement of international law. Thus, – instead of adding to legal certainty – consolidated versions might create a false sense of security for both taxpayers and national tax administrations, considering that public international law disregards the content of consolidated versions for legal purposes.

This problem is further exacerbated by the fact that some countries, pursuant to their domestic law, do afford legal relevance to consolidated versions. In such a case,

94. OECD, *Action 15 Final Report, supra* n. 9, para. 64.

the relationship between the two layers of law must be assessed carefully. While the constitutional law of some states gives general primacy to international law, other states apply the 'later in time' principle. For these latter countries, a consolidated version containing deviating wording could prevail over the MLI. Where the deviation in the wording results in a violation of international law, such practice has become known as a 'treaty override' and can formally be defined as 'the enactment of domestic legislation intended by the legislature to have effects in clear contradiction to international treaty obligations'.[95] While a treaty override constitutes an infringement of international law, and while it may trigger certain sanctions in response, such a violation does not necessarily result in the invalidity of a consolidated version, as its effects depend on a state's constitutional law.[96] Such an approach would subsequently prevent the uniform application of the MLI and would therefore be contrary to the instrument's express object and purpose.

Moreover, due to the complexity of the MLI, consolidated versions that are not drafted carefully have a notable potential for mistakes. If both states decide to draft one and the two versions deviate, further problems will arise. The potential for conflict can be decreased significantly if the countries involved cooperate in the preparation of a mutual consolidated version. However, while a procedure of this kind may definitely help to mitigate the difficulties generally associated with consolidated versions, their legal nature is not affected, as a close cooperation between the states does not guarantee the accuracy of consolidated versions. Even if the consolidated version becomes part of a mutual agreement between the two competent authorities, it does not achieve more legal weight. In many countries, courts ignore mutual agreements when they have to apply tax treaties. Otherwise, courts would give up checking whether acts merely produced by the administrations are in line with the tax treaty which usually is approved by the legislature.

Furthermore, language issues may arise when drafting a consolidated version, considering that the MLI's only authentic languages are English and French, and a considerable number of treaties are not authoritative in one of these languages. Therefore, the different language versions of the agreements to be considered may give rise to interpretation issues.

Whether the production of consolidated versions results in an increase of legal certainty may well be called into question in view of the problems which can be associated with them and which were discussed extensively in the previous paragraphs. While consolidated versions may facilitate the assessment of the current legal situation when drafted carefully, they may also create a false sense of security, as their wording can deviate from the wording that can be derived from the underlying treaty and the MLI. Therefore, the value of consolidated versions should be subject to a critical review.

95. K. Vogel & A. Rust, *Introduction*, in *Klaus Vogel on Double Taxation Conventions*, 4th ed. (E. Reimer & A. Rust eds., Wolters Kluwer 2015), para. 155.
96. Vogel & Rust, *supra* n. 95, paras 158 et seq.

4 CONCLUSION

In order to successfully address BEPS concerns, broad participation of the international community is required. Thus, the MLI aims at modifying the greatest number of treaties possible. In order to attract a maximum number of states, flexibility is of paramount importance, as reaching a single agreement without the possibility of unilateral adjustment is highly unlikely, given the existence of different tax systems and dissimilar tax policies. Flexibility is guaranteed by a variety of mechanisms. One of the major challenges related to the development of a flexible multilateral treaty involved ensuring that mechanisms and procedures were developed and put in place to achieve full transparency. One of the measures intended to ensure clarity and transparency is the requirement to make notifications. Each substantive provision of the MLI is structured the same and contains one or more notification clause(s), requiring parties to notify certain circumstances to the depositary. That way, parties are allowed to modify or exclude specific treaty provisions to accommodate a different country position. In order for the modification or exclusion to be effective, it must be communicated to the depositary by means of a notification. Article 29(1) of the MLI provides for an exhaustive list of required notifications by reference to the provisions in which they are set out.

Another tool that could help to address the challenges that result from the flexible approach adopted by the MLI, is the preparation of consolidated versions of treaties. Formally, a consolidated version consists of the content of an amendment, or amendments if more than one, being incorporated into the content of the base publication, and reflects the precise changes made to an existing bilateral agreement and the level of commitment undertaken by the parties in cases where the MLI provides for flexibility. Despite not being legally required by international law or the MLI itself, countries may resort to such versions to avoid or mitigate confusion and uncertainty that would otherwise occur. As many bilateral treaties are simultaneously affected by the modifications, cross-references to specific articles are not possible and the assessment of the applicable legal situation may involve significant difficulties.

Thus, the preparation of consolidated versions may appear useful for various reasons. However, these versions will have to be drafted carefully and various aspects will have to be taken into consideration. Furthermore, one must bear in mind that consolidated versions could contain a considerable potential for conflict, particularly in situations where the content of the consolidated version deviates from the content that can be derived from the MLI and the underlying agreement. Moreover, language issues can arise, as the MLI's authentic languages are English and French, and a considerable number of treaties are not authoritative in one of these two languages.

CHAPTER 10

Consequences of Withdrawal from or Termination of the Multilateral Instrument

Benedikt Hörtenhuber[*]

1 INTRODUCTION

Before signing the Multilateral Instrument (MLI)[1] it is crucial to carefully examine - in addition to the binding contractual rights and obligations - whether there is a predetermined contractual clause which makes it possible for the parties to withdraw from the MLI. Article 37 of the MLI contains a specially designated provision for withdrawal from the MLI. However, the MLI does not contain an explicit provision on the termination of the MLI itself. Nevertheless, the Vienna Convention on the Law of Treaties (hereinafter 'Vienna Convention')[2] contains several provisions that deal with the withdrawal from, or termination of a treaty. However, the Vienna Convention provision can be regarded as setting forth default rules and would apply only 'unless' the treaty (i.e., the MLI) otherwise provides. Therefore, the MLI needs to be analysed carefully in order to assess the legal consequences in the event of a withdrawal from, or a termination of the MLI. The legal relevance of the Vienna Convention provisions with regard to the termination will mainly depend on the question as to whether an implicit right of termination could be derived from the content and the nature of the MLI itself.

* The author would like to thank Univ.-Prof. Dr DDr. h.c. *Michael Lang*, Hon.-Prof. Dr *Heinz Jirousek* and *Nathalie Bravo*, LLM for their valuable inputs.

1. OECD, *Multilateral Convention to Implement Tax Treaty Related Measures to Prevent Base Erosion And Profit Shifting* (November 2016).
2. United Nations, *Treaty Series* (1980), vol. 1155, at 331. The Vienna Convention on the Law of Treaties (the Vienna Convention) was drafted by the International Law Commission (ILC) of the United Nations and entered into force on 27 January 1980; it has been ratified by 114 states. For the full list, *see* https://treaties.un.org/doc/Publication/MTDSG/Volume II/Chapter XXIII/XXIII -1.en.pdf, accessed 13 July 2017.

Each future contracting party must face the legal consequences in the event of a withdrawal from, or a termination of the MLI or the underlying tax treaty. Therefore, it is necessary to clearly understand how the contractual rights and obligations are intended to be implemented in the bilateral tax treaty relationship to determine the succeeding effects of such an event. The consequences of a withdrawal from or a termination of the MLI will mainly depend on how these modifications in the tax treaties are implemented.

The reasons for a withdrawal from or a termination of the MLI can differ widely and range from a change in the political system to the conclusion of a later treaty. Therefore, this issue is highly significant not only for the signing contracting parties, but also for further governments that will be bound by the contractual rights and obligations through the MLI. Each potential signatory to the MLI should therefore check in advance as to the contractual rights and obligations, and consider the consequences in the event of a withdrawal from, or a termination of the MLI.

2 IMPLEMENTATION AND EFFECTIVENESS OF THE MLI

2.1 Negotiation and Signature

The facilitators of the OECD Base Erosion and Profit Shifting (BEPS) project agreed on the implementation of a MLI, which is intended to modify a variety of bilateral tax treaties.[3] This MLI 'should be negotiated through an International Conference open to G20 countries, OECD members and other interested countries and convened under the aegis of the OECD and the G20. The mandate of the Conference should be limited in scope (implementing the BEPS Action Plan) and in time (no more than two years)'.[4] This International Conference - through a mandate[5] of the OECD and G20 - developed the MLI to tackle BEPS-related topics in tax treaties.[6] The negotiations concerned the contractual content of the MLI. The members of the ad hoc group determined the contractual text of the MLI. The negotiation process of the OECD/G20 mandate was

3. OECD, *Developing a Multilateral Instrument to Modify Bilateral Tax Treaties – Action 15: 2015 Final Report*, OECD/G20 Base Erosion and Profit Shifting Project (2015). For a further example, *see also* N. Bravo, *The Proposal for a Multilateral Tax Instrument for Updating Tax Treaties*, in *Base Erosion and Profit Shifting (BEPS)* (M. Lang, P. Pistone, A. Rust, J. Schuch & C. Staringer eds., Linde 2016), at 328; S. Bendlinger, *Multilateral Instrument to Automatically Adjust Existing Bilateral Tax Treaties*, Steuer und Wirtschaft International (SWI), at 2 (2017); J. Hattingh, *The Multilateral Instrument from a Legal Perspective: What May Be the Challenges?*, 71 Bull. Int'l. Taxn. 3/4 (2017); H. Jirousek, *Where Will International Tax Law Move?*, SWI, at 332–334 (2017); C. Silberztein & J. Tristram, *OECD: Multilateral Instrument To Implement BEPS*, 23 Int'l. Transfer Pricing J. 5, at 347–353 (2016).
4. OECD, *Developing a Multilateral Instrument to Modify Bilateral Tax Treaties – Action 15: 2014 Deliverable*, OECD/G20 Base Erosion and Profit Shifting Project (2014), at 14.
5. OECD, *Action 15: A Mandate for the Development of a Multilateral Instrument on Tax Treaty Measures to Tackle BEPS*, OECD/G20 Base Erosion and Profit Shifting Project (2015), at 3–9.
6. OECD, *Action Plan on Base Erosion and Profit Shifting* (2013); OECD, *Addressing Base Erosion and Profit Shifting* (2013). *See also Base Erosion and Profit Shifting, supra* n. 4.

successfully concluded, and the MLI was published on 24 November 2016.[7] The new instrument, the Multilateral Convention to Implement Tax Treaty Related Measures to Prevent BEPS (commonly referred to as the 'Multilateral Instrument'),[8] is supposed to swiftly implement BEPS-related issues into various bilateral tax treaties around the world. An Explanatory Statement[9] with regard to the MLI was also drafted and published together with the MLI, and 'is intended to clarify the operation of the Convention'.[10]

This Convention, the MLI, must be signed by the states and jurisdictions and is subject to ratification, acceptance or approval pursuant to Article 27(2) of the MLI. Although the MLI opened for signature by 1 January 2017, the first official signing ceremony took place on 7 June 2017 in Paris.[11] To date, sixty-eight states or jurisdictions[12] have already signed the MLI.

As defined in Article 2(1)(d) of the MLI, the term 'signatory' as used in the MLI means a 'State or jurisdiction which has signed this Convention but for which the Convention is not yet in force'.[13] Once the state or jurisdiction has signed the MLI, the signatory must deposit its instrument of ratification, acceptance or approval. This state or jurisdiction becomes a party to the MLI if the MLI enters into force pursuant to Article 34 (Entry into Force). A signatory subsequently becomes a party to the MLI if the MLI has entered into force for that state. The difference between a party and a mere signatory of the MLI is essential to the contractual rights and obligations, as well as the follow-up consequences of a withdrawal from, or a termination of the MLI. Therefore, the date of entry into force will be critical when ascertaining the legal consequences. Having said this, the deposit of the instrument of ratification will mainly depend on the national ratification process of the concerned contracting state or jurisdiction.

2.2 Entry into Force

The MLI must enter into force for each signatory thereof in order to implement the tax treaty-related measures to prevent BEPS into the notified tax agreements. Article 34 of the MLI, which specifies the point in time when the MLI enters into force, provides as follows:

7. OECD, *Countries Adopt Multilateral Convention to Close Tax Treaty Loopholes and Improve Functioning of International Tax System*, OECD Press Release (24 November 2016).
8. OECD, *Multilateral Convention to Implement Tax Treaty Related Measures to Prevent Base Erosion and Profit Shifting* (2016).
9. OECD, *Explanatory Statement to the Multilateral Convention to implement Tax Treaty Related Measures to Prevent Base Erosion and Profit Shifting* (2016).
10. OECD, *Explanatory Statement*, *supra* n. 9, para. 12.
11. OECD, *Countries Adopt Multilateral Convention*, *supra* n. 7; Meeting of the OECD Council at Ministerial Level on 7–8 June 2017.
12. For the full list of signatories, *see* http://www.oecd.org/tax/treaties/beps-mli-signatories-and-parties.pdf (accessed 13 January 2017).
13. Article 2(1)(d) MLI.

1. This Convention shall enter into force on the first day of the month following the expiration of a period of three calendar months beginning on the date of deposit of the fifth instrument of ratification, acceptance or approval.
2. For each Signatory ratifying, accepting, or approving this Convention after the deposit of the fifth instrument of ratification, acceptance or approval, the Convention shall enter into force on the first day of the month following the expiration of a period of three calendar months beginning on the date of the deposit by such Signatory of its instrument of ratification, acceptance or approval.

Under Article 34(1), the MLI itself will enter into force three month after at least five states or jurisdictions which have already signed the MLI, have deposited their instrument of ratification, acceptance or approval of the MLI.[14] Thus, a minimum of at least five deposited instruments of ratifications, acceptance or approval are necessary in order for the MLI itself to enter into force for the first time. However, this minimum number of potential signatories will not be an actual problem, as the OECD organized a signing ceremony in June 2017. The real issue is that the signatories must complete their national ratification processes and deposit their instruments of ratification. This ratification process can vary from state to state and will mainly depend on the provisions of the applicable national constitutional law. The implementation of the political choice to sign and ratify the MLI may be an expedited process in some cases, or could take months - or even years - in other states or jurisdictions.

The time period between the deposit of the fifth instrument and the first day of entry into force of the MLI itself is at least three calendar months, and ends on the first day of the month following the expiration of this three-calendar-month period.[15] The first day the month following the deposit of the fifth instrument, in addition to the three-month-time expiration indicated, is consequently the decisive date for the entry into force of the MLI itself and is also the equally decisive date for the entry into force of the first five signatories that have deposited their instruments of ratification, acceptance or approval. Therefore, the first valid day of entry into force for each signatory is the first day of the month following a three-calendar-month period after the deposit of the fifth ratification, acceptance or approval of the MLI.

Once the MLI itself has entered into force, the entry into force date for each further signatory is determined based on an individual calculation pursuant to Article 34(2) of the MLI. The date of entry into force for the first five signatories that have deposited their instruments of ratification, acceptance or approval, is the same as the date of entry into force of the MLI itself. The decisive date for subsequent signatories

14. Pursuant to Art. 27(2) MLI ('This Convention is subject to ratification, acceptance or approval.').
15. Consider the following sample calculation of the time expiration of the period of three calendar months: deposit of ratification on 28 January 2017 + three calendar months beginning on the date of deposit (28 January 2017) → 28 April 2017 + first day of the month following the expiration → 1 May 2017 (date of entry into force). Under Art. 4(2) of the European Convention on the calculation of time limits, the last day of the last month is decisive if a corresponding day is missing. For example: deposit of ratification on 31 January 2017 + three calendar months beginning on the date of deposit (31 January 2017) → 30 April 2017 + first day of the month following the expiration → 1 May 2017 (date of entry into force).

will be calculated in the same manner, but starting from each individual date of deposit of the respective instrument of ratification. Therefore, the entry into force for each signatory is an ongoing process as soon as five signatories have deposited their instruments of ratification. As the MLI itself has entered into force, the entry into force date for each individual states or jurisdiction will depend on the deposit of its instrument of ratification and begins on the first day of the month following the expiration of the three-calendar month period.

The MLI enters into force for each signatory after the instrument of ratification has been deposited and the specified time period has expired. The previous signatory consequently becomes a party to the MLI. Under Article 2(1)(b) of the MLI, the term 'party' means a state or jurisdiction for which the MLI 'is in force pursuant to Article 34 (Entry into Force)'.[16] From that point on, every notified agreement for the avoidance of double taxation[17] between the parties is covered by means of a 'covered tax agreement'.[18] As of the date on which the MLI enters into force with respect to a covered tax agreement, the parties must comply with the rights and obligations as provided for in the MLI.

2.3 Entry into Effect

Once the MLI has entered into force pursuant to Article 34 thereof, the tax treaty-related measures of the MLI (hereinafter 'the MLI provisions') are not immediately applicable. The MLI provisions will have effect with respect to covered tax agreements when these provisions enter into effect pursuant to Article 35 of the MLI. Before that, the MLI provisions are not applicable with respect to a covered tax agreement. However, the legal commitment to the MLI provisions with respect to covered tax agreements occurs when the MLI enters into force pursuant to Article 34 thereof. On the other hand, Article 35 of the MLI solely determines the point in time when the MLI provisions will have effect with respect to the covered tax agreement.[19] Pursuant to Article 35(1)(a) of the MLI, the provision concerning 'taxes withheld at source' will have effect on or after the first day of the next calendar year when the MLI enters into force with respect to a covered tax agreement.[20]

With regard to 'all other taxes', under Article 35(1)(b) of the MLI, the relevant provisions of the MLI will have effect for a taxable period beginning on or after the

16. Article 2(1)(b) MLI.
17. Also commonly called a 'tax treaty' or 'double taxation agreement'. The states or jurisdictions must make a notification to the depositary listing all tax agreements that are to be covered by the MLI.
18. Article 2(1)(a) MLI.
19. Article 35(1) MLI (providing that '[t]he provisions of this Convention shall have effect in each Contracting Jurisdiction with respect to a Covered Tax Agreement' on the – in (a) and (b) – prescribed dates after a specific time period (next calendar year, period of six calendar months).
20. Article 35(1)(a) MLI ('with respect to taxes withheld at source on amounts paid or credited to non-residents, where the event giving rise to such taxes occurs on or after the first day of the next calendar year that begins on or after the latest of the dates on which this Convention enters into force for each of the Contracting Jurisdictions to the Covered Tax Agreement').

expiration of a period of six calendar months.[21] Furthermore, the point in time for the date of entry into effect can vary under special rules in Article 35 of the MLI concerning notifications and reservations, as well as the entry into effect of Part VI of the MLI pursuant to Article 36 thereof.[22]

However, the most significant consequence of the entry into effect of the MLI pursuant to Article 34 is that, from that moment, the tax treaty-related MLI provisions are deemed to have modified and affected the covered tax agreements. The new BEPS-related provisions coexist with the covered tax agreements and supersede the existing provisions of the covered tax agreements to the extent of the scope of the MLI. This specific manner of implementing the MLI provisions is decisive for the resulting legal consequences in the event of a withdrawal from, or a termination of the MLI.

2.4 Relationship Between the MLI and Covered Tax Agreements

After the MLI enters into force and also enters into effect, the covered tax agreements are affected through the MLI and are legally binding. In this context, the question arises as to the relationship[23] between the provisions of the MLI and the superseded provisions of the covered tax agreements. This relationship could be described as a coexistence[24] of the MLI and the existing bilateral tax treaties. One approach to deal with the relationship could be to explicitly define the relationship by so-called comparability clauses.[25] Another way to determine the relationship between the MLI and the covered tax agreements could be to follow the general principle of jurisprudence, such that the newer provisions apply only to the extent of the scope of the MLI provisions.[26] Article 30 of the Vienna Convention stipulates the relationship in the case of provisions of 'successive treaties dealing with the same subject matter'. However, in the most common case of identical parties under both treaties, the default rule in Article 30(3) of the Vienna Convention, i.e., the *lex posterior derogat legi priori* rule, will apply. This principle, which is laid down in public international law, states that '... the earlier treaty applies only to the extent that its provisions are compatible with those of the

21. Article 35(1)(b) MLI ('with respect to all other taxes levied by that Contracting Jurisdiction, for taxes levied with respect to taxable periods beginning on or after the expiration of a period of six calendar months (or a shorter period, if all Contracting Jurisdictions notify the Depositary that they intend to apply such shorter period) from the latest of the dates on which this Convention enters into force for each of the Contracting Jurisdictions to the Covered Tax Agreement').
22. For details, *see* Art. 35, paras 5, 6 and 7 MLI. *See also* Chapter 9 in this book regarding notifications and reservations; for the provisions regarding Part IV *see* Art. 36 MLI.
23. For details, *see* Chapter 6 in this book regarding the relationship between tax treaties and the multilateral instrument. *See also* Bravo, *supra* n. 3, at 330–340; L.E. Schoueri & R.A. Galendi, *Interpretative and Policy Challenges Following the OECD Multilateral Instrument (2016) from a Brazilian Perspective*, 71 Bull. Intl. Taxn. 6, at 340–343 (2017); N. Bravo, *The Multilateral Tax Instrument and Its Relationship with Tax Treaties*, 8 World T.J. 3, at 291–293 (2016); F. Haase, *Das sog. Multilaterale Instrument*, Internationale Wirtschafts-Briefe (IWB), at 16–22 (2017).
24. For the approach taken in the MLI, *see* OECD, *Explanatory Statement*, *supra* n. 9, para. 13.
25. These issue will be addressed in more detail in Chapter 6 of this book.
26. OECD, *Action 15 Deliverable*, *supra* n. 4, at 33.

latter treaty'.[27] This approach is also taken in the MLI, as it 'will be applied alongside'[28] the underlying tax treaties (in the MLI, referred to as covered tax agreements).[29]

Furthermore, Article 30 of the MLI provides for the opportunity for subsequent modification of covered tax agreements that apply without any prejudice to the MLI.[30] Therefore, it can be stated that the approach taken in the MLI is in accordance with the aforementioned international law rules.

Once the provisions of the MLI have entered into force and thus have 'modified' the covered tax agreements, the modified covered tax agreements become applicable for the taxpayer and the tax authorities only from the subsequent date of entry into effect. Subsequent modifications of the modified covered tax agreement are possible pursuant to Article 30 of the MLI. Furthermore, there are several possibilities with regard to options, reservation and further notifications.[31] Therefore, the date of signature, entry into force and entry into effect, as well as the manner of implementing and the effectiveness of the MLI, are crucial for assessing the contractual rights and obligations with respect to the affected covered tax agreements. The following two parts of this chapter will focus on the legal basis, the procedural requirements and, in particular, on the consequences of a withdrawal from, or a termination of the MLI.

3 WITHDRAWAL FROM THE MLI

3.1 Specific Provision in Article 37 of the MLI

The MLI contains a specially designated provision regarding withdrawal from the MLI, namely Article 37, which provides as follows:[32]

> 1. Any Party may, at any time, withdraw from this Convention by means of a notification addressed to the Depositary.
> 2. Withdrawal pursuant to paragraph 1 shall become effective on the date of receipt of the notification by the Depositary. In cases where this Convention has entered into force with respect to all Contracting Jurisdictions to a Covered Tax Agreement before the date on which a Party's withdrawal becomes effective, that Covered Tax Agreement shall remain as modified by this Convention.

27. Article 30(3) Vienna Convention.
28. OECD, *Explanatory Statement*, *supra* n. 9, para. 13.
29. OECD, *Action 15 Deliverable*, *supra* n. 4, at 33 ('In the silence of the multilateral treaty, the applicable customary rule, codified in Article 30(3) of the VCLT, 4 is that when two rules apply to the same matter, the later in time prevails (lex posterior derogat legi priori). Accordingly, earlier (i.e., previously concluded) bilateral treaties would continue to apply only to the extent that their provisions are compatible with those of the later multilateral treaty.').
30. Article 30 MLI ('The provisions in this Convention are without prejudice to subsequent modifications to a Covered Tax Agreement which may be agreed between the Contracting Jurisdictions of the Covered Tax Agreement.').
31. These issues are addressed in more detail in Chapters 8 and 9 of this book [options, reservations, and notifications].
32. For purposes of this chapter, the withdrawal described here deals only the withdrawal from the MLI pursuant to Art. 37 of the MLI and not with the withdrawal from the tax treaty on a bilateral basis.

3.2 Procedural Requirements

This specific provision in the MLI concerning withdrawal from the MLI pursuant to Article 37 sets forth the procedural requirements for a party's withdrawal from the MLI.

3.2.1 Any Party

First, a withdrawal from the MLI is possible only for a party to the MLI. Therefore, only parties to the MLI may give notice of a withdrawal, which means all states and jurisdictions for which this MLI 'is in force pursuant to Article 34 (Entry into Force)'[33] may withdraw from the MLI. A signatory may not withdraw from the MLI pursuant to Article 37, as this state or jurisdiction is not a party to the MLI. If a signatory wants to reverse its decision, that signatory must not deposit its instrument of ratification, acceptance or approval. However, the withdrawing signatory may have to reverse its national ratification, approval or acceptance process under its own constitutional law. If the signatory has already deposited its instrument of ratification, but has not yet become a party to the MLI only because the three-month period has not yet expired, a withdrawal pursuant to Article 37 would then be necessary.

3.2.2 At Any Time

Under Article 37 of the MLI, any party may withdraw from the MLI 'at any time', so there is no time limitation or a particular point in time (such as a notice date). The only stipulation is that the MLI have entered into force for the withdrawing party pursuant to Article 34 thereof. If the signatory has deposited its instrument of ratification, but the MLI itself has not entered into force pursuant to Article 34 thereof, the withdrawal is legally impossible. In such a case, the question arises as to whether the deposit of the instrument of ratification could be reversed by a signatory. Consequently, the MLI itself must enter into force for the first time in order to allow the parties the right to withdraw pursuant to Article 37 thereof. Before that date, a withdrawal pursuant to Article 37 is not possible.

3.2.3 Notification Addressed to the Depositary

Moreover, a withdrawal calls for certain formal requirements. A withdrawal requires a 'notification addressed to the Depositary'. A withdrawal from the MLI must be effected through a notification pursuant to Article 29 thereof addressed to the depositary. The depositary is defined in Article 39 of the MLI and is to be the Secretary-General of the OECD.[34] Pursuant to Article 39(2)(f) of the MLI, the depositary must notify all other parties and signatories within one calendar month of 'any withdrawal from this

33. Article 2(1)(b) MLI.
34. Article 39(1) MLI.

Convention pursuant to Article 37 (Withdrawal)'.[35] Thus, not only parties to the MLI are informed about a party's withdrawal, but signatories are notified, as well. However, the time period for forwarding the notification of the withdrawal to all other parties and signatories constitutes a time of uncertainty.

3.2.4 Effective Date of the Withdrawal

The most crucial issue regarding the withdrawal concerns the effective date of the withdrawal from the MLI and not the notification of this event. Therefore, Article 37(2) of the MLI provides that the withdrawal becomes effective on the date of receipt of the notification by the depositary.[36] Therefore, the decisive date for assessing the legal implications concerning a withdrawal is the point in time when the depositary – pursuant to Article 39 – receives the notification of the withdrawal from the withdrawing party. The date of receipt of the notification by the depositary is the effective date for the party's withdrawal from the MLI, and is therefore essential when determining the legal consequences. The time period not exceeding one calendar month between the receipt of the notification by the depositary and the forwarding of the information about the withdrawal to all parties and signatories about the effective date of the withdrawal, constitutes an element of uncertainty for the remaining parties and signatories. This is because the legal consequences become effective on the date of receipt of the withdrawal by the depositary, and not when all the other parties and signatories receive this notification about the withdrawal from the MLI.

In this context, a general issue arises concerning incorrect or undelivered notifications. For details, *see* Chapter 9 of this book.[37]

3.3 Consequences of a Withdrawal

The consequences of a withdrawal from the MLI essentially depend on an already created legal situation through the implementation of the MLI provisions in the covered tax agreements. Therefore, the legal situation in the covered tax agreement is decisive as from the effective date on which the depositary receives the notification of the party's withdrawal from the MLI. Special attention must be given to the effective date of the withdrawal pursuant to Article 37 of the MLI and the date of entry into force pursuant to Article 34 of the, in order to assess the existing legal situation. The date of entry into effect pursuant to Article 35 of the MLI is not a crucial element for the assessment of the consequences of a withdrawal from the MLI.[38]

35. Article 39(2)(f) MLI.
36. Article 37(2) MLI.
37. *See* Chapter 9 of this book [dealing with notifications].
38. For more information, *see* the explanation below. *See also* OECD, *Explanatory Statement*, *supra* n. 9, para. 353 (stipulating that the covered tax agreement shall remain as modified by the MLI and 'regardless of whether those modifications have come into effect pursuant to Article 35').

3.3.1 Covered Tax Agreement Shall Remain as Modified by the MLI

Pursuant to the second sentence of Article 37(2) of the MLI, the legal consequences are as follows:

> In cases where this Convention has entered into force with respect to all Contracting Jurisdictions to a Covered Tax Agreement before the date on which a Party's withdrawal becomes effective, that Covered Tax Agreement shall remain as modified by this Convention.[39]

Under this provision, the affected covered tax agreement shall remain as modified by the MLI. Each affected 'covered tax agreement'[40] before the effective date of a party's withdrawal – including all modifications made while a party to the MLI – shall remain as modified by the MLI. Insofar as the MLI has entered into force pursuant to Article 34 thereof among contracting jurisdictions[41] to a covered tax agreement, these modification made in the covered tax agreements remain unaffected by the withdrawal. Once the MLI enters into force, these provisions still coexist within the bilateral tax agreement relationship even after the withdrawal from the MLI. If these MLI provisions have already entered into effect, such provisions are applicable and also affect the underlying tax agreements. Even if the MLI provisions have solely entered into force, but have not yet entered into effect, the covered tax agreement has already been modified and these provisions will entry into effect on the designated date, and will also be applicable as from that date. A withdrawal from the MLI would not modify covered tax agreements retroactively which have been modified by the MLI. These MLI provisions that have entered into force pursuant to Article 34 thereof to a covered tax agreement shall remain unaffected by the withdrawal, even if these modifications have not entered into effect pursuant to Article 35 of the MLI.

3.3.2 Withdrawal Will Not Affect Contractual Duties in the Covered Tax Agreement Between the Contracting Jurisdictions

The covered tax agreements will remain as modified by the MLI. The modifications were made through the implementation of the MLI provisions in the covered tax agreement. These MLI provisions coexist alongside the underlying tax treaties.[42] The modifications concerning the tax treaties are effected on the date on which the MLI enters into force pursuant to Article 34 thereof to a covered tax agreement. Once the MLI enters into force with respect to a covered tax agreement, the provisions of the MLI have been implemented into the affected tax treaty relationship. The MLI provisions to

39. Article 37(2), 2nd sentence MLI.
40. Pursuant to Art. 2(1)(a) MLI.
41. Article 2(1)(c) MLI (defining a contracting jurisdiction as 'a party to a Covered Tax Agreement').
42. The MLI may also modify multilateral treaties like the Nordic Multilateral Tax Treaty (Convention between Denmark, Finland, Iceland, Norway, and Sweden for the avoidance of double taxation with respect to taxes on inheritances and gifts). In general not only bilateral tax treaties are covered, but also agreements for the avoidance of double taxation between two or more states or jurisdictions.

prevent BEPS thus modify the covered tax agreement. The implementation of the MLI provisions into the tax treaty relationship through the entry into force event is an irreversible one-time process (executed clause).[43] The covered tax agreement remains as modified by the MLI 'and regardless of whether those modifications have come into effect pursuant to Article 35'.[44] Therefore, it is not relevant as to whether (or not) the provision of the MLI have entered into effect pursuant to Article 35 of the MLI, as the covered tax agreements have already been modified by the entry into force of the MLI.

The applicability of the tax treaty-related BEPS provisions that have been implemented in the bilateral tax treaty relationship, remains unchanged, and these MLI provisions become applicable as from the date of the entry into effect. Any further modification of the tax agreement (former covered tax agreement) – such as the full cancellation of the MLI provisions in the tax treaties – must be done on a bilateral basis and in accordance with the rules of the underlying tax treaty.[45] '[A] unilateral decision to withdraw from the Convention would not reverse the modifications already made to that Covered Tax Agreement'.[46] Therefore, any amendments concerning bilateral agreed covered tax agreements are at the discretion of the contracting jurisdictions. A unilateral decision to withdraw from the MLI cannot modify a bilateral agreed tax treaty modification.[47] As long as the MLI provisions affect the tax treaty and those provisions are not terminated on a bilateral basis, the contractual agreed modifications thereof must be respected and remain unchanged.

3.3.3 *Effects of the Withdrawal Are Forward-Looking (Ex Nunc)*

The effects of the withdrawal are only forward-looking, and influence the contractual rights and obligations for the former party to the MLI in future. At this time, the effective date of the withdrawal – the date on which the depositary receives[48] the notification – is essential and releases the former party from future contractual rights and obligations. The withdrawal of a party 'would ensure that the Convention would not modify any tax agreements with states and jurisdictions that join the Convention after the date of withdrawal since they would not fall within the definition of 'Covered Tax Agreements'.[49] In this context, the question arises as to whether the expression 'join the Convention' could be equated with the date of signature, the date of the ratification, the date of deposit or with the date of entry into force. If a state or jurisdictions seeks to become a member of the MLI, that state or jurisdictions must sign and ratify the MLI pursuant to Article 27. This signatory becomes a party to the MLI if

43. Consequences of the termination, *see* section 4.5.
44. OECD, *Explanatory Statement, supra* n. 9, para. 353.
45. OECD, *Explanatory Statement, supra* n. 9, para. 353.
46. OECD, *Explanatory Statement, supra* n. 9, para. 353.
47. OECD, *Explanatory Statement,* para. 353 ('This approach replicates the approach taken in amending protocols to bilateral tax treaties in which the bilaterally agreed amendments cannot be unilaterally reversed by means of withdrawal from the protocol.').
48. *See* Chapter 9 of this book [dealing with notifications].
49. OECD, *Explanatory Statement, supra* n. 9, para. 353.

the MLI 'is in force pursuant to Article 34 (Entry into Force)'[50] for that state. Consequently, the wording 'join the Convention' can be equated with the date when the MLI 'has entered into force with respect to all contracting jurisdictions to a Covered Tax Agreement'.[51]

A withdrawal pursuant to Article 37 releases the withdrawing party from any further obligation to modify tax agreements which have not entered into force pursuant to Article 34 of the MLI before the date on which a party's withdrawal becomes effective. Thus, all notified tax agreements from signatories or later notified tax agreements from any other parties will be not affected in any way. This is why the depositary informs - in addition to all parties - the signatories of the MLI, because if the signatory has notified a tax agreement with the withdrawing party, that future party knows that the tax agreement with the withdrawing party will not be covered by the MLI. However, the covered tax agreements that have already entered into force shall remain as modified by the MLI.

3.3.4 Future Changes to the MLI Itself Will Not Affect the Leaving Party's Tax Agreements

After a withdrawal from the MLI pursuant to Article 37 thereof, the leaving party will be relieved of any future adjustment concerning the contractual rights and obligations of the MLI itself. Therefore, a future modification of the MLI will not affect any tax agreements of the already withdrawn party.[52] However, any modifications made during the sustained contractual relationship (therefore all covered tax agreements for which the MLI has entered into force) shall will remain unchanged. The MLI provisions in the bilateral tax treaty relationship are independent of the existence of the MLI itself. These MLI provisions are part of the bilateral contractual relationship - the so-called coexistence of the MLI provisions and the underlying tax treaty. The unilateral decision of a withdrawal from the MLI cannot reverse the modifications already made to that covered tax agreement. Any further modification of the tax treaties or of the coexisting MLI provisions would be at the discretion of the concerned states or jurisdiction.[53]

3.3.5 Entry into Effect Pursuant to Article 35 of the MLI Is Not Decisive

The decisive date for the effectiveness of a withdrawal from the MLI is the date of the receipt by the depositary of the notification regarding the withdrawal. Each covered tax agreement for which the MLI has entered into force pursuant to Article 34 thereof before the effective date of a party's withdrawal, will remain as modified by the MLI. For the contractual rights and obligations, it is not necessary that the provisions of the MLI have entered into effect pursuant to Article 35 thereof before the effective date of the withdrawal, as the provisions of the MLI have already been implemented into the

50. For the legal definition of the term 'party', *see* Art. 2(1)(b) MLI.
51. Article 37(2), 2nd sentence MLI. *See also* OECD, *Explanatory Statement, supra* n. 9, para. 354.
52. Regarding future changes of the MLI, *see* Chapter 11 of this book.
53. OECD, *Explanatory Statement, supra* n. 9, para. 353.

covered tax agreements.[54] Thus, the situation could arise where a party withdraws from the MLI and the implemented MLI provisions enter into effect pursuant to Article 35 thereof on a date after the effective date of the party's withdrawal.

3.3.6 *Termination of Rights and Obligations under the MLI*

A withdrawing state or jurisdiction is no longer a party to the MLI. Therefore, all contractual rights and obligations regarding the MLI itself cease to exist. The leaving party is no longer a member of the conference of the parties pursuant to Article 31 of the MLI and therefore cannot derive any rights and obligations. Furthermore, the withdrawing party is not permitted to propose an amendment to the MLI pursuant to Article 33 thereof. Moreover the submission of notifications and reservations are no longer possible due to a lack of a legal basis under the MLI. However, all rights and obligations concerning the MLI provisions in the covered tax agreement remain unchanged. The contractual relationship with respect to the MLI itself entirely ceases to exist.

3.3.7 *Withdrawal Will Not Terminate the MLI*

The withdrawal of a party will not terminate the MLI itself under Article 55 of the Vienna Convention.[55] This event affects only the contractual rights and obligations between the leaving and the remaining parties, and will not terminate the MLI itself.[56] However, if the fifth member of the MLI[57] were to withdraw from the MLI, the number of parties to the MLI would fall below the number necessary for its entry into force. Before a withdrawal becomes possible for the first time, the MLI must entry into force pursuant to Article 34 thereof, as only a party may withdraw from the MLI.

Once the MLI has entered into force and the number of parties falls below the minimum number, there are two possible solutions: the MLI remains in force for the sake of the stability of the treaty[58] or the necessary number could be interpreted as a minimum participation and the MLI would be deemed to expire.[59] The MLI has no provision dealing with this case. Due to the fact that the object and purpose of the MLI do not require a limit for its applicability, the MLI will not be terminated (or even suspended).[60] Every time new states or jurisdictions could join the MLI, and therefore

54. OECD, *Explanatory Statement*, *supra* n. 9, para. 353.
55. Article 55 Vienna Convention: Article 55 – Reduction of the parties to a multilateral treaty below the number necessary for its entry into force ('Unless the treaty otherwise provides, a multilateral treaty does not terminate by reason only of the fact that the number of the parties falls below the number necessary for its entry into force.'). *See also* T. Giegerich, *Art. 55*, in *Vienna Convention on the Law of Treaties: A Commentary*, para. 10 (O. Dörr & K. Schmalenbach eds., Springer-Verlag Berlin Heidelberg 2012).
56. Giegerich, *supra* n. 55, para. 3.
57. The minimum number for entry into force of the MLI amounts to the 'fifth instrument of ratification, acceptance or approval' pursuant to Art. 34(1) MLI.
58. Giegerich, *supra* n. 55, para. 5.
59. Giegerich, *supra* n. 55, para. 3.
60. Giegerich, *supra* n. 55, paras 11 et seq.

there is no need for a termination of the MLI merely because the number of parties falls below the necessary number for the first time entry into force of the MLI itself.

3.3.8 Summary of Main Findings

The date of entry into force pursuant to Article 34 of the MLI with respect to each concerned covered tax agreement is decisive for the legal consequences of a withdrawal from the MLI. The provisions of the MLI become legally effective in all covered tax agreement for which the MLI has entered in force pursuant to Article 34 thereof after the expiration of the time period under Article 35 thereof. The affected 'agreement for the avoidance of double taxation' remain as modified by the MLI as before the effective date of withdrawal. Therefore, the provisions of the MLI can also entry into effect after the effective date of the withdrawal. Every further modification of the bilateral tax treaty relationship must be made at the discretion of the contracting states of the underlying treaty. If two contracting states or jurisdiction would like to also erase the modifications made through the MLI or modify their tax treaty, they must effect this on a bilateral contractual basis. A unilateral modification of a bilateral agreed treaty is not permitted. Therefore, every state or jurisdictions should consider the consequences of a withdrawal from the MLI before signing and ratifying the MLI. Once the MLI has entered into force with respect to a covered tax agreement, the modifications made by the BEPS-related MLI provisions to the tax agreement relationship remain unaffected even after a withdrawal from the MLI.

3.4 Example

State *A* signs the MLI on 7 June 2017 and consequently becomes a signatory to the MLI pursuant to Article 2(1)(d) of the MLI. The MLI must be ratified, accepted or approved by the signing State *A*, and this instrument of ratification, acceptance or approval must be deposited via a notification addressed to the depositary pursuant to Article 39 of the MLI. Once the MLI itself has entered into force for the first time, State *A* becomes a party to the MLI pursuant to Article 2(1)(b) thereof as soon as the MLI is in force pursuant to Article 34(2) thereof for State *A*. State *A* is now a party to the MLI.

State *B* also signs and ratifies the MLI and becomes a party thereto one month after State *A* has become a party to the MLI. The MLI has entered into force for both contracting states with respect to a notified covered tax agreement. At that time, the MLI has not yet entered into effect with respect to this covered tax agreement due to the time gap pursuant to Article 35 of the MLI (six month/next taxable period). One month after the covered tax agreement of States *A* and *B* has entered into force pursuant to Article 34 of the MLI, State *B* withdraws from the MLI. The withdrawal becomes effective on the date of receipt of the notification by the depositary. The covered tax agreement will remain as modified by the MLI under Article 37(2) thereof because the covered tax agreement has already entered into force pursuant to Article 34(2) of the

MLI. After the expiry of the time period in Article 35 of the MLI, the provisions of the MLI in the covered tax agreement become effective, although State *B* has already withdrawn from the MLI.[61]

4 TERMINATION OF THE MLI

4.1 Absence of Specific Provisions in the MLI

Termination of the MLI requires that the MLI have already entered into force pursuant to Article 34(1) thereof.[62] The MLI contains no specific provisions for the termination of the MLI. In this context, the question arises as to what the expression 'termination' in fact means in the sense of the MLI. On the one hand, it could be interpreted as a complete termination of the MLI itself along with all MLI-related provisions in all modified covered tax agreement, although they were implemented in the underlying tax treaty relationship. On the other hand, the termination could be seen as a 'simultaneous withdrawal' of all parties to the MLI, so that the covered tax agreement remain as modified by the MLI and only the MLI itself is terminated with all the contractual rights and obligations regarding the MLI.

Therefore, the question arises as to whether the general rules of the Vienna Convention would be applicable with respect to the termination of the MLI. The Vienna Convention provisions concerning the consequences of a termination would only apply '[u]nless the treaty otherwise provides or the parties otherwise agree'.[63] In this context, the question arises as to whether implicit provisions regarding the 'termination' and the consequences could be derived from the context and the object of the MLI itself, or whether the general rules of the Vienna Convention would otherwise be applicable.

4.2 Fundamental Principles of the Vienna Convention

The Vienna Convention on the Law of Treaties[64] is a codification of existing international customary law and was written down through the efforts of the ILC.[65] The Vienna Convention is generally applicable to the MLI under Article 2 of the Vienna Convention, because the Vienna Convention includes written treaties between states;[66] thus multilateral treaties are also covered by the Vienna Convention. The subsequent explanations assume that the Vienna Convention is applicable for all parties to the MLI.

61. OECD, *Explanatory Statement, supra* n. 9, para. 353 ('regardless of whether those modifications have come into effect pursuant to Article 35').
62. Article 34(1) MLI ('This Convention shall enter into force on the first day of the month following the expiration of a period of three calendar months beginning on the date of deposit of the fifth instrument of ratification, acceptance or approval.').
63. Article 70 Vienna Convention.
64. The Vienna Convention was signed in Vienna on 23 May 1969 and entered into force on 27 January 1980. It has been ratified by 114 states. For a full list of Vienna Convention participants, *see* United Nations, *Treaty Series* (1980), vol. 1155, at 331.
65. O. Dörr, *Introduction*, in *Vienna Convention on the Law of Treaties: A Commentary, supra* n. 55, para. 13; International Law Commission (ILC).
66. For the scope of the Vienna Convention, *see* Art. 2 thereof.

If the Vienna Convention have not been ratified by a state, the Vienna Convention can be seen as a written form of international customary law and the rules are therefore also applicable to non-Vienna Convention states.[67]

The MLI contains no explicit rule regarding its own termination. Therefore, the general rules of the Vienna Convention would apply if there is no implicit rule regarding the termination in the MLI. The relevant provisions for a termination of or a withdrawal from a treaty could be taken from Article 54 (Termination of or withdrawal from a treaty under its provisions or by consent of the parties) of the Vienna Convention, which provides as follows:

> The termination of a treaty or the withdrawal of a party may take place:
>
> (a) in conformity with the provisions of the treaty; or
> (b) at any time by consent of all the parties after consultation with the other contracting States.

4.2.1 Termination in Conformity with the Provisions of the Treaty

The first type of the termination 'in conformity with the provisions of the treaty' requires that the treaty contain a provision with regard to its termination. Admittedly, the MLI contains no specific or general provision about the treatment of the termination. The only provision which deals with the termination of contractual rights and obligations could be found in the provision regarding the withdrawal pursuant to Article 37 of the MLI. If the expression 'termination' is interpreted as a simultaneous withdrawal of all parties, the provisions and also the consequences of the withdrawal could be applied correspondingly to the termination. However, in the event of a simultaneous withdrawal from the MLI, the MLI itself would still exits and therefore a termination cannot be equated with a simultaneous withdrawal of all parties. On the other hand, the expression 'in conformity with the provisions of the treaty [MLI]' could also be interpreted as a right of termination that is derived from the nature of the treaty itself and is in accordance with the object and purpose of the MLI. Therefore, the consequences of a termination will, in principle, correspond with the consequences of a withdrawal. However, if one were to assume that there is no implicit provision in the MLI, Article 56 of the Vienna Convention[68] would be applicable.

4.2.2 Termination of the Treaty by Consent of All Parties

The other way to terminate a treaty within the meaning of the Vienna Convention is a termination 'by the consent of the parties' pursuant to Article 54(b) of the Vienna Convention. If it is the consent of all parties to the MLI to terminate this MLI, they could

67. M. Lang, *The Interpretation of the Multilateral Instrument*, SWI, at 11 (2017); H. Loukota, *The Legal Relevance of BEPS in Light of the Vienna Convention on the Law of Treaties*, SWI, at 437 (2016).
68. Article 56 Vienna Convention – Denunciation of or withdrawal from a treaty containing no provision regarding termination, denunciation or withdrawal.

terminate the MLI because they are the 'masters of their treaty'.[69] Therefore, the possibility to terminate the MLI exists at any time by the consent of all parties.[70] However, in this case the question arises as to what happens to modified covered tax agreement of a former withdrawing party.[71]

4.2.3 Treaty Containing No Provision Regarding Termination

The MLI contains no provision regarding the termination of the treaty. Therefore, attention should be paid to Article 56 (Denunciation of or withdrawal from a treaty containing no provision regarding termination, denunciation or withdrawal) of the Vienna Convention, which provides as follows:

> 1. A treaty which contains no provision regarding its termination and which does not provide for denunciation or withdrawal is not subject to denunciation or withdrawal unless:
>   (a) it is established that the parties intended to admit the possibility of denunciation or withdrawal; or
>   (b) a right of denunciation or withdrawal may be implied by the nature of the treaty.
> 2. A party shall give not less than twelve months' notice of its intention to denounce or withdraw from a treaty under paragraph 1.

Under Article 56 of the Vienna Convention, a treaty is not subject to denunciation or withdrawal if the treaty contains no provisions regarding its termination, denunciation or withdrawal, unless one of the two mentioned conditions in (a) and (b), above, is fulfilled. The first condition of Article 56 of the Vienna Convention is that the treaty contains no provision regarding its termination, denunciation or withdrawal. However, as Article 37 of the MLI stipulates the possibility of a withdrawal, this condition is not fulfilled. Under Article 56(a) of the Vienna Convention, the parties to the MLI have not intended to admit the possibility of a withdrawal for a party. Moreover, if the MLI were not to offer Article 37, there could - under Article 56(b) of the Vienna Convention - be a kind of withdrawal-right implied by the nature of the treaty itself.

Once the MLI for provides the possibility of a withdrawal pursuant to Article 56(1)(a) of the Vienna Convention, the right to terminate the MLI could not be prohibited under international customary law. Thus, if any party wants to break from the contractual rights and obligations of the MLI, there is always the possibility of a withdrawal, and therefore there is no need for resort to Article 56(2) of the Vienna Convention.[72]

69. Giegerich, *Art. 54*, in *Vienna Convention on the Law of Treaties: A Commentary*, *supra* n. 55, para. 10.
70. Giegerich, *Art. 54*, *supra* n. 69, paras 20 et seq.
71. For possible solutions, *see* section 4.5 Consequences of a Termination.
72. Article 56(2) Vienna Convention applies only if there is no explicit right of a withdrawal from the underlying treaty.

4.2.4 Brief Summary

There is no specific provision regarding a termination of the MLI. It is questionable as to whether a termination right could be derived from the content and the nature of the treaty itself. However, any party has the right to give notice of its unilateral decision to withdrawal from the MLI. In addition, the MLI could also be terminated if this were by the consent of all parties to the MLI.

4.3 Reasons for the Termination

4.3.1 Necessary Number of Contracting Parties: Article 55 of the Vienna Convention

As mentioned[73] relating to Article 55 of the Vienna Convention,[74] the reduction of the necessary number of parties below the number of parties necessary for its entry into force would not automatically terminate the MLI.[75] The necessary number is decisive only for the entry into force of the MLI pursuant to Article 34(1) of the MLI[76] and will therefore not terminate the MLI only because the necessary number of five parties falls below this limitation. Furthermore, the MLI is open for signature ad infinitum, so that the number of contracting parties could vary significantly over time. Under Article 55 of the Vienna Convention, the MLI will not be terminated merely by the reason that the number of parties falls below the necessary number for the entry into force of the MLI itself.[77]

4.3.2 Conclusion of a Later Convention: Article 59 of the Vienna Convention

Another reason for the termination of the MLI could be the conclusion of a later convention relating to the same subject matter pursuant to Article 59 of the Vienna Convention.[78] This reason for a termination could be done only under the strict conditions of Article 59 of the Vienna Convention.[79] 'The conclusion of a later treaty by

73. Regarding consequences of a withdrawal from the MLI: Art. 55 will not terminate the Multilateral Instrument.
74. Article 55 Vienna Convention: Article 55 – Reduction of the parties to a multilateral treaty below the number necessary for its entry into force ('Unless the treaty otherwise provides, a multilateral treaty does not terminate by reason only of the fact that the number of the parties falls below the number necessary for its entry into force.'). *See also* Giegerich, *Art. 55, supra* n. 55, para. 10.
75. Giegerich, *Art. 55, supra* n. 55, para. 3.
76. The minimum number for entry into force of the MLI is the 'fifth instrument of ratification, acceptance or approval' pursuant to Art. 34(1) of the MLI.
77. Giegerich, *Art. 55, supra* n. 55, paras 11 et seq.
78. In this regard, *see* Chapter 11 of this book (dealing with future changes to the MLI).
79. For further literature, *see* T. Giegerich, *Art. 59*, in *Vienna Convention on the Law of Treaties: A Commentary, supra* n. 55. *See also* conditions in Art. 59 VCLT.

all the Parties is ... the termination or suspension of their earlier incompatible treaty by implicit consent'.[80] Regarding future changes to the MLI, *see* Chapter 11 of this book.

4.3.3 *Termination as a Consequence of a Breach of the MLI: Article 60 of the Vienna Convention*

Article 60(2) of the Vienna Convention[81] contains a special provision regarding the termination of a multilateral treaty as a consequence of a breach of contract. As a result of a material breach by one of the parties to the MLI, the other parties to the MLI are – by unanimous agreement – entitled 'to suspend the operation of the treaty in whole or in part or to terminate it either: (i) in the relations between themselves and the defaulting State, or (ii) as between all the parties ... '.[82] Under Article 60 of the Vienna Convention, a termination as a consequence of a breach of the contractual rights and obligations of the MLI is possible. However, this also requires the consent of all other parties, except for the defaulting state, by a unanimous agreement to terminate the MLI.[83]

In this context, the question could arise as to whether subsequent modifications – for example a treaty override, an acting against the minimum standard[84] or the termination or amendment of the underlying tax agreement – could be regarded as a breach of contract under the MLI. Article 30 of the MLI stipulates that these provisions are 'without prejudice to subsequent modifications to a Covered Tax Agreement'.[85] Under the definition of a covered tax agreement in Article 2(1)(a) of the MLI, a covered tax agreement is 'an agreement for the avoidance of double taxation'. Therefore, subsequent modifications in terms of Article 30 of the MLI could be interpreted such that these modifications refer only to the underlying tax agreement and not to the coexisting MLI provisions in the bilateral tax relationship.

However, another possible interpretation is that the MLI provisions are without any prejudice to any modifications in the bilateral tax relationship. The MLI provisions coexist within the bilateral tax relationship and modify the covered tax agreement. Also

80. Giegerich, *Art. 59, supra* n. 79, para. 1.
81. Article 60 Vienna Convention – Termination or suspension of the operation of a treaty as a consequence of its breach ('2. A material breach of a multilateral treaty by one of the parties entitles: (a) the other parties by unanimous agreement to suspend the operation of the treaty ... (b) a party specially affected by the breach [...] 3. A material breach of a treaty, for the purposes of this article, consists in: (a) a repudiation of the treaty not sanctioned by the present Convention; or (b) the violation of a provision essential to the accomplishment of the object or purpose of the treaty.').
82. Article 60(2)(a) Vienna Convention.
83. T. Giegerich, *Art. 60*, in *Vienna Convention on the Law of Treaties: A Commentary, supra* n. 55, paras 52 et seq.
84. *See* Chapter 5 of this book.
85. Article 30 MLI – Subsequent Modifications of Covered Tax Agreements ('The provisions in this Convention are without prejudice to subsequent modifications to a Covered Tax Agreement which may be agreed between the Contracting Jurisdictions of the Covered Tax Agreement.').

the consequences with regard to withdrawal stipulates that the covered tax agreement 'shall remain as modified by [the MLI]'.[86] As a consequence, subsequent modifications of a covered tax agreement are, in principle, possible. The consequence of a breach of the contractual rights and obligations concerning the modified bilateral tax treaties would be at the discretion of the contracting parties to the MLI, but would not constitute a material breach of the MLI.[87] Thus, a termination as a breach of contract in terms of Article 60 of the Vienna Convention is not the case, because subsequent modifications of a covered tax agreement are possible. However, the breach of obligations under international law must be resolved as between the parties to the MLI.

4.4 Procedural Requirements

The MLI contains no specific provision regarding procedural requirements for a termination of the MLI. Thus, the rules of the Vienna Convention would be applicable to the termination of the MLI, unless the MLI otherwise provides. There are different ways to terminate a multilateral treaty which would depend on the reason for the termination. In order to enable a termination of the MLI, the procedure pursuant to Article 65 of the Vienna Convention should be considered.[88]

4.4.1 Notification

First, the party that seeks to terminate the MLI under the provision of the Vienna Convention 'must notify the other parties of its claim' pursuant to Article 65(1) of the Vienna Convention. Such notification must 'indicate the measure proposed to be taken with respect to the treaty and the reasons therefor'.[89] A notification of the termination must be given in a written form under Article 67(1) of the Vienna Convention.[90] With regard to the MLI, the notification could either be transmitted under the rules of the Vienna Convention or could potentially also be submitted by using the instrument of a notification pursuant to Article 39(2)(g) of the MLI[91] addressed to the depositary.

86. So the consequences of a withdrawal with respect to a covered tax agreement in Art. 37(2) of the MLI shows that the MLI modifies the covered tax agreement, and therefore Art. 30 of the MLI could be interpreted so as to refer to subsequent modifications also of the MLI provisions in the bilateral tax relationship (covered tax agreement).
87. However, subsequent modification of the MLI provisions in the bilateral tax relationship could constitute a breach of the contractual obligations to the MLI to, for example, implement the minimum standard.
88. Article 65(1) Vienna Convention.
89. Article 65(1) Vienna Convention.
90. H. Krieger, *Art. 65*, in *Vienna Convention on the Law of Treaties: A Commentary*, *supra* n. 55, para. 30. *See* Art. 67(1) Vienna Convention ('The notification provided for under article 65 paragraph 1 must be made in writing.').
91. Article 39(2)(g) MLI ('any other communication related to this Convention').

4.4.2 Objection

Any party to the MLI has the right to raise its objection against the termination. If unanimous agreement is necessary and the termination is by the consent of all the parties, the termination can be performed smoothly.[92] However, if 'objection has been raised by any other party, the parties shall seek a solution through the means indicated in article 33 of the Charter of the United Nations'.[93] A possible solution to this dilemma could be the unilateral decision to withdraw from the MLI for each termination-seeking party instead of trying to reach consent for a termination of the MLI, because the consequences for the withdrawing party with respect to the covered tax agreement are almost the same.[94]

4.4.3 Expiry of at Least a Three-Month Period

The time period for any other parties to raise their objection against the termination of the MLI should be at least three months.[95] Every party to the MLI receives the notification from the terminating party and should therefore be able to deal with the potential new situation, even if no party has raised any objection. The exact time period can vary and could also be longer or even shorter in special urgent circumstances.[96] If no party has raised any objection prior to the expiry of the time period, the notifying party 'may unilaterally take the measure proposed'.[97] 'The treaty in question is not terminated just because a State initiates the procedure according to Arts 65-68. ... The travaux preparatoires do not give a clear answer to the question, leaving room for an interpretation according to which the operation of the treaty may be suspended even though the treaty itself remains in force during the settlement procedure.'[98] The procedural requirements for the termination of the MLI are partially regulated by the Vienna Convention. The procedure for the termination of the MLI and a withdrawal pursuant to Article 37 of the MLI reflect a similar operation.

4.5 Consequences of a Termination

A termination of the MLI would release all contracting parties from fulfilling their contractual duties with regard to the MLI. The already created legal situation in the affected covered tax agreement shall remain unaffected by the termination of the

92. Krieger, *supra* n. 90, para. 34; Art. 65(2) Vienna Convention ('... no party has raised any objection, the party making the notification may carry out [the termination'.]).
93. Article 65(3) Vienna Convention. *See also* Krieger, *supra* n. 92, paras 45 et seq.
94. However, in the event of a withdrawal, the MLI still exists, but the consequences for the covered tax agreement are comparable.
95. Article 65(2) Vienna Convention.
96. Krieger, *supra* n. 92, paras 36 et seq.
97. Krieger, *supra* n. 92, para. 43.
98. Krieger, *supra* n. 92, para. 44.

MLI.[99] In spite of preserving modifications, the current parties to the MLI could also agree to terminate the coexisting MLI provisions in their bilateral tax treaty relationship, so that their former tax treaties are applicable again. However, a termination of the MLI could not have any effect on the tax agreements of already withdrawn parties, as the unilateral decision by a MLI party could not modify a bilateral agreed tax treaty modification. That would be possible only if the *existence* of the MLI itself were to be a precondition for application. As this is not the case, the tax treaty-related MLI provision in the covered tax agreement are independent from the MLI itself, because they have been implemented into the bilateral tax treaty relationship.

This view would also be supported by the consequences of a withdrawal from the MLI, because the covered tax agreement shall remain as modified by the MLI and the covered tax agreement is without prejudice to subsequent modifications pursuant to Article 30 of the MLI. This shows that the MLI provisions modify the covered tax agreement and are part of the bilateral tax treaty relationship and are therefore independent from the existence of the MLI itself. Subsequent modifications of a covered tax agreement, which have been affected by the provisions of the MLI, are possible even before the termination of, or a withdrawal from the MLI.

Once the MLI has been terminated, the MLI provisions would still be part of the bilateral tax agreement relationship (former covered tax agreement). If there is consent by all parties to also delete all MLI provision in the process of the termination of the MLI, this rescission could also be performed, but nevertheless requires a separate agreement. As a general rule – and in accordance with the provisions of the withdrawal and the treaty itself – the MLI-related measures in the covered tax agreement would remain unaffected after a termination, and any further modifications in the tax agreements are at the discretion of the contracting jurisdictions. Therefore, once the MLI has entered into force and is subsequently terminated, the MLI provisions could last in some bilateral tax treaties ad infinitum.

4.5.1 Consequences of the Termination of the MLI: Article 70 of the Vienna Convention

Article 70 (Consequences of the termination of a treaty) of the Vienna Convention provides as follows:

> 1. Unless the treaty otherwise provides or the parties otherwise agree, the termination of a treaty under its provisions or in accordance with the present Convention:
>   (a) releases the parties from any obligation further to perform the treaty;
>   (b) does not affect any right, obligation or legal situation of the parties created through the execution of the treaty prior to its termination.
> 2. If a State denounces or withdraws from a multilateral treaty, paragraph 1 applies in the relations between that State and each of the other parties to the treaty from the date when such denunciation or withdrawal takes effect.

99. For the legal consequences of a withdrawal from the MLI, *see* Art. 37(2) MLI ('Covered Tax Agreement shall remain as modified by this Convention').

The consequences of the termination of a treaty are regulated in Article 70 of the Vienna Convention. These rules regarding a termination in accordance with the Vienna Convention will apply 'unless the treaty [MLI] otherwise provides' or 'the parties [to the MLI] otherwise agree'. The provisions of Article 70 of the Vienna Convention regarding the consequences of a termination of a treaty are 'are dispositive and subject to party autonomy'.[100]

4.5.2 Unless the Treaty Otherwise Provides

The provisions under Article 70 of the Vienna Convention are dispositive, and therefore these provisions concerning the consequences of a termination apply only if the treaty concerned (i.e., the MLI) provides no rule regarding termination. In this context, it is questionable whether the MLI 'otherwise provides'. The MLI contains no explicit provision for the termination of the MLI, but the consequences of a withdrawal from the MLI are prescribed. This raises the question as to whether the provisions regarding withdrawal could be applied by analogy to the consequences of a termination. As indicated in the definition of a termination, the term 'termination' could be interpreted as a simultaneous withdrawal from the MLI. In contrast to an act of termination with a simultaneous withdrawal, the MLI itself would remain without any parties. Therefore, a termination could not be placed on a level with a simultaneous withdrawal. However, all contractual rights and obligations concerning the treaty-related MLI provisions in the covered tax agreement for the leaving parties are almost the same. Therefore, it could be said that the treaty provides analogous consequences for the termination with regard to the tax treaty-related MLI provisions. Due to the contractual rights and obligations concerning the MLI itself, the provision in accordance with Article 70 of the Vienna Convention should apply.

4.5.3 Unless the Parties Otherwise Agree

The provisions on the consequences of the termination of a treaty under Article 70 of the Vienna Convention would not apply if 'the parties otherwise agree'. The consequences of a termination are subject to party autonomy.[101] This means, in context of the MLI, that all parties to the MLI could agree 'otherwise'. In this situation, there are no formal procedural requirements for such an 'agreement'. However, the agreement must be decided by the consent[102] of all the parties to the MLI in accordance with Article 54(b) of the Vienna Convention.[103] If the consent of all the parties to the MLI is

100. S. Wittich, *Art. 70*, in *Vienna Convention on the Law of Treaties: A Commentary*, *supra* n. 55, para. 3.
101. Wittich, *supra* n. 100, para. 3.
102. Wittich, *supra* n. 100, para. 10.
103. Article 54 Vienna Convention ('The termination of a treaty or the withdrawal of a party may take place: (a) in conformity with the provisions of the treaty; or (b) at any time by consent of all the parties after consultation with the other contracting States.').

also to delete the MLI-related provision in the affected tax agreement, they could effect this unanimous agreed modification. However, this modification could affect only current parties to the MLI (or the parties to such an agreement) and cannot affect the position of third parties. Consequently, the termination could not affect the MLI-related provisions in tax agreements of former parties which had already withdrawn from the MLI earlier. Accordingly, the situation may arise where all parties to the MLI agree by consent to terminate also the tax treaty-related MLI provision in their tax agreements, but the MLI-related provision are still in force in another tax agreement of former withdrawn parties. So once the MLI has entered into force pursuant to Article 34 of the MLI with respect to a covered tax agreement, the MLI-related provisions could remain in some bilateral tax relationships ad infinitum.

4.5.4 Releases the Parties from Any Obligation Further to Perform the MLI

The consequences of a termination are determined in Article 70 of the Vienna Convention and would apply with regard to the MLI only 'unless the parties otherwise agree'. Pursuant to Article 70(1)(a) of the Vienna Convention, the termination of the treaty (MLI) terminates the contractual rights and obligations relating to the treaty itself. As a consequence, the termination releases the parties to the treaty from fulfilling their contractual duties with respect to this treaty.[104] The termination of the MLI has, for the parties, an ex nunc effect to the contractual rights and obligations concerning the MLI itself.[105] After a termination of the MLI, the MLI could not modify any tax agreements going forward. However, the MLI provisions in the affected covered tax agreements could become effective pursuant to Article 35 of the MLI after the date of termination if these provisions entered into force pursuant to Article 34 of the MLI before the effective date of the termination.

4.5.5 Does Not Affect Any Right, Obligation or Legal Situation of the Parties Created Through the Execution of the Treaty Prior to Its Termination

Nevertheless, the act of termination does not affect the legal situation outside the operation of the treaty.[106] Consequently, modifications made by the tax treaty-related provisions of the MLI in the concerned tax agreements will remain unaffected by a termination. The MLI provisions still coexist alongside the bilateral tax agreement. Nonetheless, the modifications made by the execution of the MLI are part of the bilateral contractual tax treaty relationship and do not constitute a contractual right or obligation in respect with the treaty itself (the MLI). The contractual obligation with regard to the MLI is to modify the covered tax agreement. Once the amendments have

104. Wittich, *supra* n. 100, para. 21.
105. Wittich, *supra* n. 100, para. 22 ('legal consequences of termination to non-retroactive effects ex nunc.').
106. The general rules would apply in these circumstances: pacta sunt servanda.

been made in the covered tax agreement, the contractual obligations concerning the implementation of the tax treaty-related BEPS measures would be achieved.

Therefore, the tax treaty-related MLI provisions to tackle BEPS could be regarded as executed clauses.[107] Accordingly, the legal consequences of the termination have 'non-retroactive effects ex nunc'.[108] '[T]he (legal and factual) acts carried out in the application and implementation of the treaty remain in force and valid'.[109] The legal situation created through the MLI – which is independent of the MLI itself – is not affected by the termination.[110] Any right, obligation or legal situation that could not survive without the terminated treaty is gone as a consequence of the termination.[111] The MLI provisions in the affected covered tax agreements survive, because in the case of a withdrawal of the MLI, these provisions also remain unaffected. The BEPS-related MLI provisions are part of the tax treaty relationship and are independent of the existence of the MLI.

4.5.6 Subsequent Modification of Tax Treaties

Once the parties to the MLI have withdrawn from the MLI or have terminated the MLI, all further changes are at the discretion of the contracting jurisdictions.[112] It is depends on the relationship of the contracting states as to whether they would want to amend their tax agreement along with the coexisting BEPS-related MLI provisions. However, if the tax agreements have been modified through the MLI, one state cannot unilaterally modify the bilaterally agreed tax treaty including the MLI provision. 'This approach replicates the approach taken in amending protocols to bilateral tax treaties in which the bilaterally agreed amendments cannot be unilaterally reversed by means of withdrawal from the protocol'.[113]

5 CONCLUSION

The MLI is supposed to allow a simultaneous modification of a variety of existing tax treaties. The implementation of the MLI has the same effect as an individual renegotiation of thousands of bilateral tax treaties. Once the MLI has entered into force pursuant to Article 34 of the MLI with respect to a covered tax agreement, the modifications made through the MLI will remain unaffected even after a withdrawal from, or a termination of the MLI has occurred. Therefore, each signatory should consider in advance the contractual rights and obligations of the MLI and, in particular, also the consequences in the event of a withdrawal from, or a termination of the MLI. After such an event, all modifications made to the affected tax treaties through the MLI

107. Wittich, *supra* n. 100, para. 21.
108. Wittich, *supra* n. 100, para. 22.
109. Wittich, *supra* n. 100, para. 22.
110. Wittich, *supra* n. 100, paras 24 et seq.
111. Wittich, *supra* n. 100, para. 25.
112. OECD, *Explanatory Statement*, *supra* n. 9, para. 353.
113. OECD, *Explanatory Statement*, *supra* n. 9, para. 353.

shall remain as modified by the MLI. Any further amendments to the tax treaty relationship would be at the discretion of the contracting jurisdictions. Therefore, each state or jurisdiction should bear in mind the legal consequences of the implemented BEPS-related MLI provisions before signing the MLI.

CHAPTER 11

Future Changes to Covered Tax Agreements and of the Multilateral Convention to Implement Tax Treaty-Related Measures to Prevent BEPS

Nathalie Bravo[*]

1 INTRODUCTION

Treaties can be altered only by agreement between the parties. For bilateral treaties, unanimous consensus of the parties to amend the corresponding treaty is required.[1] On the other hand, multilateral treaties may be revised without the consensus of all the parties, unless the respective multilateral treaty provides otherwise.[2] As the

* The author wishes to thank Univ.-Prof. Dr DDr. h.c. Michael Lang, Prof. Scott Wilkie, Dr Kasper Dziurdź, Dr D.M. Broekhuijsen and Pedro G. Lindenberg Schoueri, LLM for their insightful comments and suggestions.

1. The rule that a bilateral treaty might not be revised without the consent of the other party (unanimity for bilateral treaties) is recognized as customary law. For more information: I. Sinclair, *The Vienna Convention on the Law of Treaties*, at 107 (Manchester University Press 1984); K. Odendahl, *General Rule Regarding the Amendment of Treaties*, at 701–702, in *Vienna Convention on the Law of Treaties: A Commentary* (O. Dörr & K. Schmalenbach eds., Springer-Verlag 2012); UN Treaty Section of the Office of Legal Affairs, *Handbook of Final Clauses of Multilateral Treaties*, at 95 (United Nations Publications 2003).
2. In general, parties to a multilateral treaty are not obliged to conclude future amending agreements. This principle is recognized in Art. 40(4) of the Vienna Convention under which amending agreements do not bind parties to a multilateral treaty if they do not become also parties to the amending agreements. For details, *see* M. Villiger, *Commentary on the 1969 Vienna Convention on the Law of Treaties*, at 524 (Martinus Nijhoff Publishers 2009); P. Sands, *Article 39 Convention of 1969*, at 970, in *The Vienna Conventions on the Law of Treaties: A Commentary* (O. Corten & P. Klein eds., Oxford University Press 2011); K. Ardault & D. Dormoy, *Article 40 Convention of 1969*, at 983, in *The Vienna Conventions on the Law of Treaties: A Commentary* (O. Corten & P. Klein eds., Oxford University Press 2011); Odendahl, *supra* n. 1, at 701–702, 706, 710 and 714.

Multilateral Convention to Implement Tax Treaty Related Measures to Prevent Base Erosion and Profit Shifting (BEPS), commonly referred to as the Multilateral Instrument (MLI),[3] will coexist with the tax treaties it modifies (hereinafter 'covered tax agreements'),[4] the parties to the MLI may agree either to change the provisions of the covered tax agreement or to change the provisions of the MLI.

This chapter analyses the various forms in which international tax rules may be revised after the MLI enters into force. For this purpose, the chapter first reviews the forms in which covered tax agreements may be amended (section 2). Second, it scrutinizes the context, as well as the object and purpose of the MLI to determine whether subsets of parties to the MLI have the power to modify the international tax rules introduced through this instrument without restrictions (section 3). Third, it analyses the forms in which the provisions derived from the MLI may be changed among all of its parties (sections 4 and 5). The analysis will be based on the provisions of covered tax agreements, the MLI and the Vienna Convention on the Law of Treaties (hereinafter 'the Vienna Convention')[5] as the convention that establishes the supplementary rules applicable to treaties when they do not regulate certain matters.[6] Additionally, common practice in international law will be taken into account.

2 AMENDMENT OF COVERED TAX AGREEMENTS

The MLI will not govern all the tax treaty relations among the parties. Instead, it will modify the provisions of covered tax agreements that differ from the output of the BEPS Project.[7] Many provisions of covered tax agreements will, therefore, remain unchanged by the MLI. The provisions of covered tax agreements not modified by the MLI will

3. OECD, *Multilateral Convention to Implement Tax Treaty Related Measures to Prevent Base Erosion And Profit Shifting* (2016).
4. A covered tax agreement is defined in Art. 2 of the MLI as:

> 'an agreement for the avoidance of double taxation with respect to taxes on income (whether or not other taxes are also covered):
>
> i) that is in force between two or more:
>   A) Parties; and/or
>   B) jurisdictions or territories which are parties to an agreement described above and for whose international relations a Party is responsible; and
>
> ii) with respect to which each such Party has made a notification to the Depositary listing the agreement as well as any amending or accompanying instruments thereto (identified by title, names of the parties, date of signature, and, if applicable at the time of the notification, date of entry into force) as an agreement which it wishes to be covered by this Convention'.

   For details, *see* Chapter 1 of this book.
5. *Vienna Convention on the Law of Treaties* (22 May 1969).
6. As Pauwelyn indicates, if a treaty does not establish special rules contracting out of general international law rules on amendment and modification, then the rules of general international law are applicable. J. Pauwelyn, *The Role of Public International Law in the WTO: How Far Can We Go?*, Amer. J. Int'l. L. 95, at 547 (2001).
7. For a more detailed analysis, *see* N. Bravo, *The Multilateral Tax Instrument and Its Relationship with Tax Treaties*, 8 World T. J. 3, at 291 (2016).

continue to be the exclusive interest of the parties to the covered tax agreement, which, in exercise of their sovereign rights, may decide to amend them.

Although it is possible to arrive to this conclusion from an analysis of the functioning of treaties, Article 30 of the MLI refers to the subsequent modification of covered tax agreements, stating that: 'The provisions in this Convention are without prejudice to subsequent modifications to a covered tax agreement which may be agreed between the Contracting Jurisdictions of the Covered Tax Agreement.' Article 30 eliminates any doubts that might arise as to the power of the parties to a covered tax agreement to amend the provisions of their tax treaty that will not be modified by the MLI. Thus, if the parties to a covered tax agreement reach the consensus that amendments to the referred provisions are needed to regulate their tax treaty relations in a different fashion, they are welcome to do so.

As both the OECD and UN Model Conventions do not contain provisions on the amendment of tax treaties modelled after them, normally tax treaties do not contain a provision regarding their amendment either.[8] Because the provisions of the Vienna Convention codify customary law and treaty practices, its provisions are applied to treaties unless the parties to the treaties contract out from the provisions of the Vienna Convention. Thus, to update tax treaties, their parties generally follow the provisions of the Vienna Convention regarding the amendment of treaties.

Article 39 of the Vienna Convention enshrines the general principle that treaties may be amended by agreement between the contracting states,[9] in the following terms: 'A treaty may be amended by agreement between the parties. The rules laid down in Part II apply to such an agreement except in so far as the treaty may otherwise provide.' Article 39 is the only provision of the Vienna Convention that applies to the amendment of bilateral treaties, including bilateral tax treaties. This article, however, does not establish a procedure for the adoption of the amendments. In this sense, Article 39 of the Vienna Convention grants leeway to the parties to a bilateral treaty to amend their treaty in accordance with the procedure that they may consider appropriate.[10]

The only clear rule that can be derived from Article 39 of the Vienna Convention in connection to the amendment of bilateral treaties is that both of the parties must always reach consensus. The parties to a bilateral treaty cannot unilaterally amend the provisions of that treaty. The result of a unilateral measure aimed at amending a bilateral treaty may breach the treaty and lead to the termination of the treaty relation.

The form that amending agreements can take varies widely.[11] An amending agreement may take the form of an amending treaty, an amending protocol, an oral agreement, an exchange of diplomatic notes or a resolution of the conference of the parties.[12] Until now, the common practice to amend tax treaties has been that the parties renegotiate the provisions of their tax treaty and, after reaching a unanimous

8. That is normally the case for bilateral treaties as it is believed that the amendment of bilateral treaties should not create major problems due to the involvement of only two countries.
9. Odendahl, *supra* n. 1, at 699.
10. Odendahl, *supra* n. 1, at 702 ('The form of the amending agreement is left to the States Parties' discretion; they may choose whatever form they deem appropriate.').
11. Odendahl, *supra* n. 1, at 703.
12. Villiger, *supra* n. 2, at 513; Sands, *supra* n. 2, at 972; Odendahl, *supra* n. 1, at 701–702.

consensus on the scope and wording of the new provisions, they sign and ratify an amending protocol. As amending treaties, including amending protocols, are subject to Article 39 of the Vienna Convention, the formalities related to the signature and ratification set out in Part II of the Vienna Convention apply to the amending protocols to tax treaties.

Therefore, it is foreseeable that amendments to the provisions of covered tax agreements that will not be modified by the MLI will be conducted in the form previously described. That is, the parties will renegotiate the provisions of their covered tax agreement and conclude an amending protocol, following the provisions of Part II of the Vienna Convention.

The considerations made in this section apply to the provisions of covered tax agreements that will not be modified by the MLI. The question as to whether the parties to the MLI will have the power to modify the provisions of covered tax agreements as modified through the MLI remains unanswered. The following section will analyse this possibility in detail.

3 MODIFICATIONS OF PROVISIONS OF COVERED TAX AGREEMENTS AS MODIFIED THROUGH THE MLI

3.1 Interpretation of Article 30 of the MLI with Regard to Provisions of Covered Tax Agreements as Modified Through the MLI

Article 30 of the MLI recognizes that the parties to the MLI may conclude subsequent modifications to covered tax agreements. As analysed in section 2, the scope of Article 30 of the MLI is clear in connection to provisions of covered tax agreements that will not be modified by the MLI. However, it is less clear whether provisions of covered tax agreements modified by the application of the MLI are also within the scope of Article 30.

Article 30 of the MLI does not distinguish in its wording between subsequent modifications to the provisions of the covered tax agreements that will not be directly affected by the MLI and subsequent modifications to the provisions of the covered tax agreements as modified through the MLI. Yet, the wording is only the beginning of the interpretation process of treaty provisions. Under Article 31 of the Vienna Convention, when interpreting treaty provisions, it is necessary to also take account of the context, as well as the object and purpose of the treaty as a whole, and furthermore any other available means of interpretation. If a certain meaning of Article 30 of the MLI would go against both the context and the object and purpose of the MLI as a whole, it might not have been intended by the parties. The wording of Article 30 of the MLI allows for any subsequent modifications to a covered tax agreement, but just as this neutral wording makes no distinction between different kinds of modifications, the context and the object and purpose could favour a distinction and, therefore, speak for a narrower meaning of the wording.

The Explanatory Statement on Article 30 of the MLI supports the view that the scope of the article also covers the provisions of covered tax agreements as modified through the MLI. The Explanatory Statement indicates that the MLI 'is not intended to freeze in time' the covered tax agreements, and that the parties to a covered tax agreement 'may of course decide to further amend the underlying agreement after it has been modified by the Convention'.[13] The statement is further explained in the Explanatory Statement on Article 1 of the MLI, which reads as follows:

> The right of the Contracting Jurisdictions to further amend their Covered Tax Agreements is intended to remain unaffected, *irrespective of whether the further modifications relate to provisions that have been modified by the application of the Convention*. This is reflected in Article 30 of the Convention, which provides that subsequent modifications to Covered Tax Agreements may be agreed between the Contracting Jurisdictions.[14]

The Explanatory Statement clarifies that the intention of the treaty makers was to allow the parties to modify the provisions of covered tax agreements after they have been modified through the MLI. Thus, after the MLI enters into force, two or more of its parties may conclude new agreements that will have effect among them alone with the purpose of further modifying the covered tax agreements as modified through the MLI.

Under Article 30(4)(a) of the Vienna Convention,[15] the subsequent modification would apply with priority over the modified covered tax agreement.[16] The later treaty in time prevails as a consequence of the *lex posterior* principle enshrined in the mentioned article of the Vienna Convention.[17] The *lex posterior* principle is the corollary of the contractual freedom of the states, which are free to change their intention over time. As a consequence, the latest expression of the intention of the contracting states must prevail over the earlier,[18] which results in the modification of

13. OECD, *Explanatory Statement to the MLI*, para. 310 (2016).
14. OECD, *Explanatory Statement to the MLI* (2016), *supra* n. 13, para. 33 (emphasis added).
15. Article 30(4) Vienna Convention provides as follows: 'When the parties to the later treaty do not include all the parties to the earlier one:

    (a) As between States parties to both treaties the same rule applies as in paragraph 3;
    (b) As between a State party to both treaties and a State party to only one of the treaties, the treaty to which both States are parties governs their mutual rights and obligations'.

    Article 30(3) provides as follows: 'When all the parties to the earlier treaty are parties also to the later treaty but the earlier treaty is not terminated or suspended in operation under article 59, the earlier treaty applies only to the extent that its provisions are compatible with those of the later treaty.'
16. The International Law Commission (ILC) recognized the application of Art. 41 together with Art. 30 of the Vienna Convention in *Summary records of the sixteenth session 746th Meeting*, at 155, Yearbook of the International Law Commission, 1964 Vol. I. *See also* M. Fitzmaurice & O. Elias, *Contemporary Issues in the Law of Treaties*, at 323 (Eleven International Publishing 2005).
17. For further explanation of the *lex posterior* principle, *see* OECD, Directorate for Legal Affairs, *Multilateral Convention to Implement Tax Treaty Related Measures to Prevent Base Erosion and Profit Shifting: Functioning under Public International Law*, para. 16 (2017), available at: http://www.oecd.org/tax/treaties/legal-note-on-the-functioning-of-the-MLI-under-public-international-law.pdf (accessed on 3 July 2017). *See also* Bravo, *supra* n. 7, at 287.
18. A. McNair, *The Law of Treaties*, at 219 (Oxford at the Clarendon Press 1961).

the provisions of the earlier treaty (the respective covered tax agreement as modified through the MLI) that conflict with the later treaty (the subsequent modification).[19]

As limitations cannot be found in either Article 30 of the MLI or the Explanatory Statement, it seems that the treaty makers did not intend to establish limitations on the power of the parties to the MLI to further change the provisions of the modified covered tax agreements. In this sense, the parties to the MLI seem to remain free to contract out from the provisions of this instrument,[20] even if the agreed changes reverse their commitments to curtail BEPS opportunities.

This interpretation of Article 30 of the MLI can be based on the fact that subsequent modifications to the covered tax agreements as modified through the MLI would, in general, affect only the tax relations of pairs of states.[21] Based on the sovereignty of the states, which is protected through the MLI,[22] parties to the instrument would be free to update their tax treaty relations among themselves alone as required by their common economic interests and tax policies. That is, the mutual consent of states that have concluded a covered tax agreement already modified by the MLI could be changed in the future through subsequent agreements.

If this were to be the case, parties to the MLI that have also joined the Inclusive Framework for BEPS Implementation (hereinafter 'the Inclusive Framework') still would have the political commitment to fulfil the minimum standards set out in the BEPS Actions.[23] The Inclusive Framework has, among other things, the task of monitoring the implementation of the four BEPS minimum standards, two of which can be implemented through the MLI,[24] namely provisions to prevent treaty abuse (BEPS Action 6 and Articles 6 and 7 of the MLI)[25] and provisions to improve the mutual agreement procedure (BEPS Action 14 and Article 16 of the MLI).[26] The monitoring of the BEPS minimum standards will 'ensure that all members, as well as jurisdictions of relevance, will comply with the standards in order to ensure a level playing field'.[27] If a subsequent modification were to seek to pull back the fulfilment of the minimum

19. O. Dörr, *Termination or Suspension of the Operation of a Treaty Implied by Conclusion of a Later Treaty*, in *Vienna Convention on the Law of Treaties: A Commentary*, *supra* n. 1, at 1012.
20. G. Vidigal, *From Bilateral to Multilateral Law-making: Legislation, Practice, Evolution and the Future of Inter SE Agreements in the WTO*, 24 Eur. J. Int'l. L. 4, at 1029 (2013).
21. The OECD Directorate for Legal Affairs seems to refer to this characteristic of the interaction between the MLI and the Covered Tax Agreements. OECD, Directorate for Legal Affairs, *supra* n. 17, para. 18.
22. OECD, *Developing a Multilateral Instrument to Modify Bilateral Tax Treaties, Action 15 – 2015 Final Report, OECD/G20 Base Erosion and Profit Shifting Project*, at 13 (2015).
23. For a list of the parties to the MLI, *see* http://www.oecd.org/tax/treaties/beps-mli-signatories-and-parties.pdf (accessed on 3 July 2017). For a list of the members of the Inclusive Framework, *see* https://www.oecd.org/tax/beps/inclusive-framework-on-beps-composition.pdf (accessed on 3 July 2017).
24. For details, *see* Chapter 5 of this book.
25. For details on the monitoring power of the Inclusive Framework on BEPS Action 6 on Preventing the Granting of Treaty Benefits in Inappropriate Circumstances, *see* http://www.oecd.org/tax/treaties/beps-action-6-preventing-the-granting-of-treaty-benefits-in-inappropriate-circumstance-peer-review-documents.pdf (accessed on 3 July 2017).
26. For details about the monitoring power of the Inclusive Framework on BEPS Action 14 on More Effective Dispute Resolution Mechanisms, *see* http://www.oecd.org/tax/beps/beps-action-14-on-more-effective-dispute-resolution-peer-review-documents.pdf (accessed on 3 July 2017).
27. OECD, *Background Brief: Inclusive Framework on BEPS*, at 13 (2017).

standards implemented through the MLI, the Inclusive Framework could take steps to ensure that those parties to the MLI comply once again with their commitment to curtail BEPS opportunities.

Under this interpretation of Article 30 of the MLI, parties could conclude subsequent modifications to the covered tax agreements as modified through the MLI to, for example, change the MLI's principal purposes test rule in whatever form they may consider more appropriate – or even abolish it. No legal limitations could be found in the MLI that would preclude such a modification. The only possible limitation that could preclude such a modification may derive from the commitments accepted within the Inclusive Framework. However, one should bear in mind that this is a political commitment rather than a legal one.

Nonetheless, parties are compelled to apply treaties in good faith and interpret them in accordance with the ordinary meaning to be given to their terms based on their context and in light of their object and purpose.[28] Therefore, as shown below, an alternative interpretation of Article 30 of the MLI can be constructed taking into account the context and the object and purpose of the MLI. The grounds for an alternative interpretation of Article 30 of the MLI will be reviewed below.

3.2 Are There Grounds for an Alternative Interpretation of Article 30 of the MLI?

A purpose of the MLI is to multilaterally coordinate international tax treaty rules in order to eliminate BEPS. The coordinating character of the MLI is evident from the preamble of the instrument, which includes the following statements:

> Conscious of the need to ensure swift, co-ordinated and consistent implementation of the treaty-related BEPS measures in a multilateral context;
> ...
> Recognising the need for an effective mechanism to implement agreed changes in a synchronised and efficient manner across the network of existing agreements for the avoidance of double taxation on income without the need to bilaterally renegotiate each such agreement ... .

These statements show that the MLI creates a multilateral context to facilitate states interested in avoiding BEPS to incorporate in their treaty network the relevant output of the BEPS project. All parties to the MLI thus share the common multilateral interest of combating BEPS. Despite the high level of flexibility guaranteed in the MLI through optional provisions, alternative provisions and reservations, several of its measures aim at preserving and protecting this multilateral interest.[29]

Among the measures adopted by the treaty makers to preserve the common multilateral interest of the parties to the MLI, or in order words, to preserve the multilateral context created through this instrument, is the establishment of a closed

28. Articles 26 and 31 Vienna Convention.
29. P. Valente, *BEPS Action 15: Release of Multilateral Instrument*, 45 Intertax 3, at 220 (2017).

list of permitted reservations[30] which will apply across a party's entire set of covered tax agreements. Parties to the MLI are not allowed to formulate the reservations that they may consider more appropriate to favour their own individual interests vis-à-vis the corresponding treaty partner. They may only formulate those reservations that the treaty makers have considered acceptable from a tax policy perspective in the fight against BEPS and in respect of all the parties' covered tax agreements.

Moreover, under Article 28(9) of the MLI, parties to the MLI may withdraw their reservations at any time. They may also replace their reservations at any time under the condition that the new reservations have a more limited or restrictive scope than the original reservations. Indeed, Article 28(9) of the MLI provides as follows:

> Any Party which has made a reservation in accordance with paragraph 1 or 2 may at any time withdraw it or replace it with a more limited reservation by means of a notification addressed to the Depositary. Such Party shall make any additional notifications pursuant to paragraph 6 of Article 29 (Notifications) which may be required as a result of the withdrawal or replacement of the reservation ... .

As the purpose of a reservation is the exclusion or modification of the legal effects of the provision of a multilateral treaty in its application to the party that formulates it,[31] when a party withdraws a reservation it accepts the entire application of the treaty provision to which the reservation relates.[32] Moreover, when a party replaces a reservation, it limits the legal effects of the reservation and accepts the partial application of the treaty provision.[33]

In the context of the MLI, when Article 28(9) permits the withdrawal and replacement of reservations at any time, it aims that the party that withdraws or replaces the reservation expands its commitment to curtail BEPS practices. This explains why Article 28(9) establishes as a condition for the replacement of a reservation that the new reservation have a more limited scope. If the new reservation were to have a broader scope than the original one or, in other words, encourages BEPS, the new reservation would not be permitted. Once a party has committed to combat BEPS, whether through the implementation of provisions that are minimum standards or through the implementation of provisions that are optional, the MLI does not allow this party to diminish the scope of its commitments by replacing its reservations.

Putting it in more practical terms, if a party has formulated a reservation to the entirety of a provision of the MLI, that party may withdraw that reservation (which means that the provision will apply to all its covered tax agreements) or may replace that reservation with another one that will apply only to a set of its covered tax agreements (e.g., those covered tax agreements that already contain a provision addressing the same issue in similar terms). However, a party that has formulated such

30. Article 28(1) MLI; OECD, *Explanatory Statement to the MLI* (2016), *supra* n. 13, paras 14, 15 and 264.
31. Article 2(1)(d) Vienna Convention.
32. ILC, *Guide to Practice on Reservations to Treaties*, at 11, Yearbook of the International Law Commission, 2011 Vol. II, Part Two, Guideline 2.5.7.
33. ILC, *supra* n. 32, Guideline 2.5.10.

a reservation in connection to a set of its covered tax agreements could not replace that reservation with one that has a broader scope, such as a reservation that would exclude the application of the totality of the article to all of its covered tax agreements.[34]

Replacing a reservation with another one having a broader scope will be equivalent to the formulation of late reservations.[35] This practice is expressly prohibited in Article 28(5) of the MLI. The only situations in which the formulation of late reservations is allowed under the MLI is when a new covered tax agreement is included under the scope of the MLI and that covered tax agreement is the first one to fall under a reservation and when a party chooses to apply the mandatory binding arbitration after it has become a party to the MLI. Except for these particular cases, reservations may be made only at the time of the signature of the instrument or at the time of the deposit of the instrument of ratification, acceptance or approval.[36] As with the replacement of a reservation with one that will have a broader scope than the original one, the formulation of late reservation seems to be expressly prohibited in the MLI in order to eliminate the possibility for parties to restrict their commitment to curtail BEPS practices after the ratification and entry into force of the instrument.

In this context, one should also consider the MLI provision that deals with the withdrawal of the parties from the instrument. Under Article 37 of the MLI, parties may withdraw from the MLI at any time by means of a notification addressed to the depositary. However, the provisions of the covered tax agreements as modified through the MLI will remain modified after the withdrawal becomes effective.[37] Article 37 establishes a different result than the residual rules of the Vienna Convention dealing with the withdrawal from a treaty.[38] Under the residual rules of

34. OECD, *Explanatory Statement to the MLI* (2016), *supra* n. 13, para. 282.
35. Villiger, *supra* n. 2, at 309; A. Pellet, *Article 22 Withdrawal of Reservations and Objections to Reservation*, in *The Vienna Conventions on the Law of Treaties*, *supra* n. 2, at 582.
36. Article 28(5) MLI ('Reservations shall be made at the time of signature or when depositing the instrument of ratification, acceptance or approval, subject to the provisions of paragraphs 2, 6 and 9 of this Article, and paragraph 5 of Article 29 (Notifications). However, for a Party which chooses under Article 18 (Choice to Apply Part VI) to apply Part VI (Arbitration) after it has become a Party to this Convention, reservations described in subparagraphs p), q), r) and s) of paragraph 1 of this Article shall be made at the same time as that Party's notification to the Depositary pursuant to Article 18 (Choice to Apply Part VI).').
37. Article 37 MLI:

> '1. Any Party may, at any time, withdraw from this Convention by means of a notification addressed to the Depositary.
> 2. Withdrawal pursuant to paragraph 1 shall become effective on the date of receipt of the notification by the Depositary. In cases where this Convention has entered into force with respect to all Contracting Jurisdictions to a Covered Tax Agreement before the date on which a Party's withdrawal becomes effective, that Covered Tax Agreement shall remain as modified by this Convention'.

38. Scholars acknowledge that multilateral treaties may provide that the withdrawal of a party does not release it from its treaty obligations. *See* e.g., Villiger, *supra* n. 2, at 874 ('In the case of multilateral treaties, the treaty itself may regulate the consequences of termination, *i.e.*, if one party denounces or withdraws from the treaty, it will not be released from its obligations.')

Also, Ascensio deals with this matter ('Certain treaties furthermore foresee the extension of certain effects of the treaty beyond the date at which it ends for the denouncing party. The ILC *travaux* cite the example of Article XIX of the Convention on the Liability of Operators of Nuclear Ships of 25 May 1962, under which responsibility for a nuclear incident will continue for a

Articles 54, 56[39] and 70 of the Vienna Convention, when a party withdraws from a treaty, it is liberated from its obligation to execute the treaty towards the rest of the parties, while the rest of the parties remain bound by the treaty in their mutual relations.[40] As the MLI provides for a special rule dealing with the withdrawal from this instrument, the effects derived from the rules of the Vienna Convention cannot apply.

According to the Explanatory Statement, the purpose of Article 37 of the MLI is to prevent a party to the MLI from unilaterally reversing its effects and thereby producing unilateral changes to a covered tax agreement already modified through the MLI.[41] Nonetheless, the author believes that Article 37 of the MLI also contributes to preserving the multilateral context created with the purpose of combating BEPS practices. Once the tax treaty-related BEPS project output is implemented in the covered tax agreements of a party, the treaty provisions as modified through the MLI remain in place, even if that party decides to detach from the MLI. For the parties, it is not possible to contract out from the commitment to combat BEPS practices solely by withdrawing from the instrument. They would also need to renegotiate all the modified treaties. This might prove difficult if their treaty partners would still be parties to the MLI and politically committed to tackling BEPS.

Hence, although not expressly established in the wording of Article 30, an interpretation of this provision based on the context and the object and purpose of the MLI as a whole would permit the conclusion that only subsequent modifications to the provisions of the covered tax agreements as modified through the MLI with a similar or a more far-reaching scope in the fight against BEPS may be accepted. This interpretation would find support in the idea that, as stated in its preamble, the MLI creates a multilateral context where all the parties commit to implementing tax treaty rules that seek to curtail BEPS practices to achieve a level playing field. The main object and purpose of the MLI, thus, is to curtail BEPS practices through the implementation of coordinated and consistent tax treaty provisions. In this context, if parties to the MLI were to conclude new agreements to adopt provisions that reduce the scope of the accepted multilateral commitment to tackle BEPS, those agreements would probably be incompatible with the object and purpose of the MLI as a whole.

---

certain time after the termination of the Convention for ships the operation of which was licensed while the Convention was in force. The denunciation provision of the Geneva Conventions (Art. 63/62/142/158) also illustrates this case; it specifies that if the denouncing party is a State involved in a conflict, the denunciation "shall not take effect until peace has been concluded, and until after the operations connected with release and repatriation of the persons protected by the presentation have been terminated".'.). H. Ascensio, *Article 70 Consequences of the Termination of a Treaty*, in *The Vienna Conventions on the Law of Treaties*, *supra* n. 2, at 1589.

39. The Vienna Convention presumes that a withdrawal from a treaty is not possible, unless its provisions so provide, the consent of all the parties is obtained, it can be established that the parties intended to admit the possibility of withdrawal or the right of withdrawal can be implied from the nature of the treaty. Articles 54 and 56 Vienna Convention.
40. V. Chapaux, *Article 54 Termination of or Withdrawal from a Treaty under Its Provisions or by Consent of the Parties*, in *The Vienna Conventions on the Law of Treaties*, *supra* n. 2, at 1242; Villiger, *supra* n. 2, at 68 and 874.
41. OECD, *Explanatory Statement to the MLI* (2016), *supra* n. 13, para. 353.

This interpretation would also find support in the limitations related to reservations provided in the MLI and the effects given to the withdrawal from the instrument, as a withdrawal from the MLI as such does not allow the withdrawing party to liberate itself from its obligation to execute the treaty towards the rest of the parties and, thus, to apply its covered tax agreements in the form in which they existed before they were modified through the MLI. Through these mechanisms the treaty makers of the MLI have expressly prohibited parties to the MLI to reduce their commitments to curtail BEPS practices. Even though a limitation of subsequent modifications cannot be found in Article 30 of the MLI, the intention of the parties, the context and the object and purpose of the MLI would favour an interpretation under which parties to the MLI may not contract out from their multilateral commitment to curtail BEPS practices, unless, of course, they withdraw from the MLI. Thus, if a state were to decide to make a multilateral commitment to curtail BEPS by joining the MLI, it could not expect to be in the same legal position as if it would have never joined the MLI, and if a state decides to go against this commitment by creating BEPS opportunities, it cannot expect to find support for, or legal approval of, such conduct in Article 30 of the MLI. Although it could be argued that this view encourages parties to withdraw from the MLI, it might just as well encourage parties not to create new BEPS opportunities, which is part of the object and purpose of the MLI, of the monitoring process implemented within the Inclusive Framework[42] and of the whole BEPS Project.[43]

Under this interpretation of Article 30 of the MLI, parties, for example, could conclude subsequent modifications to the covered tax agreements as modified through the MLI to change the MLI's principal purpose test rule only if the modification maintains the commitment of the parties to curtail BEPS practices. In this sense, parties could modify the wording of the principal purpose test rule as long as it has a similar or a more far-reaching scope against BEPS practices. Parties could also replace the principal purpose test rule with a detailed limitation-on-benefits rule together with anti-conduit mechanisms. However, a subsequent modification could not abolish the principal purpose test rule without replacing it.

Under this interpretation of Article 30 of the MLI, if a subsequent modification of covered tax agreements as modified through the MLI were to be incompatible with the context and the object and purpose of the MLI, although illegitimate,[44] it would still be a valid treaty.[45] Under Article 30(4)(a) of the Vienna Convention, the subsequent modification in this case would also apply with priority over the covered tax agreement as modified through the MLI. However, the rest of the parties to the MLI could claim the international responsibility of the defaulting parties. Under Articles 30(5)[46] and

42. OECD, *Background Brief: Inclusive Framework on BEPS*, *supra* n. 27, at 11.
43. OECD, *Addressing Base Erosion and Profit Shifting*, at 48–50 (2013).
44. Subsequent agreements are illegitimate if they affect the enjoyment by the other parties to the multilateral treaty of their rights or affect the performance of their obligations under the treaty. Subsequent agreements are also illegitimate if they are incompatible with the object and purpose of the treaty as a whole.
45. Odendahl, *supra* n. 1, at 721; Fitzmaurice & Elias, *supra* n. 16, at 308.
46. Article 30(5) Vienna Convention ('Paragraph 4 is without prejudice to article 41, or to any question of the termination or suspension of the operation of a treaty under article 60 or to any

60(2)[47] of the Vienna Convention, the rest of the parties to the MLI may claim the suspension of the instrument with regard to the defaulting parties (whether in whole or in part), or its termination (whether in the relations between themselves and the defaulting parties, or as between the defaulting parties and all the other parties).

Nonetheless, this interpretation is not without criticism. It is not easy to determine whether subsequent modifications would have the same or a more far-reaching scope than the provisions of the MLI. The benchmark is not easy to establish because provisions that look totally different can provide for equal commitments to curtail BEPS practices, as is the case for the principal purpose test rule in comparison to the detailed limitation-on-benefits rule together with anti-conduit mechanisms. Although a comparison of the effects of the subsequent modification and the effects of the provisions of the MLI and the BEPS Final Reports could serve this purpose, the conclusion could still be inexact or wrong.

Moreover, it could always be argued against this interpretation that Article 30 of the MLI allows parties to contract out from the provisions of this instrument because it does not intend to freeze the tax treaty network. And unlike what has been a common practice, Article 30 of the MLI does not expressly prohibit subsequent modifications if they are inconsistent with the MLI or if they run contrary to its object and purpose.[48] Consequently, the alternative interpretation of Article 30 of the MLI asserted in this section might not be the one intended by the treaty makers. In this regard, the OECD Directorate for Legal Affairs recently published a note titled 'Multilateral Convention to Implement Tax Treaty Related Measures to Prevent Base Erosion and Profit Shifting: Functioning under Public International Law' (hereinafter 'the note issued by the OECD Directorate for Legal Affairs'), which indicates that the 'mutual consent between the two jurisdictions on these issues can continue to be modified in the future ... the key concept is the evolution of the mutual consent between the two jurisdictions which may be expressed in different legal forms'.[49]

question of responsibility which may arise for a State from the conclusion or application of a treaty the provisions of which are incompatible with its obligations towards another State under another treaty.').

47. Article 60(2) Vienna Convention ('A material breach of a multilateral treaty by one of the parties entitles: (a) The other parties by unanimous agreement to suspend the operation of the treaty in whole or in part or to terminate it either: (i) In the relations between themselves and the defaulting State, or (ii) As between all the parties; (b) A party specially affected by the breach to invoke it as a ground for suspending the operation of the treaty in whole or in part in the relations between itself and the defaulting State; (c) Any party other than the defaulting State to invoke the breach as a ground for suspending the operation of the treaty in whole or in part with respect to itself if the treaty is of such a character that a material breach of its provisions by one party radically changes the position of every party with respect to the further performance of its obligations under the treaty.').

48. For a more detailed analysis of the type of provision contained in multilateral treaties commonly referred to as obedience clauses, *see* N. Bravo, *The Proposal for a Multilateral Framework for Updating Tax Treaties*, at 336–339, in *Base Erosion and Profit Shifting (BEPS): The Proposals to Revise the OECD Model Convention* (M. Lang, A. Rust, J. Schuch, C. Staringer, P. Pistone, A. Storck & J. Owens eds., Linde 2016).

49. OECD, Directorate for Legal Affairs, *supra* n. 17, para. 19.

3.3 Notifications Regarding Subsequent Modifications

Subsequent modifications to the provisions of the covered tax agreements as modified through the MLI are comparable to a withdrawal or replacement of reservations. Although a withdrawal or replacement of reservations would have effects towards all covered tax agreements covered by the reservations made by the relevant party, whereas a subsequent modification, in principle, would have effects only towards a single covered tax agreement, in both cases substantive changes to covered tax agreements are produced. The Explanatory Statement to the MLI indicates that allowing the replacement of one reservation by another has '[t]he purpose of allowing a party to accept further modifications to be made' to its covered tax agreements.[50] It thereby expressly refers to modifications of covered tax agreements. Consequently, the Explanatory Statement recognizes that similar effects as through the withdrawal or replacement of reservations can be achieved through a subsequent modification to the provisions of the covered tax agreements as modified through the MLI, and vice versa. That is, parties to the MLI may decide to further change their covered tax agreements as modified by the MLI, either through the withdrawal or replacement of reservations or through the conclusion of subsequent agreements.

Withdrawals and replacements of reservations must be notified to the depositary. The depositary, in turn, is obliged to notify these new circumstances to the rest of the parties and signatories to the MLI. Indeed, under Article 39(2)(c) of the MLI, the depositary must notify the parties and signatories within one calendar month of any 'withdrawal or replacement of a reservation pursuant to Article 28 (Reservations)'. Only after the withdrawal or replacement of a reservation has been notified to the rest of the parties and signatories, will it become effective.[51] The depositary has the obligation to notify the rest of the parties and signatories of the MLI of the withdrawal or replacement of reservations, so they are informed of the modifications to the covered tax agreements produced by the referred means, irrespective of whether such changes may affect them or not.[52,53] As subsequent modifications to the provisions of the covered tax agreements as modified through the MLI have similar effects as

50. OECD, *Explanatory Statement to the MLI* (2016), *supra* n. 13, para. 282.
51. Article 22(3)(a) of the Vienna Convention provides as follows: 'Unless the treaty otherwise provides, or it is otherwise agreed:

> (a) The withdrawal of a reservation becomes operative in relation to another contracting State only when notice of it has been received by that State'.

The MLI does not provide otherwise or contracts out from Art. 22(3) of the Vienna Convention.
52. Article 39(2) MLI ('The Depositary shall notify the Parties and Signatories within one calendar month of ... .').
53. In this sense, although a replacement of a reservation to the entirety of a provision, by a reservation that excludes only the covered tax agreements that already contain a provision addressing the same issue in similar terms will, in principle, not affect the parties and signatories that already have a similar provision in the covered tax agreement with the party that replaces the reservation, they should still be notified by the depositary of the replacement of the reservation.

withdrawals or replacements of reservations, it would be consistent that the same obligations to notify the rest of the parties and signatories to the MLI apply to all these mechanisms.

Irrespective of which interpretation is given to Article 30 of the MLI (*see* sections 3.1 and 3.2), the author believes that as the commitment to combat BEPS practices is a multilateral one, all parties to the MLI would have an interest in knowing if a subgroup of them intends to produce a subsequent modification. Therefore, parties that intend to undertake a subsequent modification should notify the depositary about their intention to alter the respective provisions and the content of the intended modification. Under Article 39(2)(g) of the MLI, which permits the depositary to send other notifications and communications to the parties and signatories not specifically listed in the MLI as long as they are related to the instrument, the depositary should within one calendar month produce the respective notifications.

This idea of notifying the rest of the parties and signatories of the MLI of subsequent modifications would be consistent with Article 41 of the Vienna Convention, which establishes the possibility to modify multilateral treaties among certain parties only, commonly referred to as inter se agreements. Under Article 41(2) of the Vienna Convention, parties that intend to undertake an inter se modification must notify the rest of the parties to the multilateral treaty about their intention to alter its provisions among themselves alone and the content of the intended modification, independently of whether the possibility to undertake the modifications is expressly allowed in the corresponding treaty.[54] This obligation is waived only if the treaty expressly provides that a notification will not be required - which is not the case with the MLI.

As Austry, Avery Jones, Baker et al. have pointed out, one could argue that the provisions of the MLI will be inserted in the text of the covered tax agreements, in which case subsequent modifications will not affect the MLI, but will exclusively affect the relevant covered tax agreements. On the other hand, as those authors have also pointed out, one could argue, instead, that the provisions of the MLI will not cease to apply after the MLI enters into force because its provisions will not be inserted in the text of the covered tax agreements,[55] in which case subsequent modifications will not exclusively affect the covered tax agreements, but could also affect the MLI (inter se modifications). The residual concept of amending or modifying treaties is set out in

54. Article 41(2) Vienna Convention ('Unless in a case falling under paragraph l(a) the treaty otherwise provides, the parties in question shall notify the other parties of their intention to conclude the agreement and of the modification to the treaty for which it provides.').
55. S. Austry, J. Avery Jones & P. Baker, *The Proposed OECD Multilateral Instrument Amending Tax Treaties*, 70 Bull. Int'l. Taxn. 12, at 683 (2016).

Articles 39,[56] 40[57] and 30[58] of the Vienna Convention. Under these articles, the modification of the provisions of a treaty results in a new instrument that coexists with the amended treaty as long as the latter is not terminated by the amending treaty.[59] The situation that arises when the amended treaty and the amending treaty coexist is that of successive treaties dealing with the same subject matter.[60] To resolve conflicts between successive treaties dealing with the same subject matter, parties to the treaties should give priority to the amended treaty or to the amending treaty based on compatibility clauses or the *lex posterior* principle.[61]

Now, it is necessary to review the MLI to determine whether the treaty makers expressly or implicitly deviated from the residual concept established in the Vienna

---

56. Article 39 of the Vienna Convention, applicable to bilateral and multilateral treaties, provides that an amending treaty is a new and legally distinct treaty from the treaty it amends. *See* Art. 39 Vienna Convention as quoted in section 2.
57. Article 40 of the Vienna Convention, applicable only to multilateral treaties, provides that an amending treaty will exist and apply alongside the amended treaty. Article 40 is based on the idea that the relationship between the amended treaty and the amending treaty is that of successive treaties dealing with the same subject matter. Both premises found their expression in Art. 40(4) and (5) of the Vienna Convention. Scholars such as Villiger and Sand acknowledge that Art. 40(4) and (5) rephrase to some extent Art. 30 of the Vienna Convention:

    '4. The amending agreement does not bind any State already a party to the treaty which does not become a party to the amending agreement; article 30, paragraph 4(b), applies in relation to such State.
    5. Any State which becomes a party to the treaty after the entry into force of the amending agreement shall, failing an expression of a different intention by that State:

    (a) be considered as a party to the treaty as amended; and
    (b) be considered as a party to the unamended treaty in relation to any party to treaty not bound by the amending agreement'.

    See Villiger, *supra* n. 2, at 526; Sands, *supra* n. 2, at 970–971.
58. Under Art. 30 of the Vienna Convention, conflicts between the amended treaty and the amending treaty will be resolved in the following way: (i) in cases of bilateral treaties, the amended treaty and the amending treaty apply to the extent that the provisions of the amended treaty are compatible with those of the amending treaty; (ii) in cases of multilateral treaties, between parties to the amended treaty and the amending treaty both treaties will apply to the extent that the earlier treaty is compatible with the later treaty; but between parties to the amended treaty alone and parties to the amended treaty and the amending treaty solely the amended treaty will apply. Art. 30(3) and (4) Vienna Convention.
59. ILC, Summary records of the 16th session, 745th, 746th, 747th, 752nd, 753rd, 754th and 764th Meetings, *supra* n. 16, at 132–167, 189–204 and 267–274; ILC, Summary records of the 18th session 859th and 860th Meetings, at 112–128, Yearbook of the International Law Commission, 1966 Vol. I, Part II. The position of the ILC is summarized by Villiger in the following way: 'Strictly speaking, it is not the former treaty which is altered, rather a new treaty is concluded which supersedes (but does not substitute itself for) the previous one'. Villiger, *supra* n. 2, at 512. Also, Sands summarizes the position of the ILC as follows: 'General practice indicates that a treaty is to be amended by a separate treaty, which is only binding on the parties to the second treaty. The relationship between the two treaties is subject to the rules relating to successive treaties on the same subject matter, in accordance with Art. 30 of the Vienna Convention.' Sands, *supra* n. 2, at 969.
60. ILC, *Summary records of the 16th session, 747th Meeting, supra* n. 59, at 154. For details regarding potential conflicts between Covered Tax Agreements and the MLI, *see* Bravo, *supra* n. 7, at 282–291.
61. Sir H. Waldock, *Third Report on the Law of Treaties*, at 53, Yearbook of the International Law Commission, 1964 Vol. II.

Convention, in which case only the rules of the MLI would apply. The treaty makers were apparently aware that by withdrawing from the MLI, the provisions of the covered tax agreement as modified through the MLI would cease to have effect if the residual rules of the Vienna Convention were to be followed.[62] Thus, Article 37 of the MLI stipulates different effects in order to avoid unilateral changes to a covered tax agreement.[63] This deviation from the residual rule on withdrawal, together with the fact that the provisions of the covered tax agreements are 'replaced' by the provisions of the MLI,[64] could indicate that the treaty makers intended to deviate from the residual concept of amending or modifying treaties, as well.

However, certain provisions of the MLI are not intended to replace or be added to covered tax agreements, or do not always do so. Article 15 of the MLI defines a person closely related to an enterprise and is relevant for the application of Articles 12–14.[65] Article 15 of the MLI is an example of a provision that does not replace provisions of a covered tax agreement.[66] Moreover, some of the provisions of Articles 5, 7 and 13 of the MLI provide that they will 'apply to',[67] which – according to the Explanatory Statement – implies that 'the provision of the Convention [i.e., the MLI] is intended to change the application of an existing provision without replacing it'.[68] Similarly, some of the provisions of Article 16 provide that they will apply 'in the absence of',[69] which – according to the Explanatory Statement – means that the provision of the MLI 'will apply only in ... the absence of an existing provision of the Covered Tax Agreements'.[70] Finally, Articles 3, 4, 6, 7, 8, 9, 10, 11, 14, 17 and 26 (the last of which is applicable to the whole mandatory binding arbitration procedure: Articles 18–25) and some of the provisions of Article 16 establish that they will apply 'in place of or in the absence of'. If one or both parties fail to notify the relevant provisions of the covered tax agreements

---

62. Indeed, as indicated above, the residual rules of Arts 54, 56 and 70 of the Vienna Convention provide that a withdrawing party is liberated from its obligation to execute the treaty towards the rest of the parties, while the rest of the parties remain bound by the treaty in their mutual relations.
63. Under Art. 37 of the MLI, the covered tax agreements as modified through the MLI of a withdrawing party will remain modified after the withdrawal becomes effective.
64. The possibility that the provisions of covered tax agreements may be 'replaced' by the provisions of the MLI is established in the following articles of the MLI: 3(6), 4(3)(e) and (4), 6(5), 7(17)(a) and (e), 9(8), 10(6), 11(4), 14(4), 16(6)(a) and (b)(i), 17(4) and 26(1).
65. Articles 12–14 are included in Part IV of the MLI dealing with the avoidance of permanent establishment status. In particular Art. 12 deals with the artificial avoidance of PE status through commissionaire arrangements and similar strategies, Art. 13 deals with the artificial avoidance of PE status through the specific activity exemptions and Art. 14 deals with the splitting up of contracts.
66. Article 15 of the MLI does not contain a compatibility clause or a notification clause. It should apply every time parties apply Arts 12–14 of the MLI. Therefore, only if parties made reservations to Arts 12–14 of the MLI, may they also reserve the right for Art. 15 not to apply to their covered tax agreements. Art. 15(2) MLI.
67. More specifically, these provisions are contained in Arts 5 (Options A and B), 7(4) and 13(4) of the MLI.
68. OECD, *Explanatory Statement to the MLI* (2016), *supra* n. 13, para. 15.
69. The provisions of the MLI that may apply in the absence of an existing provision in the covered tax agreements are those established in Art. 16(2) and (3).
70. OECD, *Explanatory Statement to the MLI* (2016), *supra* n. 13, para. 15.

correctly,[71] the provisions of the MLI do not replace but 'supersede' the relevant provisions of the covered tax agreements.[72] The Explanatory Statement states that 'the provision of the Convention [i.e., of the MLI] will prevail over that existing provision [of the covered tax agreement], superseding it to the extent that it is incompatible with the relevant provision of the Convention'.[73] According to the Explanatory Statement, this approach reflects the *lex posterior* principle enshrined in Article 30(3) of the Vienna Convention.[74]

The Explanatory Statement further indicates that the MLI 'will not function in the same way as an amending protocol to a single existing treaty, which would directly amend the text of the covered tax agreements; instead, it will be applied alongside existing tax treaties modifying their application in order to implement the BEPS measures'.[75] This has been emphasized by Jirousek,[76] Herrington and Lowell[77] and explained in more detail in the note issued by the OECD Directorate for Legal Affairs:

> The approach taken in the MLI follows the general legal principle that when two rules apply to the same subject matter, the later in time prevails (*lex posterior derogat legi priori*). Accordingly, to the extent that they are incompatible, a subsequent treaty (i.e., the MLI) prevails over a previously concluded treaty between the same Parties on the same subject matter (i.e., a Covered Tax Agreement).[78]

Thus, the author believes that the MLI follows the residual concept set out in Articles 39, 40 and 30 of the Vienna Convention, which corresponds to the second approach proposed by Austry, Avery Jones, Baker et al. If this view of the author, as well as of Pistone and Govind,[79] is followed, subsequent modifications to the covered tax agreements as modified through the MLI are, in fact, inter se modifications of the MLI.

According to the International Law Commission, the purpose of the notification of inter se agreements is to give to the rest of the parties to the treaty 'a reasonable opportunity of satisfying themselves that the inter se agreement does not exceed what is contemplated by the treaty'.[80] Therefore, the notification should be sent to the rest of

71. The compatibility clauses determine whether the provisions of the MLI should replace, change, apply in the absence of, or prevail over similar provisions in covered tax agreements. The compatibility clauses work together with the notification clauses.
72. The fact that the provisions of covered tax agreements will be 'superseded' by the provisions of the MLI despite the parties' failure to notify the relevant provisions of the covered tax agreements correctly, is established in the following articles of the MLI: 3(6), 4(4), 7(17)(a) and (e), 9(8), 10(6), 11(4), 14(4), 16(6)(a) and (b)(i), 17(4).
73. OECD, *Explanatory Statement to the MLI* (2016), *supra* n. 13, para. 15.
74. OECD, *Explanatory Statement to the MLI* (2016), *supra* n. 13, para. 16.
75. OECD, *Explanatory Statement to the MLI* (2016), *supra* n. 13, para. 13.
76. H. Jirousek, *Wohin entwickelt sich das internationale Steuerrecht?*, 27 Steuer und Wirtschaft International (SWI) 7, at 333 (2017).
77. M. Herrington & C. Lowell, *The Evolving World of Global Tax Planning: Part II*, 24 Int'l. Transfer Pricing J. 2, at 92 (2017).
78. OECD, Directorate for Legal Affairs, *supra* n. 17, para. 16.
79. *See* Chapter 6 of this book.
80. ILC, *Final Draft of the Vienna Convention Commentary*, at 232, para. 3, Yearbook of the International Law Commission, 1966 Vol. II.

the parties only when the inter se agreements have reached 'a mature stage'.[81] As before that stage the rest of the parties would not have enough information to determine whether the modification 'is in conformity with the original treaty',[82] it would be 'unnecessary and even inadvisable'[83] to notify the rest of the parties to the multilateral treaty of the inter se modification before it reaches 'a mature stage'. The notification is needed, as the rest of the parties to a multilateral treaty do not participate in the process of inter se modifications.

To this effect, the notifications of intended subsequent modifications to the rest of the parties and signatories of the MLI would help in the evaluation of whether such a modification would affect the rights and obligations of the rest of the parties. Likewise, the notification of the subsequent modification would allow the other parties to evaluate whether they want to join the agreement and thereby transform a bilateral subsequent modification into a new multilateral treaty that modifies several covered tax agreements, whether they want to conclude a similar agreement with regard to their covered tax agreements,[84] or whether they may want to start an amendment procedure among all the parties to the MLI to adopt the same changes. For this reason, modifications intended to be concluded only among certain parties may, in fact, be relevant to all the parties and signatories of the MLI.

4 AMENDMENTS OF THE MLI

The procedure for the amendment of multilateral treaties normally includes two main phases, commonly referred to as the adoption procedure (steps (1) through (4) in the illustration, below) and the ratification procedure (steps (5) and (6) in the illustration, below). Both of them are composed of several steps and requirements.

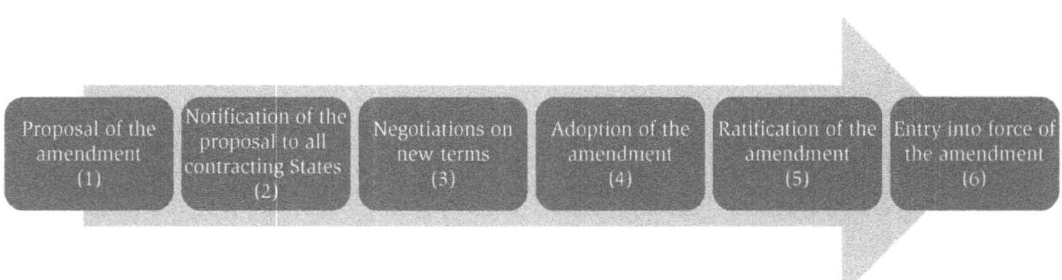

The provisions of a multilateral treaty may be amended following the procedure as provided in its own text. Provisions establishing a procedure for the amendment of multilateral treaties vary extensively. Some provisions are very detailed and expressly deal with all steps of the amendment procedure, while others are not exhaustive and

81. ILC, *supra* n. 80, at 235, para. 3.
82. Odendahl, *supra* n. 1, at 726.
83. ILC, *supra* n. 80, at 235, para. 3.
84. Villiger, *supra* n. 2, at 536.

refer only to certain steps of the procedure.[85] When a multilateral treaty does not contain an amendment procedure or the amendment procedure is not detailed enough, the residual rules of Articles 39 and 40 of the Vienna Convention may apply.[86,87]

The provision that establishes the amendment procedure for the MLI is contained in Article 33. It provides that any party to the MLI may suggest amendments to the text of the instrument and that, once a party to the MLI has proposed an amendment, a conference of the parties may be convened with the aim of studying the merit of the amendment. The exact wording of Article 33 of the MLI is as follows:

> 1. Any Party may propose an amendment to this Convention by submitting the proposed amendment to the Depositary.
> 2. A Conference of the Parties may be convened to consider the proposed amendment in accordance with paragraph 3 of Article 31 (Conference of the Parties).

Additionally, Article 31(3) of the MLI sets forth the form in which the notification of a proposal for amendment must be done by the depositary. The depositary must communicate to all the parties about the proposal and convene a conference of the parties if one-third of them supports the proposal within six calendar months, counted from the date of the communication. Signatory states for which the MLI has not yet entered into force may be invited to participate in the conference of the parties,[88] as they may also have an interest in the amendment. The notification provided for in Article 31(3) ensures that all parties and signatories that could be affected by changes to the provisions of the MLI are aware of the initiation of a reviewing procedure.[89]

To determine whether Article 33 in conjunction with Article 31 of the MLI are exhaustive and deal with the different steps of the two phases of an amendment procedure, i.e., the adoption procedure and the ratification procedure, it is convenient to compare these provisions with one that is assessed by the UN Office of Legal Affairs as very detailed, as it deals with most of the steps of an amendment procedure. Such a comparison will permit one to draw a conclusion as to whether Articles 33 and 31 of the MLI are sufficient to allow the parties to complete an amendment procedure or whether parties will also need to apply the residual rules of the Vienna Convention.

---

85. Odendahl, *supra* n. 1, at 712; ILC, *supra* n. 80, at 232, para. 2.
86. A. Aust, *Modern Treaty Law and Practice*, at 272 (Cambridge University Press 2009); Villiger, *supra* n. 2, at 522; UN Treaty Section of the Office of Legal Affairs, *supra* n. 1, at 95.
87. The text of Art. 40(1) of the Vienna Convention supports this ('Unless the treaty otherwise provides, the amendment of multilateral treaties shall be governed by the following paragraphs.').
88. OECD, *Explanatory Statement to the MLI* (2016), *supra* n. 13, para. 312. This is in line with the spirit underlying Art. 40(2) of the Vienna Convention, under which all states that have expressed their consent to be bound by the multilateral treaty subject to an amendment should participate in the amendment procedure. This is exactly the reason why Art. 40(2) of the Vienna Convention refers to contracting states instead of referring to the parties to the treaty: 'Any proposal to amend a multilateral treaty as between all the parties must be notified to all the contracting States, each one of which shall have the right to take part in.
    (a) The decision as the action to be taken in regard to such proposal;
    (b) The negotiation and conclusion of any agreement for the amendment of the treaty'.
89. Odendahl, *supra* n. 1, at 713.

According to the UN Treaty Section of the Office of Legal Affairs, Article 12 of the Optional Protocol to the 1989 Convention on the Rights of the Child on the Involvement of Children in Armed Conflict (hereinafter 'the Optional Protocol to the 1989 Convention')[90] is an example of a very detailed provision dealing with most of the steps of the amendment procedure of a multilateral treaty.[91] This provision includes detailed information about the following steps of the amendment procedure:

- notification of a proposal for amendments;
- adoption of the amendment by the parties to the treaty, including the manner in which the consent of the parties to be bound by the amendment must be reached;
- entry into force of the amendment; and
- effects of the amendment.

Regarding the notification of a proposal for amendment, Article 12 of the Optional Protocol to the 1989 Convention provides that the UN Secretary General must communicate the proposed amendment to the parties and request that they indicate whether they favour a conference of the parties to consider and vote upon the proposal. If, within four months counted from the date of such a communication, more than one-third of the parties favour the conference, the UN Secretary General must convene it under the auspices of the UN. Regarding the adoption of the amendment, the Optional Protocol to the 1989 Convention provides that the majority of the parties present and voting at the conference is necessary for its adoption. Additionally, the Optional Protocol to the 1989 Convention provides that after the voting has taken place, the amendment must be submitted to the UN General Assembly for its final approval.

Concerning the entry into force of the amendment, the Optional Protocol to the 1989 Convention indicates that it will enter into force only after the UN General Assembly has approved the amendment and two-thirds of the parties have accepted it. Finally, as regards the effects of an amendment, the Optional Protocol to the 1989 Convention specifies that the amendment will be exclusively binding on the parties that have accepted it, whereas the parties that have not accepted the amendment will be bound only by the text of the Convention and earlier accepted amendments.

A comparison of Article 12 of the Optional Protocol to the 1989 Convention with Articles 33 and 31 of the MLI allows one to conclude that the MLI does not expressly deal with all steps of the amendment procedure. Articles 33 and 31 of the MLI cover the initiation of the amendment procedure. However, they do not set forth the adoption procedure of an amendment, including the number of votes needed to adopt an amendment. They do not provide the entry into force procedure, this is, whether ratification will be a requirement for the entry into force of an amendment (some

90. *Optional Protocol to the 1989 Convention on the Rights of the Child on the Involvement of Children in Armed Conflict* (25 May 2000), Art. 12.
91. UN Treaty Section of the Office of Legal Affairs, *supra* n. 1, at 98.

treaties allow their amendment by a decision of the body or the plenary meeting without requiring subsequent ratification; *see* section 5 below) and, if the ratification will be a requirement, what is the number of parties to the MLI that must ratify the amendment before the amendment enters into force. Finally, they do not specify the effects of an amendment to the text of the instrument, i.e., whether the amendment will bind the parties to the MLI that have not accepted the amendment, or whether the amendment will bind only the parties that have completed the ratification procedure[92] (some treaties provide that their amendment will apply to all the parties to the original treaties, irrespective of whether they have accepted the amendment or not; *see* section 5 below). As Articles 33 and 31 of the MLI do not expressly deal with all the relevant steps of the amendment procedure, the conference of the parties will need to apply the residual rules of the Vienna Convention set out in its Articles 39 and 40 or agree to apply a different amendment procedure.

Indeed, during the time when the conference of the parties meets, the parties to the MLI will need to agree on the procedure they will follow for the adoption and ratification of the amendments and vote on whether to adopt the amendments. As the MLI does not establish the number of votes or the precise majority needed to reach agreements,[93] the two-thirds voting majority established in Article 9(2) of the Vienna Convention should apply.[94] As indicated above, Articles 39 and 40 of the Vienna Convention are applicable if a multilateral treaty does not contain an amendment provision or if the amendment provision of the multilateral treaty does not cover all relevant steps of an amendment procedure. Under the residual rule in Article 39 of the Vienna Convention, Part II of that Convention must apply to amending agreements (Articles 6–25).[95] Article 9(2) of the Vienna Convention indicates that '[t]he adoption of the text of a treaty at an international conference takes place by the vote of two thirds of the States present and voting unless by the same majority they shall decide to apply a different rule'. Therefore, the two-thirds majority under Article 9(2) of the Vienna Convention must be applied to determine whether the amendments to the provisions of the MLI will be adopted or not.

Nonetheless, the parties to the MLI could agree to apply a different voting majority than that established in Article 9(2) of the Vienna Convention, for example, consensus or unanimous consensus. For this purpose, a two-thirds majority of the votes of the parties to the MLI present and voting will be decisive.[96] The reason is that

92. Aust, *supra* n. 86, at 267; UN Treaty Section of the Office of Legal Affairs, *supra* n. 1, at 99.
93. The only information regarding the procedure to be used by the conference of the parties for the discussion of relevant matters is provided in the para. 312 of the Explanatory Statement to the MLI. This paragraph indicates that the conference of the parties may meet in person. However, remote meetings are also allowed, including the use of videoconference, teleconference, taking decisions through written procedure and any other form approved by the parties.
94. M. Lang, *Die Auslegung des multilateralen Instruments*, 27 SWI 1, at 20 (2017); F. Hoffmeister, *Adoption of the Text*, in *Vienna Convention on the Law of Treaties A Commentary*, *supra* n. 1, at 145.
95. ILC, *supra* n. 80, at 232, para. 4.
96. Villiger, *supra* n. 2, at 161.

by following a different voting majority than that established in Article 9(2) of the Vienna Convention, the parties to the MLI would implicitly amend the amendment procedure of the MLI.[97]

As consensus is the rule followed within the OECD Committee on Fiscal Affairs[98] and within the Inclusive Framework,[99] the parties to the MLI may attempt to reach consensus for amending the provisions of the instrument. Consensus means that the parties must approve the text of the amending treaty or abstain from voting against it. The OECD Committee on Fiscal Affairs and the Inclusive Framework use consensus because it is considered that agreements by consensus respect the sovereignty of states. On the other hand, the parties to the MLI could attempt to reach unanimous consensus for amending the instrument. Unanimous consensus means that *all* the parties that participated in drafting the text of the amending treaty must approve it. The reason for this would be that the MLI modifies covered tax agreements, and in order to revise bilateral and regional tax treaties unanimous consensus is a requirement.[100] However, it seems unlikely that the parties to the MLI would decide to apply unanimity when amending the instrument, as unanimous consensus can be difficult to reach and if it could not be reached, the provisions of the MLI would be frozen in time.

The parties to the MLI could also agree to apply a different amendment procedure than that provided for in Articles 39 and 40 of the Vienna Convention.[101] In such a case, they would also implicitly amend the amendment procedure of the MLI. Some alternative amending procedures are analysed in section 5.

If the conference of the parties does not agree to follow a different procedure than that provided in the Vienna Convention, under Articles 39 and 40 of the Vienna Convention, once agreement to amend the provisions of the MLI has been reached, ratification, acceptance or approval must follow. Reaching agreement on the text of the amending treaty does not mean that the amending treaty will bind the parties. In order to achieve this effect, the parties must complete the ratification procedure.

As Article 33 of the MLI does not determine the number of instruments of ratification, acceptance or approval required before an amendment will enter into force, the parties to the MLI would need to discuss this and include it in the text of the amending treaty. The number of instruments of ratification, acceptance or approval could be the same as that established in the MLI for its entry into force, or a different number. Under Article 34 of the MLI, the instrument will 'enter into force on the first

97. A. Zimmermann, *Amending the Amendment Provisions of the Rome Statute*, 10 J. Int'l. Crim. Just. 1, at 211 (2012).
98. M. Bennet, *The OECD's BEPS Final Report, Part II: OECD as a Standard-Setting Organization*, 67 Tax Exec. 22, at 23 (2015).
99. OECD, *Background Brief: Inclusive Framework on BEPS*, *supra* n. 27, at 5 and 6.
100. Article 9(1) Vienna Convention ('The adoption of the text of a treaty takes place by the consent of all the States participating in its drawing up except as provided in paragraph 2 [referred to the adoption of the text of a treaty at an international conference for which the vote of two thirds of the States present and voting is required]'.).
For more information, see H. Blix, The *Rule of Unanimity in the Revision of Treaties: A Study of the Treaties Governing Tangier*, 5 Int'l. & Comp. L. Q. 3, at 447 (1956).
101. Odendahl, *supra* n. 1, at 712; Ardault & Dormoy, *supra* n. 2, at 981.

day of the month following the expiration of a period of three calendar months beginning on the date of deposit of the fifth instrument of ratification, acceptance or approval'.

Once the number of instruments of ratification, acceptance or approval needed for the entry into force of the amendments is reached, under Article 40(4) of the Vienna Convention, the amending treaty would apply only to the parties to the MLI that have completed the ratification procedure of the amending treaty.[102] In this case, the parties to the MLI would be divided in two categories, namely: (i) those that have ratified the MLI and the amending treaty, to which both treaties will apply to the extent that the MLI is compatible with the amending treaty; and (ii) those that have ratified only the MLI, to which only the provisions of the MLI would apply.[103] Moreover, under the rule applicable to successive treaties relating to the same subject matter set out in Article 30(4)(b) of the Vienna Convention, between the parties to the MLI alone and the parties to the MLI and the amending treaty, only the MLI would apply, as the MLI would be the only treaty to which both would be parties.

5 ALTERNATIVE AMENDMENT PROCEDURES OF MULTILATERAL TREATIES

The conference of the parties to the MLI has the option to choose and apply a different procedure than that established in Articles 39 and 40 of the Vienna Convention, in which case the parties would implicitly amend Article 33 of the MLI. The following paragraphs will examine amendment procedures of multilateral treaties that deviate from the traditional approach set out in Articles 39 and 40 of the Vienna Convention. These alternative procedures have been adopted to swiftly update treaty provisions and to avoid the situation where different regimes apply to the parties to multilateral treaties depending on whether or not they have already ratified subsequent amending agreements.[104] Therefore, the conference of the parties could consider amending Article 33 of the MLI to adopt an amendment procedure similar to those analysed below, if the parties wish to avoid the application of different regimes by the parties to the MLI.

Some multilateral treaties provide that an amendment may be adopted by the decision of a specified majority - the percentage varies from treaty to treaty, although frequently it is two-thirds or three-fourths of the parties - and that, once adopted, it will bind all the parties to the treaty, unless they explicitly declare in written form within a certain time period their disapproval of the amendment. This type of amendment procedure is known as tacit consent or an opt-out procedure.[105] The Convention on

102. Article 40(4) provides in this regard: 'The amending agreement does not bind any State already a party to the treaty which does not become a party to the amending agreement; article 30, paragraph 4(b), applies in relation to such State.'
103. Villiger, *supra* n. 2, at 524.
104. UN Treaty Section of the Office of Legal Affairs, *supra* n. 1, at 99.
105. For details, *see* J. Brunnée, *Treaty Amendment*, at 356-360, in *The Oxford Guide to Treaties* (D.B. Hollis ed., Oxford University Press 2014); M. Fitzmaurice & P. Merkouris, *Uniformity*

International Civil Aviation,[106] the Convention on the Facilitation of Maritime Traffic,[107] the Convention on Biological Diversity,[108] the Kyoto Protocol[109] and the Rotterdam Convention[110] are among the international agreements that provide for tacit consent or an opt-out procedure for the amendment thereof. The opt-out procedure is frequently adopted for the amendment of technical or administrative provisions that do not generate significant disagreement among the parties to a multilateral treaty.

One advantage of this approach is that it swiftly updates treaties by avoiding several steps of the traditional approach to the amendment of treaties illustrated in section 4, which can be time-consuming and sometimes even prevent the implementation of the amendments. However, the opt-out procedure has a significant disadvantage, in that it requires a by-pass of legislative approval of the amendment required in many countries by shifting the accomplishment of the domestic ratification process to the executive branch.[111] Although this might be a lesser problem when the amendments deal with technical or administrative matters, it is not the case when the amendments establish new obligations or alter the core terms of a treaty. Many parties to the MLI may be faced with constitutional constraints when seeking to adopt new obligations or alter the core terms of the instrument without the approval of their legislatures. These difficulties explain why the parties to the MLI decided to follow the amending procedure as set out in Article 33 of the MLI, applicable in conjunction with Articles 39 and 40 of the Vienna Convention, instead of adopting an opt-out procedure to produce future changes to the MLI. In this sense, it seems unlikely that the parties to the MLI would agree to amend Article 33 of the MLI to adopt an opt-out procedure.

Other multilateral treaties provide that an amendment may be adopted by the decision of a specified majority – again, the percentage varies from treaty to treaty – and that, once adopted, it will bind all of them, including those parties to the treaty that did not accept the amendment or did not ratify it.[112] This type of amendment procedure, known as a majority ratification procedure,[113] is contained in, for example, the UN Charter, the Statute of the Council of Europe,[114] the Convention Establishing the WIPO[115] and the Marrakesh Agreement Establishing the WTO.[116] For example, Article 108 of the UN Charter states that its amendments will enter into force for all UN

versus Specialization (1): The Quest for a Uniform Law of International States, in *Research Handbook on the Law of Treaties*, at 362-363 (C. Tams et al. eds., Edward Elgar Publishing Ltd. 2014).

106. *Convention on International Civil Aviation* (7 December 1944), Art. 90(a).
107. *Convention on the Facilitation of Maritime Traffic* (9 April 1965), Art. VII.
108. *Convention on Biological Diversity* (5 June 1992), Art. 30(2).
109. *Kyoto Protocol to the United Nations Framework Convention on Climate Change* (11 December 1997), Art. 21.
110. *Convention on the Prior Informed Consent Procedure for Certain Hazardous Chemical and Pesticides in International Trade* (10 September 1998), Art. 22.
111. Brunnée, *supra* n. 105, at 359.
112. Aust, *supra* n. 86, at 266.
113. For details, *see* Brunnée, *supra* n. 105, at 360-361.
114. *Statute of the Council of Europe* (10 May 1945), Art. 41.
115. *Convention Establishing the World Intellectual Property Organization* (14 July 1967), Art. 17(3).
116. *Marrakesh Agreement Establishing the World Trade Organization* (15 April 1994), Art. X(4).

members after a majority of two-thirds has adopted and ratified them.[117] A second approach to this type of amendment procedure is that, once the majority of the parties agree to an amendment, those parties that fail to ratify it will be either automatically excluded or free to withdraw from the treaty or organization. Under Article 94(b) of the Convention on International Civil Aviation, the Assembly may agree that the parties that have not ratified an amendment within a certain period after it has entered into force must cease to be a party to that Convention. On the other hand, Article 122 of the Rome Statute of the International Criminal Court[118] provides that the parties that have not accepted an amendment approved by seven-eighths of the parties may withdraw from the Statute.

Like the opt-out procedure, the majority ratification procedure has the advantage of reducing the period of time normally required for the revision of a treaty. The main difference between the opt-out procedure and the majority ratification procedure is that the former allows parties to show their disagreement to the amendment by opting-out, while in the latter the acceptance of all the parties to the treaty is presumed if a certain number of votes and ratifications are reached. The majority ratification procedure is widely used in constituting treaties of international organizations – which makes sense, as it would be inconvenient for different regimes to apply to different groups of parties. However, this procedure jeopardizes, to some extent, the sovereignty of states. Constitutional constraints may inhibit the ability of the parties to the MLI to accept new obligations or alter the core terms of the instrument without their explicit consent. These difficulties again explain why the parties to the MLI decided to follow the amending procedure as set out in Article 33 of the MLI instead of adopting a majority ratification procedure. Therefore, it seems unlikely that the parties would intend to change Article 33 of the MLI in favour of a majority ratification procedure in the future.

A common feature of the three amendment procedures described so far – i.e., the traditional approach established in Articles 39 and 40 of the Vienna Convention, the opt-out procedure and the majority ratification procedure – is that they consist of two steps: the adoption of the amendment and the entry into force of the amending treaty after ratification.[119] However, the last amendment procedure that will be introduced in this chapter is an abbreviated one, consisting of a single step. This procedure is known as amendment by consensus or majority plenary decision,[120] and consists of the adoption and entry into force of amendments once a specified majority at a plenary meeting or conference of parties has approved them.

Because the amendment by consensus also bypasses the legislative approval of the amendment required in many countries and shifts the accomplishment of the domestic ratification process to the executive branch, it is normally not used to adopt

117. *Charter of the United Nations* (26 June 1945), Art. 108: ('Amendments to the present Charter shall come into force for all Members of the United Nations when they have been adopted by a vote of two thirds of the members of the General Assembly and ratified in accordance with their respective constitutional processes by two thirds of the Members of the United Nations, including all the permanent members of the Security Council'.).
118. *Rome Statute of the International Criminal Court* (17 July 1998), Art. 121.
119. Brunnée, *supra* n. 105, at 360.
120. For details, *see* Brunnée, *supra* n. 105, at 362–363.

amendments that establish new obligations or alter the core terms of a treaty. For example, Article XIII(4) of the FAO Agreement to Promote Compliance with International Conservation and Management Measures by Fishing Vessels on the High Seas provides that the 'proposed amendment of this Agreement shall require the approval of the Conference and shall come into force as from the thirtieth day after acceptance by two-thirds of the Parties'.[121] However, this procedure does not apply to '[a]mendments involving new obligations for Parties'. For amendments involving new obligations for the parties, acceptance by each party is a requirement. Under Article XIII(4), it is assumed that all amendments involve new obligations for the parties unless the conference decides otherwise. Similar provisions are enshrined in the UNESCO Constitution[122] and the Rome Statute of the International Criminal Court for provisions of an institutional nature.[123] Thus, it also seems unlikely that the parties would agree to amend the current amendment procedure set out in Article 33 of the MLI to adopt instead an amendment by consensus or majority plenary decision procedure.

The three alternative amendment procedures described in this section are established most of the time not only with the aim of speeding up the revision of treaties, but also with the aim of avoiding different treaty regimes among the parties to multilateral treaties, even though sometimes they can jeopardize the sovereignty of states. Different treaty regimes among the parties are avoided when they are impractical or undesirable from a policy perspective, as is the case with treaties constituting international organizations and treaties on civil aviation, maritime traffic and environmental protection.

It does not seem that the MLI pursues the creation of a uniform regime of international taxation. The treaty makers not only omitted dealing with this issue in Article 33 of the MLI but actually, in the author's opinion, they encouraged the implementation of different treaty regimes among the parties to the MLI by allowing them to adopt optional provisions and different alternatives, as well as providing them with a long list of allowed reservations. Besides swiftly modifying the tax treaty network, the MLI has as an object and purpose coordinating international tax rules to combat BEPS in a multilateral context, but not to create a uniform tax regime.

Based on the object and purpose of the instrument under study, there are good reasons why the parties to the MLI have agreed on an amendment procedure based on the current Article 33 of the MLI, applicable in conjunction with Articles 39 and 40 of the Vienna Convention. Therefore, it seems unlikely that the parties to the MLI will intend to amend the provisions dealing with the amendment procedure in the future. The reasons are threefold. First, states strongly protect their sovereignty in all tax treaty-related matters. The MLI was drafted with the promise of reaching 'the appropriate balance between national sovereignty and international co-operation'.[124] Thus,

121. *Agreement to Promote Compliance with International Conservation and Management Measures by Fishing Vessels on the High Seas* (24 November 1993), Art. XIII.
122. *Constitution of the United Nations Educational, Scientific and Cultural Organization* (16 November 1945), Art. XIII.
123. *Rome Statute of the International Criminal Court* (17 July 1998), Art. 122. This Article establishes which provisions are of an institutional nature.
124. OECD, *Action 15 Final Report, supra* n. 22, at 13.

amendments of the MLI will most likely also preserve the tax sovereignty of the parties. It is possible to preserve the tax sovereignty of the parties only if they expressly adopt and ratify amending treaties. Second, the MLI modifies covered tax agreements, and for the revision of bilateral tax treaties and multilateral regional tax treaties, unanimous consensus and ratification by all the parties are required. As amendments of the MLI will most likely also have effects on the covered tax agreements, it is logical to request that the parties to a covered tax agreement unanimously agree on the form in which that treaty will end up applying. This can be guaranteed only through the traditional amendment procedure set out in Articles 39 and 40 of the Vienna Convention, under which amending agreements apply only to the parties that have adopted and ratified them. The opt-out procedure, the majority ratification procedure and the amendment by consensus procedure seek to bind all the parties to a multilateral treaty regardless of whether they have expressly agreed to the changes. Third, alternative amendment procedures are more frequently accepted by states when the provisions concerned relate to technical or administrative matters, and that is not the nature of the provisions of the MLI.[125]

6 CONCLUSION

This chapter has scrutinized the forms in which international tax rules may be revised after the MLI enters into force. For this purpose, the relevant provisions of covered tax agreements, the MLI and the Vienna Convention, as well as common practice in international law were taken into account.

Parties to the MLI may agree to change the provisions of the covered tax agreements and/or the provisions of the MLI. The provisions of covered tax agreements that are not modified through the MLI may be amended at any time. Unchanged provisions of covered tax agreements continue to be the exclusive interest of the respective parties, who – in the exercise of their sovereign rights – may amend them. Furthermore, under Article 30 of the MLI, the provisions of covered tax agreements as modified through the MLI may be subject to subsequent modifications. Based on the object and purpose of the MLI (which is to curtail BEPS practices) and its context, including the statements contained in its preamble, the design of the system of reservations and the limited effect of a withdrawal from the instrument, one can conclude that subsequent modifications will be allowed only if they have a similar or a more far-reaching scope in the fight against BEPS than the provisions of the MLI. Nonetheless, it is likely that the parties did not intend to limit their right to produce subsequent modifications, not even if through the subsequent modifications they contract out from the commitment to curtail BEPS. The MLI does not have the purpose of freezing in time the tax treaty network.

The provisions of the MLI may also be changed through amendment procedures that intend to achieve the participation of all the parties to this instrument. This type of

125. C. Chinkin & C. Kessedjian, *The Legal Relationship Between the Proposed UNIDROIT Convention and Its Equipment-Specified Protocols*, 4 U. L. Rev. 2, at 330 (1999).

procedure is covered by Articles 33 and 31 of the MLI. However, Articles 33 and 31 of the MLI do not provide for an exhaustive amendment procedure. They just cover the initiation of the amendment procedure, particularly the form in which the proposal for amendment may be put forward and the form in which a conference of the parties must be convened. As a consequence, a conference of the parties convened to amend the MLI must both: (i) discuss the procedure to be used for the adoption and ratification of the amendments; and (ii) vote on whether they agree to adopt the amendments.

Where Article 33 of the MLI is silent, the parties to the MLI will, in principle, apply the residual rules provided for in Articles 39 and 40 of the Vienna Convention, under which ratification of the amendments is required and only parties that have ratified the amendments will be bound by them. On this basis, however, they may also agree to amend Article 33 of the MLI to apply a different amendment procedure, such as the opt-out procedure, the majority ratification procedure or the amendment by consensus procedure. The author believes that the parties to the MLI will most likely stay with the current amendment procedure set out in Article 33 of the MLI. This opinion is based on three reasons, namely: (i) the sovereign autonomy of states is strongly protected in all tax treaty-related matters; (ii) amendments to the MLI will likely have effects on covered tax agreements, and thus, the parties to a covered tax agreement should unanimously agree on the form in which that treaty will end up applying; and (iii) alternative amendment procedures are more frequently used to change treaty provisions dealing with technical or administrative matters – and the provisions of the MLI are not of such a nature.

Index

J

L

M

N

O

T

U

V

www.ingramcontent.com/pod-product-compliance
Ingram Content Group UK Ltd.
Pitfield, Milton Keynes, MK11 3LW, UK
UKHW020246290926
15470UKWH00002B/762

9 789041 188366